PARLIAMENTARY SOCIALISM

A STUDY IN THE POLITICS OF LABOUR

—◦◦❧❦◦◦—

RALPH MILIBAND

Second Edition

MERLIN PRESS
LONDON

© Merlin Press 1972
First published by Allen & Unwin in 1961,
second edition published by The Merlin Press Ltd.,
Sufferance Wharf, Isle of Dogs,
London.

2nd impression 1975

Printed by
Whitstable Litho Ltd.,
Whitstable, Kent.

TO MY PARENTS

ACKNOWLEDGEMENTS

I wish to express a general and deeply-felt debt to my late teacher, colleague and friend, Harold J. Laski, and to record here my gratitude and abiding affection.

My friend John Saville has continuously given me invaluable criticism, advice and encouragement in the preparation of this book. It is scarcely too much to say that his help has often amounted to collaboration.

I also wish to thank the following colleagues and friends who have kindly read parts or the whole of this work and offered most valuable criticism: V. L. Allen, R. E. Dowse, H. R. G. Greaves, W. Goldstein, W. L. Guttsman, Russell W. Kerr, Miss Marion Kozak, M. Liebman, C. Wright Mills, Edward and Dorothy Thompson, and E. Wohlgemuth.

I should also like to acknowledge the benefit I have derived from discussion and debate with the members of my graduate seminar on Problems of Contemporary Socialism at the London School of Economics and Political Science.

I am very grateful to Miss Dorothy West for the patience and skill with which she has typed successive versions of my manuscript; and to Miss D. M. Wates and other members of the Library Staff of the British Library of Political and Economic Science for their help and courtesy.

I was able to make use of material on the history of the Labour Party collected by the Government Research Division of the London School of Economics and Political Science with the financial assistance of the Passfield Trustees, to whom I wish to record my thanks.

It may be especially necessary, given the somewhat controversial views expressed in this book, to stress that I alone am responsible for everything which appears in the following pages.

R.M.

The London School of Economics
and Political Science
December 1960

CONTENTS

—◦⬥⬥◦—

PREFACE TO THE SECOND EDITION

Save for some minor and mainly typographical corrections, the only difference between the first edition of *Parliamentary Socialism* and the present one consists in the addition of a Postscript. The reason for leaving the original text alone is not, I need hardly say, that I think it incapable of improvement but that, if I were to cover the ground again, I would want to broaden and, I hope, deepen the analysis in ways which would require not only the revision of the existing text but the writing of a new book. However, I venture to say that, considering what else is available, the work as it stands still seems to me to provide a worthwhile account of the politics of Labour in the present century.

I should like to stress that the Postscript does not attempt to bring the story up to date, in the sense of tracing in detail the history of the Labour Party from 1960 to the present day. Its purpose is rather to discuss the underlying reasons for Labour's record in the sixties, and then to say something about what I believe may and what may not be expected of the Labour Party in the coming years. In this latter respect, it will be seen that my conclusions are rather different from those which I set down in the first edition; and I welcome the chance which the re-issue of the book has given me to make a correction which I have long thought to be very necessary.

April 1972   R.M.

INTRODUCTION

◦❧❦◦

Of political parties claiming socialism to be their aim, the Labour Party has always been one of the most dogmatic—not about socialism, but about the parliamentary system. Empirical and flexible about all else, its leaders have always made devotion to that system their fixed point of reference and the conditioning factor of their political behaviour. This is not simply to say that the Labour Party has never been a party of revolution : such parties have normally been quite willing to use the opportunities the parliamentary system offered as one means of furthering their aims. It is rather that the leaders of the Labour Party have always rejected any kind of political action (such as industrial action for political purposes) which fell, or which appeared to them to fall, outside the framework and conventions of the parliamentary system. The Labour Party has not only been a parliamentary party; it has been a party deeply imbued by parliamentarism. And in this respect, there is no distinction to be made between Labour's political and its industrial leaders. Both have been equally determined that the Labour Party should not stray from the narrow path of parliamentary politics. The main purpose of this book is to analyse the consequences which this approach to politics has had for the Labour Party and the Labour movement from the time the Labour Party came into existence.

Labour's devotion to the parliamentary system does not, of course, date from the formation of the Labour Party. The Labour Representation Committee in which the Labour Party originated was itself the product of a parliamentary view of politics which had been steadily gaining in strength over the previous decades. By the time the L.R.C. was formed in 1900, there were not many people in the Labour movement to contest the view that Labour's grievances and demands could only find solution through parliamentary action, and that the parliamentary method was ideally suited, not only to the achievement of immediate gains by the working-classes, but also to the socialist reconstruction of society.

It was a view which, in the first years of the century, was coming to be more and more widely held by the leadership of all Western Labour movements.[1] Parliamentarism in the British Labour move-

---

[1] See, e.g. the excellent study of the German Labour movement in the first years of the twentieth century by Carl E. Schorske, *German Social-Democracy 1905-1917* (Cambridge, Mass., 1955); also P. Gay, *The Dilemma of Democratic Socialism: Bernstein's Challenge to Marx* (New York, 1952).

ment was only unique in that it was so much more explicit, confident and uninhibited than its Continental counterparts, and that it met with so much less resistance.

However, the establishment of a distinctive Labour Party in the House of Commons marked more than the continuation of a well established parliamentary tradition in the Labour movement. For the creation of the Labour Party gave that tradition new forms and created problems which had not existed, or which had been far less acute, so long as the Labour movement did not have its own party in Parliament.

I must make it clear that I have not tried to write a comprehensive history of the Labour Party, much less of the Labour movement. I am particularly conscious of the fact that I have had to pay less attention than I should have liked to the multitude of activities at local level which, more than anything else, have made the Labour movement a living reality, indeed a way of life. I have proceeded historically, not only because my theme obviously requires detailed historical illustration, but also and more important because Labour's integration into parliamentary politics has been a process of growth, becoming more pronounced, assuming more specific forms, and producing new tensions as the Labour Party changed from a small pressure group in the House of Commons into a party of Official Opposition and of Government. Indeed, the recent controversies over the powers of the Labour Party's Annual Conference in relation to the Parliamentary Labour Party indicate that the process is even now by no means complete. Nor would the Labour Party's integration into parliamentary politics have taken place, or taken place in the same way, had it not had its parallel in the growing integration of the trade unions into the framework of modern capitalism. This integration has not been smooth, but it has been continuous; and the crucial influence it has had on the political ways of the Labour Party explains why its various aspects occupy so large a place in the following pages.

Throughout the history of the Labour Party, its leaders have had to contend with two different sets of critics and opponents on the Left. The first of these has been the Labour Left, whose purpose has always been two-fold: to push their leaders into accepting more radical policies and programmes, and to press upon them more militant attitudes in response to challenges from Labour's opponents. The Labour Left's own acceptance of the categories of the parliamentary system has been distinguished from that of the leadership by a continuous search for means of escape from its inhibitions and constrictions. What the Labour leaders have accepted eagerly, the

Labour Left has accepted with a certain degree of unease and at times with acute misgivings.

This Labour Left has assumed a variety of political forms in different periods. From 1900 to 1932, its main political expression was the Independent Labour Party. When the I.L.P. ceased, in that year, to be a constituent body of the Labour Party, it was replaced, until 1937, by the Socialist League. In the fifties, it found expression, firstly in the Bevanite movement and then in such organizations as Victory for Socialism. But the Labour Left has always encompassed many more people than have actually joined any of its organizations. One of its main sources of strength, for instance, has always been in the trade unions, whose militant members have generally steered clear of the political organizations of the Labour Left.

This left-wing activist element in the Labour Party and the trade unions has always been in a minority. It has seldom been able to pose an effective challenge to the Labour leaders and it has never come near to capturing the Labour movement's commanding heights. Even so, organized or unorganized, it has been a force with which the Labour leaders have always had to reckon, and to which they have often been forced to make concessions; in various ways, the Left within the Labour Party has at least reduced the leaders' freedom of action.

The second set of opponents of the Labour leadership has been made up of what might be called the extra-parliamentary Left, for whom parliamentary politics has always been of secondary importance, if that. This extra-parliamentary Left too has been a permanent part of Labour's political landscape, though outside the Labour Party. Until the foundation of the Communist Party after the First World War, it was represented by a number of political groupings and organizations, such as the Social Democratic Federation and the British Socialist Party. After 1920, it came to be concentrated mainly in the Communist Party, and its impact upon the Labour movement, notably in the trade unions, cannot be discounted, despite the smallness of its numbers.

But the Labour movement is not a self-contained entity. It responds to, and is deeply influenced by, external factors, historical, economic, social and political. It is, for instance, hardly necessary to stress how much, in their eagerness to 'work' the British political system, the Labour leaders have been affected by the strategy of the traditional parties. Thus, no analysis of Labour's role in British politics would make much sense which did not include at least some consideration of the politics of Liberalism before the First World War, and of Conservatism after it. I hope that the analysis which will be found here of this interplay of contending forces may throw some useful light on the true nature of British politics in this century, as well as on the politics of Labour.

The assumption is often made in discussions of the present crisis in the Labour Party that the latter's difficulties are of recent origin. This is not so. Like Hobbes and fear, crisis and the Labour Party have always been twins—Siamese twins. And explanations which begin with recent difficulties either mistake the symptoms of the crisis, or its aggravation, for the crisis itself. Much, for instance, has been made in recent years of the Labour Party's supposed inability to 'adjust' to the circumstances and demands of the 'affluent society'. This, it has been said, explains the Labour Party's loss of appeal, as expressed in successive electoral defeats. But such an explanation would surely carry greater weight if the Labour Party had fared any better in the years of the not so affluent society, say in 1935, when the Conservative Party, having carried the main responsibility for the conduct of affairs during four years of mass unemployment, was returned to office with a parliamentary majority of well over two hundred. And what, to take another instance, is being said about the Labour Party's failure to act as an effective opposition in the fifties, or of its ambiguity of purpose in the same period, has also been said, with equal emphasis (and equal justification), ever since it came into being. In fact, what is so remarkable about the Labour Party is the similarity of the problems which have beset it throughout its history.

In suggesting the permanence and similarity of crisis, I do not wish to minimize its present gravity. Quite obviously, the Labour Party's difficulties in the last few years have been more acute than at any previous time, and it is at least unlikely that they will be resolved without causing profound changes in the Labour Party's whole character. But I do suggest that the present difficulties can only be properly understood by seeing them in the perspective of what has gone before. It is such a perspective that I have sought to provide.

CHAPTER I

LABOUR IN PARLIAMENT

'Socialism is to come through a
socialistic political party and not
through a Socialist one.'

Ramsay MacDonald, 1909

1. THE LIBERAL CONNECTION

So long had independent Labour representation in the House of
Commons been in the making that the formation of the Labour
Representation Committee in February 1900 was viewed then, and
has been viewed ever since, as a major step forward for Labour.
And so, for trade unionism, it was. But it was also a deliberate retreat
on the part of those in the Independent Labour Party who, like Keir
Hardie, had come to think that a party like theirs, with a socialist
programme, could not hope to attract sufficient support to become a
serious political force. In order to make possible an alliance with the
trade unions, the Socialists of the I.L.P. were content to agree that
the new body should only declare its purpose to be the representation of working-class opinion 'by men sympathetic with the aims and
demands of the Labour movement',[1] and to leave these aims and demands undefined. The delegates of the Marxist Social Democratic
Federation wanted the L.R.C. to declare that 'the representatives of
the working-class movement in the House of Commons' would form
there 'a distinct party based upon the recognition of the class war
and having for its ultimate object the socialization of the means of
production, distribution and exchange'.[2] None but a few of the 129
delegates to the Conference had any thought of agreeing to such
formulations.

Most of the delegates were trade unionists, representing sixty-seven
trade unions with a membership of some 570,000, or over one quarter
of the total trade union membership at the time. In the main, they
were radical Liberals, either explicitly hostile to, or with very little
sympathy for, socialism in any of its variants. They wanted indepen-

[1] Labour Representation Committee Conference Report, 1900, p. 11.
[2] ibid, p. 11.

17

dent Labour representation in the House of Commons, not because they had undergone some major ideological conversion, but because they had come to feel, slowly and hesitantly, and on the basis of their experience in the previous decade, that the working classes urgently needed reliable advocates in Parliament if their painfully-won rights were to be maintained and enhanced.[1] As the first Manifesto of the L.R.C. said, it was in the House of Commons that the power of capital was already represented. 'It is on both sides of the House. It has the ear of Ministers and can control the policy of parties. It frankly uses its powers to promote its own ends. It is fully alive to the fact that the great battles between capital and labour are to be fought out on the floor and in the division lobbies of the House of Commons.' The time had therefore come for wage-earners 'to be organized to support trade union principles and ideas by political methods'.[2]

As for the Socialists of the I.L.P., their opposition to the inscription of the doctrine of the class war on the banner of the new organization was not simply a reluctant surrender to the tactical requirements of the moment. It was also an expression of the conviction, however various its grounds, that there were no irreconcilable differences in society, that politics was not civil war carried on by other means, that there was room for manoeuvre with opponents who were not necessarily enemies, and that compromise was not only necessary but desirable. The House of Commons was not the best arena in which to fight the class war. But since they did not believe in the doctrine of the class war, as distinct from its necessary practice when conflict was forced upon the wage-earners, there was no reason why they should therefore take a poorer view of the House of Commons; the more so since the representative principle which the House of Commons had traditionally, if selectively, enshrined, had, by 1900, come to mean all but adult male suffrage. What was now needed, they felt, was to bring the working-classes more directly into politics, to persuade working men to send their own representatives to the House of Commons. Reforms desired by the Labour movement would then follow. And, the Socialists in the new Labour alliance believed, Labour would ultimately want socialist reforms; and these too would then naturally follow. In the words of Ramsay MacDonald, 'the modern State in most civilized communities is

---

[1] For evidence that the Taff Vale decision of 1901 was not the beginning of an attack on the trade unions, but the culmination of a trend, see J. Saville, 'Trade Unions and Free Labour: The Background to the Taff Vale Decision', in A. Briggs and J. Saville (Eds), *Essays in Labour History* (London, 1960) pp. 317-50.

[2] F. Bealey and H. Pelling, *Labour and Politics 1900-1906* (London, 1958) p. 33.

democratic, and in spite of remaining anomalies and imperfections, if the mass of the ordinary people are agreed upon any policy neither electors, privileged peers nor reigning houses could stand in their way'.[1]

The delegates to the 1900 Conference had pledged themselves to the return of a 'distinct Labour Group in Parliament, who shall have their own Whips, and agree upon their policy, which must embrace a readiness to co-operate with any party which for the time being may be engaged in promoting legislation in the direct interest of labour, and be equally ready to associate themselves with any party in opposing measures having an opposite tendency'.[2]

Once the Labour Representation Committee had been founded, with Ramsay MacDonald as its secretary, its members soon turned their attention to the achievement of electoral understandings, particularly with the Liberal Party. As early as May 1900, a sub-committee of the L.R.C. recommended that organizations affiliated to it 'should run their candidates to begin with in such a way as to make it possible for either the local Liberal or Conservative Associations to leave an open field for the Labour candidates'; the sub-committee also deemed it advisable 'to write to the Liberal and Conservative Whips, stating that we are supporting certain Labour candidates in certain constituencies with a view to forming a Labour Party . . . that *as a Committee we have no hostility to other political parties,* and that, so far as is possible under the conditions of our constitution, we shall be glad of their co-operation in getting these candidates through'.[3]

The proposal was formally made in September that a deputation from the L.R.C. be sent to the Whips of the Conservative, the Liberal and the Irish Nationalist parties, but a decision was deferred, by a majority of five to four. The election of 1900 then occurred before any further moves could be initiated.

Fifteen candidates were endorsed by the L.R.C. Of these, Richard Bell, the Secretary of the Railway Servants Union, and Keir Hardie were successful. Neither of them had been opposed by Liberal candidates. The lesson was bound to reinforce the Committee's propensity to alliance with the Liberals.

In fact, the history of the L.R.C. is largely the history of political manoeuvres to reach electoral accommodations with the Liberals. That this often involved the support of 'moderate' Labour candidatures in preference to socialist ones was something which the

---

[1] J. R. MacDonald, *Socialism and Society* (London, 1905) p. 135.
[2] Labour Representation Committee Conference Report, 1900, p. 12.
[3] Bealey and Pelling, op. cit. pp. 40-1. My italics.

strategists of the L.R.C. found it relatively easy to accept.[1] After protracted and secret negotiations, MacDonald and Keir Hardie reached an understanding in 1903 with Herbert Gladstone, the Liberal Chief Whip, under the terms of which the Liberal leaders agreed to use their influence to prevent local Liberal opposition to any L.R.C. candidate who supported 'the general objects of the Liberal Party'; in return, the L.R.C. was to 'demonstrate friendliness' to the Liberals in any constituency where it had influence.[2] Save for Keir Hardie, MacDonald's colleagues on the L.R.C. had known nothing of the negotiations nor did the Labour movement at large know anything about the agreement after it had begun to operate in the constituencies. Indeed, both Keir Hardie and MacDonald denied that there existed any compact with the Liberals at either national or local levels.[3]

There were naturally differences in the degree of eagerness with which the leaders of the L.R.C., some of whom were also leaders of the I.L.P., viewed the Liberal connection. But it is worth noting that they all found it much easier to contemplate association with the Liberals than with the Marxists of the Social Democratic Federation. Again, this was not only due to tactical or personal considerations. Much deeper ideological factors were involved. Keir Hardie had no love for the Liberal Party, but his affinities with a radical version of Liberalism remained strong.[4] As for MacDonald, he believed that there was no 'profound gulf' between Liberalism and Socialism. Socialism for him marked 'the growth of society, not the uprising of a class', and it was naturally to be furthered by the close collaboration of all men of good will on the basis of 'conceptions of right and wrong common to all classes'. By 1903, he was looking forward to the emergence of 'a united democratic party appealing to the people on behalf of a single, comprehensive belief in social reconstruction. The party may not be called Liberal, and it will be as far ahead of Liberalism as Liberalism itself was of its progressive predecessor Whiggism.'[5]

The leaders of the I.L.P., both for tactical and for larger ideological reasons, could not but welcome the withdrawal of the S.D.F.

[1] See, e.g. the manner in which David Shackleton, a Liberal trade unionist, was selected as L.R.C. candidate in the Clitheroe by-election of 1902, and his unopposed return to the House of Commons, ibid, Ch. V.
[2] For details of the 'MacDonald-Gladstone Entente', see ibid, Ch. VI.
[3] See Bealey and Pelling, op. cit. p. 158.
[4] See for instance his Open Letter to Lloyd George, published in the *Labour Leader* of the 7th of March, 1903, urging him to break with the Liberal Party and to become 'the recognized leader of that force in politics which desires genuine reform, and which is not bound by doctrinaire theories or traditions'.
[5] Bealey and Pelling, op. cit., p. 155.

from the L.R.C. in August 1901. From the beginning, they had considered the S.D.F. as a nuisance and a political embarrassment and they eagerly greeted Hyndman's resignation from the Executive of the S.D.F. as, in MacDonald's phrase, 'a frank acknowledgment of the complete failure of the Marxian movement' in England. And it was Hardie who wrote that 'the propaganda of the class hatred is not one which can ever take root in this country. . . . Mankind in the main is not moved by hatred but by love of what is right. *If we could have Socialism on the S.D.F. lines nothing would be changed —save for the worse.*'[1] It did not take the Bolshevik Revolution or the Communist Party's involvement with the Third International and Russia to define the attitude of the leaders of Labour to any organization which proclaimed its adherence to a revolutionary ideology. The attitude was defined from the earliest days of the Labour Party's existence. Later events only served to strengthen and refine it.

In strict electoral terms, the strategy of the L.R.C. proved highly successful. The House of Commons elected at the General Election of 1906 included twenty-nine L.R.C. members of Parliament, only five of whom had been opposed by Liberal candidates. Thirteen candidates who stood under a number of independent Socialist labels all fought in three-cornered contests and all were defeated.[2] Among the successful L.R.C. candidates were all the men who were to lead Labour in the following years, including MacDonald, Keir Hardie, Arthur Henderson,[3] Philip Snowden and J. R. Clynes. Together with the twenty-four 'Lib-Lab' members who had been elected under more direct Liberal auspices, Labour after 1906 formed a sizeable group in Parliament.

Given the history of the L.R.C., there was never any likelihood that the new Labour Party in Parliament,[4] however incisive the individual contributions of some of its members might on occasion be, would assume the character of a militant and independent opposition, with distinctive, let alone socialist, policies. The L.R.C.

[1] P. P. Poirier, *The Advent of the Labour Party* (London, 1958) p. 143. (My italics.) To which the S.D.F. retorted that 'Socialism based on the economics of the Fabian Society and the ethics of the New Testament (was) not Socialism at all, but glorified bureaucracy tempered by Christian charity' (ibid, p. 143).

[2] The S.D.F. put up eight candidates who obtained 22,000 votes.

[3] Henderson had entered Parliament in a by-election at Barnard Castle in July 1902, when he was still much more a Liberal than anything else. (See Bealey and Pelling, op. cit. pp. 152 ff.)

[4] For a description of its activities between 1906 and 1914, see J. H. Stewart Reid, *The Origin of the British Labour Party* (Minneapolis, 1955) chs. X and XI.

candidates had not, in any case, fought on a socialist platform and MacDonald had charted the course of the party two years before the election when he had written that 'if the Cabinet were anti-Imperialist, and were sound on Trade Union legislation, the Labour Party would be justified in giving it general support and in protecting it from defeat'.[1] Though this had embarrassed his colleagues, and though Hardie had written that a 'working agreement with Liberals or Conservatives would spell ruin',[2] the Parliamentary Labour Party did in fact act after 1906 as a more or less radical appendage of the Liberal Party in Parliament. There was no need until 1910 to protect the Liberal Government from defeat since the Liberals had an absolute majority over all other parties. Even so, Labour behaved much less like an opposition party than as a pressure group in the House of Commons. Its assumption of this rôle was made a great deal easier by the Government's initiation of a limited programme of social reform. The 'new Liberalism', of which Lloyd George became the apostle, was to a large extent designed, then and later, to provide a safe alternative to Labour and to anchor popular support to a party which explicitly repudiated, as the Labour Party did not, socialism of any kind.[3] For Labour to take its distance from a Liberal Government, at least one of whose members spoke a language of ringing radicalism, it would have been necessary for it to go far beyond the policies and strategy followed by the Parliamentary Party. And this its leaders would not do.

The only issue on which the Labour Party was unambiguously pledged was the legislative reversal of the Taff Vale decision of 1901, which had seriously jeopardized the unions' right to strike, but which had also been of crucial importance to the L.R.C., since it was this above all else which had persuaded more unions that they did indeed require independent representation in the House of Commons, and who therefore agreed to affiliate to the L.R.C. A Trades Dispute Act was in fact passed in 1906. That the Act ultimately met the Trade Unions' demands could legitimately be claimed as a success for the Parliamentary Labour Party. Much the same might

---

[1] Bealey and Pelling, op. cit. p. 178.
[2] Poirier, op. cit. p. 229.
[3] 'If a Liberal Government,' Lloyd·George said, 'tackle the landlord, and the brewers and the peers, as they have faced the parsons, and try to deliver the nation from the pernicious control of the confederacy of monopolists, then the independent Labour Party will call in vain upon the working men of Britain to desert Liberalism that is gallantly fighting to rid the land of the wrongs that have oppressed those who labour in it.' (J. T. Murphy, *Preparing for Power* (London, 1934) p. 101).

be said for various improvements of other Liberal measures of social reform, such as the provision of meals in schools for needy children, old age pensions and unemployment compensation. For a pressure group concerned with a limited range of specified objectives, it was not a discreditable record. For those concerned with the reconstruction of society, as many of the leaders of the parliamentary party claimed they were, it was not an impressive one. However, everything about the House of Commons taught resignation to slow advance and the Labour men were good pupils. 'Old members,' Snowden later recalled, 'smiled at the impatience of the new members. They reminded us of the time when they first came to Parliament full of an earnest enthusiasm to achieve some good purpose; but despair had entered into their hearts, and before the advent of the Labour men, they had resigned all hope of ever being able to move that cumbersome machine at any reasonable rate along the path of reform.'[1]

The Labour Party just maintained its position in the two General Elections of 1910. It won forty seats in January and forty-two in December but the apparent gain was entirely due to the transfer of the 'Lib-Lab' M.P.s of the Miners' Federation to the Labour Party. As in 1906, most successful candidates had no Liberal opponent. But the parliamentary situation was very different. The Liberal Government was returned on both occasions but now came to depend on either the Irish Nationalist or the Labour vote for a majority in the House. This gave a new kind of political relevance to Labour's parliamentary tactics, and it might have been thought to give Labour a much stronger bargaining position. In fact, the strategy of the leadership gave it less. The fixed point of that strategy was that the Government must on no account be brought down. The election of MacDonald to the Chairmanship of the Parliamentary Party in 1911, and annually thereafter until his resignation in 1914, further strengthened the bias towards alliance and accommodation with the Liberals, but the responsibility was hardly that of MacDonald alone.

In the bitter conflicts of those years—the most stormy period of British politics in this century—it was inevitable that the Labour Party should side with the Liberals against the Conservatives. What was less inevitable was that the Labour Party's voice should be reduced to a muffled plaint, which could barely be heard above the impassioned chorus of debate that rose over such issues as the reform of the House of Lords and Irish Home Rule. Neither Conservative nor Liberal protagonists in that debate found it necessary to

[1] Philip Viscount Snowden, *An Autobiography* (London, 1943) I, p. 127.

pay close attention to what the Labour Party might or might not think and do.[1]

The Labour Party had its own immediate grievances and interests. The decision of the House of Lords in the Osborne case in 1909 had placed an effective bar on the use of trade union funds for political purposes and had thus cut off the Labour Party from its most important source of revenue. This at least was a clear issue on which the Labour Party could unite. But even on matters such as these, it was content to beg rather than to demand: it was not until 1913 that the passage of the Trade Union Act of that year secured a partial reversal of the House of Lords' decision.[2] Meanwhile, however, the Government did institute in 1911 the payment of a salary of £400 a year to Members of the House of Commons.

On the fiercely controversial issue of the House of Lords, the Labour Party was unable to decide whether it wanted abolition or reform, and therefore readily supported reform. It is an index of the Labour Party's political status in those years that the Government, when it called the Constitutional Conference of 1910 to seek an agreed solution on this issue with its Tory opponents, should not have found it necessary to consult the Labour leaders, or to invite Labour to participate in the proceedings of the Conference.

Nor did the Labour Party find it easy to decide its tactics on the issue of female suffrage. Though there was, all things considered, a high measure of agreement about the justice of the women's claim to enfranchisement, there was much disagreement as to whether the Party should oppose any measure of electoral reform which did not also grant votes to women, or whether it should support some measure of reform, such as the enfranchisement of all male adults and the exercise of one vote only by each elector, and hope that the women might be taken care of later. It was only in 1912 that a resolution was passed at the Annual Conference of that year, requesting the Parliamentary Party 'to make it clear that no bill can be acceptable to the Labour and Socialist movement which does not include women'.[3]

[1] In 1910, however, Lloyd George approached MacDonald with the proposal that he should join a Coalition Government to be made up of 'moderate' Liberals and Conservatives. MacDonald tentatively agreed, and told Henderson that he had been empowered, should such a Coalition be formed, to bring in two under-secretaries. Henderson opposed participation and the scheme in any case soon collapsed. (See M. A. Hamilton, *Arthur Henderson. A Biography* (London, 1938) pp. 73-4.)
[2] Under the Act, unions were able to use funds for political purposes, provided they first obtained the authority of their members to do so by a ballot vote, and provided also that those union members who notified their unwillingness to contribute to such expenditure be exempted from the political levy.
[3] Labour Party Annual Conference Report, 1912, p. 192.

But on one thing at least the Labour leaders, except for a tiny minority which included Keir Hardie and George Lansbury, were clear; this was in their condemnation of the suffragettes' militant tactics and in their opposition to any action which did not conform to constitutional practice. As MacDonald wrote: 'The violent methods . . . are wrong, and in their nature reactionary and anti-social, quite irrespective of vote or no vote.'[1]

2. THE LABOUR LEFT

The achievements of the parliamentary party in those years were not such as to hide the limited nature of its impact and the ambiguity of its position. Whatever might be said for the inevitability of gradualness, Labour's progress bore too close a resemblance to stagnation not to produce much frustration, recrimination and criticism of the leadership.

The challenge stemmed from two quite distinct sources. The first came from the Labour Left, mainly from within the ranks of the I.L.P., and therefore inside the Labour Party; the second came from the revolutionary Left, mainly outside it. The two sets of critics had little in common, save for their common hostility to the strategy and tactics of Labour's leaders.

Most rank and file members of the I.L.P., and certainly all the activists, saw themselves as Socialist crusaders, engaged in a permanent battle against evil, and they were borne along by the fervent conviction that the outcome of the battle must be the establishment of a Socialist Commonwealth in which classes would be no more and men would finally come into their inheritance. Had the Trade Union component of the Labour alliance more openly assumed the leadership of the Labour Party, the Socialists' relative weakness in it would have appeared more clearly. As it is, the leaders of the I.L.P., by occupying positions of major influence in the direction of the L.R.C. and then of the Labour Party, helped to a considerable extent to blur the image of the Party, and to provide it, in the eyes of many activists, with some kind of socialist letters of credit. Yet, even men like Keir Hardie could not hide the fact that the Labour Party was not only a party of compromise but that the compromise gave very little to the Socialists in the way of effective political influence.

From the very beginning, there were members of the I.L.P. who were deeply suspicious of the strategy of the L.R.C., and who took a much less hostile view of bodies like the S.D.F. than did the leadership. Thus at the Dewsbury by-election of 1902, a number of I.L.P. branches, despite the clear advice of the leaders of the I.L.P., had

[1] *Socialist Review*, August 1912.

urged the Dewsbury I.L.P. to support Harry Quelch, the S.D.F. candidate. Indeed, Edward Hartley, the man whom the leaders wanted as the candidate himself supported Quelch. Hartley was certainly expressing sentiments that were not his alone when he wrote to Thompson of the *Clarion* that 'the great work of the official section of the I.L.P. at the present seems not so much to push Socialism as to try to intrigue some half a dozen persons into Parliament. There is probably not more than one place in Britain (if there is one) where we can get a Socialist into Parliament without some arrangement with Liberalism, and for such an arrangement Liberalism will demand a terribly heavy price—more than we can possibly afford.'[1] Furthermore, there was a minority within the I.L.P. which was not reluctant to consider a renewed connection with the S.D.F., even though it would not endorse the S.D.F.'s doctrines. At the 1902 Conference of the Party forty delegates (against sixty-nine) voted in favour of a consideration of the proposal.

In the main, however, the Labour Left was more concerned to strengthen its influence within the Labour Party than to look for allies outside it. One of its most constant endeavours was to circumscribe within narrow limits the freedom of action of Labour representatives in Parliament. The socialist activists in the party could not reconcile themselves to the notion that their parliamentarians should enjoy a Burkeian kind of independence. The parliamentarians on the other hand, wanted the greatest possible degree of freedom in their political activities. These divergent attitudes had very little to do with abstract principles concerning the proper working of parliamentary government or the rights and duties of Members of Parliament. Underlying the tension between activists and parliamentarians was the former's fear that the Labour Group in Parliament would, if it were not strictly controlled, backslide into opportunism, manoeuvre and compromise, and the latter's easy assumption that manoeuvre and compromise were inherent in their situation and essential to the furtherance of Labour's immediate aims.

The issue remained largely academic until the entry in 1906 of a sizeable Labour Group in Parliament. It was debated at the 1907 Annual Conference of the Labour Party and an ambiguous formula was then agreed (by 642,000 to 252,000 votes) according to which 'resolutions instructing the Parliamentary Party as to their action in the House of Commons be taken as the opinions of the Conference, on the understanding that the time and method of giving effect to those instructions be left to the Party in the House, in conjunction with the National Executive'.[2] The principle that the Annual Con-

[1] Poirier, op. cit. p. 145.
[2] Labour Party Annual Conference Report, 1907, p. 48.

ference of the Party had the right to give binding instructions to the P.L.P. was thus affirmed, while the execution of these instructions was left to the discretion of the leadership, mainly the parliamentary leadership. In practice, as experience was to show, this gave the leadership as much or nearly as much independence as it desired. On the other hand, it greatly enhanced the activists' faith in the efficacy of Conference resolutions and their ineradicable conviction that the passage of resolutions at annual conferences must automatically entail important consequences in regard to Party policy. In fact, the whole history of the Labour Party has been punctuated by verbal victories of the Labour Left which, with some few exceptions, have had little influence on the Labour Party's conduct inside or outside the House of Commons,[1] but which have always been of great importance in keeping up the hopes and the morale of the activists.

The strategy of Labour's parliamentary leaders was bound to increase the suspicion and hostility of the activists who found much more attractive the behaviour in Parliament of Victor Grayson than of their leaders. Victor Grayson was a 25-year-old member of the I.L.P. who stood as an independent 'Labour and Socialist' candidate in a by-election at Colne Valley in July 1907, without the endorsement either of the I.L.P. or of the Labour Party, but with the support of the local I.L.P. He was elected, refused to accept the discipline of the Parliamentary Party and sat as an independent member. His impassioned zeal in pressing the claims of the unemployed soon involved him in angry 'scenes' in the House of Commons, and led to his suspension from it. Grayson's activities were profoundly embarrassing to his colleagues, both because these activities were deemed to compromise the Labour Group's respectability, and also because they offered to the activists a striking contrast with the Group's own lack of impact.

It was not only the strategy of the Labour Group in Parliament which infuriated the leadership's critics. They were equally incensed by an electoral strategy which clearly continued to be dictated by

[1] In 1908, for instance, the Conference of that year passed a resolution which stated that 'the time has arrived when the Labour Party should have as a definite object, the socialization of the means of production, distribution and exchange to be controlled by a democratic State in the interest of the entire community; and the complete emancipation of labour from the domination of capitalism and landlordism, with the establishment of social and economic equality of the sexes'. The resolution was passed by 514,000 votes to 469,000 (Labour Party Annual Conference Report, 1908, pp. 76-7). Though it pleased the socialists within the Party, the resolution could hardly be said to have had any influence upon the Party's policies in the following years.

clandestine accommodations with the Liberals. Repeatedly, the Executive Committee withheld support for Labour candidates at by-elections so as to give a Liberal a straight fight against a Conservative. It did so notably at Dundee in 1908, where Winston Churchill, the Liberal candidate and newly appointed President of the Board of Trade, stood and was elected. The Labour candidate, who was only supported by the Scottish Labour Party, finished at the bottom of the poll.

In 1908, Ben Tillett, of 1889 Dock Strike fame, published a pamphlet with the suggestive title *Is the Parliamentary Party a Failure?*, in which he denounced the parliamentary leaders as 'sheer hypocrites' who 'for ten and five guineas a time will lie with the best' and who repaid 'with gross betrayal the class that willingly supports them'. Tillett's language was unrepresentative, but the unease and frustration which lay behind it were not. At the 1909 Conference of the I.L.P., a resolution was actually moved for the secession of the I.L.P. from the Labour Party; it was heavily defeated, but the victory of those whom the activists had come to see as the Old Guard did not settle matters and the parliamentary party's unswerving determination to support the Government after 1910 swelled the ranks of the critics.

So acute was this unease that Keir Hardie found it necessary to deal explicitly with those who proclaimed the necessity for a break with the Labour Party.[1] This he did in *My Confession of Faith in the Labour Alliance*. The I.L.P., he claimed, had lost nothing of its Socialist character by entering into alliance with the Labour Party. 'People,' he said, 'want more picturesqueness, more of the embodiment of the old rebellious spirit of revolt, more fighting which will quicken the pulse in connection with the work of the Party in Parliament.' This was a feeling with which he could 'most heartily sympathize'. But the Party needed more than this; it must prove to the nation that its members could be 'statesmen as well as agitators'. Moreover, he reminded the critics, no Socialist save for himself at South West Ham in 1892 had yet succeeded in winning a seat in Parliament under other than Labour Party auspices. At least the Labour label made it possible for a Socialist to get 'a sympathetic reception for both himself and his doctrines because he comes to the average man[2] as the representative of his own party, for which he is paying and over which he exercises control'.[3]

---

[1] As, e.g. Robert Blatchford, who wrote in the *Clarion* in April 1910: 'I think a Labour Party is a good thing; but the I.L.P. was a Socialist Party. In joining the Labour Party it ceased to be a Socialist Party.'
[2] 'who does not indulge over much in theories'
[3] K. Hardie, *My Confession of Faith in the Labour Alliance* (London, 1910) pp. 9 ff.

As for the Marxist critics of the Social Democratic Federation, who were thinking of forming a Socialist Representation Committee in rivalry to the Labour Party, they were, said Hardie, 'outraging every principle of Marxian Socialist tactics'; indeed, he wrote, 'the Labour Party is the only confession of orthodox Marxian Socialism in Great Britain', for the Labour Party 'practises the Marxian policy of the class struggle, following Marx's own example, and is blamed by its critics for doing so, whilst its critics, in practice, reduce Marx's great historic formula to a set of quite meaningless phrases'.[1]

For all that, Keir Hardie himself was far from easy. 'The Labour Party,' he said, 'had ceased to count: the Press ignored it; Cabinet Ministers made concessions to the Tory Party and to the Irish, seemingly oblivious of the fact that there was a Labour Party in the House.'[2] I.L.P. members of Parliament, he told the 1910 Conference of the Party, should be in the House of Commons 'not to keep governments in office or to turn them out, but to organize the working class into a great independent political power to fight for the coming of Socialism'.[3] By 1914, he had joined the critics of the parliamentary leadership.[4]

Another leading member of the I.L.P. who had long been unhappy about the Party's commitment to support of the Government was Fred Jowett. In his presidential address to the 1910 Conference of the I.L.P., he too argued that 'all this jiggery pokery of party government played like a game for ascendency and power, is no use to us. It is . . . for us to state in the clearest possible terms what we stand for and vote steadily on the merits of the questions before us, regardless of consequence, rather than barter our support for some promised measure, which may or may not realize our expectations when it is produced.'[5]

For the most part, however, the Labour Left never seriously considered secession from the Labour Party. A pamphlet published in the same year by four members of the I.L.P. National Council, led by Leonard Hall, is a good example of its frustrations. The pamphlet, entitled *Let Us Reform the Labour Party* and known as the Green Manifesto, bitterly condemned the 'suicidal "Revisionist" policy' accepted by most members of the Parliamentary Labour Group, which had 'reduced the whole Movement to acute anaemia or rabid melancholy'. 'For myself,' Leonard Hall wrote, 'I am convinced that

[1] Hardie, op. cit. p. 14.
[2] Snowden, *An Autobiography*, op. cit. I, p. 215. Hardie had not, Snowden wrote, 'the accommodating spirit which is essential in a successful Parliamentary leader' (ibid, p. 125).
[3] 1910 I.L.P. Annual Conference Report, p. 59.
[4] 1914 Labour Party Annual Conference Report, pp. 82-3.
[1] 1910 I.L.P. Annual Conference Report, p. 35.

the I.L.P. would be far more fruitfully engaged as a purely propagandist force, devoting its resources to the spreading of sound and thorough-going Socialist opinion in the country, and eschewing direct Parliamentary representation altogether, than in continuing to waste its magnificent opportunities and its potential enthusiasm on such Socialistically barren pettifogging as the Labour Parliamentarians are giving us.'[1] One of Hall's co-authors, J. M. McLachlan, wrote that the two alternatives facing the Labour movement were 'what might be termed for convenience "REVISION and REVOLUTION". The former is already in practice as the chosen policy of our Parliamentary leaders. The latter is the one which more truly harmonizes with the temperament and represents the political ideals of the rank and file of the Trade Union and Socialist movement. The movement desires the one; our leaders have chosen the other.'[2] Even so, Mr McLachlan hoped and trusted 'that no man or woman would be so cowardly as to listen to the cry "Let us leave the Labour Party". . . . The Labour Party is the one conceivable formation in which Labour can operate against Capitalism.' What was needed, however, was to return to the traditional policy of the movement and to state 'in the clearest possible manner what we stand for, and vote steadily on the questions before us, regardless of consequences'; in other words, 'a policy of steady independence which observes an impartial acceptance or rejection of measures on their merits, irrespective of the fate or convenience of a Government'.[3] This plea that the parliamentary party should vote 'on merits' was overwhelmingly defeated at the 1911 Conference of the I.L.P. But it steadily gained support and by 1914 it had become the majority view (by 233 votes to 78), only to be made irrelevant by the War.

The critics were given plenty of ideological hostages by the leadership of the Party, and particularly by MacDonald. The latter took no pains to conceal the peculiar view he held of the progress of socialism in Britain, or of the tactics which that view dictated; and MacDonald was both the main architect and the most articulate advocate of the politics of manoeuvre and compromise. Speaking to the I.L.P. Conference of 1909, he vigorously defended the strategy of the Parliamentary Party as not only necessary but desirable in principle for a minority party like the Labour Party. 'Every facility given to a minority to impose its will upon the majority is a facility which any minority could use, and not merely a Labour or a Socialist minority. To protect the conditions and the existence of democratic government is just as essential to the building up of a Socialist State as is the

[1] *Let Us Reform the Labour Party*, p. 4.
[2] ibid, p. 7.
[3] ibid, p. 14.

solution of the problem of unemployment. . . . The Party which proposes to strike at the heart of democratic government in order to make a show of earnestness about unemployment, will not only not be tolerated by the country, but does not deserve to be.'[1]

This argument from democracy, or rather from parliamentary democracy, was the trump card which the leadership constantly played against its I.L.P. critics. The latter's theoretical positions were not such as to enable them to counter it with any effect. But Macdonald went a good deal further. In his *Socialism and Government*, published in 1909, he found the conclusion 'irresistible' that the object of Socialist who were active in politics 'ought not to be to form a Socialist party, but a party that will journey towards Socialism. The Socilaist assumptions are like the light and the air. They become the conditions of the life of the people who can no more theorize and dogmatize about them, explain and rattle off their scientific formulae, than they can fly. The clamour for a Socialist party is a remnant of the revolutionary period, or a copying of methods proper to countries where parliamentary government is but a name. What is wanted here is a party which accepts the Socialist point of view and approaches the industrial problems of society with Socialist assumptions in mind. . . . Socialism is to come through a socialistic political party and not through a Socialist one. Indeed, paradoxical though it may appear, Socialism will be retarded by a Socialist party which thinks it can do better than a Socialistic party, because its methods would be contrary to those by which Society evolves.'[2]

As to the view that Labour should pursue a totally independent policy, regardless of political circumstances, MacDonald proclaimed it as altogether mistaken. 'The parliamentary method,' he wrote in September 1910, 'must take long views; it must use brains to choose time and reasons for combats, to select occasions for elections, to use circumstances.' And, he warned, rather prophetically, 'men who are oppressed by the thought of how much needs to be done, will, if the present condition of jealousy and vain criticism continues, decline to waste their lives in a Party that refuses to allow anyone to put its good principles and its excellent intentions to practical use.'[3]

It was to be expected that MacDonald should come under attack, particularly after 1911. He was, said one delegate to the 1909 I.L.P. Conference, 'a powerful leader', but 'he is leading the Labour movement in the wrong direction. The revisionist policy that he stands

[1] 1909 I.L.P. Annual Conference Report, p. 47.
[2] J. R. MacDonald, *Socialism and Government* (London, 1909) p. 12.
[3] *Socialist Review*, September 1910.

31

for is not the policy represented by the I.L.P. in the past.'[1] But what is more significant, and indicative of the weakness of the Labour Left, is that opposition to MacDonald was not greater. The weakness was not of numbers only, nor of will. It was a weakness implicit in the fact that the Labour Left shared so many of MacDonald's fundamental assumptions. But in any case, the critics were already then suffering from a disadvantage which has been a permanent element in the weakness of the Left in regard to the Labour leadership—the fact that they were critics. The critics were a threat to unity. They were rocking a fragile boat. They were letting down the team. They were not playing the game. These were, and have always remained, compelling notions in the Labour movement and Labour leaders have always taken the fullest advantage of their compulsion in dealing with the Labour Left. From 1910 onwards, however, it was not the Labour Left which constituted the main problem that faced the leadership. It was the new militancy of the industrial workers.

3. THE CHALLENGE OF MILITANCY

Replying to the authors of the Green Manifesto, MacDonald had written that 'revisionism' (which he held to be 'primarily a restatement of certain economic doctrines and forecasts of Marx') 'had little to do with the Labour Party and nothing to do with its policy'.[2] And it is certainly true that the strategists of the Labour Party were not theoretical revisionists since they had never, so to speak, been visionists. There was no coherent and official body of doctrine from which they found it necessary to extricate themselves in order to get down to what they conceived to be the serious business of politics. English 'reformists' did not seek to justify themselves with the kind of analysis of the nature and future of capitalism with which men like Eduard Bernstein sought to buttress German reformism. They did not find it necessary to argue that capitalism was no longer the prisoner of unsurmountable contradictions which must lead to ever greater crises. They had never believed that it was. They did of course believe that there was much that was wrong with capitalism, on economic, social and moral grounds. But they also believed that what was wrong with it could be gradually cured by remedial action mainly conceived in terms of growing State intervention. They assumed that, given sufficient pressure in Parliament, the State would not only further the process of redressing the economic and social

[1] 1909 I.L.P. Annual Conference Report, p. 70.
[2] *Socialist Review*, September 1910.

balance in favour of Labour, but also that, in time, this would entail a measure of collectivism so wide that it would also mean the super-session of capitalism, without strife and upheaval. Nor were most of their critics in the I.L.P. arguing from very different premisses. And since this view was only controverted by small revolutionary groupings of small numerical importance, the Labour Parliamentarians, whether orthodox or otherwise, had little need to engage in what was in any case for most of them the highly uncongenial task of theoretical debate.[1]

The theoretical confrontation, such as it was, between more or less orthodox Marxists, mainly grouped in the Social Democratic Federation, and anti-Marxists, mainly represented by the Fabians, had occurred in the eighties and nineties, and had been acted out on an extremely exiguous stage, between few participants and mostly outside the Labour movement itself. Nor had the Marxist groupings succeeded in making a greater impact in the following years. In the first decade of the century these groupings consisted mainly of the S.D.F., the Socialist Labour Party, which was formed in 1903 as a splinter group of the S.D.F., and whose strength lay mainly on the Clyde; and another splinter group of the S.D.F., the Socialist Party of Great Britain which was formed in 1905. The S.D.F. itself became the Social Democratic Party in 1907 and again changed its name to the British Socialist Party in 1911.

Under Russian conditions, the disputations between contending revolutionary factions came to have epoch-making consequences. In the British context, the differences are not really capable of rising above the level of historical footnotes. Much more important was the residue of ideas which the members of these revolutionary groupings had in common and the selfless dedication they showed in their propagation. For beyond their more complex differences, the simple message they carried was that the wage earners would achieve neither immediate reforms, nor the emancipation of their class, without a militant assertion of their strength outside Parliament.

---

[1] After the General Election of 1906, W. T. Stead, the Editor of *The Review of Reviews*, sent a questionnaire to the 51 Labour and 'Lib-Lab' Members of Parliament, asking them to set out what books they had found most useful in their early days. Of the 51, 45 replied. The most interesting feature of the answers, in the present context, is the paucity of books mentioned which are concerned with socialist theory: the answers of only two members, J. O'Grady and particularly Will Thorne, both of the S.D.F., suggest any grounding in it. For the rest, their main intellectual influences appear to have been the Bible, and writers ranging from Shakespeare and Milton to Carlyle, Ruskin, J. S. Mill and Dickens. (See *The Review of Reviews*, vol. XXXIII, June 1906, pp. 568-952.)

In essence, this was also the message which revolutionary syndicalism preached after 1910. Revolutionary syndicalism in England entailed the rejection of traditional trade unionism, with its fragmented organization, its emphasis on collective bargaining and compromise, on conciliation and respectability. It entailed the rejection of the kind of bureaucratic collectivism which was to be found at the core of Fabian thinking and which has also come to permeate much non-Fabian thinking in this period. And, thirdly, it entailed a doctrine of industrial action, based on a rejection of parliamentary action almost as dogmatic as was the Labour leaders' insistence upon its virtues. But what ultimately mattered about the syndicalist message was its emphasis upon 'direct action'. Most of the hundreds of thousands of workers involved in the bitter industrial warfare of the years which preceded the First World War had more limited aims than the syndicalists; few would have subscribed to the revolutionary vision the syndicalists held forward. But they could and did respond to the call for industrial militancy of which the syndicalists were the most vocal exponents.

Revolutionary syndicalism was of course abhorred by all Labour leaders, industrial and political. 'Let not the Labour movement' MacDonald urged in the *Socialist Review* (October 1911) 'add syndicalism to the already numerous vipers which in the kindness of its heart, it is warming on its hearthstones',[1] and in his *Syndicalism: A Critical Examination*, published the following year, he condemned it both for its ultimate ends and even more for its methods. 'Syndicalism,' he wrote, 'must be parliamentary or nothing.' The programme of revolutionary syndicalism was shaped by the belief in the class struggle as the determinant factor in society. 'But,' said MacDonald, 'any project of social reconstruction which founds itself upon reality must begin with the facts of social unity, not with those of class conflict, because the former is the predominant fact in society.'[2] As to Parliament, it was 'essential to social coherent life'; ultimately, industrial disputes would have 'at length to be settled by the House of Commons as representative of the common interest of consumers and as guardian of social order and peace'.[3]

In the same year, Philip Snowden, who had long been one of the most acid critics of the leadership on the parliamentary left, published his *Socialism and Syndicalism* and altogether dismissed the latter as obsolete and futile, together with any form of revolutionary socialism. That phrase, he said, 'has survived long after it has ceased to have any real significance, for nowadays not even the boldest

[1] *Socialist Review*, October 1911.
[2] J. R. MacDonald, *Syndicalism: A Critical Examination* (London 1912) p. 50.
[3] ibid, pp. 54, 70.

voiced Revolutionary Socialist expects that the social Revolution will be achieved in any other way than by the gradual acquisition of political power by the democracy and the gradual transformation of the capitalist system into a co-operative commonwealth.'[1]

In regard to strike action itself, however, the Labour leaders had to take account both of the temper of the times and also of the successes of militant action. In 1911, four Labour parliamentarians, including Arthur Henderson, had tabled a Bill which proposed to make strikes illegal unless thirty days' notice had been given in advance.[2] The Bill, Mr Roberts notes, had not been officially authorized either by the T.U.C. or the Labour Party, 'though', he adds, 'it probably had the support of many of the leaders of the Labour movement'.[3] But the Parliamentary Committee of the T.U.C., while stressing the need for discipline, also found it necessary to express appreciation of the gains strike action had made possible. The 1911 Conference of the T.U.C., however, was in a much more militant mood. 'No effort,' one resolution said, 'shall be spared by the forces of organized labour to arouse and maintain the discontent of underpaid workers with their conditions, and to quicken and assist their determination to use all possible means to win for themselves a living wage.'[4] And the Conference also unequivocally condemned the 'conciliation bill' introduced in the House by the four Labour M.P.s.[5] By 1913, Ramsay MacDonald was writing 'it is quite certain that up to now the power to strike has enabled organized Labour to secure the advances of wages and improvements in conditions which it has won'.[6] At the same time, he insisted that 'the Trade Union conflict has become the national conflict; the field upon which it has to be fought out is the State, not the workshop; the weapon is to be the ballot-box and the Act of Parliament, not collective bargaining'.[7]

The reconciliation, more apparent than real, between the divergent emphasis of the militants and the parliamentarians was achieved by the latter's agreement that there was much to be said for *both* industrial and political action.

Thus in his presidential address to the 1913 Labour Party Conference, G. H. Roberts, M.P., referring to 'the harsh and violent criticism of those who claim to be, but are not in uniformity with,

---

[1] P. Snowden, *Socialism and Syndicalism* (London, 1912) p. 133.
[2] B.C. Roberts, *The Trades Union Congress, 1868-1921* (London, 1958) p. 241.
[3] ibid, p. 241.
[4] ibid, p. 241; T.U.C. Annual Conference Report, 1911, p. 237.
[5] T.U.C. Annual Conference Report, 1911, p. 230.
[6] Ramsay MacDonald. *The Social Unrest, Its Cause and Solution* (London, 1913) p. 69.
[7] ibid, p. 104.

the organized Labour and Socialist Movement', admitted that 'none can avoid a sense of disappointment at the results of political action'. But the same, he claimed, was true of industrial action. 'Direct actionists affect to repudiate the representative government of modern democracy, and have aroused the suspicion that they favour violence rather than discussion and reason.' Yet, politics could not be dispensed with, and it was a reckless gamble to stake everything on a single policy of forceful action; nor had what he called the universal strike yet emerged from the realm of speculative philosophy. Both political and industrial action, he insisted, were equally necessary, and the Labour Party refused to accept the view that political action was futile and "direct industrialism" the only certain means of realizing working-class aims and aspirations.[1] And a year later, the 1914 conference was presented with a resolution which stated 'that permanent improvement among the ranks of the workers can only be fully effected by joint action on Trade Union and independent political lines'. This, said MacDonald, was a definite challenge to Syndicalism, and he therefore asked the delegates to give it 'their most enthusiastic and overwhelming support'.[2] The resolution was easily carried.

But 'Trade Union lines' did not necessarily mean militant action. On the contrary, it was coming, more and more, to mean the reverse. For one of the not very paradoxical results of the industrial unrest of those years was to hasten the search for means of averting industrial conflict. The Government was not averse to the display and even to the use of military strength against strikers. But it also wished to clip the wings of the militants by the establishment of regular machinery for the pacific settlement of disputes. In this, it found the Labour leaders valuable allies.[3] Between 1910 and 1914, trade union membership rose from two and a half to four million. And in June 1914, the miners, the railwaymen and the transport workers had formed a Triple Industrial Alliance, which promised, as Mr Roberts notes, 'to be the most formidable concentration of industrial strength ever achieved by the trade union movement'.[4] But under the guidance of trade union leaders eager for conciliation, such a growth held the promise of stability at a new level, not of upheaval.

So of course did the emergence of Labour as a parliamentary

[1] Labour Party Annual Conference Report, 1913, pp. 69 ff.
[2] Labour Party Annual Conference Report, 1914, p. 103.
[3] For attempts to achieve better 'industrial relations' before the First World War, see E. H. Phelps Brown, *The Growth of British Industrial Relations* (London, 1959) ch. VI; also Lord (G. R.) Askwith, *Industrial Problems and Disputes* (London, 1920).
[4] Roberts, op. cit. p. 267.

force. This was well realized by many influential people, particularly in the Liberal Party, who had become reconciled to the fact that Labour must be accorded some place in the political order of things because they saw Labour in the House of Commons much less as a threat than as a safety valve. Men like Lloyd George might dream of giving the Liberal Party an image that would diminish and possibly destroy the Labour Party's appeal to the working classes. But there were others who were more concerned to integrate Labour into the system on the safest possible terms, lest worse befall. Joseph Chamberlain had spoken in the eighties of the need for property to pay ransom[1]. His successors knew the Labour leaders to be scarcely less opposed to 'extremism' than they were themselves, and more likely to defeat its manifestations in the Labour movement. Nor did they have to fear that, under the leadership of men like MacDonald, there would be found in the House of Commons, as one of MacDonald's critics urged there should, 'a reflection . . . of the heat and passionate indignation that had moved large masses of people to revolt.'[2] Hence their readiness to smooth Labour's path in politics, as expressed, for instance, in their willingness to legislate for the payment of members of Parliament, a measure of far greater benefit to Labour members than to any other; as expressed too in their agreement to remove the inhibitions imposed upon Labour's participation in politics by the Osborne Judgement. And there is much significance in the fact that this latter concession should have been made in 1913, at the height of the industrial unrest: if that unrest was to be stemmed, one of the means to stem it was to strengthen the position of the Labour parliamentarians and to make it possible for them to argue, as MacDonald did at the 1914 Labour Party Conference, that so long as either of the main parties offered some concession to the Labour movement, for whatever reason, 'then irrespective of its name *and irrespective of other proposals it might make*, the Labour Party would be bound to do its level best to give that Party a chance for being responsible for the politics of

---

[1] See E. E. Gulley, *Joseph Chamberlain and English Social Politics* (New York, 1926). 'What ransom,' Chamberlain had asked in 1885, 'will property pay for the security which it enjoys? What substitute will it find for the natural rights which have ceased to be recognized?' (op. cit. p. 213); and in 1886: 'What insurance will wealth find to its advantage to provide against the risks to which it is undoubtedly subject? If the rich want their rights to be respected as they ought to be, they are bound in turn to respect the rights of their less fortunate brethren' (ibid, p. 213). See also Arthur Balfour in 1895: 'Social legislation . . . is not merely to be distinguished from Socialist legislation, but is its most direct opposite and its most effective antidote' (J. D. Kingsley, *Representative Bureaucracy* (London 1944) p. 47.
[2] Labour Party Annual Conference Report, 1914, p. 75.

the country'.[1] Similarly there was everything to be said, from the traditional parties' point of view, for having J. R. Clynes tell the delegates that 'too frequent strikes caused a sense of disgust, of being a nuisance to the community'.[2] By 1914, the more enlightened members of Britain's ruling orders had come to see the leaders of Labour *both* as opponents and as allies.

[1] Labour Party Annual Conference Report, 1914, pp. 78-9.
[2] ibid, p. 74.

CHAPTER II

LABOUR IN THE FIRST WORLD WAR

'When this war broke out organized
Labour in this country lost the
initiative. It became a mere echo of
the old governing classes' opinion.'

J. R. MacDonald, 3rd of June, 1917

1. THE GREAT ILLUSION

I T seems very odd, in retrospect, that anyone should have seriously
believed in the decade which preceded the outbreak of war that
most Labour leaders, whether in Britain, France, Germany or
Austria, would refuse to support their Governments in case of war;
and that the working classes, faced with the choice of national
as against international solidarity, would opt for the latter. Of all
the great illusions of that epoch, this was surely the greatest. It was
of course an illusion that was greatly encouraged by the rhetoric
of the parties affiliated to the Second International and by the
resolutions adopted on the subject of war by the International itself.[1]
At Stuttgart in 1907, the International had unanimously endorsed a
powerfully-worded resolution on *Militarism and International Conflicts*, which remained a fundamental text of the international
Socialist movement down to 1914, and whose concluding paragraphs
stated that 'in the case of a threat of an outbreak of war, it is the
duty of the working classes and their parliamentary representatives
in the countries taking part, fortified by the unifying activities of the
International Bureau, to do everything to prevent the outbreak of
war by whatever means seem to them most effective, which naturally
differ with the intensification of the class war and of the general
political situation'. 'Should war break out in spite of all this,' the
resolution went on, 'it is their duty to intercede for its speedy end,
and to strive with all their power to make use of the violent economic
and political crisis brought about by the war to rouse the people,

---

[1] See, e.g. J. Joll, *The Second International, 1889-1914* (London, 1955) chs.
v, vi, vii, and G. D. H. Cole, *A History of Socialist Thought, The Second
International, 1889-1914*, volume III, Part I (London, 1956) ch. II.

and thereby to hasten the abolition of capitalist class rule."[1]

Whatever ambiguities and reservations this and later resolutions might conceal, the International, and the parties affiliated to it, were at least committed to some form of action against the threat of war. The British Labour movement was a party to the commitment. The British Section of the International included the Labour Party, the I.L.P., the Fabian Society and (after 1911) the British Socialist Party. Deep though disagreement might run among them on all else, British delegates to the Congresses of the International were at least united in their belief that the international working-class movement could, and should, do all in its power to prevent the outbreak of an international conflict. At Copenhagen in 1910, it was Keir Hardie, supported by his fellow delegates from the I.L.P. and the Labour Party, who was responsible, with the Frenchman Vaillant, for an amendment to the general resolution on the issue of war. 'Among all the means to be used to prevent and hinder war,' the amendment stated, 'the Congress considers as particularly effective the general strike of workers, especially in the industries which supply the instruments of war (arms, munitions, transport, etc.) as well as popular agitation and action in their most effective forms."[2]

It was not proposed, Keir Hardie explained, that the use of the strike weapon should be unilateral; there should be a simultaneous stoppage by the workers in all belligerent countries. Nor, he said, need the strike be truly general; and he certainly did not envisage strike action as the prelude to insurrection. Even so, the specific commitment to strike action was sufficiently definite for a majority of the Congress to refuse, significantly, to enter into it, and to decide to hold the matter over for further consideration at a subsequent Congress.

On this issue, at least, the British delegates found themselves on the left of the International. Ramsay MacDonald himself, though he condemned in the pages of the *Socialist Review* the notion of the General Strike for purely industrial or revolutionary aims, did however suggest that such a strike 'is quite possible for some definite and specific object which has stirred the popular mind, and is regarded sympathetically by sections of all classes—a General Strike for instance, against an unpopular war'.[3]

There were, however, different voices before 1914. Quite apart from those who, like Robert Blatchford and H. M. Hyndman,

[1] For the full text, see Joll, op. cit., pp. 196-98. The last paragraph was the contribution of Lenin and Rosa Luxemburg.
[2] Cole, op. cit. p. 83.
[3] *Socialist Review*, October 1911, p. 121, ft. 1.

opposed the idea of working-class action against war because of their virulent anti-Germanism, there were others whose opposition was simply based on the view that, if it came to the point, Labour could do nothing about it, and should in any case not try. When, for instance, the 1912 Annual Conference of the Labour Party was asked to approve a proposal from the International (which had originated in the I.L.P. and had been supported by the whole British Section) that each national party 'investigate and report on whether and how far a stoppage of work, either partial or general, in countries about to engage in war would be effective in preventing an outbreak of hostilities',[1] this was strongly opposed in a remarkable speech by a representative trade union leader, Tom Shaw, of the Textile Workers. 'Why waste time,' asked Shaw, 'in going round asking the rank and file if they thought it would be advisable in the event of a declaration of war to declare a General Strike?' 'War between country and country,' he went on, 'is a bad thing, but in case of such a war any attempt of a General Strike to prevent the people defending their country would result in civil war which was ten times worse than war between nation and nation.' And he therefore proposed that the International be told that 'the rank and file were so much opposed to the idea of a General Strike that it was considered unnecessary to make any further inquiries'.[2]

Arthur Henderson's reply was equally illuminating. 'Personally,' he said, 'he was very largely in agreement with the remarks of Mr Shaw . . . had the resolution been committing the Movement to the principle (of the General Strike) he would have opposed it.' Since, however, the resolution was non-committal, there was no reason why it should not be unanimously carried.[3]

Austria-Hungary declared war on Serbia on the 25th of July, 1914. On the 29th, the Bureau of the International met at Brussels and was told that Austrian social-democracy was entirely powerless to affect the course of events. The Bureau decided nothing, except that the Congress should meet in Paris on the 9th of August.

Even so, British Labour leaders did, in the days before Britain actually entered the war, speak as though they attached meaning to the International's commitments. On the 30th of July, the Labour members of Parliament unanimously passed a resolution expressing the hope that 'on no account will this country be dragged into the

[1] Labour Party Annual Conference Report, 1912, p. 101.
[2] ibid, p. 101.
[3] ibid, p. 101. It was in fact carried by 1,323,000 votes to 155,000. For Labour attitudes to the Liberal Government's rearmament measures, see W. P. Maddox, *Foreign Relations in British Labour Politics* (London, 1934) pp. 44-5 and 208-10.

European conflict in which, as the Prime Minister has stated, we have no direct or indirect interest'; and the resolution also called 'upon all Labour organizations in the country to watch events vigilantly so as to oppose, if need be, in the most effective way any action which may involve us in war'.[1] On the 1st of August, the British Section of the International appealed in vehement language to its affiliated organizations to hold demonstrations against war in every industrial centre. 'Workers,' it urged, 'stand together . . . for peace! Combine and conquer the militarist enemy and the self-seeking Imperialist today, once and for all. Men and women of Britain, you have now an unexampled opportunity of rendering a magnificent service to humanity, and to the world! Proclaim that for you the days of plunder and butchery have gone by; send messages of peace and fraternity to your fellows who have less liberty than you. Down with class rule. Up with the peaceful rule of the people.'[2] The appeal was signed by Keir Hardie and Arthur Henderson. Both also spoke at a demonstration on the 2nd of August in Trafalgar Square, where a resolution was adopted which declared that 'the Government of Great Britain should rigidly decline to engage in war'.[3]

However, save for the encouragement of demonstrations, there was no attempt to give concrete meaning to Labour's proclaimed intention to oppose 'if need be, in the most effective way any action which may involve us in war'.

Need there certainly was. On the 30th of July, the Czar had signed the order for general mobilization; on the 2nd of August, Germany had declared war on France and Russia and presented its ultimatum to Belgium. On the 3rd, the Foreign Secretary, Sir Edward Grey, told the House of Commons that British commitments to France, which he now revealed after their existence had been repeatedly denied over the previous years, made it impossible for Britain to stand aside. 'There is but one way,' he said, 'in which the Government could make certain at the present moment of keeping outside this war, and that would be that it should immediately issue a proclamation of unconditional neutrality. We cannot do that. We have made the commitments to France that I have read to the House, which prevents us from doing that. We have got the consideration of Belgium which prevents us also from any unconditional neutrality . . .'[4] On the 4th of August, Britain declared war on Germany.

[1] G. D. H. Cole, *Labour in War-Time* (London, 1915) p. 24.
[2] ibid, p. 25.
[3] Labour Year Book, 1916, p. 17.
[4] H. of C., vol. 65, col. 1825, 3rd of August, 1914.

Save for the Russians and the Serbs, the socialist parliamentarians of all belligerent countries aligned themselves with their governments. On the eve of war, however, the British Section of the International was in a unique situation. Alone of the Powers involved, Britain had neither attacked nor had it been under any immediate threat of attack. The manner in which Britain had been pledged to the support of France, quite apart from the light it threw on the operation of parliamentary government in Britain, could hardly be deemed to make the Government's commitment binding on the Labour Party. Nor, whatever emotions might be engendered by the German invasion of Belgium, could this be seriously held by Socialists to constitute adequate grounds for Britain's entry into the conflict. British policy would not have been different had Germany respected Belgian neutrality; nor, it may be surmised, would the Labour Party's attitude have been different. Had there not been gallant little Belgium to defend, there would have been the gallant French ally. As to freedom and democracy, it was only after war had been declared that the Labour Party discovered that this was what the conflict was about. Until war was upon it, it had never thought of international slaughter in those terms.

The real reason for the support which most Labour leaders gave to the war was that the Government of the day decided to bring Britain into it. They simply found it unthinkable, given the dimensions of the crisis, and irrespective of its origins, to refuse .that support. They had not really tried to mobilize opposition to war before its outbreak. They were hardly likely to do so once it had begun. Like their colleagues in France, Germany and Austria, they found overwhelming the call to national identification, and responded to it the more readily in order to dispel any doubt as to Labour's patriotism.

To most trade union leaders, and to most Labour parliamentarians, the war barely posed any problem. They were for it from the beginning. On the 4th of August, a representative conference of all the most important organizations of the Labour movement, called for the purpose of forming a National Labour Emergency Committee against war, created instead the War Emergency Workers' National Committee to watch over the interests of the working classes in the new circumstances of war. On the 24th of August, the trade unions and the Labour Party declared that there should be an Industrial Truce for the duration of the war; and on the 29th, the Labour Party agreed to an Electoral Truce and placed the party organization at the disposal of the recruiting campaign.

The I.L.P. parliamentarians, on the other hand, reacted rather differently. Only two of them, J. R. Clynes and James Parker, aligned themselves with the Labour Party. The remaining five, MacDonald (who resigned the leadership of the Parliamentary Party and was replaced by Henderson), Keir Hardie, Snowden, Jowett, and Thomas Richardson, continued to oppose the ascendant mood of chauvinism, not least in Labour's own ranks,[1] and to challenge the official definitions of the causes and character of the war.

Their opposition, however, was not without very substantial qualifications. 'A nation at war must be united,' Keir Hardie wrote a few days after the outbreak of war, 'especially when its existence is at stake. In such filibustering expeditions as our own Boer War or the Italian war over Tripoli, where no national danger of any kind was involved, there were many occasions for diversity of opinion, and this was given voice to by the Socialist Party of Italy and the Stop-the-War Party in this country. Now the situation is different. With the boom of the enemy's guns within earshot, the lads who have gone forth to fight their country's battles must not be disheartened by any discordant notes at home'[2] 'We cannot go back,' MacDonald wrote in September 1914, in reply to an invitation to join the recruiting campaign in Leicester, 'nor can we turn to the right or to the left. We must go straight through. History will, in due time, apportion the praise and the blame, but the young men of the country must, for the moment, settle the immediate issues of victory. Let them do it in the spirit of the brave men who have crowned our country with honour in the times that are gone. Whoever may be in the wrong, men so inspired will be in the right.'[3]

Fred Jowett, on the other hand, maintained throughout a very different position. Speaking at Letchworth in July 1915, he said: 'How can I go on the platform along with men who think the war is right and appeal for recruits? It is impossible. My position is clear, I cannot ask for recruits for a war shapen in iniquity, into which the country has been led blindfolded, the result of imperialist aggression.' And at Leicester: 'The obligation to fight is one to

[1] In April 1915, there was formed the Socialist National Defence Committee, whose specific purpose was to counter the Socialist opponents of the war. This vociferously chauvinistic body included Dan Irving of the B.S.P., Joseph Burgess of the I.L.P., Stewart Headlam of the Fabian Society, H. G. Wells, Robert Blatchford, and some Labour members of Parliament like John Hodge, C. H. Roberts and Stephen Walsh. A year later, the Committee became the British Workers National League, dedicated to peace by victory, the retention of the German colonies in British hands and the protection of British industry. (C. F. Brand, *British Labour's Rise to Power* (London 1914) p. 76.)
[2] ibid, p. 69. In December, he also wrote: 'I have never said or wrote anything to dissuade young men from enlisting.' *Forward*, 26th of December, 1914.
[3] Cole, op. cit. p. 31.

which I, though a Member of Parliament, am not a party. The war has been entered into after Sir Edward Grey and Mr Asquith had stated definitely that the obligation was not in existence. Therefore I ask myself if it is my business to go recruiting, and I come to the conclusion that those who believe in it should do the recruiting."[1]

These differences did not much trouble the patriotic Press, which condemned all opposition to war, qualified or unqualified, as treason. Much of MacDonald's later reputation as a man of the left was born in the war, and was of immense value to him after it. As one of his biographers has noted, 'he found himself at once in renewed contact and intimacy with the I.L.P., chief spokesman of the very body which had chiefly housed those phraseologists whose enthusiasm had sometimes in recent years so embarrassed his leadership. From being so constantly suspect, he became once again the idol of the Left Wing'.[2]

The I.L.P. was, from the beginning, the main anti-war political organization in Britain. Indeed, its opposition to the war gave it a new lease of life, after a steady period of decline. On the 13th of August, it had declared, in a Manifesto on International Socialism, that 'out of the darkness and the depth we hail our working class comrades of every land. Across the roar of guns, we send sympathy and greetings to the German socialists. They have laboured unceasingly to promote good relations with Britain, as we with Germany. They are no enemies of ours, but faithful friends'; and, the Manifesto went on, 'in forcing this appalling crime upon the nations, it is the rulers, the diplomats, the militarists who have sealed their doom. In tears of blood and bitterness the greater democracy will be born . . . long live Freedom and Fraternity! Long live International Socialism!'[3]

Members of the I.L.P. refused to support the war for a variety of reasons. Some, like George Lansbury, were mainly moved by an integral form of Christian pacifism. Others were inspired by the ethical conviction that all violence was evil. Men like Fenner Brockway and Tom Johnston were pacifists but they also opposed the war on more specifically socialist grounds: they believed that it was the result of imperialist rivalries which the working class movements on either side had no cause to support.

---

[1] F. Brockway, *Socialism over Sixty Years. The Life of Jowett of Bradford* (London, 1946) p. 139.
[2] G. Elton, *The Life of James Ramsay MacDonald 1868-1919* (London, 1939) p. 250.
[3] G. D. H. Cole, *A History of the Labour Party since 1914* (London, 1948) p. 19.

To these I.L.P. opponents of the war was soon added a body of people, important not in numbers but in influence, talent and, in some cases, wealth, who came into the I.L.P., or came to be associated with it through the Union of Democratic Control, the No Conscription Fellowship or the National Council for Civil Liberties. Many of them, like E. D. Morel, one of the founders of the Union of Democratic Control, Norman Angell, C. P. Trevelyan, Roden Buxton and Arthur Ponsonby, were pacifists or liberal internationalists, or both, and some had, until the War, found themselves at home in the Liberal Party, or had been advanced radicals. For many of them, the socialism they came to profess as a result of their association with the I.L.P., and therefore with the Labour Party, was defined in terms of internationalism, open diplomacy and the democratic control of foreign affairs, coupled with a deep interest in social reform. They were, in effect, articulate representatives of that special brand of English middle-class (and upperclass) radicalism, which had been an essential part of the Liberal tradition throughout the nineteenth century. It was the I.L.P., and its attitude to the War, which made possible the marriage, or at least a liaison, between representatives of that tradition and the Labour movement. Even during the war, the influence of these men, particularly in shaping and defining Labour's 'War aims', was real. After it, that influence, at least in the realm of foreign affairs, was considerable.

Though many members of the I.L.P. went to jail as conscientious objectors when conscription was introduced, the Party itself did not seek to extend its opposition to the war beyond constitutional and legal forms and its propaganda soon came to dwell most insistently on the need to bring the war to an end by means of a negotiated peace, with, as the I.L.P. National Council put it in 1915, 'the largest possible measure of equity and the least possible loss of life'.[1] At the same time, the I.L.P. remained unwilling throughout to cut itself off from the Labour Party, or to condemn it outright for its attitude to the war. Conversely, there were enough influential members of the Labour Party, among them Henderson, to prevent the I.L.P.'s exclusion from the Labour Party itself.

As to the avowedly Marxist and revolutionary British Socialist Party, it was not until 1915 that it was able to defeat Hyndmann and its other pro-war leaders. It then declared at its Conference of that year that the supreme duty of socialists everywhere was to work for an immediate peace on such terms as would preclude a repetition

[1] Brand, op. cit. p. 73.

46

of the war.[1] More concretely, many of its members, particularly in Scotland, were actively involved in the leadership of the industrial struggles of the latter part of the war.[2]

2. JUNIOR PARTNERSHIP

A speedy restoration of peace on equitable terms had been the declared aim of the Labour Party at the beginning of the war. On the 7th of August, 1914, it had proclaimed that its duty was now 'to secure peace at the earliest possible moment on such conditions as will provide the best opportunities for the re-establishment of amicable feelings between the workers of Europe'.[3] However, both the Trade Unions and the Labour Party were immediately involved in the war effort and they very quickly made their own the view that the war must be fought until Germany had been totally defeated.

Official Labour's total involvement in the First World War has too seldom been accorded the importance it deserves in the history of the Labour movement. Until the outbreak of war, the Labour Party and the Trade Unions had been little more, in the eyes of Britain's traditional rulers, than manageable nuisances or, to the more sophisticated, than necessary evils. The war immediately gave Labour's leaders, particularly its industrial leaders, a very different and much enhanced status. For they now came to be needed (and as the war dragged on, sorely needed) as brokers and intermediaries between the Government and a labour force whose acceptance of a new industrial discipline was an essential condition of military success. They not only became, as the Webbs put it, the diplomatic representatives of the wage-earning class';[4] they also acted as the representatives of the Government in relation to the working classes. It was a dual rôle which many Labour leaders had begun to learn in the previous decades. But it was the war which gave that rôle new institutional forms. In the course of those four years of brokerage, a host of Labour representatives became deeply involved in the business of the State and, with their service in the new bureaucracy that was born of the war, acquired a stake, if not in the country, at least in the country's official business. By the

[1] Brand, op. cit. p. 74. In 1916, when Hyndmann and his followers seceded and formed the National Socialist Party, the B.S.P. Conference declared that, though war could only be abolished by the overthrow of capitalism, the conflict might yet be ended on the basis of the freedom of all nations and the prohibition of all annexations against the wishes of the peoples concerned. (ibid, p. 75.)
[2] See below, pp. 53 ff.
[3] Cole, op. cit. p. 18.
[4] S. & B. Webb, *The History of Trade Unionism,* op. cit. p. 637.

end of the war, a whole army of Labour representatives were serving on a multitude of official committees, commissions, tribunals and agencies.[1] Nor certainly did they lose the habits of mind engendered by this experience when the war came to an end.

Once it had become clear that the war would not soon be over, and that it would make enormous demands in war material, it was also realized on all sides that much more would be needed by way of Labour collaboration with the Government than an Industrial Truce and Labour support for the recruitment campaign. Although there was very little working class opposition to the war itself, neither was there any eagerness, then and even less later, to accept the abandonment of painfully won industrial rights and guarantees, such as the right to strike, to choose jobs freely or to restrict entry into skilled occupations. Nor were working class interests confined to these issues. There were grievances like the steep rise in the cost of living (if this is not too macabre a phrase in the context); or the bitterness engendered by the resistance of employers to wage demands, which was contrasted to the enormous profits that were being made, and which a Government more concerned to control labour than business did very little to check. All this and a multitude of other irritants produced by the social and economic dislocations of war made industrial discipline increasingly difficult to maintain. If popular discontents were to be kept in check and industrial agitation subdued, the Government would have to lean heavily on the Labour leaders. It was upon them above all that would devolve the task of persuading their members that militancy at home must be sacrificed to military success abroad.

This view, already expressed in the terms of the Industrial Truce, was formally embodied in the Treasury Agreement of March 1915. The Agreement committed the unions for the duration of hostilities to the abandonment of strike action and the acceptance of Government arbitration in disputes; it was also agreed that trade union restrictive practices in regard to the employment of women, girls and youths, particularly in the engineering industries, would be suspended; similarly, the unions agreed to the relaxation of the provisions of the Factory Acts relating to the employment of women and youths and to the suspension of all restrictions on the duration of the working day, on overtime, night work and Sunday work. In return, the Government announced its intention to 'conclude arrangements' for the limitation of profits of firms engaged in war work, 'with a view to securing that benefits resulting from the relaxation of trade restrictions or practices shall accrue to the State'; the

[1] See S. & B. Webb, op cit. pp. 646 ff.

Government also promised that it would 'undertake to use its influence to secure the restoration of previous conditions in every case after the war'.[1] The provisions of the Treasury Agreement were obviously of great advantage to employers in relation to their workers, while the Government, in the words of the Webbs, 'found itself unable to fulfil, with any literal exactness, the specific pledges which it had given to organized Labour'.[2]

The Treasury Agreement also provided for the creation of a National Labour Advisory Council, composed of seven trade union leaders under the chairmanship of Arthur Henderson, and intended to secure close liaison between the Government and the unions. From then onwards, as Cole notes, Henderson 'was attempting to double the parts of leader of the Labour Party in the House of Commons and *de facto* Industrial Adviser to a Government in which Labour was not represented.'[3]

This latter deficiency was soon remedied. In May 1915, at the time of an acute munitions crisis, Henderson was invited to become a member of the Cabinet in a new Coalition Government, nominally as President of the Board of Education, in fact as the Government's main political link with the Labour movement. Two other Labour M.P.'s, William Brace, of the Miners, and G. H. Roberts, of the Printers, were also offered junior offices, the former as Under-Secretary of State at the Home Office, the latter as a Government Whip. This could hardly be construed as providing Labour with a major influence in the councils of State, the more so as Henderson, though offered a seat in the Cabinet, was not to be included in the inner War Council. There was in fact a good deal of opposition in the Executive Committee and the Parliamentary Party to the proposal; but it was ultimately accepted and subsequently endorsed by overwhelming majorities at the T.U.C. Conference in September 1915, and at the Labour Party Conference (the first since the outbreak of war) in January 1916.

Opposition to participation mainly stemmed from a belief that Labour should retain some degree of independence rather than from any desire to impede its contribution to the war effort. Snowden, one of the principal critics of participation, wrote that 'the whole Labour movement will be united on one point—namely that it is the duty of the movement to help the nation in its present difficulties'; but, 'the point of difference is that some members think that the Labour Party can be much more useful outside the Government than inside it. The

---

[1] For details of the agreement, see Cole, *Labour in War-Time* op. cit. pp. 185 ff.
[2] S. & B. Webb, op. cit. p. 641.
[3] Cole, *A History of the Labour Party since 1914*, op. cit. p. 24.

acceptance of office in the Coalition Government will take away the freedom of independent criticism which at a time like this may often be the most valuable service a small party can render to the nation.'[1]

With Labour's entry into the Asquith Coalition the Labour Party became a much more 'official' party than it had ever been before. With Ministers in the Government, it was now formally committed to policies to the determination of which it only made, in the nature of its position, the most marginal of contributions.

On the other hand, its contribution to the *execution* of the Government's policies, particularly in the industrial field, grew steadily more important. Within a few weeks of the formation of the Coalition, the Treasury Agreement, which had some months earlier been acclaimed as 'opening up a great new chapter in the history of Labour in its relation with the State',[2] was superseded by the much more stringent Munitions of War Act. As Mr Roberts remarks, Lloyd George, now the head of a new Ministry of Munitions, 'no doubt shrewdly realized that once he had obtained the voluntary agreement of the unions for the policy adopted at the Treasury meetings, it would be difficult for them to oppose the Government's action in taking powers to see that the objects of the Agreement were achieved; the more so since the Labour Party was now represented in the Government'.[3] Indeed, Lloyd George carried shrewdness further: he asked the National Labour Advisory Council to draft the bill.

The Munitions of War Act provided for compulsory arbitration and virtually prohibited all strikes and lockouts, not only in industries directly engaged in war production, but in any dispute in any industry. The Act also prohibited any change in the level of wages and salaries in 'controlled' establishments without the consent of the Minister of Munitions; it provided for the abandonment of restrictive practices and forbade workers in those establishments to leave their job without a 'certificate of leave'. In return for all this, the Act also empowered the Minister to regulate the level of profits in the 'controlled' establishments.

Stringent though its provisions were, the Munitions of War Act was only another step—there were to be many more—in the complete mobilization of labour for war. Military conscription followed soon after. Though its introduction was fiercely opposed in the Labour movement,[4] it too was finally endorsed, on the advice of the

[1] Brand, op. cit. p. 34. Fred Jowett was far more explicit. He described the offer to Labour as motivated by the hope of 'making hostages of the new men'. (Brockway, op. cit. p. 145.)
[2] Roberts, op. cit. p. 277.
[3] ibid, p. 278.
[4] See Cole, op. cit. pp. 26 ff.

Parliamentary Committee of the T.U.C. and of a majority of the Labour Party Executive.

Granted support for a war to the finish, there was an inevitable logic in both industrial and military conscription, and it was a logic which the Labour leaders found irresistible. They might no doubt have tried to exact a better reward for the sacrifices they helped to impose upon the working classes and they might have demanded more vigorously that these sacrifices should be more nearly matched by employers. That they did not do so had much to do with the patriotic blackmail to which they were subjected from all sides. But the appeal of patriotism only *reinforced* the trade union leaders' propensity to pitch their claims very low. The result, as the Webbs note with unusual pungency, was that 'the Trade Unionists who had at the outset of the War patriotically refrained from bargaining as the price of their aid were, on the whole, "done" at its close'.[1]

In December 1916, Asquith was elbowed out of the Premiership and replaced by Lloyd George. The fact that Asquith's followers refused to serve under Lloyd George made it the more necessary for him that he should be able to include Labour representatives in his Coalition. The bait to Labour was accordingly made more attractive. Henderson was offered a seat in the War Cabinet, and two other Cabinet posts (the Ministry of Pensions and a new Ministry of Labour) were also offered to Labour. There were also to be some more minor Labour appointments. Lloyd George promised 'strong action' in respect of food distribution, and he announced that he intended instituting closer State control of mines and shipping. He also promised that he would not be a party to a policy of repression and persecution of opponents of the war. And another promise, not disclosed until the end of the war, was that Labour would have representation at the peace conference.[2]

The offer was accepted, but not without some opposition and misgivings. The Executive Report to the Labour Party Conference of January 1917 bluntly stated that opinion in the Parliamentary Party and the National Executive had been unanimous 'against the methods by which the break-up of the Asquith Coalition Government has been secured'.[3] As late as the 1st of December, Henderson had referred to Asquith as the indispensable man to lead Great Britain successfully to the end of the war.[4] Lloyd George, in contrast,

[1] S. & B. Webb, op. cit. p. 643.
[2] Brand, op. cit. p. 40.
[3] Labour Party Annual Conference Report, 1917, p. 43. Snowden called it 'as vile a conspiracy as ever disgraced English political life', *Labour Leader*, 14th of December, 1916, in Brand, op. cit. p. 39.
[4] ibid, p. 40.

was much distrusted. But, the Report also said, 'the national interests and the possibility of Labour securing a greater opportunity to mould policy and exercise executive authority in important administrative positions could not be ignored'; 'the presence of Members of the Party in Government,' the Report claimed, 'has kept the views of Labour prominent and possibly prevented things being decided upon which would be prejudicial to the interests of those whom the Party specially represents and which would have disturbed the unity now existing in the country to see the war through.'[1]

Anticipating criticism that 'they had been guilty of selling the Movement without getting anything in return', Henderson told the 1917 Conference that 'in a national crisis like this, if they had to associate with any form of Government, they ought to concern themselves more with what they were going to give than what they were likely to get'. And in any case, he reminded the delegates, both the minority (against participation) and the majority were agreed that a German victory would be the defeat of democracy and freedom; and the best argument for participation was that it would best assist in carrying the war to a successful conclusion.[2]

'A successful conclusion' meant war until Germany's total military defeat. Nothing in the attitudes of the Labour leaders in war-time is more remarkable than their endorsement, throughout, of the official thesis that no attempt must be made to stop the war by negotiation.

Lloyd George had assumed the Premiership on the basis of a policy of war to the finish. Labour's entry into the Coalition was an expression of its full acceptance of that policy.

Nor did the critics of participation argue at the Conference that Labour should have stayed outside the Coalition in order to play whatever role it might in the exploration of the possibility of peace by negotiation. Like Snowden, they merely suggested that participation, by giving Labour responsibility without power, would be detrimental to the interests of the Labour movement;[3] or, like Bevin, that Labour should have received assurances as to the composition of the Cabinet which, he complained, included some of Labour's bitterest enemies.[4] The Conference itself endorsed participation by a majority of six to one;[5] and it rejected by an overwhelming majority an I.L.P. proposal, which echoed an earlier proposal by neutral social-democratic parties, that a meeting of the International Socialist

[1] Labour Party Annual Conference Report, 1917, pp. 43-5.
[2] ibid, pp. 86-8.
[3] ibid, pp. 91-3.
[4] ibid, pp. 96-7. Lloyd George himself, he said, 'did not represent the sane portion of the citizens of this country'.
[5] ibid, p. 98. The vote was 1,849,000 to 307,000.

Congress should be held in Stockholm to discuss war aims.[1]

With this endorsement of Labour participation in the Lloyd George Coalition, the Labour movement remained committed until the very last stages of the war to the doctrine of peace through slaughter. Nevertheless, there is another side to the story of Labour in war-time. For, while official Labour willingly surrendered its political and industrial independence, and only met with tepid opposition to that surrender from most I.L.P. parliamentarians, it was confronted, in the second half of the war, with a marked resurgence of the militancy it had done its best to stifle before 1914.

3. THE RESURGENCE OF MILITANCY

The trade union leaders' virtual transformation into agents of the State inevitably offered new opportunities to the militant Left which it was not slow to exploit. From the beginning of 1915 onwards, when some eight thousand engineers on Clydeside struck for higher wages, the Industrial Truce was repeatedly broken in one part or another of the country. The disputes were mostly 'unofficial' and under the leadership of local shop stewards' committees, such as the Sheffield Workers' Committee or the Clyde Workers' Committee. These local initiatives not only fell foul of the Government, but of the bulk of the trade union leadership as well, which is hardly surprising since every unofficial strike constituted a repudiation of that leadership. Nor, it may be noted, did the shop stewards find any greater favour with men like MacDonald, who, though they were opposed to official Labour policy, did their best to dissociate themselves from militant industrial action.[2]

Despite constant arrests and other difficulties of industrial agitation in war-time, this unofficial rank and file movement grew. G. D. H. Cole described it as 'the most important single development in the Trade Union world during the war period',[3] and a recent writer has noted that 'never before or since has an unofficial rank and file move-

---

[1] Labour Party Annual Conference Report, 1917, p. 127.
[2] See, e.g. MacDonald in the House of Commons in March 1916 on the subject of an industrial dispute on the Clyde: 'Unfortunately . . . certain opinions, which I have come to conscientiously, have somewhat divided me from old colleagues, but I beg this House to believe me when I say that, rather than that division of opinion should make me an agent to bring men out on strike just now, I should wish that something should happen of some kind or other which would destroy every particle of influence that ever I have had with the working men of this country. Within two months of the outbreak of the War I made publicly in my own Constituency an appeal to men who are working on munitions to work honestly on munitions.' (H. of C. vol. 81, cols. 998-9, 20th of March 1916).
[3] G. D. H. Cole, *An Introduction to Trade Unionism* (London, 1918) p. 53.

ment exercised such power and influence in this country'.[1] By August 1917, the movement was sufficiently widespread to make possible the creation of a national organization, the Shop Stewards' and Workers' Committee Movement.[2]

This militant Left was, of course, directly linked, in personnel and in ideas, to the militant Left of pre-war days. But the extremely adverse conditions under which it fought its battles and disseminated its ideas steeled its spirit and gave it a new resilience. And the fact that the war *had* occurred, and had turned into a blood bath, powerfully served to confirm its hatred of the old order, and its belief that the latter's reversion to barbarism was but the final sign of its inevitable doom. Undoubtedly, the militant Left, then and later, greatly overestimated the chances of revolutionary success. Though it saw itself as the architect of revolution, its real importance lay elsewhere. It lay in the fact that it kept alive, through the war years, a tradition of militancy and a ferment of ideas which only made their full impact on the Labour movement when the war came to an end.

That the militant Left smelt revolution in the air was, to an important extent, due to its outbreak in Russia in March 1917. The repercussions of that event were immediately felt within the Labour movement, though assessments of its significance naturally varied.[3] War weariness, industrial and economic difficulties, military reverses and anti-war agitation would in any case have made 1917 a year of crisis. But the Russian Revolution both gave enormous encouragement to the Left and presented the Labour leadership with a much more insistent challenge than the Left, alone, would then have been able to pose.

The first occasion on which Labour's welcome for the Russian Revolution found organized expression was in April 1917 when, at a meeting at the Albert Hall sponsored by George Lansbury's *Herald* and attended by some twelve thousand people, the Revolution was greeted with enthusiasm, and congratulatory messages to the Russian people were passed.[4] Similar meetings were also held in Manchester, Glasgow and other cities. What was then being celebrated, however,

---

[1] B. Pribicevic, *The Shop Stewards' Movement and Workers' Control 1910-1922* (London, 1959) p. 83.
[2] See ibid, ch. VI; also G. D. H. Cole, *Workshop Organization* (London, 1923); W. A. Orton, op. cit. pp. 88-100, 115-27, 128-32; Murphy, op. cit. chs. IV-VIII; and W. Gallacher, *Revolt on the Clyde* (London, 1936) ch. VI.
[3] For a detailed account of the impact of the Russian Revolution on the Labour movement, see S. R. Graubard, *British Labour and the Russian Revolution, 1917-1924* (London, 1956).
[4] ibid, p. 18.

was much more a political than a social, let alone a socialist, revolution. Labour supporters of the war had long been made uncomfortable by the incongruity of fighting a war in the name of freedom and democracy with Czarist Russia as one of Britain's principal allies. It was natural that they should welcome the downfall of the Russian autocracy. Nor for that matter were these sentiments confined to the ranks of Labour. They were shared, at least initially, by many Liberal and Conservatives.

For the militant Left, however, the Russian Revolution, even before the Bolshevik seizure of power, was held to have deeper implications, of immediate relevance both to the issue of peace and to the chances of socialism in Britain. What these implications were was well demonstrated by the Leeds Convention of the 3rd of June, 1917, perhaps the most remarkable gathering of the period.

According to the official report of the Convention, which had been organized by a group calling itself the United Socialist Council, 1,150 delegates attended the meeting.[1] The occasion was given a special cachet by the presence of nationally known Labour figures, such as MacDonald, Snowden, Robert Smillie, Tom Mann and Ben Tillett, W. C. Anderson, Robert Williams and R. C. Wallhead.

Indeed, it was MacDonald who moved the first resolution, which congratulated the Russian people on their achievement and on having taken 'a foremost part in the international movement for working-class emancipation from all forms of political, economic and imperialist oppression and exploitation'. 'Our congratulations,' he said, 'are absolutely unstinted and unqualified. (Hear, hear.) . . . When this war broke out organized Labour in this country lost the initiative. (Hear, hear.) It became a mere echo of the old governing classes' opinions. (Hear, hear.) Now the Russian Revolution has once again given you the chance to take the initiative yourselves. Let us lay down our terms, make our own proclamations, establish our own diplomacy, see to it that we have our own international meetings.'[2]

Much more startling was the fourth resolution adopted by the Convention. This called for the formation 'in every town, urban and

---

[1] *What Happened at Leeds,* Report published by the Council of Workers' and Soldiers' Delegates (London 1917) p. 2. The Report enumerated 209 delegates as representing Trades Councils and local Labour Parties, 371 from Trade Union organizations, 294 from the I.L.P., 88 from the B.S.P., 16 from other socialist societies, 54 from various women's organizations and 118 from such organizations as Adult Schools, Co-operative Societies, the Union of Democratic Control, the National Council for Civil Liberty, Peace Societies and May-Day Committees (ibid, p. 2).

[2] ibid, p. 6.

rural district' of Councils of Workmen and Soldiers' Delegates 'for initiating and co-ordinating working-class activity'.[1]

To those who might discover in this a call to revolution, the mover, W. C. Anderson, M.P., freely admitted that 'if a revolution be the conquest of political power by a hitherto disinherited class, if revolution be that we are not going to put up in the future with what we have put up with in the past, then the sooner we have revolution in this country the better'. On the other hand, the central organization which was being set up to organize the Councils, he added, was 'not subversive, not unconstitutional unless the authorities care to make it so'.[2]

The seconder of the resolution, Robert Williams of the Transport Workers, went much further. The resolution, he said, if it meant anything at all meant the dictatorship of the proletariat. Nor was it only directed against 'the most competent, the most capable governing class of the whole world'; it was also directed against the labour leaders who had allowed themselves to be used by that ruling class against Labour. 'We want,' said Williams, 'to break the influence of the industrial and political labour "machine" and this Convention is our attempt to do so.' Parliament would do nothing for Labour. 'We,' Williams proclaimed, meaning the Convention, 'are competent to speak in the name of our own class, and damn the Constitution.' (Loud cheers.) He then drew a parallel with Russia. 'Had the Russian revolutionaries been concerned with the Constitution of Holy Russia, the Romanoffs would have been on the throne today, and I say to you: Have as little concern for the British Constitution as the Russians you are praising had for the dynasty of the Romanoffs. (Cheers.) You have a greater right to speak in the name of our people, civilian and soldiers, than have the gang who are in charge of our political destinies at this moment. . . . If you are really sincere in sending greetings to Russia, I say to you: "Go thou and do likewise". (Cheers.) The need for far-reaching, for revolutionary changes is as great in this country as it was in Russia.'[3]

The sentiments which Robert Williams expressed were obviously shared by a section, perhaps by a majority of the delegates. But they were not the sentiments of people like MacDonald, or Snowden, or Robert Smillie, the Miners' leader, who chaired the Conference, and who told the delegates at the beginning of the proceedings that 'we have not come here to talk treason. We have come here to talk reason'.[4] The Leeds Convention had fortuitously brought together

[1] *What Happened at Leeds*, p. 13.
[2] ibid, p. 15.
[3] ibid, p. 17.
[4] ibid, p. 15.

revolutionaries and constitutionalists. But the gulf between them remained as profound as it had ever been and the instoration of the Bolshevik regime in November 1917 only served to widen that gulf.

The first problem which the March Revolution in Russia had created for the leadership was that of its attitude to the meeting in Stockholm of the International Socialist Congress to discuss war aims. British participation had already been rejected by the Labour Party Annual Conference in January 1917. However, Henderson, while on an official mission to Russia, had come to believe that the meeting would in any case be held and that, as he told a Special Party Conference in August 1917, 'it would be highly inadvisable and perhaps dangerous for the Russian representatives to meet representatives from enemy and neutral countries alone'.[1]

Despite considerable opposition from the floor, Henderson prevailed and the Conference agreed (by 1,846,000 to 550,000 votes) to send delegates to Stockholm. But it also agreed, by an even larger majority, that the delegation should only consist of nominees from the Labour Party, the Parliamentary Committee of the T.U.C. and the Special Conference itself. This ran directly counter to the terms of the invitation to Stockholm and was obviously designed to prevent minority, anti-war representation. However, by the time the Conference reconvened on the 21st of August, the Government had announced that it would refuse passports to delegates, and this time the Conference itself was almost exactly divided on the issue of participation,[2] and a larger majority than on the previous occasion insisted that the socialist societies should not be allowed to send their own delegates to Stockholm. But in any case, the closeness of the vote, and the Government's refusal of passports, had given the day to the abstentionists. Their victory indicates how enduringly powerful in the Labour movement was the feeling against any kind of parley, however innocuous, with socialists from enemy countries.

Henderson's support for Labour participation at the Stockholm Conference had greatly strained his relations with his Cabinet colleagues, and led to his resignation from the Government on the 11th of August. But there was no question of a general Labour withdrawal from the Coalition. G. N. Barnes, who strongly opposed Henderson on this issue, merely stepped into his leader's place.[3]

[1] Special Labour Party Conference Report, 10th of August, 1917, pp. 9-13.
[2] The voting was 1,234,000 to 1,231,000. The access of strength to the abstentionists was mainly due to the switch of the Miners' Federation.
[3] Nor did Henderson himself want Labour to leave the Coalition, then or later. At the Labour Party Conference of January, 1918, a resolution was moved asking the Conference to declare that 'it is contrary to the interests of the working class for Labour Members of Parliament to remain members

The second, and much more important, issue raised by the Russian Revolution was its impact on the military fortunes of the Allies. Increasingly likely after March, a Russian withdrawal from the war was made certain by the Bolsheviks' accession to power. The Bolsheviks had hoped that they might pull Russia out of the war as part of a general peace settlement whose terms would be imposed upon the belligerents by their respective Labour movements. These hopes were futile since those movements continued to support, or at least failed to influence, their governments. On the 3rd of March, 1918, the Bolshevik Government signed a separate peace with Germany at Brest-Litovsk. This was a massive blow to the Allied Powers and led to bitter condemnation of Russia's 'defection', in which Labour, however, took no part. Indeed, the harshness of the terms imposed upon the Russians helped to evoke Labour sympathy for the plight of Russia,[1] and blunted somewhat the edge of criticism, already widespread in the Labour movement, of the Bolsheviks' internal policies.[2]

On the other hand, it was only the Left which spoke out unequivocally against Allied military intervention against the Bolsheviks. For the bulk of the Labour movement, it was military considerations which remained paramount in shaping its attitude to intervention. As Mr. Graubard notes, 'the great body of trade unionists preferred to remain silent on the question. While few cared openly to approve of intervention, most were reluctant in the midst of war to speak out against it'.[3] It was only with the end of the war that intervention came to be considered in other than military terms, and assumed major importance within the Labour movement. Meanwhile, the Bolsheviks were left to defend themselves and their regime as best they could. What mainly preoccupied the Labour movement in the last stages of the war was how to meet the challenge of a victory for whose sake its leaders had, over four bitter years, called upon the working classes to make such staggering sacrifices.

---

of the Coalition Government or any subsequent capitalist Government'. (Labour Party Annual Conference Report, 1918, p. 116). The mover bluntly said that 'the Labour Ministers were simply shields to prevent the Labour movement dealing with the capitalists. The Labour Party came into existence to destroy capitalism, but the Labour Ministers were bolstering it up.' (ibid, p. 116.) The resolution was strongly opposed by Henderson who agreed that there was nothing to be said in normal times for a Coalition, but insisted that Labour must stay in the Government until peace had been achieved. (ibid, p. 117.) However, no less than 722,000 votes were cast for the resolution (against 1,885,000).
[1] Graubard, op. cit. pp. 54-5.
[2] ibid, pp. 55-7.
[3] ibid, p. 66.

CHAPTER III

PARLIAMENTARISM VERSUS
DIRECT ACTION

> 'The view of the Labour Party is that
> what has to be reconstructed after the
> war is not this or that Government
> Department, or this or that piece of
> social machinery; but, so far as Britain
> is concerned, society itself.'
>
> (Labour and the New Social Order,
> 1918.)

1. LABOUR AND THE OLD SOCIAL ORDER

'The whole state of society is more or less molten,' Lloyd George had told a Labour deputation in 1917, 'and,' he had gone on to say, 'you can stamp upon that molten mass almost anything, so long as you do so with firmness and determination.... I believe the settlement after the War will succeed in proportion to its audacity.... If I could have presumed to have been the adviser of the working classes ... I should say to them: "Audacity is the thing for you. Think out new ways; think out new methods.... Don't always be thinking of getting back to where you were before the War: get a really new world".'[1]

It is conceivable that Lloyd George half believed what he said at the time he said it. It hardly committed him then to anything. The position of the Labour leaders as the war entered its last stages was more complex. They certainly did not want Labour to get back to where it was before the war. The trade unions emerged from the war greatly strengthened, in membership and status. Their leaders wanted a new deal for Labour. But they wanted to obtain that new deal by the traditional methods they knew, and which the war itself had done much to enhance. They had, while the war was still on, looked forward to the retention on a permanent and enlarged basis of the machinery of State control, arbitration and conciliation which had

[1] Labour Party Annual Conference Report, 1917, p. 163.

then been created. When the war ended, their trust in co-operation with Government and employers was undimmed, as was their determination to defeat the advocates of militant action, industrial or political.

Of course, they were now much more ready than they had been before 1914 to accept a mainly notional commitment on the part of the Labour Party to a Socialist Shangri-La: the times were not such as to facilitate resistance to the rhetoric of proletarian emancipation. But when it came to deeds, they made it clear that they had no intention of allowing the movement they controlled to embark upon militant courses they had always deemed disastrous. Nor had most of the political leaders of the Labour Party any such intention. This made it easier to achieve agreement on the terms of the new Party Constitution.

This new Constitution was adopted in February 1918. It transformed the Labour Party from a loose federation of affiliated organizations into a centralized, nationally cohesive Party, with its own individual members, organized in local constituency parties and subject to central party discipline.

The new Constitution also provided for a much larger financial contribution from the Trade Unions, whose predominant influence was clearly reflected in the structure of the National Executive Committee. Under the old Constitution, the affiliated Socialist societies had elected their own representatives to the Committee and they had been allotted three seats on it (the Trade Unions had eleven). Under the 1918 Constitution, there was to be an Executive of twenty-three members, of whom thirteen were to represent all nationally affiliated organizations as a single group, including Socialist societies and Trade Unions; five were to represent the local Labour Parties; four seats were reserved to women; the Treasurer was to be elected separately. But, while nominations were to be made separately for each section, it was the whole Annual Conference, where the Trade Unions wielded an overwhelming majority of votes, which was to elect the representatives of all groups.

These arrangements, with the particular distribution of power they entailed between the trade unions and the political wing of the alliance, were naturally much disliked by the Labour Left, which found itself condemned to permanent tutelage. On the other hand, the Left derived some consolation and hope from the inclusion in the Party Constitution of the famous socialist Clause 4 which formally committed the Party 'to secure for the workers by hand or by brain the full fruits of their industry and the most equitable distribution thereof that may be possible, upon the basis of the common ownership of the means of production[1] and the best obtainable system of popular administration and control of each industry and service'.

The Labour Party's announcement that it now was a socialist party was to create a serious problem for the I.L.P., which that body was never able to resolve. The I.L.P.'s *raison d'être* after 1900 had been to transform the Labour Party into a party committed to socialism. The Labour Party now said that it was. But, more and more in the course of the twenties, the I.L.P. found itself compelled to carry on its diverse activities on the wholly justified assumption that the Labour Party's conversion to socialism was as much a thing of the future as it had been before 1918. This made for acute conflict. At the same time, the creation of constituency Labour Parties was naturally bound, in time, to reduce the role of the I.L.P., whose local units had until then been the main centres of socialist propaganda in the constituencies. They now had competitors, ideologically much more diluted than was the I.L.P.

However, all this was for the future. In 1918, the Labour Party's commitment to socialism on the basis of common ownership, which the Labour Left had so long desired, seemed unambiguous enough to raise lively hopes that Labour had finally done with its own version of Liberalism And so in fact it had. But what had replaced it was not socialism, but Labourism, of which the Labour Party's statement of policy, *Labour and the New Social Order* of 1918, was the manifesto.

Labour and the New Social Order bravely asserted that what had to be reconstructed was not 'this or that piece of social machinery' but 'society itself'. It also expressed the desirability of 'the socialization of industry' and the Labour Party's wish to see achieved 'a genuinely scientific reorganization of the nation's industry, no longer deflected by industrial profiteering, on the basis of the Common Ownership of the Means of Production'.

In its concrete proposals for public ownership, *Labour and the New Social Order* advocated the nationalization of the land ('to be applied as suitable opportunities occur') and the immediate nationalization of railways, mines, the production of electric power, the Industrial Insurance Companies, as well as canals, harbours and steamship lines; it also saw 'the key to Temperance Reform in taking the entire manufacture and retailing of alcoholic drink out of the hands of those who find profit in promoting the utmost possible consumption'; while the need to extend municipal ownership was also stressed. The document further insisted on the State's responsibility for the provision to every citizen of a minimum standard of health, education,

[1] In 1929, this was amended to read 'the means of production, distribution and exchange', see below, p. 158.

leisure and subsistence, and for guaranteeing employment to 'every willing worker, by hand or by brain'; it was also proposed that the wide extension of social services and education should be financed by steeply progressive taxation; and there was also to be a new system of taxation on inheritance and an immediate Capital Levy to pay off part of the War Debt.

The full implementation of all the proposals contained in *Labour and the New Social Order* would, of course, have left the bulk of the means to life in private hands, even though under some measure of State control. In this sense, the new programme was much less the manifesto of a new social order, altogether different, economically and socially, from the old one, than an explicit affirmation by the Labour Party of its belief that piecemeal collectivism, within a predominantly capitalist society, was the key to more welfare, higher efficiency, and greater social justice. Shorn of its rhetoric, *Labour and the New Social Order* was a Fabian blueprint for a more advanced, more regulated form of capitalism, which had been in the making over the past decades and whose image had been given more definite shape by the war. With the adoption of *Labour and the New Social Order*, the Labour Party became the most consistent advocate of State action to control and humanize the operation of private enterprise, to extend the social services, to guarantee employment, to secure a more ample life for working men and women, and to create greater opportunities for the latter's sons and daughters.

Nevertheless, and however short its concrete proposals might fall of a socialist programme, *Labour and the New Social Order* marked a considerable step forward for the Labour Party; sufficiently so to make innumerable men and women, who did want an altogether new and differently based social order, feel that here at least was a real beginning. And indeed, even though the implementation of Labour's programme would not have ushered in a socialist society, it would have made a vast difference to the character and texture of the old one. It is because the document held this promise that it reconciled so many socialists to its limitations and created a basis of agreement between socialists and social reformers in the Labour Party. In fact, it was only in the fifties that this basis of agreement really began to crack. Until then, the existence of two fundamentally different views of the Labour Party's purpose was sufficiently blurred to suggest a common purpose, at least in programmatic terms.

The authors of *Labour and the New Social Order* fervently believed in the continued validity of parliamentary government as the means of achieving the new society they declared to be their aim. Nor had they much to propose by way of constitutional reform. In January 1918, the Party Conference had agreed without debate to a resolution which declared 'that a hereditary chamber such as the House of Lords should be abolished'; more remarkable, it had also expressed 'its confirmed opposition to any form of Second Chamber, whether elected by the House of Commons or otherwise'.[1] However, the final draft of *Labour and the New Social Order* failed to embody this decision. Instead, it said, in a wonderfully devious phrase, that 'the Party stands . . . for the complete abolition of the House of Lords, and for a most strenuous opposition to any machinery for revision of legislation taking the form of a new Second Chamber, whether elected or not, having in it any element of Heredity or Privilege'.

As for electoral reform, the passage of the Representation of the People Act of February 1918 had virtually introduced universal manhood suffrage and enfranchised a substantial number of women. At another Conference in June 1918, the Labour Party was therefore content to reaffirm its belief in full adult suffrage and to ask that 'the best practical arrangements' should be made to ensure that 'every minority has its proportionate and no more than its proportionate representation'.[2]

More immediately relevant was the Party's demand for the complete removal of all the war-time restrictions 'the day after Peace is declared' on freedom of speech, of publication, of the press, of travel, of choice of place of residence and employment. 'What marks off this Party most distinctly from any of the other political parties,' *Labour and the New Social Order* said, 'is its demand for the full and genuine adoption of the principle of Democracy.'

But the fact remained that a long time must elapse, as no one in the Labour Party doubted, before there would be a chance for a Labour Government to try and implement any of Labour's proposals. After the election of December 1918[3], the problem was not what Labour would do when it came to office, but what it would do to prevent Labour's opponents from exploiting their parliamentary majority for the purpose of trampling into the dust Labour's hopes of a new deal.

'Hang the Kaiser', and Lloyd George's famous pledge of a 'fit country for heroes to live in', were by no means the only themes of

---

[1] Labour Party Annual Conference Report, January 1918, p. 136.
[2] Labour Party Annual Conference Report, June 1918, p. 67.
[3] At the Election, the Labour Party proposed a 'Peace of Reconciliation'; the immediate withdrawal of the Allied Forces from Russia; freedom for Ireland and India; the end of conscription; the nationalization of land and of 'vital public services' such as mines, railways, shipping, armaments and electric power; a special tax on capital; and heavily graduated direct taxation.

the 'Coupon Election' of December 1918. 'Bolshevism' too, as Mr Mowat notes,[1] was one of the major themes of the campaign. This was the first of a succession of election campaigns in which Conservatives and Liberals raised the Bolshevik bogey and sought to persuade the electorate that the Labour Party was, for all practical purposes, Bolshevik-led and inspired.[2] Neither this, nor the tag of 'pacifism' that was attached to some of its leading members, prevented the Labour Party from making very substantial gains. Out of some 11 million votes cast (57.6 per cent. of the electorate), Labour polled nearly 2.5 million (22 per cent.) as compared with 400,000 in the last pre-war election of 1910. The Coalition candidates had polled over 5 million votes and 484 of them were returned, of whom 338 were Conservatives. Labour was now the largest Opposition Party in the House, though only with 60 members, followed by the Asquith Liberals, who had 26.

In a different perspective, Labour's results had a very different connotation. Of its 60 members, 49 were trade union M.P.s, of whom no less than 25 had been candidates sponsored by the Miners' Federation. Only 3 I.L.P. candidates had been elected (out of 50), while the local Labour Parties, who had put 140 candidates in the field, returned 7 members. All the most prominent I.L.P. candidates, including MacDonald, Snowden and Jowett, were defeated, as were also Henderson and Lansbury. It is hardly likely that the election of MacDonald, Snowden or Henderson[3] would have made a great deal of difference to the actual influence of the Labour Party in the House of Commons. But their presence there might have helped the Parliamentary Party to make a greater impression *on the Labour movement*. As it is, the poor performance of the Party in Parliament[4] helped the case of those on the Left who argued that if Labour was content to rely on its parliamentary strength, it would not be able to make an even marginal contribution either to the peace settlement or to the shape of the post-war settlement at home: if anything was to be done to compel the Government to redeem even a few of the lavish pledges which had been made to the working classes, it would have to be done by outside pressure on a Government and employers determined to concede as little as possible.

[1] C. L. Mowat, *Britain Between the Wars 1918-1940* (London, 1955) p. 5.
[2] 'The Labour Party,' Lloyd George said in his closing speech of the campaign, 'is being run by the extreme pacifist, Bolshevist group' (ibid, p.5).
[3] Henderson re-entered the House of Commons in August 1919, after winning a by-election at Widnes.
[4] The Leader of the Parliamentary Party from 1917 to 1921 was William Adamson; he was succeeded in 1921 by J. R. Clynes. Both men were extreme moderates, and mediocre parliamentarians to boot.

Labour's resources for the purpose were far from negligible. Trade union membership, which had been 5.5 million in 1917 (as compared with 4 million in 1914), had risen to 6.5 million in 1918 and had leapt to 8 million in 1919. The core of that membership was made up of a deeply class conscious, highly militant segment of the working classes. Nor, once the jingoist mood of the General Election had passed and been replaced by the disillusionments of peace-time, did the election results provide an accurate measure of Labour's support. Ineffectual though it was in the House of Commons, Labour was a power in the country—provided it chose to exercise that power.

2. THE FEAR OF ACTION

There are few years in the history of the Labour movement more important than the immediate post-war years. It was then that Labour could have claimed an altogether different place in the scheme of things and made a really profound indent in the old order. It was also then that its leaders rejected the opportunity.

1919 was a year of bitter discontent, and it showed the organized workers to be a live, militant force, unrevolutionary in its ultimate aims, but ready for bold leadership on political as well as on industrial issues. The temper of a majority of trade union leaders was very different. The militancy of their followers did not make them feel stronger: it struck them with apprehension. They held a formidable instrument in their hands. Much of their energy was devoted to persuading their members that it should not be used. Again and again, pressure from the rank and file for resolute action was deflected and neutralized.

Yet a great deal could have been extracted at the end of the war from a Government much less confident than its pronouncements suggested. In the first months of 1919 at any rate, there were concessions to be had, provided the demand for them was pressed sufficiently hard, the more so since the Government was not even sure it could rely on the rank and file of the Army and of the police.[1] The

[1] Early in 1919, the War Office sent a secret circular to the commanding officers of troops stationed in Britain asking, *inter alia*, whether troops would 'respond to orders for assistance to preserve the public peace', whether they would 'assist in strike breaking', and whether they would 'parade for draft overseas, especially to Russia'. (See W. H. Crook, *The General Strike* (Chapel Hill, 1931) pp. 240-42.) The circular came into the possession of the *Daily Herald*, which published it in May 1919. For the Government's embarrassed explanations, see ibid, pp. 242-3. For disaffection in the police force in 1918 and 1919, see V. L. Allen, 'The National Union of Police and Prison Officers', in *Economic History Review*, vol. XI, No. 1, 1958. It was only in August 1919, with the failure of a badly mismanaged police strike, that the police force was firmly brought to heel.

one inestimable advantage the Government had was that it was dealing with men who feared to answer its challenge. The Government had a weak hand. But the Labour leaders did not dare play their aces. So the Government won the game.

The issue, it is worth stressing again, was not revolution and socialism, but direct industral action for limited and specific purposes. The two cases in which that issue was most sharply posed were the future of the mines and British intervention in Russia.

The battle for the mines was a battle which Labour could not afford to lose without losing much else. Success in imposing nationalization upon the Government and the coal owners would have meant much more than the reorganization of one industry on a new basis. It would also have meant a spectacular assertion of Labour's strength and a concrete proof of its determination to achieve a new deal.

The strength of the argument for the nationalization of the mines was in any case recognized by many whose sympathies did not lie with Labour or with public ownership generally. This was one issue on which Labour could rely on much public sympathy. As for the miners, they voted for strike action by a six to one majority on the 13th of February, 1919, if their demand for State ownership and the democratic control of the mines, as well as for higher wages and shorter hours, was not met. And the miners' resolve was enhanced by their membership, with the railwaymen and the transport workers, of the Triple Alliance.

The Government's reaction to the threat was, firstly, to call a National Joint Industrial Conference of employers and representatives of Labour to discuss ways of improving 'industrial relations'; and, secondly, to propose the appointment of a Royal Commission on the Mines, the Commission to include the miners' president, Robert Smillie, and two other Labour representatives; and Lloyd George also proposed that the miners should be able to nominate three other members of the Commission.

Not without great difficulty and as it turned out, disastrously, the miners' representatives were persuaded by their leaders to accept this offer to postpone strike action until the Sankey Commission had issued an Interim Report on wages and hours.[1] On the 20th of March, the Commission's Interim Report conceded the miners' claim for higher wages and shorter hours and, though it refused to commit

---

[1] Frank Hodges, the Secretary of the Miners' Federation, later recalled that he and Robert Smillie 'threw in the whole weight of our argument and our influence to get the men and delegates to accept the Royal Commission. Hours, days, were spent in this tussle, and in the end we won.' (F. Hodges, *My Adventures as a Labour Leader* (London, n.d.) p. 80.)

itself to nationalization, said that 'even upon the evidence already given, the present system of ownership and working in the coal industry stands condemned, and some other system must be substituted for it, either nationalization or a method of unification by national purchase and/or by joint control'. Much encouraged, the Miners' Federation again decided to postpone strike action.

The Government thus achieved its main object, which was to gain a precious measure of time, and it went on buying more with repeated promises that it was prepared to adopt the Commission's Report 'in the spirit as well as in the letter and to take all necessary steps to carry out its recommendations without delay'.

These were rash words. The Commission's sittings had turned into a massive indictment of the coal owners[1] and though it finally issued on the 23rd of June no less than four sets of recommendations, all of them were in favour of at least the public ownership of coal itself, while the Chairman of the Commission and the Labour representatives also agreed to the nationalization of the industry.[2]

The Government had no intention of accepting these recommendations. It delayed its answer until it felt safe. Finally, on the 18th of August, Lloyd George announced in the House of Commons that it would not act on the basis of the Commission's Report. The challenge to the miners and to the whole Labour movement was unmistakable. The question was whether Labour would use its industrial power to coerce the Government. By then, the same question had already been extensively canvassed—in connection with British intervention in Russia.

In March 1919, the Miners' Federation had demanded the withdrawal of British troops from Russia. In April, the miners, supported by other unions, had moved an emergency resolution to the same purpose at a joint Conference of the Labour Party and the T.U.C., convened to discuss Labour's attitude to the proposed Covenant of the League of Nations. The resolution was endorsed by the Conference. But its movers also proposed that *action* should be taken to compel the Government to carry out this, and other demands contained in the resolution.[3] The Chairman of the Conference, G. H. Stuart-Bunning, who was also the Chairman of the Parliamentary Committee of the T.U.C., refused to accept this part of the resolution, because it implied taking industrial action, a course to which, he

[1] See A. Gleason, *What the Workers Want. A Study of British Labour* (New York, 1920) pp. 33 ff.
[2] For an analysis of the Sankey Commission Report, see R. Page Arnot, *The Miners: Years of Struggle* (London, 1953), chs. VII and VIII.
[3] i.e. the lifting of the blockade against Germany, the ending of conscription, and the release of conscientious objectors from prison.

said, the political section of the Labour movement could not be committed.[1] Soon after, the leaders of the Triple Industrial Alliance called upon the Parliamentary Committee to summon a special National Congress to discuss the action that should be taken.

The last thing the Parliamentary Committee wanted was to be pushed into militant action, over Russia or anything else. Instead of calling a special Congress, it decided to seek 'clarification' from the Government on its Russian policy. A deputation from the Committee saw Bonar Law,[2] the Leader of the House of Commons, on the 22nd of May, and was told that the Allies did not intend to interfere in the internal affairs of Russia, that British forces would be withdrawn as soon as possible, but that, on the other hand, the Government would meanwhile continue to help Koltchak against the Bolsheviks.[3] A majority of the Parliamentary Committee found this satisfactory enough to justify the Parliamentary Committee refusing to call a special conference.[4] Nor was the Left, despite protest and pressure, able to have the decision reversed.

The first occasion on which the issue of direct action was properly joined was at the Labour Party Annual Conference, which opened on the 25th of June, 1919, two days after the publication of the Sankey Commission Report. 'Many resolutions,' the Executive's Report to the Conference noted, 'have been received at the Head Office, indicating that there are some sections of the Movement anxious that an organized attempt to defeat the Government's political policy by direct industrial action should be discussed by a joint Conference representative of both the political and industrial movements.'[5]

For its own part, the National Executive approached the subject of direct action with extreme caution and was well content to leave the initiative to the trade unions themselves. 'If,' it said, 'the British Labour movement is to institute a new precedent in our indusrial history by initiating a general strike for the purpose of achieving not industrial but political objects, it is imperative that the Trade Unions, whose members are to fufil the obligations implied in the new policy and whose finance it is presumed are to be involved, should realize

[1] Roberts, op. cit. p. 320.
[2] Lloyd George being away at the Peace Conference in Paris.
[3] 'We are helping Koltchak,' said Bonar Law. 'We have already taken steps to make it clear to him that unless it is made quite clear that his success will not mean the establishment of some autocratic government, that his success will mean the calling of a Free Assembly in Russia, which will decide for themselves what their form of government is to be, we are free to change our attitude, and cease to give even the support we are giving now' (Graubard, op. cit. p. 73).
[4] ibid, p. 73.
[5] Labour Party Annual Conference Report, 1920, p. 27.

the responsibilities such a strike movement would entail and should themselves determine the plan of any such new campaign."[1]

In his presidential address to the Conference, the Chairman of the Party, J. McGurk, of the Miners' Federation, was more explicitly hostile to the notion of direct action. Referring to the movement 'that was already afoot to employ the strike weapon for political purposes', he said that this 'would be an innovation in this country which few responsible leaders would welcome . . . We are either constitutionalists or we are not constitutionalists. If we are constitutionalists, if we believe in the efficacy of the political weapon (and we do, or why do we have a Labour Party?) then it is both unwise and undemocratic because we fail to get a majority at the polls to turn round and demand that we should substitute industrial action.' The political weapon, said Mr McGurk, had not failed; it could not be given a fair trial so long as the workers did not realize much more clearly 'that they hold the power of political salvation in their own hands and through their own party'. 'If they are not yet politically conscious, if they fail to give their support to constitutional political action by the Labour Party, it appears to me to be less likely that they will be ready to give their adhesion to industrial action to enforce political demands and ideas.'[2]

In conjunction with the assertion that direct action was in any case unconstitutional and undemocratic, this was an argument that was to be used again and again in the course of the debates. Rather than draw strength from the support Labour *had* received at the Election, in spite of the special and transient circumstances in which it had been held, men like Mr McGurk chose to dwell on the fact that Labour had not done better, and to use this as proof that the workers, despite the evidence of the previous months, would not follow a militant leadership. But the opponents of direct action also sought to defeat the Left by narrowing the alternatives open to the Labour movement to constitutional, meaning parliamentary, action on the one hand, and revolution and civil war on the other. Because of their dislike of it, these opponents invested direct action with the most extreme meaning, so as to inhibit and discourage their rank and file. Thus James Sexton, of the Dock Labourers, also pointed to the results of the General Election to question the feasibility of direct action. But he then immediately went on to argue that direct action would be *too* effective and plunge the country into civil war, 'which would destroy all their organizations for generations to come'. Much better, he pleaded, to wait until the next General Election came along. Even if it meant waiting for four years, 'what then?'

[1] Labour Party Annual Conference Report, 1919, p. 27.
[2] ibid, p. 113.

Four years of 'good, sound legislation' (presumably to be introduced by the Government as a result of Labour's parliamentary pressure) was infinitely preferable to 'rushing civil war'. Supposing they destroyed the Government by a national strike, asked Sexton, 'what were they going to put in its place?'

But there was another fear to which James Sexton gave expression —the fear that direct action, which would necessarily strengthen the influence of a hated Left, would also threaten the supremacy of the unions' traditional leadership. 'They were,' said Sexton, 'letting loose an element that was rife today in the Trade Union Movement, that would take advantage of the confusion, and make it impossible for them to exercise any controlling power . . . They had no machinery to control what they destroyed. Their only machinery would be revolution. It was all very well to talk of revolution. He was a revolutionist of a social character and believed in social revolution. But he did not believe in letting mad dogs loose and that was what they were asking for.'[1]

In fact, the direct actionists were not, for the most part, revolutionaries, determined upon the overthrow of the existing order. They did not see direct action as a strategy of revolutionary change but as a means of pressure, for specific and limited purposes, incomparably more effective than parliamentary action. They might speak of coercing or even of 'overthrowing' the Government. But they were not thinking of capturing power from it. Once the Government appeared to have retreated on the issue of intervention, as it seemed to do in August,[2] their pressure for action immediately relaxed.

On the other hand, they did accept their opponents' claim that direct action was 'unconstitutional', and went on to argue that, even so, it was necessary. Robert Williams, himself a member of the National Executive, bluntly said that 'there were members sitting on the Parliamentary Committee of the Trades Union Congress who were more reactionary than the British Government'; their action 'was only directed to promote a sort of smoke screen to protect and hide the reactionary conduct of the Government'. As to the argument that certain forms of action were unconstitutional, it was his 'first conviction', he said, that 'inexorable circumstances would compel them to revolutionize their tactics'. In any case, 'was the war against Russia constitutional war? Had war been formally declared? Had the credits been voted?'[3]

For the Miners, Robert Smillie took over where Williams left off

[1] Labour Party Annual Conference Report, 1919, p. 119.
[2] see below, p. 74.
[3] Labour Party Annual Conference Report, 1919, p. 116.

and asserted that the Executive Committee of the Labour Party 'feared more than anything else what had come to be called direct action' and thus 'taken up exactly the position of every exploiter and capitalist and politician in this country at the present time'. Where, he asked, did political questions end and Trade Union questions begin? And, like Williams, he answered those who said industrial action was unconstitutional by asking whether the Government's action was constitutional. 'Had they not deceived the people? Were they not returned to power under false pretences? Did not every member of their Committee believe that the present Government was sitting in its place through fraud?' If so, 'was the great Labour Movement not to take any action to get rid of a Government that was sitting there through fraud and deceit?'[1]

Fred Bromley, of A.S.L.E.F., went a good deal further than this and put forward a view seldom heard at Labour Party Conferences. 'They were told,' he said, 'they had not a majority in favour. Could any man or woman then point to any progressive measure in the world that had waited for the majority to bring it about . . . These things had always been done by the intelligent progressive minorities and they would do so again . . . If they were going to wait until the worker had clear issues and truthful statements put before him on which to vote they would never get anywhere . . . Let them give the rank and file a lead. They were waiting for it. It was the leaders who were too respectable, who did not like to be roasted in the capitalist Press, who liked to be called level-headed Trade Unionists.'[2]

The Parliamentary Party too naturally came in for sharp criticism. It had, said Herbert Morrison, a delegate of the London Labour Party, been a failure in the present Parliament; they had to realize that the war against Russia was not a war against Bolshevism or against Lenin, but against the international organization of Socialism and the organization of the Trade Union Movement itself. 'As such (it) should be resisted with the full political and industrial power of the whole Trade Union Movement . . . their great necessity was to overturn the Government; that was the immediate need.'[3]

In replying to the critics of the Parliamentary Party, W. Adamson, its Chairman, fell back on the argument that the Labour members had done all they could, given the paucity of their numbers. His real point, however, was that there was only one way in which more could be done: that was for Labour 'to get into the constituencies and to attempt to convince the people that the time had come for Labour being represented there in great numbers, that the time had

[1] Labour Party Annual Conference Report, 1919, p. 118.
[2] ibid, pp. 120-1.
[3] ibid, p. 128.

71

come for Labour to form the Government of the country'.[1] The motion for the reference back of the Parliamentary Report was actually 'negatived'.[2] Nevertheless, it was ultimately the direct actionists who carried the day.

The Conference had before it a composite resolution which instructed the National Executive to consult the Parliamentary Committee of the T.U.C. 'with the view to effective action being taken' to enforce their demands 'by the unreserved use of their political and industrial power'.[3]

The debate on the resolution went over much the same ground that had already been covered in the discussion of direct action, and was mainly notable for a speech by J. R. Clynes against it. Clynes insisted that he fully believed in the use of the 'great Trade Union weapon' for industrial ends,[4] but that 'he refused to use that weapon for so clearly and obvious a political purpose as that mentioned in the resolution'. He too argued that the election results had proved that 'the working men were not ready for their appeal'. But he also asked the delegates to remember that they hoped to see one day a Labour and Socialist Government. 'Were they going to concede to every other or any other class the right they were claiming to exercise? Did it mean that any class which could exercise the power should have the right to terrorize a Labour Government by the use of any means or manoeuvres that it could apply? . . . The blow which they were threatening would not be a blow at a Government but a blow at democracy. It would be a hurt to themselves, it would do greater and more permanent harm to the true interests of the working class than to any other class in this country . . . Millions of men in the street could not be there long without mischief, riot, disorder, disturbance, and bloodshed.'[5]

What Clynes was asking was that Labour should deliberately forbear to use its power over urgent issues in the expectation that its opponents, in grateful memory of that forbearance, would also behave nicely when Labour came to office. It was a remarkable view, but by no means an unusual one, of the manner in which traditional elites acquit themselves in politics when their power, property and privileges are threatened.

However, despite all warnings of chaos to come, the resolution was passed—by 1,893,000 votes to 935,000,[6] a notable majority,

[1] Labour Party Annual Conference Report, 1919, p. 132.
[2] ibid, p. 132.
[3] ibid, p. 156.
[4] In actual fact, Clynes had been a leading advocate of industrial conciliation in the previous months.
[5] Labour Party Annual Conference Report, 1919, p. 161.
[6] ibid, p. 161.

mainly due to the split in the trade union vote. But the advocates of inaction were far from defeated. The National Executive agreed on the 9th of July by fourteen votes to five to press for a special conference 'for the purpose of discussing *whether*, and by what means direct industrial action should be taken . . .'[1] But a majority of the Parliamentary Committee continued to oppose any such action and refused to convene the special conference. As the vote of the National Executive indicated, their resistance did not lack support in that body.

Henderson himself had not spoken at the Labour Party Conference on the issue of direct action, but he too was strongly opposed to it. 'To force upon the country by illegitimate means the policy of a section, perhaps of a minority of the community,' he wrote at the time, 'involves the abrogation of Parliamentary Government, establishes a dictatorship of the minority, and might easily destroy eventually all our constitutional liberties. It is moreover a two-edged policy. When Labour conquers political power and accepts responsibility for the machinery of Government, I cannot see it prepared to admit, say the followers of Sir Edward Carson, or the medical profession, to set the Executive at defiance of any process of direct action.'[2]

[1] V. L. Allen, *Trade Unions and the Government* (London, 1960) p. 156. My italics.

[2] *Daily Herald*, 14th of July 1919, in Graubard, op. cit. p. 79. For his own part, MacDonald adopted a more ambiguous view on the subject. On the one hand, he wrote that 'the power which the I.L.P. seeks to gain is the power of public opinion' (*The Labour Leader*, 25th of September, 1919); on the other hand, in his *Parliament and Revolution*, published in 1919, he suggested that direct action, in very rare cases, was not incompatible with the sovereignty of Parliament, but was intended to 'limit its liberty to abuse its sovereignty' and to 'convert the masses from an attitude of passivity between elections to one of activity when it is necessary . . . there is nothing "unconstitutional" in this—nothing that does violence to any intelligent conception of Parliamentary government'. But direct action was only to be resorted to 'should circumstances arise when active political sections in the community are convinced that Parliamentary powers are being abused and that in the interest of representative government the abuse must be ended, if public opinion will give sufficient support and the object to be aimed at is of such a nature as to allow the weapon to be used effectively, which in most cases means swiftly' (J. R. MacDonald, *Parliament and Revolution* (London, 1919) p. 70). No parliamentary constitutionalist could reasonably have asked for more inhibiting qualifications. Snowden was more direct. 'Industrial action for the specific purposes named,' he wrote, 'could be justified on the ground that the intervention in Russia and the continuance of conscription by the Government were themselves unconstitutional acts, unsupported by the country, and were violations of the pledges on which the Government was returned to power' (*The Labour Leader*, 21st of August, 1919).

Faced with the obstruction of the Parliamentary Committee, a conference of Triple Alliance delegates decided on the 25th of July (by 217 votes to 11) to proceed on their own and they recommended the constituent unions to ballot their members on the issue of strike action.[1] On the 29th, Winston Churchill, the Secretary of State for War, announced that the withdrawal of British troops from Russia, which he claimed to have been decided by the Government at the beginning of the year, was in progress; and that Labour's other grievances (the continuation of conscription, the threat of the use of troops in labour disputes and the continued imprisonment of conscientious objectors) had already been dealt with, or were being dealt with. On the 12th of August, another Conference of the Triple Alliance decided that strike action was no longer necessary. On the 19th, Lloyd George announced the Government's rejection of the Sankey Commission Report. As the hesitation and doubts within the Labour movement had become more obvious, so had the Government's confidence increased.

In the course of these months three things had been clearly demonstrated: firstly, that a majority of Labour leaders remained as timid and cautious after the war as they had been before, in some ways more; secondly, that a substantial segment of the organized working class was far ahead of its leadership in its willingness to challenge the Government; and thirdly, that while the Left wielded far greater influence than it had done before 1914, and could win temporary majorities at Conferences, it was not in a position to supplant the traditionalists. Whatever episodic defeat these might sustain, they remained in control of Labour's political and industrial machine.

At the T.U.C. Conference in September 1919, the Parliamentary Committee immediately faced angry criticism over its refusal to convene a special Congress and a motion for the reference back of its Report, moved in scathing terms by Robert Smillie and seconded by Robert Williams, was carried by 2,586,000 votes to 1,876,000.[2] But opposition to the leadership's attitude was expressed even more clearly on the straightforward issue of direct action.

A special resolution, asking the Congress to declare 'against the principle of industrial action in purely political matters' was introduced by Tom Shaw, M.P., and debated later in the week. Shaw accused both Smillie and Williams of seeking to foment a revolution with the ultimate purpose of establishing a government on the Soviet model;[3] his seconder, Arthur Hayday, less flamboyantly argued that

[1] Allen, op. cit. p. 156.
[2] T.U.C. Annual Conference Report, 1919, p. 231.
[3] ibid, p. 289.

redress through the ballot-box was possible'.[1] Nevertheless, when the opponents of the resolution moved the previous question, it was carried, by a comfortable majority.[2] Yet, these votes were more in the nature of consolation prizes for the Left than substantial victories.

By the time the Government announced in August that it would not nationalize the mines, the hesitations of the previous months had had their effect, even on the miners. On the 3rd of September, a Conference of the miners' delegates stated that they did not 'at this stage' recommend industrial action. Instead, they invited the T.U.C. 'to declare that the fullest and most effective action be taken to secure that the Government shall adopt the majority report of the Commission as to the future governance of the industry'.[3] The commitment was vague and the miners had no difficulty in obtaining an overwhelming majority in their support from the T.U.C. Conference. It was also agreed there to call a special Congress two months hence to decide what action should be taken, if the Government had not by then yielded. What this meant in effect was that nothing much, and certainly nothing effective, would be attempted. Yet the outcome of the railway dispute at the beginning of October showed that the Government could be moved, if Labour chose to use its strength, or even to threaten its use.

Negotiations with the Government over the railwaymen's national programme of wages, hours and conditions of work had gone on throughout the year. Until September, the Government had only had to deal with threats it could afford to ignore so long as they were not followed by concrete action. But when final deadlock appeared to be reached on the 16th of September, a national railway strike was called for the 26th. The railwaymen's leaders (J. H. Thomas was the General Secretary of the N.U.R.) insisted that the strike was purely economic and were deeply reluctant to see it spread. The Government for its own part insisted that the strike *was* a strike 'against the life of the community' and that it 'must be resisted and fought with all the resources of the country'.[4] It then proceeded to mobilize those resources with all the appearance of

---

[1] T.U.C. Annual Conference Report, 1919, pp. 291-2. Note also Arthur Henderson's appeal to the Congress, as the fraternal delegate from the Labour Party, to 'give the political side of the movement such a trial as you have never given it before', and his warning that to display 'a withdrawal of confidence in the political and constitutional method' would be the greatest calamity for Labour 'just at this momentous period in our history, when the position is so promising . . .' (ibid, p. 311).

[2] ibid, p. 300.

[3] Arnot, op. cit. p. 215.

[4] Allen, op. cit. p. 174.

grim determination. This was the bogey which the chairman of the T.U.C., G. H. Stuart-Bunning, had agitated when defending the Parliamentary Committee against its critics. 'If the Government fought,' he had said at the T.U.C. Conference, 'it meant revolution . . . a desperate gamble with the lives of men, women and children. . . .' This indeed is how the Government talked, with appeals to 'Fight for the Life of the Community', while *The Times* likened the strike with the war against Germany, and insisted that it must be fought to a finish.[1]

No sooner however was the Government faced with the real possibility that the strike *would* spread[2] than it agreed to a settlement which gave the railwaymen much, though not all, that they had asked. The Labour leaders, though under strong rank and file pressure, had throughout been on the side of conciliation. But the threat that they would finally have to invoke their power was sufficient to force the Government to retreat before them.

In the case of the miners, the story was very different. The special Congress which met in December was faced with the fact that the Government's position was unchanged. It then decided to launch an 'educational campaign' on the theme of 'The Mines for the Nation'. Four weeks later the Miners' Executive, realizing that the campaign would produce no results, asked the Parliamentary Committee to convene a special conference of the T.U.C. to consider the calling of a General Strike to achieve the nationalization of the mines. By then, the Parliamentary Committee had no reason to fear that this would be endorsed. Indeed the miners themselves were now divided on the issue. At a conference on the 10th of March, the day before the Congress met, the miners' delegates voted for direct action, but only by 524 to 344.[1] The Congress itself decided against it by 3,732,000 votes to 1,050,000. In so doing, it settled the issue, and much else as well, for twenty-five years.

3. LABOUR'S FLING

At the end of April 1920, Soviet-Polish hostilities were resumed with the launching of a Polish offensive over a wide front. Not surprisingly in view of their record, the move was widely construed

---

[1] Allen, p. 175.

[2] On the 4th of October, it was warned by representatives of unions likely to be affected by the strike that 'unless a more reasonable attitude is adopted . . . it will be impossible to avert a widespread extension of the strike with all its consequences' (ibid. p. 177).

[3] Arnot, op. cit. p. 218.

as having been inspired by the British and French Governments[1] and trade union reaction was prompt. London dockers refused to load the *Jolly George* with ammunition and other supplies for Poland. An emergency resolution, moved by Ernest Bevin at the Dockers' Conference the following week, congratulated the dockers and called upon the whole Labour movement 'to resist their labour being used to perpetuate these wicked ventures'.[2] Following the Dockers' lead, the Executive of the National Union of Railwaymen asked its members to refuse to handle supplies destined for Poland.[3]

The Labour parliamentarians appeared more ineffectual than ever. Clynes's best effort was to suggest that the dispute be submitted to the League of Nations, which the Government refused to do, just as it refused to put pressure upon the Poles to desist from their military ventures. It was hardly to be expected that the Government would be willing to exert itself, since the Polish armies went from success to success and entered Kiev on the 12th of June. However, success did not last. By the end of the month, the Poles were in full retreat and the Labour Party Conference, which met at Scarborough on the 22nd of June, 1920, was therefore content to endorse an Executive resolution on the Peace Treaties and the Condition of Europe which demanded, *inter alia*, the recognition of Russia, the cessation of all 'direct and indirect attack', the lifting of the blockade and the encouragement of trade with Russia.[4] An amendment moved on behalf of the British Socialist Party, which asked for 'the organization of a general strike that shall put an end once and for all to the open and covert participation of the British Government in attacks on the Soviet Republic',[5] was defeated by an 'overwhelming majority',[6] after a speech in which Ernest Bevin had warned the delegates against ill-prepared movements that must result in failure. 'The Trade Union movement,' he said, 'was not a military force where men had to go blindly, at the orders of the leaders, one way or another.'[7]

And yet, the Labour Party and the trade unions were threatening, just over a month later, to do precisely what so many of their leaders

---

[1] 'The marionettes are in Warsaw,' the *Daily Herald* wrote on the 30th of April, 'but the strings are pulled from London and Paris' (Graubard, op. cit. p. 91).
[2] ibid, p. 92.
[3] This, however, was rescinded when the manager of the Great Northern Railway announced that anyone hindering the company from fulfilling its contracts would be dismissed (ibid, p. 93).
[4] Labour Party Annual Conference Report, 1920, p. 132.
[5] ibid, p. 138.
[6] ibid, p. 142.
[7] ibid, p. 144.

had said could not be done and must never be attempted: it was mobilizing its forces outside Parliament for a major and deliberate challenge to the Government.

By the beginning of July, the Polish armies were streaming out of Russia, with the Red Army in pursuit. On the 12th of July, the British Government, on behalf of the Allies, asked the Russians to sign an immediate armistice. The Russians agreed to direct negotiations with the Poles. Though the latter expressed willingness to discuss an armistice, they refused to discuss a peace settlement except in concert with their French and British Allies. The talks broke down and the Russians resumed their advance into Poland. On the 3rd of August, the British Government warned the Russians that they would come to the aid of Poland if the advance continued. War seemed imminent.

It is at this point that the Labour Party acted. On the 4th of August, Henderson, as Secretary of the Party, sent out telegrams to all affiliated local Labour Parties and Trades Councils warning of the 'extremely menacing possibility' of an extension of the Polish-Russian war, and strongly urging local parties to organize 'citizen demonstrations' for the following Sunday, the 8th of August, to protest against intervention and the supply of men and ammunition to Poland. They were also asked to demand the immediate raising of the blockade and the resumption of trade relations, to send resolutions to the Prime Minister and the Press, and to 'deputize' their Members of Parliament.[1]

Within twenty-four hours there also appeared a manifesto signed by a representative group of party leaders exonerating the Russians from responsibility in the crisis and warning 'the responsible governments, the diplomats, and the various foreign ministers, that Labour in this country will not co-operate in a war as allies of Poland'.[2]

But the Party was moving rapidly beyond a determination not to co-operate. Special peace demonstrations were held throughout the country on Sunday, 8th of August. The Labour Party's appeal, according to the Executive Committee Report to the 1921 Party Conference, 'met with an unparalleled response', and it was evident, the Report added, 'that Labour had mobilized public opinion rapidly and successfully'.[3]

On the following day, a joint meeting of the Parliamentary Committee of the T.U.C., the Executive Committee of the Labour Party and the Members of the Parliamentary Party, was held at the House of Commons and agreed (with 'surprising unanimity', the Report

[1] Graubard, op. cit. p. 104.
[2] ibid, p. 104.
[3] Labour Party Annual Conference Report, 1921, p. 11.

noted) to a resolution expressing the conviction that 'war is being engineered between the Allied Powers and Soviet Russia on the issue of Poland'. 'Such a war,' the resolution went on, 'would be an intolerable crime against humanity'; the Government was therefore warned *'that the whole industrial power of the organized workers will be used to defeat this war'*; it was further proposed 'that the Executive Committees of affiliated organizations throughout the country be summoned to hold themselves ready to proceed immediately to London for a National Conference; *that they be advised to instruct their members to "down tools" on instruction from that National Conference;* and that a Council of Action be immediately constituted to take such steps as may be necessary to carry the above decision into effect.'[1] It was at this meeting that the Council of Action, representing all shades of Labour opinion, was formed, while local Councils of Action also mushroomed all over the country.[2]

When the Council of Action met the Prime Minister on the 10th of August, it was assured of the Government's peaceful intentions. The Government's only concern, according to Lloyd George, was for a settlement which preserved Poland's independence. In the House of Commons that same afternoon, Lloyd George was equally conciliatory: new talks between the Poles and the Russians had been arranged for the following day; even if the talks failed because of Russian intransigence, there would be no question of sending British troops to Poland, though the Government might supply arms to its Polish ally, consider the imposition of economic pressure on Russia, and give generous assistance to General Wrangel who was still fighting the Bolsheviks in Russia. It was, Lloyd George also said, ridiculous for Labour to suggest that what was involved was a reactionary attack on a revolutionary socialist state.[3]

With the assurance, which even Lloyd George would have found it difficult to repudiate, that British troops would in no circumstances intervene, Labour had gained its main point. This fact robbed of some of its drama the National Conference of more than one thousand delegates[4] who met in London on the 13th of August. The meeting, in the words of the Executive Report to the 1921 Party Conference, was 'one of the most striking examples of Labour unanimity, determination and enthusiasm in the history of the

---

[1] Labour Party Annual Conference Report, 1921, p. 11. My italics.
[2] According to the Executive Committee's Report to the 1921 Conference, some 350 local Councils of Action were formed. (Labour Party Annual Conference Report, 1921, p. 17.)
[3] H. of C., vol. 133, vols. 253 ff.
[4] There were 689 delegates representing trade unions and 355 from Constituency Labour Parties and Trades Councils.

Movement'.[1] Though the crisis had passed (or, more likely *because* it had passed), the meeting offered some of the most cautious and orthodox Labour leaders an opportunity to adopt highly uncharacteristic postures. Thus Clynes: 'No Parliamentary or political measures, we felt, could be effective in themselves to save the country from being committed to war against its will. We felt that, as statesmen, contrary to their promises, had failed to establish an effective League of Nations to save us from war, we must be saved from war by an effective League of Labour action working upon lines to make it impossible to send a ship, a gun, a man, to send material or money for this nefarious purpose.'[2]

J. H. Thomas, who moved a resolution asking the delegates to approve the formation of the Council of Action, was even more dramatic. 'No Parliamentary effort,' he told the delegates, 'could do what we are asking you to do, and desperate as are our measures, dangerous as they are, we believe that the disease is so desperate and dangerous that it is only desperate and dangerous methods that can provide a remedy.' Giving effect to the resolution, he warned, did not mean embarking on a 'mere strike': 'It means a challenge to the whole Constitution of the Country.' (Cheers.)[3] A. G. Cameron, the Chairman of the Labour Party, told the delegates that 'constitutionalism can only exist as long as it does not outrage the conscience of the community. . . . If the day comes when we do take this action, and if the powers that be endeavour to interefere too much, we may be compelled to do things that will cause them to abdicate, and to tell them that if they cannot run the country in a peaceful and humane manner without interfering with the lives of other nations, we will be compelled, even against all constitutions, to chance whether we cannot do something to take the country into our own hands for our own people.'[4]

J. H. Thomas's resolution was carried unanimously, the delegates rising and singing the 'Red Flag' and the 'International' as the vote was taken.

On the following Monday, the 16th of August, Lloyd George said in the House of Commons that the policy of the Government in

---

[1] Labour Party Annual Conference Report, 1921, p. 11.

[2] The Council of Action, Report of the Special Conference on Labour and the Russian-Polish War (1920) p. 12.

[3] ibid, p. 16. It was the same Thomas who had written in July 1919 that 'we ought clearly to recognize that if Labour is going to govern—and I believe it will—we can't have some outside body attempting to rebel against Parliamentary institutions without it recoiling on our own heads' (Graubard, op. cit. p. 79).

[4] ibid, p. 18.

regard to Poland and Russia 'appear to differ in no way from that enunciated at the Labour Conference'.[1] This was obviously not true as far as the recognition of Russia and the re-establishment of commercial relations were concerned. But it had come near enough to being true in regard to war with Russia.

How decisive Labour's reaction had been in averting war it is impossible to tell. But it can hardly be doubted that it was a factor of some importance. In May 1919, an ex-Czarist general, General Golovin, had been told by the Secretary of State for War, Winston Churchill, that 'the question of giving armed support was, for him, the most difficult; the reason for this was the opposition of the British working-class to armed intervention'.[2] Labour's attitude in August 1920 provided ample confirmation of Churchill's fears.

The Labour leaders themselves had no doubt, or claimed to have no doubt, of the efficacy of their threats. Indeed, far from feeling somewhat shamefaced about their challenge to the Government once the crisis had passed, they exultantly asserted that it was their willingness to adopt so unusual a posture which had compelled the Government to change its policies. At the end of August, MacDonald wrote that 'we must hammer in the fact that it was Labour's action that saved us from war. Until that took place, everything was making for war'.[3] J. H. Thomas went further. In his presidential address to the T.U.C. Conference in September 1920, he said that 'during the past few weeks we have gone through what is, perhaps, the most momentous period of the Trade Union and Labour movement in our long history; a period which found, for the first time, a united and determined working-class effort to challenge the existing order of Parliamentary Government . . . That our action was bold none can deny; that it definitely challenged the Constitution there can be no doubt . . . I speak for the whole of the movement when I say that dangerous as was our remedy—and it was dangerous—it was justified by the result.'[4]

Labour was not in fact called upon to challenge the Constitution and it is impossible to tell how its leaders would have behaved had the Government actually embarked on offensive operations against Russia. That they had no revolutionary intentions is plain enough.

[1] H. of C., vol. 133, col. 595. 'The swinging of a sledge hammer against an open door is merely made for purpose of display,' Lloyd George also said.
[2] *Daily Herald*, 3rd of July, 1920. This was part of a report of Churchill's conversations with General Golovin which the *Herald*'s correspondent in Moscow was said to have discovered there. The report was highly compromising and increased even further Labour's bitter feelings towards Churchill. (See Graubard, op. cit. p. 100.)
[3] *Forward*, 28th of August, 1920.
[4] T.U.C. Annual Conference Report, 1920, p. 62.

Still, the threats were made, in the full consciousness that they were an attempt to coerce the Government by extra-parliamentary means. There are various factors—of which the Government's long record of duplicity over intervention is one and pressure from the left is another—which help to explain the unprecedented—and never to be repeated—adoption of a strategy which most Labour leaders had so long and so bitterly condemned. But the factor which requires the greatest emphasis was the Labour leaders' profound conviction that, in opposing war with Russia, they were the authentic interpreters of the 'national interest' as distinct from any class interest. It is significant in this context that, at a second interview with Lloyd George on the 12th of August, Ernest Bevin should have claimed that the Council of Action represented no political party, and that he should have got very angry when the Prime Minister insisted that it did. The less the Labour leaders felt the issue to be of special importance to Labour and the more they were able to divest it of a socialist content, the bolder and more resolute they became. It was when the class element was paramount, as it was in the case of the miners, that they were seized with something like political paralysis.

It is not really paradoxical that the Labour leaders should have viewed the Russian issue in 'national' rather than in socialist terms. For, of the various reasons which caused them to oppose intervention, the nature of Russia's regime did not rank very high. They opposed intervention because, as Ernest Bevin put it, 'whatever may be the merits or demerits of the theory of government of Russia, that is a matter for Russia, and we have no right to determine their form of government, any more than we would tolerate Russia determining our form of government'.[1] The Left opposed intervention because Russia was ruled by the Bolsheviks—the orthodox leaders largely despite that fact.

4. LABOUR AND COMMUNISM

There were of course nuances in the antipathy which most Labour leaders brought to their appreciation of Bolshevik Russia: while some never failed to couple their protests at Allied intervention with expressions of abhorrence of Bolshevism and all its works, others, like MacDonald, were willing to make allowances for the difficulties the Bolsheviks faced.[2] Where they were virtually unanimous was in

[1] A. Bullock, *The Life and Times of Ernest Bevin* (London, 1960), p. 134.
[2] For an analysis of MacDonald's attitude to Bolshevik Russia in the postwar years, see M. Liebman, 'Ramsay MacDonald et La Révolution Russe' in *Revue de l'Institut de Sociologie*, Number 4, 1956.

their belief that the international influence of the Bolsheviks on the Labour movements of the West should be vigorously countered. In fact, British Labour, and particularly MacDonald and Henderson,[1] played a central rôle in the resurrection, if not in the rehabilitation, of the Second International, which they saw, in MacDonald's words, as 'the only real bulwark against Bolshevism short of military execution';[2] and both men also led the opposition to any flirtation of the Labour Party with the Third International. This latter task was made a great deal easier for them by Lenin's approach to the problem of what socialist strategy and tactics were appropriate to Western Europe and Britain.

It was Henderson who, as Secretary of the Labour Party, had sent out invitations immediately after the War to Labour organizations all over the world asking them to meet in conference for the purpose of reconstituting the Second International. The Conference met in Berne in February 1919; its most important decision, in the present context, was the adoption, against the wishes of a sizeable minority which did not include the British delegates, of a Swedish resolution on *Democracy and Dictatorship*. This was the first of many attempts to formulate a theoretical social-democratic alternative to Bolshevism, of which it was also an implicit condemnation.[3] 'In full agreement with all previous Congresses of the International,' the resolution stated, 'the Berne Conference firmly adheres to the principles of Democracy. A reorganized society more and more permeated with Socialism cannot be realized, much less permanently established, unless it rests upon the triumphs of Democracy and is rooted in the principles of liberty.' 'Those institutions which constitute Democracy,' the resolution went on, 'freedom of speech and of the press, the right of assembly, universal suffrage, a government responsible to Parliament, with arrangements guaranteeing popular co-operation and respect for the wishes of the people, the right of association, etc.—these also provide the working classes with the

---

[1] For Henderson's rôle, see M. A. Hamilton, *Arthur Henderson, a Biography* (London, 1938) pp. 192 ff.

[2] *The Labour Leader,* 14th of August, 1919.

[3] This was one of the reasons for the minority's adoption of a rival resolution which bitterly attacked the war-time record of the pro-war socialists and warned against 'any kind of stigma which may be applied to the Russian Soviet Republic'. The resolution also deplored 'any decision which would make the meeting of the working classes of all countries more difficult in the future' and expressed the wish 'to reserve free entry into the International for the Socialist and Revolutionary Parties of all countries conscious of their class interests'. The resolution was supported by the Dutch, Norwegian, Irish and Spanish delegates, by the French majority, by half the Austrian delegation, and by one Greek. (Cole, *A History of the Labour Party since 1914,* op. cit. p. 99.)

means of carrying on the class struggle.' 'True socialization,' the resolution also stated, 'implies methodical development in the different branches of economic activity under the control of the democracy . . . since . . . effective socialist development is only possible under democratic law, it is essential to eliminate at once any method of socialization which has no prospect of gaining the support of the majority of the people.'[1]

There were many socialists in most countries of Western Europe who strongly recoiled from these comfortably innocuous formulations, but who were nonetheless unwilling to subscribe to the appeals to revolution of the Third International, whose first Congress was held in Moscow in March 1919.

In Britain, these people were mainly to be found in the I.L.P. A number of them would have wished to subdue whatever reservation they had and get the I.L.P. to affiliate to the Third International; others would have been willing to affiliate conditionally, if that were possible, but were already hoping that the formation of a new, all-inclusive International would make a choice between the Second and the Third unnecessary. At its Annual Conference in 1920, the I.L.P. did decide to disaffiliate from the Second International, by 529 votes to 144. But it rejected unconditional affiliation to the Third by 472 votes to 206, and decided to explore further the terms under which the I.L.P. might be admitted to it.[2]

The 1920 Annual Conference of the Labour Party, on the other hand, rejected by 2,940,000 votes to 225,000 a proposal from the British Socialist Party that the Labour Party should affiliate to the Third International.[3] A demand for the withdrawal of the Labour Party from the Second was also defeated, but much less decisively.[4]

MacDonald, Henderson and Snowden had persistently confronted those in the I.L.P. who favoured affiliation to the Third International, or who hoped that a new International which included the Bolsheviks could be formed, with the assertion that the latter were utterly uncompromising on the issue of violent revolution and the instoration of the dictatorship of the proletariat, and that they would expect that anyone who wished to associate with them should subscribe to these notions. Most of those who looked with qualified favour upon the Third International or who hoped that an all-inclusive organization might be formed had no wish to subscribe

[1] For full text of the Resolution, see Labour Party Annual Conference Report, 1919, pp. 198-9.
[2] I.L.P. Annual Conference Report, 1920, p. 86.
[3] Labour Party Annual Conference Report, 1920, p. 174.
[4] By 1,010,000 votes to 516,000, with more than half the delegates not voting (ibid, p. 174).

to them; they were therefore compelled to argue that the Bolsheviks were much more flexible than their enemies suggested, and that in any case an effort should be made to find formulations that would be acceptable to all sides.[1]

The Bolsheviks themselves proved such hopes to be futile. A T.U.C. and Labour Party delegation which went to Russia in April 1920 included two prominent members of the I.L.P., R. C. Wallhead and Clifford Allen. Both, after discussions with the Russian leaders, came out against affiliation to the Third International, on the ground that their hosts *were* indeed committed to violence. 'This question of the absolute certainty of the use of violence,' Wallhead wrote, 'was insisted upon even more strongly in conversation than in the written reply, and the idea of the establishment of Socialism by other than force was scouted as a childish dream.'[2]

In July, the Executive Committee of the Third International provided an authoritative statement of its views in the form of a reply to the I.L.P.'s questions to it. This was a remarkable document.

'In what respect,' the I.L.P. had asked, 'does Communism differ from other forms of Socialism?' 'There are no other forms of Socialism,' the Executive sternly replied; 'there is only Communism. Whatever else goes under the name of socialism is either wilful deception of the lackeys of the bourgeoisie or the self-delusion of persons or groups who hesitate between the proletariat and the bourgeoisie; who hesitate between a life and death struggle and the rôle of assistants to the expiring bourgeoisie.'[3]

As to the precise nature of that struggle the Executive categorically stated that 'the bourgeoisie cannot be defeated without civil war'. 'Nor,' it added, 'is it possible to conduct civil war successfully without the organization of the proletarian dictatorship.'[4] Indeed, the Executive considered that 'in no country can the dictatorship of the proletariat be applied better and more directly than in Great Britain'.[5] Though it admitted the theoretical possibility that Britain might evolve organs of revolutionary power other than the Soviets, it also said that experience provided no encouragement for this belief.[6] There was no section of the Labour movement which found

[1] Thus George Lansbury, who wanted a new International, told the 1920 Labour Party Conference that he had, in the course of a two and a half hour interview, argued with Lenin against the necessity of 'wading through blood to achieve the revolution', to which Lenin had replied: 'I don't believe you can do it your way, but if you can, well, do it' (ibid, p. 174).
[2] Report of the National Administrative Committee of the I.L.P., April 1920 (London 1920) Appendix 3.
[3] *The I.L.P. and the Third International* (London, 1920) p. 33.
[4] ibid, pp. 45-6.
[5] ibid, p. 33.
[6] ibid, p. 44.

it possible to endorse, and shape its policies in accordance with, these formulations—except the Communist Party, then in the process of formation.

It was on the 10th of August, at the height of the crisis over intervention in Russia, that the National Executive Committee of the Labour Party received a letter from the Chairman and Secretary of the Provisional Committee of the Communist Party, which had come into being at a National Convention held on the 31st of July and the 1st of August.[1] The letter asked for affiliation to the Labour Party, a move that was then strongly supported by the Third International and which Lenin himself had proclaimed as correct against some of the irreconcilables in the constituent bodies of the new party. It also set out three resolutions adopted at the Convention, which defined the objects, methods and policy of the Party.

The first of these declared 'for the Soviet (or Working Council) system as a means whereby the working class shall achieve power and take control of the forces of production'; 'for the dictatorship of the proletariat as a necessary means for combating the counter-revolution during the transition period between Capitalism and Communism'; these means were seen 'as steps towards the establishment of a system of complete Communism wherein all the means of production shall be communally owned and controlled'; and the resolution also stated the Communist Party's adherence to the Third International.

In the second resolution, the Communist Party repudiated 'the reformist view that a Social Revolution can be achieved by the ordinary method of Parliamentary Democracy, but regards Parliamentary and electoral action generally as providing a means of propaganda and agitation towards the Revolution'. Communist representatives, the resolution also said, were to be considered as holding a mandate from the Party, and not from the constituency for which they happened to sit; and they would, if they violated Party decisions, be called upon to resign from Parliament, or a municipality, and from the Party.

Read in conjunction with these, the third resolution was not without its humorous aspect. It said: 'That the Communist Party shall be affiliated to the Labour Party.'[2]

[1] For a description of the difficult negotiations between the British Socialist Party, the Socialist Labour Party and the Workers' Socialist Federation, which resulted in the formation of the Communist Party, see H. Pelling. *The British Communist Party* (London, 1958) pp. 5-14, and Graubard, op. cit. pp. 115-29.
[2] Labour Party Annual Conference Report, 1921, pp. 18-19.

One month later, Henderson, on behalf of the Executive, rejected the application on the ground that the objects of the Communist Party 'did not appear to be in accord with the constitution, programme and principles of the Labour Party'.[1]

To this, the C.P. replied with a series of questions. Did the Labour Party Executive rule that acceptance of Communism was contrary to the Party's constitution, principles and programme? Did it 'decisively and categorically' reject the Soviet system and the dictatorship of the proletariat? Did it propose to exclude from its ranks 'all those elements at present in the Labour Party, who hold this means to be necessary in order to achieve the political, social and economic emancipation of the workers', and did it 'impose acceptance of Parliamentary constitutionalism as an article of faith on its affiliated societies?'[2]

The answer to every one of these questions was of course 'Yes', though Henderson merely replied that there was an 'insuperable difference' between the two parties; and to the Communist Party's demand that it should be allowed to press for its policies within the Labour Party like other of its constituent bodies who believed in 'the broad principle of independent political action', Henderson, quoting from authoritative Communist statements, replied that the C.P.'s main concern was 'with disrupting the Labour Party and conducting an intensified campaign within its ranks against its policy and methods'.[3]

There never was any ground for thinking that the Labour leaders, industrial or political, would ever be willing to accept the Communist Party as a constituent body of the Labour Party. The differences were indeed 'insuperable'. What is more significant is that the leadership's attitude should have been endorsed by the vast majority of Labour's rank and file. Do what it might, the Communist Party's ardent courtship of the working classes remained unrequited. How unrequited was well demonstrated by its total failure to benefit from the catastrophic defeat which the Labour movement suffered on the 15th of April, 1921, 'Black Friday'.

In February 1921, the Government had announced that it proposed to decontrol the coalmines and restore full responsibility for their management to the owners. Private control was actually resumed on the 1st of April. The terms which the owners offered the miners included the resumption of the old system of district, as opposed to national, agreements, and drastic wage reductions. The Miners'

---

[1] Labour Party Annual Conference Report, 1921, pp. 19-20.
[2] ibid, p. 20.
[3] ibid, p. 20.

Federation refused these terms and appealed for support from the Triple Alliance. On the 1st of April too, the Government declared a state of emergency under the Emergency Powers Act which had been passed in 1920, and appeared to prepare for war.

On the 8th of April, the leaders of the railwaymen and the transport workers agreed to call for a railway and transport strike, beginning on the 12th of April. On the other hand, the same leaders were deeply concerned that the miners should reopen negotiations with the Government. They met the Prime Minister and some of his colleagues on the 9th of April, and were assured that this would be possible provided the safety-men returned to the pits to safeguard them against flooding. Under very considerable pressure from their allies, the miners' leaders agreed to this concession, and thus relieved the Government and the owners of a major worry. A conference between the miners and the mine-owners, under the chairmanship of the Prime Minister, was then arranged for the 11th of April. One of the effects of the resumption of negotiations was the postponement of the strike. This was another round to the Government.

The negotiations failed. The miners would not accept district agreements and the Government refused to accept a national pool for the equalization of wages, which would have required the resumption of State control over the mines. On the 13th of April, the Triple Alliance agreed that the strike should begin on the 15th. On the 14th, the National Council of Labour, comprising the Executive of the Labour Party, the Executive Committee of the Parliamentary Labour Party, and the General Council of the T.U.C.,[1] appealed to the whole Labour movement for solidarity with the miners.

It was on the same evening, however, that the Secretary of the Miners' Federation, Frank Hodges, addressing a meeting of M.P.s at the House of Commons, appeared to suggest, in reply to a question, that the miners would, after all, consider district agreements on a temporary basis. With his customary adroitness, Lloyd George seized upon this, and, though Hodges was repudiated by his Executive next day, so did the leaders of the railwaymen and the transport workers. Unable to persuade the miners' leaders that they should reopen negotiations, they decided to cancel their strike notices. Thus died the Triple Alliance.

[1] It was in 1920 that the T.U.C. agreed to set up a General Council to replace the Parliamentary Committee as the central organ of the Trade Union movement, with functions of co-ordination much wider than those of the Parliamentary Committee. For the re-organization, see V. L. Allen, 'The Re-organization of the Trade Union Congress, 1918-1927' in *The British Journal of Sociology*, vol. XI, No. 1, pp. 24-41 (March 1960).

There were certainly organizational weaknesses in the Triple Alliance which had prevented it from ever functioning properly. Nor were the miners' leaders the easiest of allies with whom to prepare for battle. Much more important, however, is the fact that the leaders of the railwaymen and of the transport workers, crippled by lack of confidence in their own strength, were throughout desperately eager to avert a challenge to the Government. There was, as G. D. H. Cole noted at the time, a 'failure of courage'. But that failure was not the product of a character deficiency; it was inherent in the limited view which the trade union leaders took of their purpose. They could only have acted otherwise if they had been driven by a purpose which transcended the immediate issues involved; if they had seen themselves, that is, as soldiers in a much wider battle, upon whose outcome must depend Labour's place in society. When it came to concrete action, this is not how they viewed themselves. The skill they knew was that of patient negotiators, oppressed by the fear that to insist on even half a loaf must spell disaster, and therefore eager to settle for crumbs.

'Black Friday' was a stunning blow to the Labour movement and it provided the new Communist Party with a dramatic opportunity for the denunciation of the Labour leaders. Meeting within a week of what it described as 'the greatest betrayal of the workers of Britain', a special delegate conference of the Party called 'upon the rank-and-file who were no party to this betrayal, to drive their betrayers from their official positions' and urged 'the rank-and-file of the Triple Alliance and of the other organized workers to take hold of this lesson and to prepare against a repetition of this disaster by reorganizing the unions on a class basis and with a class war policy'.[1]

This and similar appeals were entirely unsuccessful. There were no revolts against the trade unions' official leadership. Nor was there any access of strength to the Communist Party. In fact, the personal virulence and the indiscriminate character of its denunciations[2] probably strengthened the loyalty of the rank and file to their leaders. The root trouble of the Communist Party was not, however, its language, or even its tactics, but the fact that there was no following in the Labour movement for an alternative leadership organized as a distinct political formation outside the Labour Party.

[1] Graubard, op. cit. p. 169.

[2] E.g. the C.P. made no disinction between J. H. Thomas (who sued *The Communist* for libel and was awarded £2,000 in damages) and Robert Williams, who had joined the C.P. on its foundation and was now expelled from it.

Many trade unionists were entirely willing to press their own leaders for militant action, and to respond to any call that might be made upon them by those leaders. But they were not prepared to support, vote for,[1] or enlist in an avowedly revolutionary party. Labour militants did not subscribe to the view expressed by Frank Hodges at the 1922 Conference of the Labour Party that the Communists were 'intellectual slaves of Moscow, unthinking, unheeding, accepting decrees and decisions without criticism or comment, taking orders from the Asiatic mind'.[2] Indeed, a good many of them did accept Harry Pollitt's description of the Communist Party as an 'integral part of the working-class movement', whose affiliation to the Labour Party would give the latter a 'heave-up' it greatly needed.[3] But this is as far as they would go, and they were never more than a relatively small minority. At no time in the following years had the Labour leaders any difficulty in mustering large majorities for the defeat of the Communist Party's repeated demand for affiliation. The demand itself was an implicit recognition of the assured monopoly which the Labour Party had on the allegiance of that part of the working class which had been weaned away from support of the Conservative or Liberal Parties. The influence of the C.P. in the Labour movement, then and later, is not to be gauged by its numerical strength, if only because so many of its members were experienced and tireless organizers and propagandists But the fact that it did remain a tiny party shows how small was the appeal, even to the activists in the Labour movement, of the revolutionary doctrine the Communist Party preached. Had that appeal been greater, had it clashed less with a long tradition of *un*revolutionary militancy, neither the Communist Party's tactics, nor its allegiance to the Third International, nor the massive propaganda directed against it from all sides, would have stood in the way of its growth, if not into a large party, at least into a sizeable one. After all, none of these things prevented this from happening elsewhere, for instance in France. But then, 30,000 Communards had been slaughtered in Paris at about the time the secret ballot was introduced in Britain.

At the Labour Party Conference of June 1921, affiliation was

---

[1] At a by-election in Caerphilly in August 1921, the Labour candidate, who was a prominent member of the I.L.P., increased the Labour vote from 11,496 in December 1918 to 13,699. The Conservative-Liberal candidate came next with nearly 9,000 votes, as compared with 9,482 votes that had been cast for a Liberal in 1918. The Communist candidate polled 2,592 votes (*The Times*, 26th of August 1921).

[2] Labour Party Annual Conference Report, 1922, p. 198.

[3] ibid, p. 196.

rejected by 4,115,000 to 224,000.[1] A bare six days later, the Communist Party again applied, and was again promptly refused. On the 17th of November, 1921, its Chairman wrote again and this time proposed that representatives of the two parties should meet to discuss the 'difficulties' in the way of affiliation. The Executive Committee, rather surprisingly, consented, and a meeting duly took place. It was there agreed that a questionnaire from the Labour Party be submitted to the C.P. This was duly sent on the 6th of January, 1922, and the Communist Party replied on the 17th of May. This questionnaire, and the replies to it,[2] remain practically the only form of direct dialogue there has ever been between the two parties, and it showed conclusively (though proof was hardly needed) that they spoke different languages altogether.

The Constitution of the Labour Party, the questionnaire said, 'emphasizes the fact that the object of that Party is the achievement of the "political, social and economic emancipation of the people by means of Parliamentary Democracy" '. On the other hand, the Communist Party adhered to the Soviet system 'which is understood as being incompatible with Parliamentary Democracy', and to the Third International, many of whose Theses and regulations 'are regarded as inconsistent with the Constitution and objects of the Labour Party'. Had the Communist Party, the questionnaire asked, somewhat ingenuously, 'made any changes in its Constitution and objects?'

In reply, the Communist Party reaffirmed its adherence to the Soviet system and its affiliation to the Communist International, with its Theses and Statutes. 'The Communist Party, however, does not understand adhesion to the principles of the Soviet system to mean non-participation in parliamentary action. It regards the Soviet system as the system which must supersede Parliamentary Democracy after the coming to power of the workers. In the meantime, the Communist Party proposes to use the opportunity provided by Parliament for advancing the class struggle towards "the common ownership of the means of production".'

The second question referred to the Labour Party's 'fundamental principle', 'to confine its operations to lawful means'; 'it has never given encouragement to the idea of attempting to secure the power

---

[1] Labour Party Annual Conference Report, 1921, p. 167. 'Though the delegates were depressed,' Beatrice Webb noted, 'they were not exasperated or revolutionary. Quite the contrary; the trend of opinion was toward the Right, the pendulum was once more swinging back to political action. It was a "Clynes-Henderson conference"; the I.L.P. being in abeyance and the Communists a despised minority' (*Beatrice Webb's Diaries*, op. cit. p. 211).
[2] Labour Party Annual Conference Report, 1922, pp. 77-80.

of Government by means contrary to the law of the land for the time being'. Was that also the position of the Communist Party?

There was nothing, the C.P. replied, in the Constitution of the Labour Party to bear out the view that it would never under any circumstances contemplate extra-legal action for the attainment of its declared objects. Any discussion of the use of extra-legal means to obtain a political end must obviously be of a theoretical nature; the circumstances of any given time of crisis must and would determine the form an agitation would take. The Labour Party itself, the reply added, had, in August 1920, advised a 'down tools' policy which the Government would certainly have proclaimed unlawful had the threat been put into operation. Such a policy 'directly contravened the first principle of Parliamentary Democracy which insists that public discontent shall find expression only through the recognized machinery of the ballot box'.[1]

Once again, the Communist Party also reaffirmed that it would conform to the Constitution of the Labour Party, though 'without prejudice to its right of criticism of policy or tactics, in common with all affiliated bodies'. The C.P. did not 'disguise its opposition to much of the policy and many of the statements' of spokesmen of the Labour Party and it would claim the same right to express dissent within the ranks of the Labour Party 'as is constantly exercised by other and more moderate sections of the Labour Party'.

As might have been expected, the Executive found none of all this satisfactory and refused to reverse its earlier decisions. Its attitude was again endorsed at the Party Conference, this time by 3,086,000 votes to 261,000.[2]

By 1921, industrial militancy was on the wane. Having failed to assert their full power during the post-war boom, the unions now found their task made more difficult by slump, falling wages and mass unemployment. In 1920, the aggregate number of working days lost in strikes was 85,872,000. In 1921, it was 19,850,000. Labour had now entered the long, long winter of its discontent. And it was to the politicians of the Labour Party that it turned for relief.

[1] Commenting upon this, the Executive denied that it had taken any steps in connection with the Council of Action 'which were either illegal or unconstitutional'.
[2] Labour Party Annual Conference Report, 1922, p. 199.

CHAPTER IV

FROM OPPOSITION TO OFFICE

> 'A Constitution which enables an
> engine-cleaner of yesterday to be a
> Secretary of State today is a great
> Constitution.'
>
> **J. H. Thomas,** *The Times,* **8th of**
> **March, 1924.**

1. THE PARLIAMENTARY EMBRACE

THE Lloyd George Coalition finally came to an end in October
1922. Its demise was not the result of popular agitation or of
parliamentary defeat; nor was it the result of pressure by the Labour
Party. The Coalition had been born of intrigue and it died of
intrigue; it ceased to exist and Lloyd George ceased to be Prime
Minister because a sufficient number of influential Tories felt that
the time was ripe for a period of unalloyed Conservative rule.

Bonar Law, Lloyd George's successor, went to the country on
the 15th of November and was returned with a Conservative majority
of 88 over all other parties, there being 347 Conservatives in the
new House, elected on a popular poll of nearly 5½ million. The total
Liberal poll was 4.1 million but Liberal parliamentary representation was almost equally split between 60 Asquith Liberals and 57
National Liberal followers of Lloyd George.

The most important feature of the election was Labour's increase
of two million votes, with large gains in most parts of the country,
particularly in the industrial areas of Scotland, in Yorkshire, in
Northumberland, in South Wales, and also in London. For the first
time, Labour's popular poll of 4.2 million, as compared with 2.2
million in 1918, exceeded that of the Liberals. Labour had put
forward 414 candidates, of whom 142 were returned. Five Communists also stood, all in Scotland, and one of them, J. T. Walton
Newbold, was elected for Motherwell.[1]

---

[1] Another member of the Communist Party, S. Saklatvala, a Parsee, was
elected for North Battersea, though he stood as a Labour candidate. It was
only in 1924 that membership of the Communist Party was declared to be
incompatible with membership of the Labour Party (see below, p. 117).

Labour's Election Manifesto had proposed heavier taxation on the rich and the creation of a War Debt Redemption Fund, by a special graduated levy on fortunes exceeding £5,000; it had also proposed an extension of the social services and a 'National Scheme of Housing'; and the Manifesto recalled that Labour's industrial policy involved the prompt nationalization of the mines and the nationalization of railways. The document had also made the specific point that Labour's programme was 'the best bulwark against violent upheaval and class wars'. 'Democratic government,' it said, 'can be made effective in this country without bloodshed or violence. Labour's policy is to bring about a more equitable distribution of the nation's wealth by constitutional means'; and, it had been careful to point out, 'this is neither Bolshevism nor Communism, but common sense, and justice. This is Labour's alternative to Reaction and Revolution.'[1]

One of the results of the General Election of 1922 was to show that the Labour Party had become a possible channel for a political career to professional men who, for one reason or another (and the reasons were endlessly various) no longer found either the Liberal or the Conservative Party satisfactory vehicles for their private and public aspirations. The Parliamentary Labour Party had until then born the stamp of its trade union origins and the trade unionists were still in a majority in 1922.[2] But it now included a sizeable number of M.P.s who were neither trade unionists nor of the working classes and who lent Labour in Parliament a new kind of respectability. The Labour movement had by no means been free from careerists before; nor certainly had a working class origin been a guarantee of political purity. But after 1922, the opportunities became greater—and so did the temptations.

The election of 1922 marked the return to the House of Commons of a number of leading Labour figures, exiled since 1918; MacDonald, Snowden, Jowett and Lansbury came back; so did the Labour leaders in the previous Parliament, notably Clynes and Thomas; the main casualty was Henderson, who lost his seat at Widnes, but won a by-election at East Newcastle in January 1923.

The election results appeared particularly satisfactory to the I.L.P. From five, the number of M.P.s who were also members of the I.L.P. not only rose to thirty-two, but also included some representatives of the I.L.P.'s militant Left, among them James Maxton, David Kirkwood, Thomas Johnston and Emmanuel Shin-

---

[1] The Manifesto was signed by Sidney Webb, the Chairman of the Party, Ramsay MacDonald, its Vice-Chairman, and Arthur Henderson, its Secretary. For full text, see Labour Party Annual Conference Report, 1923, pp. 263-4.
[2] i.e. 85, of whom 42 were miners' representatives.

well. The I.L.P. was then in any case entering a period of great activity, particularly in the field of propaganda and education; it seemed likely that the arrival of a militant Clydeside contingent, well to the left of its leaders and greatly determined to make the House of Commons resound with the echo of working class grievances, would help to give a sharply radical inflection to the Parliamentary Labour Party.

In fact, the new recruits were effectively contained by their own leaders, who held that containment to be one of their prime tasks.[1] The 'wild men' could not easily be prevented from making occasional parliamentary scenes and from getting themselves suspended,[2] much to the embarrassment, annoyance and disapproval of many of their leaders and colleagues. But it was not they who shaped the strategy of the Party. They only continued, as their predecessors had done ever since the foundation of the Labour Party, to make its bark appear, at least to the uninstructed, much more frightening than it had ever a chance of becoming under its real controllers.

But the disapproval of their colleagues was only one of the influences which transformed many of the erstwhile agitators into subdued parliamentarians. There were other influences, no less potent. There was the House of Commons itself. David Kirkwood, one of the 'wild men', wrote later that, before he entered the House of Commons in 1922, he knew little of 'the Great Ones, the Powerful Ones, the Lordly Ones' but felt that 'they and the world they represented were crushing my fellows down into poverty, misery, despair and death'.[3] When he entered the House, however, he found that 'it was full of wonder. I had to shake myself occasionally as I found myself moving about and talking with men whose names were household words. More strange was it to find them all so simple and unaffected and friendly'.[4] Violently attacked over unemployment, Bonar Law 'showed no resentment' and expressed pleasure at hearing Kirkwood's Glasgow accent;[5] denounced as a 'Uriah Heep', Stanley Baldwin, the Chancellor of the Exchequer,

[1] This was particularly true of MacDonald: 'I was agreeably surprised,' Lord Inchcape noted after meeting him at dinner at Lord Morley's in 1923, 'to find how reasonable he is. He said he was bringing the wild socialist Labour members to heel' (H. Bolitho, *James Lyle Mackay, First Earl of Inchcape* (London, 1936) p. 226, in Mowat, op. cit. p. 149).

[2] In the most dramatic of these scenes, Maxton and a few other I.L.P.'ers were suspended for accusing the Conservatives of murder for their support of cuts in grants to child-welfare centres. The I.L.P.'ers remained suspended for seven weeks. For this and other incidents, see Brockway, *Socialism over Sixty Years,* op. cit. pp. 194-203.

[3] D. Kirkwood, *My Life of Revolt* (London, 1935) p. 200.

[4] ibid, p. 202.

[5] ibid, p. 202.

was gently reproachful and thus 'pierced a link in my armour that had never been pierced before';[1] and a Conservative member, having heard Kirkwood make a 'flaming speech' about the poverty of crofters in the Hebrides, told him, so the latter records in wonder, 'I could not vote for you, but I should like to help those men if I may,' and gave him a five-pound note.[2]

It was not only inside the House of Commons that 'the Great Ones, the Powerful Ones, the Lordly Ones' were simple, unaffected and friendly towards men like Kirkwood: no Society function was really complete in 1923 without the presence of one of the rebels from the Clyde, or at least of some other Labour Member of Parliament.[3]

However, important though were the climate of the House of Commons and the 'aristocratic embrace' in taming so many Labour members, such influences would not have been nearly so effective had these members brought with them to Westminster, not only social indignation, but a clearly defined socialist ideology. This they conspicuously lacked. John Paton, who was very close to the Clydesiders, accurately said of them that while they all 'claimed to be socialists of varying degree . . . in their mental backgrounds, experience and training, in their habits of thought . . . they would be ranged probably in a dozen different groupings'. 'All of them,' he also wrote, 'could and did claim to be "rebels" against the evil social conditions . . . but of none of them could it be said in any literal sense that he was a revolutionary.'[4] So little were they revolutionaries that they enthusiastically voted for Mac-Donald in the election to the leadership of the Parliamentary Party,[5] not only because Clynes was a mediocrity while MacDonald had a magnificent presence, not only because Clynes had been pro-war

---

[1] ibid, p. 202.

[2] ibid, p. 206. See also Robert Smillie in 1924: 'In my young and callous days I was probably a little prejudiced in favour of my own class, and hot with resentment against those whom I regarded as their oppressors. But experience teaches, and I now know that a gentleman is a gentleman, whatever his rank in life may be, and may always be trusted to act as such' (R. Smillie, *My Life for Labour* (London, 1924) p. 133).

[3] So much so that at the 1923 Conference of the I.L.P., John Wheatley, against the wishes of the Agenda Committee, put forward a resolution which recommended that Labour M.P.s should 'not accept the hospitality of political opponents at public dinners and society functions' (I.L.P. Annual Conference Report, 1923, p. 143). For Beatrice Webb's attempts to 'groom' the wives of Labour politicians to hold their own in political society, see *Beatrice Webb's Diaries*, op. cit. pp. 200 ff.

[4] J. Paton, *Left Turn* (London, 1936) pp. 145-6.

[5] It was Emmanuel Shinwell, one of the I.L.P. 'rebels', who proposed Mac-Donald. The voting was 61 for MacDonald and 56 for Clynes.

and MacDonald anti-war, more or less, but because they thought of him as the worthy standard-bearer of their own cause. 'You Clyde men,' Henderson told Kirkwood, 'are determined to put MacDonald in. Well, if you do, it will be only a few years before you will be trying to put him out.'[1] In fact, it was only a few weeks before they came to regret their choice. It was trade union Members who opposed MacDonald, most likely because they too thought him a man of the left.

MacDonald himself was above all determined that the Labour Party in Parliament should say nothing and do nothing which might suggest that, as Churchill had said in 1920, it was not 'fit to govern'. What this required, in his view, was an emphasis upon the Labour Party's moderation, its reasonableness, its 'national' perspective, as distinct from, indeed as opposed to, any class bias.

In so emphasizing the Labour Party's moderation, its leaders were doing no violence to their social philosophy. On the contrary, their strategy was a natural consequence of the particular version of the socialism they professed. Thus in his presidential address to the 1923 Party Conference, Sidney Webb claimed that, whatever might have been the case in the past, the accusation that the Labour Party was unfit to assume the responsibilities of office would not now be made by 'any instructed person of candour'; but the Labour Party, when in due course it came to be entrusted with power, would naturally not want 'to do everything at once . . . once we face the necessity of putting our principles first into bills, to be fought through Committee clause by clause; and then into the appropriate administrative machinery for carrying them into execution . . . the inevitability of gradualness cannot fail to be appreciated'. This 'translation of Socialism into practicable projects, to be adopted one after another' was, said Webb, just the task in which they had been engaged for a whole generation, with the result that, 'on every side, fragments of our proposals have already been put successfully into operation by Town and County Councils and the national Government itself, and have now become accepted as commonplaces by the average man. *The whole nation has been imbibing Socialism without realizing it! It is now time for the subconscious to rise into consciousness.*'[2]

Socialism here meant that piecemeal collectivism had made measurable strides in the past decades. The Labour Party, Webb believed, must seek, through the instrument of parliamentary govern-

---

[1] Kirkwood, op. cit. p. 195.
[2] Labour Party Annual Conference Report, 1923, pp. 175-80. My italics. Note in contrast, the rather pessimistic outlook of the Webbs' *The Decay of Capitalist Civilization* (London 1923), especially pp. 176 ff.

ment, to formalize and accentuate a trend which was both irresistible and largely devoid of class content. 'For we must always remember,' he also told the 1923 Conference, 'that the founder of British Socialism was not Karl Marx but Robert Owen, and that Robert Owen preached not "class war" but the doctrine of human brotherhood . . .'[1] It is hardly surprising that, with this philosophy, Webb should have found the militant resolutions of constituency workers, to whom he was in any case emotionally unsympathetic, both irrelevant and mischievous. Seven years later, he described the constituency parties as 'frequently unrepresentative groups of nonentities dominated by fanatics and cranks, and extremists', without whose containment by the Trade Union block vote 'it would be impracticable to continue to vest the control of policy in Labour Party Conferences'.[2] It is unlikely that he felt very differently about the activists in 1924. And, sharing his assumptions, his colleagues had no difficulty in seeing themselves as engaged in an enterprise whose success militancy could only jeopardize.

In December 1923, Stanley Baldwin, who had replaced the mortally sick Bonar Law in May, fought an election on the issue of Protection and lost the Conservatives nearly a hundred seats. Only 259 of his men were elected to the new House. The Liberals had 159, as against 117. Labour gained most seats and came back with 191 members. The popular vote, on the other hand, was much more steady. The Conservatives polled 5,483,277 votes as against 5,559,122 in 1922; the combined Liberal vote was 4,299,121 (4,113,012) and Labour polled 4,356,757, some 130,000 more than in 1922.

The Labour Party, though most of its leaders were staunch Free Traders, had refused to fight the election on that issue. Its Election Manifesto had proclaimed Labour's will to cure unemployment[3] by a large programme of public works (which was also advocated by the Liberals), and to provide 'adequate maintenance for those who could not obtain employment'. Unlike the 1922 Election Manifesto, the one issued in 1923 did not mention public ownership; it only spoke of 'the establishment of a National System of Electrical Power Supply, the development of Transport by road, rail and canal, and the improvement of national resources by Land Drainage, Reclamation, Afforestation, Town Planning and Housing Schemes'. The Manifesto also repeated an earlier proposal for a non-recurring

[1] Labour Party Annual Conference Report, 1923, p. 180.
[2] *Beatrice Webb's Diaries*, 19th of May, 1930, in McKenzie, op. cit. p. 506.
[3] In October 1923, unemployment stood at 1,350,216 or 11.7% of workpeople insured (Mowat, op. cit. p. 165).

graduated War Debt Redemption Levy on all individual fortunes in excess of £5,000. In foreign affairs, Labour had promised support for the League of Nations and proposed the calling of an international conference for the revision of the Treaty of Versailles and especially of war debts and reparations. It had also promised the resumption of diplomatic and commercial relations with Russia.[1] In the campaign, Labour candidates had insisted that Labour would inject a different tone and style, as well as a different content, into the business of government.[2]

Hardly anyone, inside the Labour Party or out, had expected that the election of 1923 would produce a Labour Government. Nor, of course, had Labour won the election. There was no strict constitutional reason why either the Conservatives or even the Liberals, should not have been asked to form a Government, either in coalition or with a pledge of parliamentary support from one to the other. It is true that Protection had sharply divided the two parties and that the election result could be construed as a vote against Conservative Protectionist proposals. Even so, it seems unlikely that the two parties would not have found some way of composing their differences had their leaders seriously believed that a Labour Government might seek to use the political opportunities which even its minority position allowed to the detriment of the traditional order of things.

Some people did so believe, or wrote and spoke as if they did, during the election[3] and immediately after. As in the two previous elections, persistent attempts were made to paint the Labour Party as bent on red revolution. It was the declared view of Winston Churchill, the defeated Liberal candidate for West Leicester, that 'the enthronement in office of a Socialist Government will be a serious national misfortune such as has usually befallen great States only on the morrow of defeat in war'.[4] The *English Review* was even more flamboyant. 'We stand now at a moment,' it wrote, 'when the sun of England seems menaced with final eclipse. For the first time in her history the party of revolution approach their hands to the

---

[1] For text of Manifesto, see Labour Party Annual Conference Report, 1924, pp. 192-3.

[2] E.g., MacDonald: 'We are going to develop our own country, we are going to work it for all it is worth to bring human labour into touch with God's natural endowments and we are going to make the land blossom like a rose and contain houses and firesides where there shall be happiness and contentment and glowing associations.' (R. W. Lyman, *The First Labour Government 1924* (London, 1953) p. 61.)

[3] See ibid, p. 37.

[4] ibid, p. 82.

helm of the State, not only, as in the seventeenth century, for the purpose of overthrowing the Crown, or of altering the Constitution, but with the design of destroying the very basis of civilized life.'[1]

Both the Liberal and Conservative leaders, though they were urged from many quarters to act so as to prevent Labour from taking office, took a more sober view of the situation. There was, after all, the fact that Labour was in a minority and, as Asquith told the Liberal Parliamentary Party on the 18th of December, 'whoever may be for the time being the incumbents of office, it is we, if we understand our business, who really control the situation . . . if a Labour Government is ever to be tried in this country, as it will be sooner or later, it could hardly be tried under safer conditions'.[2] Neville Chamberlain too believed that Labour should be given office because an alliance between Tories and Liberals to keep Labour out of office would only, he felt, strengthen it for the future, while Labour in office 'would be too weak to do much harm but not too weak to get discredited'.[3]

2. OFFICE AND ITS PURPOSE

That Labour would accept office was never much in doubt; nor that it would take office alone. The General Election had taken place on the 6th of December, 1923. A joint meeting of the National Executive of the Labour Party and the General Council of the T.U.C. on the 13th of December expressed its 'complete confidence in Mr J. Ramsay MacDonald, M.P., as leader of the Parliamentary Labour Party, being assured that should he be called upon to assume high office he will in all his actions consider the well-being of the nation in seeking to apply the principles of the Labour movement'.[4] On the same day, the National Executive Committee declared that 'should the necessity for forming a Labour Government arise, the Parliamentary Party should at once accept full responsibility for the government of the country without compromising itself with any form of coalition'.[5]

[1] Lyman, op. cit. p. 81.
[2] *The Times*, 19th of December, 1923. In the House of Commons, Asquith was more diplomatic. '. . . . With a House of Commons constituted as this House is,' he had said, 'it is idle to talk of the imminent dangers of a Socialist regime. In legislation, as in all important matters of administration, the House of Commons is and must remain supreme.' (H. of C., vol. 169, col. 315, 17th of January, 1924.)
[3] K. Feiling. *The Life of Neville Chamberlain* (London, 1946) p. 111.
[4] McKenzie, op. cit. p. 307. Later the same day, the Executive Committee of the Parliamentary Labour Party 'unanimously endorsed the resolution of confidence in Mr. MacDonald passed by the joint meeting'. (ibid, p. 307.)
[5] Labour Party Annual Conference Report, 1924, p. 4.

This settled, however, there were divergent approaches to the question of office. On the left, there was the wish that a Labour Government should propose bold measures to deal with unemployment and housing, and put forward nationalization measures as well. This would no doubt lead to parliamentary defeat, but it would also force the Tories and the Liberals to fight the next election on issues of Labour's own choosing and present the electorate with clear and distinctive political alternatives.[1] Not the least advantage of this strategy, it was argued on the Left, was that it would finally expose the Liberals at the natural allies of the Conservatives, and rob them of any politically confusing distinctiveness.

This was not how MacDonald and his colleagues saw matters. 'We are not going to undertake office in order to prepare for a General Election,' MacDonald told a victory demonstration at the Albert Hall on the 8th of January, 1924 : 'we are going to take office in order to do work.'[2] To Lord Parmoor, however, he had written immediately after the Election that 'I want to gain the confidence of the country and shall suit my policy accordingly'.[3]

The strategy of the future Government was in fact decided, privately and secretly, at a meeting at Sidney Webb's house attended by MacDonald, Snowden, Thomas, Henderson and Webb himself. 'The conversation,' Snowden later recalled, 'turned upon what we might be able to do in the first session. There would be two courses open to us. We might use the opportunity for a demonstration and introduce some bold Socialist measures, knowing, of course, that we should be defeated upon them. Then we could go to the country with this illustration of what we would do if we had a Socialist majority. This was a course which had been urged by the extreme wing of the party, but it was not a policy which commended itself to reasonable opinion. I urged very strongly to this meeting that we should not adopt an extreme policy but should confine our legislative proposals to measures that we were likely to be able to carry . . . We must show the country that we were not under the domination of the wild men.'[4]

By February 1924, MacDonald had lowered his sights even

---

[1] This was precisely what some Conservatives feared. 'In the King's Speech,' wrote Lord Derby, 'they would put forward a number of very attractive propositions. No matter whether they could pass them or not the public would see a programme of measures which they would like carried out. Our own people would be in a great hole . . .' (R. S. Churchill, *Lord Derby 'King of Lancashire'* (London, 1960) p. 547.)

[2] *The Times*, 9th of January, 1924.

[3] E. Estorick, *Stafford Cripps* (London, 1949) p. 70.

[4] Snowden, op. cit. II, pp. 595-6.

further. 'We hope to continue only so long in office, but certainly so long in office,' he told the House of Commons, 'as will enable us to do some good work that will remove many obstacles which would have hampered future Governments if they found the problems that we have now to face.'[1]

Baldwin did not immediately resign. He met the new Parliament on the 15th of January and was duly defeated on the 21st. The King asked MacDonald to form a Government on the 22nd.[2] On accepting office, Macdonald, according to Lord Stanfordham, the King's Private Secretary, 'assured the King that, though he and his friends were inexperienced in governing and fully realized the great responsibilities which they would now assume, nevertheless they were honest and sincere and his earnest desire was to serve his King and Country. They may fail in their endeavours; but it will not be for want of trying to do their best.'[3] The King in turn assured MacDonald that he might count upon his assistance in every way. In the course of the interview, the King referred to 'the unfortunate incident at the recent Meeting at the Albert Hall, presided over by Mr Ramsay MacDonald, at which the *Marseillaise* and the *Red Flag* were sung'. MacDonald's reply is sufficiently revealing to be quoted in full. 'Mr Ramsay MacDonald spoke very openly and said he was sure the King would be generous to him and understand the very difficult position he was in *vis-à-vis* to his own extremists;[4] and he could assure His Majesty that, had he attempted to prevent the *Red Flag* being sung on that occasion, a riot would inevitably have ensued. Moreover, there was a very serious possibility on Monday night of the *Red Flag* being sung in the House of Commons and it had required all his influence and that of his moderate and immediate friends to prevent this taking

[1] Lyman, op. cit. p. 106.
[2] 'Today 23 years ago dear Grandmamma died,' the King wrote in his diary that day; 'I wonder what she would have thought of a Labour Government.' (Harold Nicolson, *King George the Fifth* (London, 1952) p. 384.) After meeting his Labour ministers, the King wrote to Queen Alexandra on the 17th of February: 'I have been making the acquaintance of all the Ministers in turn and I must say they all seem to be very intelligent and they take things very seriously. They have different ideas to ours as they are all socialists, but they ought to be given a chance and ought to be treated fairly.' (ibid, p. 389.)
[3] ibid, p. 384.
[4] At the meeting at Webb's house, MacDonald had already, according to Snowden, expressed concern 'that we should have a good deal of trouble with the extreme section, who would press upon us and expect us to do all kinds of impossible things'. (Snowden, op. cit. II, p. 596.)

place; they had got into the way of singing this song and it will be by degrees that he hopes to break down this habit.'[1]

As far as the formation of the Ministry was concerned, MacDonald was given as much freedom as Conservative and Liberal Prime Ministers had enjoyed. There was no attempt on the part of any of the executive bodies of the Party to intervene. 'Nothing,' Snowden later wrote, 'was said (at Webb's house) about the allocation of Ministerial offices beyond that this should be left to the Prime Minister, Webb urging that we should follow in this respect the usual constitutional practice.'[2] After that meeting, Henderson privately expressed to Snowden 'some misgiving about leaving the appointment of Ministers wholly to MacDonald, and hoped that he would consult us freely upon this important matter before finally coming to a decision'.[3] In fact, MacDonald retired to Lossiemouth, where his golfing companion was General C. B. Thompson, who became Air Secretary. Of those people whom MacDonald chose to consult, it was Lord Haldane who appears to have had the most influence. Lord Haldane's conversion to Labour, if such it was,[4] was not much more than two years old and he had written to Baldwin immediately after the General Election (though this was not known at the time) that 'the King's Government has to be carried on, and I think that you are the only man who has a chance of doing this successfully'.[5]

The ministerial appointments were conspicuously respectable. Only two Ministers, John Wheatley, at the Ministry of Health, and F. W. Jowett, at the Office of Works, represented the radicals of the I.L.P.[6] Former Liberals fared better. Lord Haldane was Lord

[1] Nicolson, op. cit. p. 384.
[2] Snowden, op. cit. II, p. 596.
[3] ibid, p. 597.
[4] In October 1927, Beatrice Webb recalled that Lord Haldane had told her he had joined the Labour Party 'because the Labour Party is the most idealistic of the three parties'. She then added: 'But he is always contemptuous of the way they express their idealism and even of the ideals themselves and he abhors all the Labour Party's specific proposals—alike in home and foreign affairs.' (M. Cole Ed., *Beatrice Webb's Diaries 1924-1932* (London, 1956) p. 158.)
[5] Lyman, op. cit. p. 101. In return, Baldwin had 'begged' Haldane 'to join the Labour Government and help them out' (ibid, p. 101).
[6] One much noted omission was that of George Lansbury. According to his biographer (Postgate, op. cit. p. 225), MacDonald had offered him the Ministry of Transport, which he refused because he was not to be in the Cabinet. 'Merited or unmerited,' Snowden wrote later, 'the stigma of "Poplarism" still clung to him' (op. cit. II, p. 760). In September 1921, the Mayor of Poplar and twenty-nine Labour councillors, of whom Lansbury was one, had gone to prison for refusing to levy 'precepts' for the L.C.C., on the ground that the Borough could not levy these in addition to the rates it

Chancellor, C. P. Trevelyan was President of the Board of Education, Noel Buxton went to the Ministry of Agriculture and Colonel Josiah Wedgwood to the Duchy of Lancaster. Lord Parmoor, formerly a Tory, became Lord President of the Council. The connection with Labour of some other appointees was not even peripheral: H. P. Macmillan, a prominent Tory barrister, became Lord Advocate on a special 'non-political' basis. More remarkable still was the appointment of Lord Chelmsford, a life-long Conservative and a former Viceroy of India, as First Lord of the Admiralty. Arthur Henderson went to the Home Office and Sidney Webb to the Board of Trade. J. H. Thomas became Colonial Secretary[1] and Stephen Walsh, who had been an extreme patrioteer during the War, went, appropriately enough, to the War Office.[2] Less appropriately, perhaps, William Leach, an I.L.P. pacifist, was appointed Under-Secretary of State for Air under Lord Thompson. Snowden was Chancellor of the Exchequer and Clynes Lord Privy Seal. Tom Shaw, of the Textile Workers, became Minister of Labour. MacDonald took the Foreign Secretaryship as well as the Premiership.

Much more consciously and deliberately than most of his immediate colleagues, MacDonald, as he had told the King, was now more than ever concerned to emancipate the movement he led from those inopportune but deeply embedded prejudices which fostered the view that a Labour Government must behave altogether differently from its predecessors. MacDonald held precisely the opposite view. Now, he felt, was the Labour Party's great chance to dispel any suspicion that it was a party of revolt and to show 'the country' how free a Labour Government was from any class bias. At the Albert Hall demonstration on the 8th of January, he had assured his audience and the country that he was not 'thinking of party; I am thinking of national well-being'; this had also been stressed by Clynes, who said that 'Labour will not be influenced,

needed for the relief of distress caused by unemployment. The Council's action was effective: it led to legislation for a greater equality of rate burdens between poor boroughs and rich ones. It was not, however, regarded with approval by most Labour leaders. During the conflict, J. H. Thomas accused the Poplar councillors of being 'wastrels'. (For the episode, see Postgate, op. cit. Ch. XVI.)

[1] He was said to have introduced himself to the heads of departments at the Colonial Office with the statement 'I am here to see that there is no mucking about with the British Empire'. (Lyman, op. cit. p. 106.)

[2] *He* was supposed to have told the generals: 'I know my place. You have commanded Armies in the field when I was nothing but a private in the ranks'. (ibid, p. 106.) Another account has it that he opened the first meeting of the Army Council with the words: 'Gentlemen, always remember that we must all be loyal to the King' (H. Dalton, *Call Back Yesterday* (London, 1953) p. 147).

should it be trusted with the power of government, by any consideration other than that of national well-being'.[1] This was to be the constant theme of Ministers' speeches throughout the life-time of the Government. And implicit in this insistence on Labour's concern for the 'national well-being' was the acceptance of the view that the national well-being was not compatible with the vigorous advancement of remedies for working-class ills and grievances.

The education of the Labour movement into the meaning of political orthodoxy and into a keener sense of the 'national interest' was one of the main tasks the first Labour Government set itself, and it pursued it with greater resolution than any other. Much resolution was needed. For a good many members of the Party and even of the Parliamentary Party were still far from attuned in 1924 to the idea that a Labour Government's first task was to conciliate its opponents.

The process of education took a variety of forms. One of them concerned dress. It was a sure instinct which made MacDonald insist that his ministers must follow tradition in this as in every other respect and dress up in ceremonial habit to receive their seals of office from the King, not that much insistence was in most cases needed[2]. There were of course indignant protests in the left wing press and among the activists of the constituency parties,[3] but these and other protests on cognate matters (like Ministers' salaries) were brushed aside without much difficulty as naïve and trivial, and showing a deplorable lack of appreciation of what was required of the King's ministers. Ministers themselves might protest that it was only with reluctance that they complied with tradition and etiquette. In fact, not a few of them, not to speak of their wives and daughters, revelled in the ceremonial and social functions[4] of those whom Robert Owen once aptly called the gay and splendid, and found in their admittance to that world conclusive proof that they were the symbols as well as the architects of vast social changes, in truth more easily perceptible to them than to so many who had made their elevation possible.

[1] *The Times*, 9th of January, 1924.
[2] Only Jowett and Wheatley refused, at least on that occasion. (Brockway, op. cit. p. 208.) But Beatrice Webb describes a gay luncheon party at the Webbs on that day at which 'we were all laughing over Wheatley—the revolutionary—going down on both knees and actually kissing the King's hand'. She also noted that 'Uncle Arthur was bursting with childish joy over his H.O. seals in the red leather box which he handed round the company' (*Beatrice Webb's Diaries*, op. cit. p. 2).
[3] Ten constituency parties sent in resolutions or amendments to resolutions on the issue of Labour Ministers and ceremonial dress at that year's Party Conference. (Labour Party Annual Conference Report, 1924, p. 20.)
[4] See J. Scanlon. *The Decline and Fall of the Labour Party* (London 1932) pp. 62 ff.

Of all the heady experiences which office entailed for Ministers of 'humble origin', there were few more intoxicating than closer proximity to the King and the Royal Family. Leading members of the Labour Party had on occasion met the King and Queen privately,[1] and ordinary Labour backbenchers (and their families) had received their due quota of invitations to such functions as Buckingham Palace garden parties. But office was something different. 'As we stood waiting for His Majesty, amid the gold and crimson of the Palace,' Clynes later wrote, 'I could not help marvelling at the strange turn of Fortune's wheel, which had brought MacDonald the starveling clerk, Thomas the engine-driver, Henderson the foundry labourer and Clynes the mill-hand, to this pinnacle beside the man whose forebears had been kings for so many generations. We were making history.'[2] The experience was not calculated to sharpen the Labour Ministers' antagonism to what has more recently been called The Establishment.[3]

Nor of course was it intended to.

With Labour in office, a Consultative Committee of twelve backbenchers and three Ministers was established to maintain liaison between the Government and its followers. According to Lord Snell, who was a member of it, the Committee met 'almost every day'. Its functions, he recalls, 'was to interpret (the Government's) policy to the members of the party, to receive their suggestions and criticisms, to make them known to the Prime Minister or the heads of departments, and generally to keep the Party united and keen'.[4]

The Committee included one or two members of the I.L.P. Left[5] and, according to John Scanlon, who saw it at close quarters, 'week after week a steady succession of Ministers were summoned to appear' before it and did.[6] Though it was represented by the Conservatives as a 'quite unconstitutional body',[7] it was able to achieve little, save on details of administration, and not much there;[8] it certainly played no part in the determination of the strategy or of the policies of the Government. On the other hand, it is worth noting that the Labour ministers were still sufficiently new to

[1] Snowden, op. cit. II, p. 661.
[2] J. R. Clynes, *Memoirs* (London, 1937) I. p. 343.
[3] See also the chapter entitled 'Some Cherished Memories of the Royal House', in J. H. Thomas's *My Story* (London, 1937).
[4] Lord Snell, *Men, Movements and Myself* (London, 1955) p. 216.
[5] Such as Tom Johnson, the Editor of *Forward*, and R. C. Wallhead. Its Chairman was Robert Smillie; its Vice-Chairman, George Lansbury.
[6] J. Scanlon, op. cit. p. 72.
[7] McKenzie, op. cit. p. 429.
[8] Scanlon, op. cit. p. 72.

ministerial experience not to treat the questions of the Committee as unwarranted intrusions upon their work. By 1929, they had learnt.

An unofficial body of left wing I.L.P. Members of Parliament, whose secretary was Fenner Brockway, was also formed during the life-time of the Government.[1] According to Brockway, its criticisms of Government policy were bitterly resented by MacDonald.[2] There is no evidence that it was ever able to make any impression on him or on most of his colleagues. 'In spite of theoretical checks,' one Labour M.P. wrote later, 'the Cabinet remained a body apart and quite uncontrolled.'[3]

This independence not only worried a number of backbenchers but also the activists in the constituency parties, and these also thought that the Labour M.P.s themselves were too free from extra-parliamentary checks. In consequence, a large number of resolutions from constituency parties appeared on the agenda of the 1924 Party Conference, demanding stricter control both of the Cabinet and of the Parliamentary Party.[4] One of these, supported by eight constituency parties, asked the Conference to agree that the P.L.P. and the members of the Government should be 'directly responsible to the Annual Conference of the Party, and that between Conferences the activities and policies both of the Parliamentary Labour Party and the Labour Government as such, shall also be subject to the fullest control of the Executive Committee of the Labour Party'.[5] Another asked that the next Conference should set up machinery 'of a nature by which it can enforce its decisions upon a Labour Government';[6] a third, that, 'in the event of future Labour Governments, the power of appointing Ministers of the Crown be taken away from the Prime Minister and placed in the hands of the Parliamentary Labour Party'.[7] 'These naïve exhortations,' one writer has recently said,[8] 'reflected a pathetic failure to understand the nature of the parliamentary system.' It may be, on the other hand, that it is precisely because they understood the nature of the parliamentary system, and feared the use their orthodox leaders would make of the freedom it conferred upon them, that the authors of these resolutions placed them, of course unavailingly, upon the Conference agenda.

---

[1] F. Brockway, *Inside the Left* (London, 1942) p. 152.
[2] ibid, p. 152.
[3] L. Macneil Weir, *The Tragedy of Ramsay MacDonald* (London, n.d.) p. 260.
[4] Labour Party Annual Conference Report, 1924, pp. 22-4.
[5] ibid, p. 22.
[6] ibid, p. 23.
[7] ibid, p. 23.
[8] McKenzie, op. cit. p. 431.

By virtue of the strategy it had imposed upon itself at the time of its formation, the Government moved, in home affairs, within an extremely narrow domain of administrative and legislative reform. Having decided from the start that it could not do much and that it must not even try, it didn't.

It had, of course, the golden excuse of its minority position and it exploited that excuse for all it was worth, in fact for more than it was worth. For the Government's minority position was not the most important reason for its timidity.[1] Much more important was the conviction of most of its members that their first task was to dispel any apprehension as to the Government's radicalism.

However, the Government's record of reform was not altogether barren. Its most notable achievement was John Wheatley's Housing Act, which paved the way for a substantial increase over the following years in municipal house building. Similarly, there were some very modest improvements in the provision and administration of unemployment benefits and old-age pensions; an Agricultural Wages Act, though emasculated during its passage through Parliament, was of benefit to agricultural workers; under the impulse of Charles Trevelyan, the Board of Education pursued more liberal policies in regard to such matters as scholarships, grants and maintenance allowances, and local authorities were encouraged to do the same. In July 1924, Snowden announced Government support of about £28 million for road building, municipal works and the standardization of electricity frequencies.

As for the first Budget to be introduced by a Labour Chancellor, an anticipated surplus of £38 million enabled Snowden to reduce a variety of duties, including those on sugar, tea, coffee and cocoa. Protective advantages, notably for the motor car industry, were abolished; so was the special tax on Corporation profits. The latter, he wrote later, 'although fairly remunerative' was 'never a popular tax',[2] least of all no doubt with the Public Companies it affected. Snowden was well entitled to claim,·as he did not fail to do in his Budget speech, that the Budget was 'vindictive against no class and no interest'.[3] Its reception, he recollected, 'was everything I could have desired. It relieved the feelings of the rich, who had feared that there might be drastic impositions upon their class'.[4]

[1] Note, in this connection, MacDonald's remark in September 1924 that, even if he were Prime Minister for fifty years, 'the pledges I have given you from my heart would still be unfulfilled — not because I fainted or failed, but because the corn was still green' (J. Clayton, *The Rise and Decline of Socialism in Great Britain 1884-1924* (London, 1926) p. 213.)

[2] Snowden, op. cit. II, p. 645.

[3] ibid, p. 646.

[4] ibid, p. 647.

FROM OPPOSITION TO OFFICE

Whatever might be claimed for the Government's record in home policy—and plenty was—its achievements were distinctly meagre when set against mass unemployment and massive deprivation. The Government could not of course have been expected to cure all. But it could have been less complacent about the difficulties of doing more, and sought more purposefully to push back its frontiers of action. Its failure to do more for the unemployed, either in terms of benefits or in the provision of work, suggested that it lacked the quality of effective indignation. Its followers, as many resolutions to the 1924 Party Conference showed, had the indignation; what they lacked was the influence.

Nor was it only the Government's sins of omission which angered the activists; they found even less excuse for the sins it committed because of its determination to prove that it was 'fit to govern' and that it had, in as full a measure as its opponents, what the French call *le sens de l'état*.

One way in which it proved this was in its handling of strikes affecting 'essential services'. In any such strike in the past, employers had normally been able to count on the Government's hostility to the strikers and on its willingness, where appropriate, to act as a strike breaker by the use of troops. The Labour Government had no hostility to strikers, only to strikes;[1] though it never actually used troops in strikes, it repeatedly made it clear that it would not hesitate to do so and, on one occasion, when faced with the threat of a transport strike in London, prepared for the use of emergency powers under the Emergency Powers Act.[2]

The use of troops by the Government in industrial disputes had always been bitterly resented by the Labour movement, and so was the Emergency Powers Act itself. Resolutions to the 1924 Labour Party Conference were loud in their disapproval of the Government's readiness to behave like its predecessors. One of these resolutions viewed 'with the utmost gravity the attitude of the Labour Government toward recent industrial disputes' and warned that 'any measure put forward by a Labour Government to jeopardize the

[1] In his preface to the 1924 edition of his *Socialism: Critical and Constructive*, MacDonald wrote that 'public doles, Poplarism, strikes for increased wages, limitations of output, not only are not Socialism but may mislead the spirit and the policy of Socialism' (Lyman, op. cit. p. 233). For MacDonald's bitter anger when strikes did occur, see Dalton, op. cit. I, p. 148. Sidney Webb reported Henderson as saying to him 'that the epidemic of Labour revolts reminds him (from police information) of what was happening in Russia in 1917 against the Kerensky Government'. (M. Cole Ed., *Beatrice Webb's Diaries, 1924-1932*, op. cit. p. 18.) Webb himself commented that 'those little bands of wrecking Communists are undoubtedly at work' (ibid, p. 18).
[2] Allen, op. cit. pp. 230-5; also Lyman, op. cit. pp. 217-23, and Bullock, op. cit. I, pp. 237-47.

interests of the workers during an Industrial Dispute will be met by bitterness and hostility on the part of those who look to the advent of Labour in power as a means for putting into operation the full interests of the working class'.[1] Another asked that 'with the possibility of the Labour Government being turned out of office at any time', it should 'at once repeal all the Anti-Labour Laws on the Statute Book, such as the Emergency Powers Act, and those dealing with the right of the troops and the police to interfere in industrial disputes, etc., etc.'[2]

These exhortations too were no doubt naïve. When the Government fell, Josiah Wedgwood, Chancellor of the Duchy of Lancaster, was able to tell his successor that the emergency supply and transport schemes which had been worked out by previous administrations remained intact. 'I haven't destroyed any of your plans,' said Wedgwood; 'in fact I haven't done a bloody thing about them.'[3]

In this instance, the constituency activists were only echoing widespread disapproval. When the Government invoked the Emergency Powers Act in the transport strike,[4] a joint meeting of the General Council of the T.U.C. and the Labour Party Executive Committee issued a statement deploring the Government's intention and urging that, if the Act was to be used at all, it should be used for the purpose of carrying on the ordinary transport services, with 'ordinary men at the wages and conditions asked for', pending the report of a Committee of inquiry into transport difficulties in London.[5]

Nor were trade union leaders happy with the Government's determination to keep them at arm's length so as to emphasize its 'national' character. As Mr Allen notes, 'having union leaders as members of the Government did not assist matters, for they were among those who were most conventional and endeavoured to stand above class differences'.[6]

While in opposition, Labour had been critical of many aspects of military administration. Indeed, the Labour Year Book recorded that the Party in Parliament had in 1923 kept up 'an all-night struggle' on the Committee stage of the Army Annual Bill, and

[1] Labour Party Annual Conference Report, 1924, p. 21.
[2] ibid, p. 21.
[3] J. Symons, *The General Strike* (London, 1957) p. 19.
[4] A Privy Council meeting was hurriedly held at Knowsley Hall, Lord Derby's residence, where the King was staying, and his signature obtained to the Proclamation (Allen, op. cit. p. 232). There was surely something very symbolic about the Proclamation being signed in the residence of a former Conservative Minister, who was also one of the richest men in England.
[5] Allen, p. 232.
[6] ibid, p. 236.

had moved amendments 'for the abolition of the death penalty in the Army, for the setting up of Courts of Appeal, for giving recruits the right to indicate their unwillingness to do duty in the case of a trade dispute, etc.'[1]

In 1924, it was the Labour Government which was responsible for the introduction of the Army and Air Force Annual Bill. A number of amendments, most of them identical to those which had been moved the year before and voted for by the Party, were reintroduced. The Government opposed them but announced that the Army Council had been asked to go into the whole question of service and report to the Cabinet during the ensuing year. To protests that the Army Council was out of touch with the people and the rank and file of the Army, the Minister replied that 'it is quite wrong to refer to the Army Council as a purely military organization, a body of obscurantists whose minds cannot possibly be open to the more democratic or progressive views that are, I suppose, specially associated with certain hon. Members of this House'.[2]

It was George Lansbury who moved the amendment concerning the right of recruits to refuse duty in connection with trade disputes. This was an amendment, he said, which had been moved on a considerable number of occasions by members of the Labour Party. 'I am not going to find fault with the hon. and right hon. Gentlemen on the Front Bench, who have a perfect right to consider that they must take a different line to that which they took previously,' but, he added, 'I think one of the faults of the system under which affairs are managed in this House is that men, when they accept office, are expected immediately to change their attitude towards great public questions.'[3]

Fearful of innovation at home, the Government had even less thought of blazing new trails in colonial and defence policy. Some ministers accepted continuity of policy in these matters as the inevitable consequence of the Government's minority, position—others, as a matter of conviction. J. H. Thomas, the Colonial Secre-

[1] Labour Year Book, 1924, p. 127.
[2] H. of C. vol. 171, col. 2319, 2nd of April, 1927.
[3] ibid, vol. 171, col. 2374. 67 Members voted against the Government on this occasion. Beatrice Webb had noted in her Diary on the 15th of March that 'one of the unpleasant features of this Government has been the willingness of convinced and even fanatical pacifists to go back on their words once they are on the Treasury Bench as Under-Secretaries for the War Services. Hot-air propaganda in mean streets and industrial slums combined with chill moderation on the Treasury Bench and courtly phrases at Society functions may be the last word in political efficiency; but it is unsavoury, and leads, among the rank and file, to deep discouragement. Even Sidney is depressed' (op. cit. p. 15).

tary, undoubtedly spoke from the heart when, in proposing the toast of 'The Empire' at the British Empire Exhibition, he proclaimed that the Government 'intended above all else to hand to their successors one thing when they gave up the seals of office, and that was the general recognition of the fact that they were proud and jealous of, and were prepared to maintain, the Empire';[1] or when he told the Newport Chamber of Commerce that 'you have for the first time a Government composed in the main of humble working men, men who hitherto have played the rôle of propagandists and who are now face to face not only with the responsibilities of office, but with the responsibilities of the knowledge of what this great Empire means. Men faced with these responsibilities can never again be the indifferent propagandists that they were in the past. They must remain for all time responsible politicians keeping only in mind the great interest of the country.'[2]

Thomas's fellow ministers were less crude in their imperial rhetoric, but his sentiments were nonetheless a fair reflection of the Government's colonial policies, or rather of the colonial policies it endorsed. Whether in relation to India, or Egypt, or any other of Britain's dependencies, the Government gave no sign that it had any qualms about imperial rule. It is true that Gandhi, after a serious illness, was released from jail during the life-time of the Labour Government. On the dubious assumption that this would not have happened had a Conservative Government been in office, his release must be counted as the one departure in Imperial affairs[3] from what was otherwise indistinguishable from Conservative policy and attitudes.

As for defence policy, the Government, as *The Times* put it, showed 'a real largeness of view in rising above the deep-rooted prejudice of many among their adherents about "unproductive expenditure" upon armaments'.[4] The previous Government had

[1] *The Times*, 16th of May, 1924.

[2] *The Times*, 22nd of March, 1924. Thomas also added the following: 'I once wrote a book "When Labour Rules". It was a foolish thing to do. It was in the days when I was bothered about material things and wanted money . . . It is only cowards that fail to face facts. It is only cowards that pretend that consistency is a virtue.'

[3] To this should also perhaps be added the fact that, rather than use troops in the repression of tribal disturbances in Iraq, aircraft for the bombing of tribal villages was used. This method, William Leach, the Under-Secretary of State for Air, explained to his critics, was much more sparing of life for both sides since advance notice of the bombing could be given. (H. of C. vol. 175, col. 1491, 3rd of July, 1924.) 'I cannot honestly say,' he had admitted a few days earlier, 'that we have made any change in the policy of the late Government' (ibid, col. 925).

[4] *The Times*, 22nd of February, 1924.

decided upon the construction of eight cruisers. In February, it was announced that the Labour Government had decided to proceed with the building of five cruisers and two destroyers 'in view of the serious unemployment'. But it was also decided, on the advice of Haldane and for purely military considerations, to abandon the plans for the strengthening of the naval base at Singapore. As to the development of the air force, the programme initiated by the previous administration was pursued under the aegis of Lord Thompson.

On the other hand, the Government, with MacDonald in charge of the Foreign Office, deployed greater activity in its handling of international affairs than in any other field of policy. At the London Conference in July 1924, agreement was reached on the ending of the French occupation of the Ruhr, while MacDonald, having endorsed the Dawes Plan on German reparations, persuaded the French and the Germans to accept it too. Even at the time, Mac-Donald's diplomacy evoked strong criticism both in the I.L.P. and in the trade unions, which is not surprising since much of that diplomacy entailed the abandonment, as E. D. Morel said, 'of convictions and pledges which have been the inspiration of the party for the last five years'.[1] The Labour Party was officially opposed to the policy of reparations: the Dawes Plan was based upon it. The Labour Party was pledged to the revision of the Treaty of Versailles: MacDonald repeatedly assured the French that his diplomacy involved no such revision.

As for the second aspect of Labour's diplomacy—European security, the strengthening of the League of Nations, and disarmament, the Government rejected the Draft Treaty of Mutual Assistance which provided for collective aid to victims of aggression, regional security arrangements, and graduated disarmament; however, British delegates at Geneva, and particularly Henderson, played an important rôle in the drafting of the Protocol for the Pacific Settlement of International Disputes, which also provided for the application of sanctions against an aggressor, but laid the main emphasis upon more elaborate procedures for international arbitration than had been provided in the Covenant of the League of Nations. Agreement was reached on the Protocol just before the Government fell: its successor refused to ratify it.[2]

Even if one leaves aside the fact that there was nothing distinctively 'Labour' about these diplomatic ventures, their net importance, as diplomatic ventures, was small. But their importance in relation to the Labour movement was real. For, whatever the critics might say,

---

[1] *New Leader*, 25th of July, 1924.
[2] For evidence that the Labour Government itself was divided on the Protocol and might have hesitated to ratify it, see Lyman, op. cit. p. 176.

they showed to the mass of Labour supporters, as MacDonald put it in his opening election speech in December (the speech was also being broadcast) 'this extraordinary phenomenon of a Labour Government that has met kings and rulers of the earth, that has conducted itself with distinction and with dignity (cheers); this Labour Government that has met ambassadors, that has faced the rulers of Europe on terms of equality; this Labour Government that has sent its representatives forth and its representatives have been held as statesmen . . .'[1] It was a revealingly defensive kind of pride; and so were the cheers which punctuated MacDonald's remarks. But then most Labour supporters *were* defensively proud of their statesman-like leaders 'who had faced the rulers of Europe on terms of equality'.

3. NO GRATITUDE AT THE TOP

The most important, and the really distinctive, part of the Labour Government's foreign policy was its recognition of Russia almost as soon as it came to office, and its decision to negotiate a treaty for the settlement of all outstanding questions between the two countries.

On the 6th of August, after months of laborious negotiations and repeated threats of collapse, an agreement had been reached, the House of Commons was informed, on a General and also on a Commercial Treaty with Russia. Under one provision of the General Treaty, the British Government agreed to recommend to Parliament the guaranteeing of a loan to Russia upon the satisfactory settlement of British bondholders' claims upon nationalized property, a matter over which the British negotiators had shown an extremity of concern possibly worthy of a better cause. The loan was made conditional upon the settlement of claims and that settlement, it was specified, must be acceptable to the holders of at least half the value of British bondholdings.[2]

This caution, designed in part to appease the Opposition, was not rewarded. The Government's Russian policies came under bitter Liberal and Conservative attack and the treaties, particularly the proposed loan guarantee, were denounced as a further proof of Labour's affinities with the Bolshevik regime. All that was required after the conclusion of the Russian Treaties was an issue upon which to bring down the Government. But it was MacDonald himself who chose to invite defeat—on a different issue.

[1] *The Times,* 14th of October, 1924.
[2] Another condition of the loan was a Soviet undertaking to cease all Communist propaganda in colonial territories.

In view of the Government's meticulous observance of constitutional rules and procedures, however trivial, there is a certain irony in the fact that the issue on which it left office should have been its opponents' claim that it had been guilty of grave constitutional impropriety. It is perhaps just as ironical that the supposed dereliction should have arisen over the decision, confirmed in the House of Commons on the 6th of August, to prosecute J. R. Campbell, the Editor of the Communist *Workers' Weekly,* under the Incitement to Mutiny Act of 1797, for exhorting soldiers to 'let it be known that, neither in the class war nor in a military war, will you turn your guns on your fellow workers'.

On the 13th of August, however, the Government, having come to doubt the wisdom of a prosecution, said that it now accepted the view that 'the object and intention of the article in question was not an endeavour to seduce men in the fighting forces from their duty . . . but it was a comment upon armed military force being used by the State to repress industrial disputes'.[1] Treasury Counsel also stated in Court that 'it has been possible for the Director of Public Prosecutions to accept that alleged intention of this article more easily because the defendant is a man of excellent character with an admirable military record'.[2]

When the House of Commons met on the 30th of September, both Conservatives and Liberals harassed the Government with accusations of interference with the course of justice at the dictation of its left wing. MacDonald did not improve matters by first suggesting to the House that he had not been consulted on the institution or the subsequent withdrawal of the prosecution, and then explaining later that, in saying this, he 'had gone a little further than I ought to have gone'. The Tories, who had originally intended to put down a vote of censure, decided to support a Liberal demand for a Select Committee of Investigation. MacDonald chose to treat this as a matter of confidence and the Government was duly defeated on the 8th of October. Having thus refused to court defeat on a major issue of policy, the Prime Minister invited defeat on an issue that was, save for the immediate political purposes of Labour's opponents, altogether bogus : the Campbell case played next to no part in the election campaign.

MacDonald's decision to resign and to have an election was

[1] Lyman, op. cit. p. 238. It was the Attorney General, Sir Patrick Hastings, who had agreed to the prosecution. But the initial steps appear to have been taken at the War Office; the papers were then passed to the Home Office and thence to the Director of Public Prosecutions (Scanlon, op. cit. p. 77). It would not appear that either the Secretary of State for War or the Home Secretary were consulted by their respective departments.

[2] Lyman, op. cit. p. 238.

entirely his own and many explanations have been offered for it. One of them was that he was weary, and had been considerably rattled by the charge that the gift of a car and a block of shares for its upkeep from a wealthy biscuit manufacturer, Sir Alexander Grant, had been made in connection with the baronetcy Sir Alexander later received. Beatrice Webb recorded in her Diary on the 24th of September that 'J.R.M. talked gloomily about his "being sick of it" ', with particular reference to criticism from the left. He also said that he would not welcome a majority at the next Election and thought 'it would be a grave misfortune, as the Party (not the Cabinet!) was not fit to govern'.[1]

The Government sought to conduct its campaign on what a Labour Party publication called *Labour's Great Record* at home and abroad and offered in *Labour's Appeal to the People* what was coming to be a familiar mixture of cautious rhetoric, pious exhortation and piecemeal collectivism.[2]

It was not however Labour which chose the issues or set the pace of the campaign. It was the Opposition; and particularly the Tories, who concentrated on Labour's Russian policies, and turned the election into a scare campaign designed to suggest that, with Labour in office, Britain was in dire peril of more or less imminent Bolshevization.[3]

It is at the height of that campaign, on Friday, 24th of October (polling day was Wednesday, the 29th), that the Foreign Office published the Zinoviev letter, or rather a copy of the alleged letter (no original was ever produced), together with a strong letter of protest

[1] *Beatrice Webb's Diaries, 1924-32*, op. cit. p. 43. Baldwin believed that MacDonald decided to stand or fall by the Campbell motion in order to avoid debate on the Russian treaties and on unemployment. (G. M. Young, *Stanley Baldwin* (London, 1952) p. 83.)

[2] For text, see *The Times*, 13th of October, 1924. 'We appeal to the People,' the Appeal concluded, 'to support us in our steadfast march—taking each step only after careful examination, making sure of each advance as we go—and using each success as the beginning of further achievements towards a really Socialist Commonwealth . . .'

[3] One of the most virulent exponents of this view was Winston Churchill. On the 22nd of October, he was speaking of the 'Socialist Movement' as 'from beginning to end, a foreign-minded movement. It has been lifted bodily from Germany and Russia'. (*The Times,* in Graubard, op. cit. p. 275.) On the 27th he recalled 'the story of Kerensky, how he stood there, like Mr. MacDonald, pretending that he meant to do the best he could for his country, and all the time apologizing behind the scenes to the wild, dark, deadly forces which had him in their grip'. (*The Times,* in Lyman, op. cit. p. 259); see also *Socialist Review*, November, 1924 and C. Higbie, *A Study of the British Press in Selected Political Situations, 1924-1938*, unpublished Ph.D. thesis (London, 1950), ch. II.

to the Russian Chargé d'Affaires, which thus gave the Zinoviev letter the appearance of authenticity.

The letter, supposedly addressed to the Central Committee of the Communist Party and signed by Zinoviev, the President of the Presidium of the Third International, urged that the 'proletariat of Great Britain must show the greatest possible energy in the further struggle for ratification' of the Russian Treaties as a means of furthering 'the revolutionizing of the international and British proletariat'. It also commended closer contacts between British and Russian workers so as to make it easier 'to extend and develop the propaganda of ideas of Leninism in England and the Colonies'. There were also references to the spreading of revolutionary disaffection in the Army by the creation of Communist cells, to preparations for a revolutionary seizure of power in the event of a threat of war, and to much else similarly bloodcurdling.[1]

The Zinoviev letter had first been received at the Foreign Office on the 10th of October, and it had been sent to MacDonald, who was then campaigning in the country, on the 15th. On the 17th, the Foreign Office received instructions from MacDonald that the greatest care should be taken to ascertain whether the document was authentic or not. However, he also gave instructions—rashly, it might be thought—that if the letter was found to be authentic, it should be published at once, and that, in any case, a draft letter of protest to the Russian Chargé d'Affaires should be prepared immediately, so as to save time. The draft protest was sent on to him on the 21st; he received it on the 23rd and sent it back with amendments on the 24th. The Foreign Office published the letter, with the protest, on the same evening, well in time for the morning papers of Saturday 25th; before, Snowden was even to suggest later, it had received MacDonald's amended draft.[2] MacDonald himself telegraphed the Foreign Office on Saturday 25th to ascertain the facts concerning the publication of the documents, and was assured that he had initialled the draft, and that this had been taken to mean that he wanted it published.

It was the *Daily Mail* which had come into possession of the letter in circumstances that have never been really fully elucidated.[3]

[1] See W. P. and Z. Coates, *A History of Anglo-Soviet Relations* (London, 1943), ch. VIII for a detailed analysis of the whole episode and for internal evidence suggesting that the letter was a forgery.

[2] Snowden, op. cit. II, p. 710-15.

[3] Thomas Marlowe, who was then Editor of the *Daily Mail*, wrote to the *Observer* in March, 1928 that a telephone message 'from an old and trusted friend' had been left on his desk on the 23rd of October, which ran as follows: 'There is a document in London which you ought to have. It shows the relations between the Bolsheviks and the British Labour Party. The Prime

Its intention to publish the letter was given to MacDonald as one of the motives for allowing publication by the Foreign Office; Sir Eyre Crowe, the Permanent Under-Secretary, wrote to the Prime Minister on the 25th of October that he had wished to spare the Government from the charge that 'information vitally concerning the security of the Empire had been deliberately suppressed during the elections'.[1] The propriety of this solicitude, in the light of MacDonald's instructions, may well be doubted, and Lord Morrison can hardly be said to err on the side of exaggeration when he writes that 'it could also be argued that the Foreign Office, in the absence of a minute of instruction, should not have acted'.[2] It is in fact hard to doubt that the Prime Minister's hand was forced by one or more of his subordinates.

The Zinoviev letter was eagerly presented by Labour's enemies as further evidence that, by negotiating the Russian Treaties, the Government was acting, consciously or otherwise, as the Trojan horse of Bolshevism and that, whatever the Labour leaders might say, there was little if anything to distinguish them from the Communists.

In their indignant repudiation of this view, the Labour leaders could point, justifiably enough, to their consistent record of opposition to the Communist Party and to the Third International, and to the bitter attacks they had endured from both. They could also point to the overwhelming vote by the Annual Conference of the Party, on the eve of the election, against Communist affiliation.[3] Indeed, the Conference had also agreed to further measures designed to isolate the Communist Party: by 2,456,000 votes to 654,000, it had declared that no member of the Communist Party would henceforth be eligible for endorsement as a Labour candidate for Parliament or any local authority;[4] and, even more drastically, it had agreed, but only by 1,804,000 votes to 1,546,000,[5] that no member of the Communist Party was to be eligible for membership of the Labour Party.

In any case, the whole record of the Labour Government should

Minister knows all about it, but is trying to avoid publication. It has been circulated today to Foreign Office, Home Office, Admiralty and War Office.' (W. P. and Z. Coates, op. cit. p. 191.)

[1] Nicolson, op. cit. p. 82.

[2] H. Morrison, *Government and Parliament* (London, 1954) p. 66. It also seems likely that Lord Morrison is mistaken in stating that 'Mr. MacDonald could not be got hold of on the telephone'. (ibid, p. 65.)

[3] The voting was 3,185,000 to 193,000 (Labour Party Annual Conference, 1924, p. 131).

[4] ibid, p. 131.

[5] ibid, p. 131.

have been sufficient to prove how true was the Labour leaders' contention that their party was not only opposed to revolution, violence and exacerbation of class conflict, but that it was the best bulwark against them.

However, the Labour Party could not, in 1924, easily compete with its opponents in the matter of anti-communism. Whatever parliamentary and trade union leaders might say to show how real was their abhorrence of communism, revolution and the Bolsheviks, their opponents could always, given sufficient ingenuity and unscrupulousness, find something or other which could be interpreted as showing that Labour *was* soft on Communism, or at least not as hard as its opponents.

Yet, the results of the poll suggested that the red scare did little damage to the Labour Party. Its real advantage to the Tories was that it frightened into their camp many people who might have otherwise voted Liberal, and that it made more difficult the discussion of serious issues.

The Labour Party had not, in any meaningful sense, won the election of December 1923; nor did it, in any meaningful sense, lose that of October 1924. True, it had a net loss of 40 seats, but its popular poll went up by well over a million, from 4,348,379 to 5,482,620.[1] The real losers were the Liberals whose total poll fell by more than 1.25 million and whose representation was reduced from 158 to 42. The real victors were the Tories, whose poll went up by more than 2 million to 7,400,000 and who returned 415 members.

At first sight, it may seem odd that the Labour Party should, relatively speaking, have done so well, considering that the Government had tried to do so little to give concrete meaning to its announced ethos, and done a great deal that ran counter to it.

This, obviously, is not how the mass of Labour voters judged it. Whatever disappointment they might feel was tempered by the thought that the Government's minority position *was* a sufficient excuse for its failings. That the Government had *been* at all was in itself an element in favour of Labour's leaders. There was much that could be held against them on socialist grounds. But then most Labour supporters were not socialists, only anti-Conservatives. And, for those who did not want to vote Conservative, there was now no serious alternative to the Labour Party, just as there was no longer any serious alternative to the Conservative Party for those who would not vote Labour.

[1] Labour contested 515 seats as against 428 in 1923 and 16,000,000 people voted on an 80% poll as compared to 14,500,000 on a 74% poll in 1923. For an analysis of Labour's results, see Graubard, op. cit. pp. 282 ff.

This political crystallization had been in the making since the beginning of the century and even before. At long last, after decades in which political alignments had failed to reflect social and economic reality, one main party of property and privilege had come to confront the political party of organized labour. The Tory Party—and this was an essential element of its strength— could still draw support from masses of people, including a substantial part of the working classes, who had neither property nor privilege. But the political contours of a class alignment had now come to be drawn much more sharply than ever before. On the other hand, the confrontation, though it primarily derived definition from its class content, was between property and labour, not between property and socialist labour. Everything was in that distinction, as was dramatically demonstrated in the General Strike of 1926.

CHAPTER V

THE GENERAL STRIKE

'I rely, in the name of the General Council, on every
man and every woman . . . to fight for the soul of
Labour and the salvation of the miners.'

Ernest Bevin, 1st of May, 1926

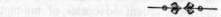

1. RED FRIDAY—AND AFTER

WRITING in September 1925, Beatrice Webb had recorded in
her diary her husband's belief 'that the Conservative Government
will go forward in our direction; that, exactly as the Labour
Government failed to go rapidly forward, so the Conservative
Government will find itself prevented from going backward. Public
opinion will insist on the *middle* way—but it will be a collectivist
middle way'.[1]

What Sidney Webb presumably meant was that the Tories would
not seek to dismantle wholesale the apparatus of State intervention
that had come to be a familiar part of the British economic and social
landscape since the years of war. It was not an entirely unrealistic
view, nor was the implication that there was, at this level, more
common ground between Conservative and Labour leaders than
was suggested by the rhetoric of either. On the other hand, it was
a view which failed to make due allowance for the fact that the interventionist propensities of a Tory Government would necessarily be
directed to the protection of its own clientele, that it would, in other
words, have an overwhelming bias in favour of property and against
labour. No doubt, if Stanley Baldwin could have defended property
without offending labour, he would, being a kindly man, have been
quite happy to do so. Unfortunately, this was not possible, least of all
when it again came to conflict over the coal industry.

The coal industry, for long the sick man of British capitalism,
was in a particularly bad state in 1925.[2] As far as the coal owners

---

[1] *Beatrice Webb's Diaries, 1924-1932*, op. cit. p. 73. 'In his heart of hearts,'
she also wrote, 'I think he still believes in Fabian permeation of other parties
as a more rapid way than the advent of a distinctly Socialist Government. A
strong Socialist H.M.O., *very seldom in office*, he thinks would be the like-
liest instrument of progress' (ibid, p. 73). Italics in text.
[2] See Arnot, op. cit. pp. 352-8.

and the Government were concerned, there was an obvious solution to the problem—a substantial reduction in wages. This was the genesis of the General Strike.

From the point of view of the Government, it was particularly unfortunate that a major conflict with Labour should have occurred over coal. For the coal owners were the least attractive representatives of British capitalism and were felt, far outside the ranks of Labour, to be a serious embarrassment to the creation of a 'better climate' in industry; and the miners' spokesmen were among the least yielding of trade union leaders; the new Miners' Secretary, A. J. Cook, was one of the most ardent advocates of militant resistance both to the owners and to the Government. In 1925, furthermore, there was every appearance that the miners enjoyed the solid support of their trade union colleagues. After the disappointments of 1924, the notion that the unions must look to their own combined industrial strength for the protection of their members had acquired a new measure of popularity: in the coalfields and in the trade unions generally, the National Minority Movement, led by Communists and designed to bring about a broad alliance of militants within the unions, was gaining marked support.[1]

The first result of the trade unions' apparent determination to stand by the miners was a victory which, though partial, was more definite than any since the War.

On the 31st of July, 1925[2] (Red Friday, as it was jubilantly called in the Labour movement), the Government had been forced to grant a subsidy to the coal industry, as an alternative to the cut in wages upon which the mine owners insisted and which the miners' leaders refused. As late as the 29th, the Prime Minister had told these leaders that the Government would not grant any subsidy and that the coal industry 'must stand on its own economic foundations'; and he had also made it clear that 'all the workers of this country have got to take reductions in wages to help put industry on its feet'.[3] On the 30th, at a Special Conference of Trade Union Executives, convened by the General Council of the T.U.C., a thousand delegates had endorsed the General Council's intention to place an embargo on coal movements from midnight, 31st of July, and

[1] Note also the *rapprochement* between the British and Russian Trade Union movements. In April 1925, an agreement was reached between them for the creation of a joint Committee for the purpose of mutual consultation and assistance.

[2] This was the date, the owners had decided, on which was to be terminated the National Wage Agreement which had been in force since the 18th of June, 1924.

[3] Arnot, op. cit. pp. 376-7.

had empowered it to call a strike, on any scale deemed requisite, should the deadlock continue. Instructions for the embargo, involving railways, docks and wharves, waterways, locks and road transport, had gone out the same evening. The Government had maintained its attitude until the last moment. At the last moment, however, it capitulated and agreed to a subsidy until the 1st of May, 1926, during which period there was to be yet another inquiry (the fifth since the end of the war and the third within two years) into the problems of the industry.

That this temporary settlement represented a defeat for the Government was recognized on all sides. And it was also recognized that its capitulation had only been made possible by the solidarity of the other unions with the miners, coupled with the Government's lack of preparedness to cope with a strike, had one occurred.[1]

Ominously, there were, on the morrow of the unions' success, some voices in the Labour movement to deplore the manner in which it had been achieved. J. H. Thomas, for instance, was 'far from happy' over the 'magnificent victory' of the miners and considered nothing more dangerous for the future of the country than that employers and Government should be compelled to concede through force, what they refused to concede through reason.[2] And, speaking to an I.L.P. Summer School immediately after the settlement, Ramsay MacDonald said that the Government had 'simply handed over the appearance, at any rate, of victory to the very forces that sane, well-considered, thoroughly well-examined Socialism feels to be probably its greatest enemy', meaning, as he explained next day, 'the Communists'.[3]

These, however, were discordant sentiments in a general chorus of self-congratulation, only qualified by the recognition that Red Friday, as Herbert Smith, the President of the Miners, said, was

---

[1] As Baldwin pithily put it to his biographer, when asked why the Government had granted the subsidy: 'We were not ready', (Young, op. cit. p. 99). Also T. J. Jones: 'The Government was, in fact, buying time to prepare the national defences (sic) against the possible recurrence of this threat' (T. J. Jones, *Lloyd George* (London, 1951) p. 217).

[2] Crook, op. cit. p. 296.

[3] Arnot, op. cit. p. 386. In the New York *Nation* of the 26th of August, he wrote that 'had the lockout (of the miners) taken place the industries of our country would have been paralysed within a week . . . the prospect was undoubtedly appalling, and the sections which believe that governments only yield to force, and that direct action against society offers great prospects for improvements in working class conditions, naturally feel that they have scored a fine triumph. They are now able to say that a threat of direct action wrung £10,000,000 from the tax-payers . . . the mishandling of the Government . . . handed over the honours of war to those who may be inclined to toy with revolution.' (Crook, op. cit. p. 294.)

'only an armistice', whose ultimate outcome would depend largely on 'how we stand between now and the 1st of May as an organization in respect of unity'.[1] No one in fact doubted, the trade union leaders least of all, that there must occur another and more decisive trial of strength when the subsidy came to an end. The composition of the four-man Samuel Commission[2] gave no ground for believing that its recommendations would be favourable to the miners. Nor in any case was there anything to suggest that this Government would be more ready than its predecessors to carry out recommendations to which the coal owners were strongly opposed. Most important of all, there were the preparations, official and semi-official, which were soon under way for the creation of a massive strike-breaking apparatus.

Less than two months after the settlement, it was announced to the newspapers that '. . . numerous suggestions have been made from various quarters for organizing those citizens who would be prepared to volunteer to maintain supplies and services in the event of a general strike'; such an organization, the announcement said, 'has already been constituted and is at work in many metropolitan boroughs, while steps are being taken to create corresponding organizations in all the principal centres of the Kingdom'. 'Certain funds,' it also said, 'have been placed by a few patriotic citizens at the disposal of the council' and these had been supplemented by contributions from many large and small firms.[3]

This Organization for the Maintenance of Supplies (O.M.S.) was an ostensibly private and voluntary body.[4] Care had been taken to exclude from its leadership representatives of finance and industry. Instead, its Council was given an impressive appearance of neutrality by a former Viceroy of India, Lord Hardinge, who was its president, Sir Rennel Rodd, a former ambassador, and Admiral Jellicoe, both of whom were vice-presidents, and by a number of other eminent retired military and naval officers.

O.M.S. was at great pains to emphasize that it was non-political and non-party, that it had no aggressive or provocative aims, that it was not formed to oppose the legitimate efforts of trade unions

---

[1] Arnot, op. cit. p. 383.

[2] Sir Herbert Samuel himself, Sir William Beveridge, General Sir Herbert Lawrence, then a managing partner of the banking house of Glyn Mills & Co., and Kenneth Lee, the chairman of the textile firm of Tootal, Broadhurst, Lee & Co.

[3] *The Times*, 25th of September, 1925.

[4] This did not prevent the Home Secretary from stating that the 'promoters' had consulted him as to their desire to form some such organization, or from giving it his blessing.

to better the conditions of their members; indeed, it was 'in complete sympathy with any constitutional actions to bring about a more equitable adjustment of social and economic conditions'; all it wanted was to defeat any attempt to 'inflict severe privation on the great mass of the people who have no direct part in the actual dispute'. No strike-breaking organization, it must be admitted, could have said fairer than that.

The organization was also much concerned to keep its distance from the British Fascists, who were armed, practised a weekly drill, and engaged in other even more spectacular activities.[1] Though welcoming the co-operation of other 'patriotic' societies in promoting the particular aims of O.M.S., Lord Hardinge stated, there could only be co-operation with the Fascists 'if they abandoned their quasi-military formation and made it clear that they would act under authority as citizens, and only then on requisition by a Constitutional Government'.[2] This was also the wish of the Government, whereupon Brigadier-General Blakeney, the president of the British Fascists, and Rear-Admiral Armstrong, the vice-president, and a majority of their committee, decided that 'at the present moment effective assistance to the state can best be given in seconding the efforts of the O.M.S.'[3]

In the succeeding months, O.M.S. enlisted volunteers as special constables, as workers to maintain public services, as transport drivers, messengers and cyclists, or for general duties requiring no technical skill. By the time the organization was handed over to the Government, on the eve of the General Strike, it was said to have recruited some hundred thousand volunteers and to have had a number of them secretly trained, on private industrial railroads and in the grounds of specially designated private residences, as locomotive and lorry drivers.[4]

[1] Such as the kidnapping of Harry Pollitt, the raiding of Communist headquarters in London and the breaking up of Communist meetings. (Crook, op. cit. p. 299.) For Pollitt's adventures see H. Pollitt, *Serving My Time* (London, 1940) pp. 200-1. Pollitt's assailants were caught, tried and acquitted. At the 1925 Conference of the Labour Party, a resolution was passed condemning the verdict as 'merely an instance of class prejudice on the part of juries' and calling for an alteration in the law to ensure adequate representation of the workers on juries. (Labour Party Annual Conference Report, 1925, p. 299.)

[2] Crook, op. cit. p. 301.

[3] ibid, p. 302. The Fascists also decided to give an earnest 'of their law-abiding propensities by taking a name less likely to be associated with unconstitutional action'. The name they chose was that of Loyalists, under whose auspices they planned to form a league 'of workers of all classes' (ibid, p. 302).

[4] ibid, p. 300.

For its own part, the Government had quickly got down to the organization of an emergency supply and transport service, and to the planning of a detailed administrative framework, extending down to local authorities, and also covering the use of air, naval and army personnel, in preparation for a General Strike.[1] In October, the Home Secretary told the Commons that the Government's plans were ready to be put into operation. In November, he said that the Government had its own elaborate organization for the maintenance of supplies, and he emphasized again the Government's readiness in February 1926.

All these vast preparations, unparalleled in peace time, had their origin, it must be stressed, in one fact and in one fact alone: the Government's determination that the coalowners should not be prevented from reducing the miners' wages. But this was not the main reason why the Government was now mobilizing its resources. Nor was it mobilizing because, as its members claimed, 'the community' or parliamentary government or democracy were in danger. Had the Government been forced to make some concessions to the miners—and that is all they and the other trade union leaders wanted—it would have been found that the Constitution remained quite unimpaired, and the Government itself would no doubt have claimed either that its concessions were not concessions at all, or that they were an admirable example of humanity and commonsense. All Governments are adept at making a virtue of ineluctable necessity. Stanley Baldwin could have been expected to do so with consummate artistry—had he been forced to.

The real danger was the access of strength which must accrue to organized labour as a whole if the miners, aided by their fellow workers, should succeed in their battle against the owners. With that access of strength, labour's acceptance of the whole burden of Britain's post-war crisis would have been in the gravest jeopardy. *That* is what the Government was preparing against.

Labour did not prepare.

At the Annual Conference of the T.U.C. in September 1925, the mood of the delegates, the speeches from the platform, and the tone of the resolutions, had been distinctly militant. In a presidential address notable for its left-wing sentiments, A. B. Swales had insisted that 'a militant and progressive policy, consistently and steadily pursued, is the only policy that will unify, consolidate, and inspire our rank and file' and he had asked that the General Council be given 'full powers to create the necessary

[1] For a detailed analysis of the Government's plans, see ibid, pp. 303-10.

126

machinery to combat every movement by our opponents'.[1] The following day, a resolution was actually moved from the floor to confer on the General Council powers to levy all affiliated members, to order its members to strike and to arrange with the Co-operative societies for the distribution of food, etc., in the event of a strike.[2]

This motion, supported by A. J. Cook for the miners, was strongly opposed by J. H. Thomas, J. R. Clynes and Ernest Bevin, the first two on the ground that the General Council had already as much power as was tolerable to its affiliated members, Bevin on the ground that such a decision ought not to be rushed.[3] The motion was not put to a vote. Those who opposed it merely asked that it should be referred to the General Council for further consideration, and so it was.[4] This decision set the pattern for all that followed. Negotiations for setting up a new Industrial Alliance hung fire throughout the following months, and were ultimately abortive. An attempt to enlist the help of the Co-operative movement was equally unsuccessful. On the 1st of May, three days before the General Strike was due to start, Bevin himself complained that no preparations had been considered until the 27th of April, when an Advisory Committee, of which he was a member, was set up for the purpose.[5]

All the same, it would be quite erroneous to think that the outcome of the General Strike was determined, or even substantially affected, by the General Council's lack of power, or by its failure to prepare. When it came to the point, the General Council had all the power it needed, and the lack of preparations was amply made up by the initiative and enthusiasm of the rank and file. The failure to prepare is only important as a sign of the leaders' hesitation to face the Government's challenge. They did not prepare precisely because they knew of the Government's own preparations. At the inquest which was held on the General Strike in January 1927, Walter Citrine and J. H. Thomas put the point very clearly. 'It was known,' Citrine said, 'that preparations had been made so elaborately by the Government as to make the possibilities of success much less than in 1925.'[6] As to Thomas, he argued that it was impossible to prepare 'deliberately and calculatedly' for a General Strike. 'You know perfectly well,' he told the Conference of Union Executives, 'that two things would follow.

[1] T.U.C. Annual Conference Report, 1925, pp. 67-8.
[2] ibid, p. 380.
[3] ibid, pp. 384-9.
[4] ibid, p. 395.
[5] T.U.C. General Council, *The Mining Crisis and the National Strike, 1926* (London, 1927) p. 138.
[6] ibid, p. 171.

First you could not get into any negotiations that would be likely to bring peace; and secondly, the other side would anticipate every move. You cannot, in these matters, assume that the other people are taking no notice. They were entitled to take notice.'[1] It was not a frame of mind to induce much energetic action.

Nor was a lead to be expected from the political side of the Labour movement. The Labour Party Conference of October 1925 was a much more sedate affair than the T.U.C. Conference, with the leaders well in the saddle, and much more determined to guard their followers from Communist contamination than to warn them of the dangers to come.

At that Conference, the ineligibility of members of the Communist Party to membership of the Labour Party was reaffirmed by 2,870,000 votes to 321,000[2] and an appeal to affiliated trade unions not to send Communists as delegates to Labour Party Conferences was endorsed by 2,692,000 votes to 480,000.[3]

The Government too was concerned with the Communists. At the Conservative Party Conference in the beginning of October 1925, Baldwin had announced to delegates much incensed by the Government's capitulation the previous July, that proceedings were being considered against the leaders of the Communist Party. Soon after, twelve leading members of the Party were arrested and charged with sedition under the Incitement to Mutiny Act of 1797. This time, though J. R. Campbell was one of the accused, there was no Campbell case. The accused were tried at the Old Bailey. Seven of them were sentenced to six months' imprisonment, five to a year. There was much indignant protest in the Labour movement, but the Communist leaders remained locked up, conveniently from the Government's point of view.

The Samuel Commission's Report was issued on the 10th of March, 1926. The Report made a number of proposals for the future reorganization of the industry. But, as Mr Symons notes, 'all of the points favourable to the miners were distantly beneficial . . . . the suggestions unfavourable to them were to be put into effect immediately'.[4] The Commissioners were strongly opposed to the continuation of the subsidy beyond its authorized term (30th of April). They recognized that 'any material fall in wages will . . . on the facts presented elsewhere in this Report, bring real wages at the present cost of living below pre-war level, for a large propor-

[1] *The Mining Crisis,* op. cit. p. 154.
[2] Labour Party Annual Conference Report, 1925, p. 181.
[3] ibid, p. 189.
[4] Symons, op. cit. p. 34.

tion of the miners'. This, however, did not prevent the Commissioners from recommending that the miners' wages *should* be cut, though not by as much as the mine owners proposed. They also agreed that the coalowners' proposals for the introduction of longer working hours would be undesirable. But they suggested that the miners might be given the choice between greater wage cuts without a change in working hours, or less severe reductions with some increase in working hours. Should the miners prefer the latter, the Commissioners said, 'Parliament would no doubt be prepared to authorize it'.

At a joint meeting with the members of the T.U.C. Special Industrial Committee[1] on the 12th of February, the miners' leaders had restated their fundamental opposition to wage reductions, the lengthening of hours, and any interference with the principle of national wage agreements. As a result of another such joint meeting on the 26th of February, the Industrial Committee had approved the issue of a circular to all affiliated unions which stated that 'while it would be premature at the present stage to attempt to formulate any detailed policy which may have to be pursued, the Committee has already affirmed the attitude of the Trade Union movement as expressed in July last, namely, that it would stand firmly and unitedly against any attempt to degrade further the standard of life in the coalfields'. There was to be no reduction in wages, no increase in working hours, and no interference with the principle of National Agreements. 'This,' the statement concluded, 'is the position of the Trade Union Movement today.'[2]

Though the Samuel Commission did recommend wage reductions and left open the possibility of longer working hours, the T.U.C.'s firm commitment did not long survive the publication of the Report. 'It was at once recognized,' the General Council later said, 'that this must greatly influence the whole situation.'[3] What this meant was made clear on the 8th of April. Pressed by the miners' leaders for a reaffirmation of its previous pledges, the Industrial Committee now merely reaffirmed 'its previous declaration in support of the miners' efforts to obtain an *equitable settlement* of outstanding

---

[1] This Committee had been set up in July 1925 to co-ordinate the other unions' activities with those of the miners' leaders. The Committee was reappointed in September 1925, with J. H. Thomas as one of its members.
[2] *The Mining Crisis,* op cit. p. 61.
[3] ibid, p. 61. Ramsay MacDonald, for his part, thought the Report 'a conspicuous landmark in the history of political thought' (J. G. Murray, *The General Strike of 1926* (London, 1951) p. 70). In contrast, a National Conference of Action, organized by the National Minority Movement, met on the 12th of March and urged the creation by the T.U.C. of a National Congress of Action and of Councils of Action by Trades Councils.

difficulties'. It also said that negotiations between the coalowners and the Miners' Federation 'should be continued without delay in order to obtain a clear understanding with regard to the Report of the Royal Commission, and to reduce points of difference to the smallest possible dimensions'. And it also expressed its willingness 'to assist in any way possible to reach a settlement'.[1]

The Committee had in fact decided, despite its earlier pledges, that there *was* room for negotiations on wages and hours, and Herbert Smith, the Miners' President, was told on the same evening that the Industrial Committee would not be committed to the miners' three points.[2] So as to leave no doubt on the matter, the Committee placed on record in a letter to the Miners' Executive that 'the Committee fully realize the seriousness of the present position but they are of the opinion that matters have not yet reached the stage when any final declaration of the General Council can be made'.[3]

On the following day, however, a Miners' delegate conference again said that it stood by the three points[4] and thus 'bound its officials', as the General Council's Report aggrievedly noted later, 'to refuse any consideration of the possibility of revisions of wages and working conditions'.[5]

The coalowners had none of the hesitations of the General Council. They made it repeatedly clear that they would be satisfied with nothing less than wage reductions. On the 13th of April, after a meeting with the miners' leaders which ended in deadlock, they gave notice that they would no longer conduct wage negotiations on a national basis, but try to reach agreement with individual miners' districts associations, which meant in fact that they would not negotiate at all. Such intransigence drew a protest from the Industrial Committee and a reiteration of its previous declaration 'to render the miners the fullest support in resisting a degradation of the standard of life and to obtain an equitable settlement of their case with regard to wages, hours and national agreements'.[6]

Undeterred, the owners gave notice on the 18th of April, without stating new terms of agreement, that the current agreement would end on the 30th. In contrast, J. H. Thomas was saying on the 19th that 'to talk at this stage as if in a few days all the workers of the country were to be called out was not only letting loose passions that might be difficult to control, but it was not rendering the best service either to the miners or anyone·else . . . instead of organizing,

[1] Crook, op. cit. p. 331. My italics.
[2] *The Mining Crisis,* op. cit. p. 152.
[3] ibid, p. 62.
[4] ibid, p. 62.
[5] ibid, p. 62.
[6] ibid, p. 63.

mobilizing, and encouraging the feeling that war was inevitable, let them concentrate on finding a solution honourable and satisfactory to all sides'.[1]

On the 20th of April, the owners further said that there was not 'the slightest foundation for the rumours that the coalowners had decided, or are prepared, to agree to the principle of a national minimum wage'.[2] As the Miners' Federation said later, 'from first to last there was never any possibility of the forces arrayed against the miners accepting anything but lower wages, longer hours and district agreements—*Unless compelled to do so by the united strength of the working class . . . this from the spring right on through the struggle the General Council failed to see*'.[3] 'Feared to see' would be more accurate.

There would be no point in detailing here the frantic and abortive efforts which the Negotiating Committee made in the following days to avert a final breakdown of negotiations.[4] Faced with the mineowners' intransigence, the Committee naïvely appealed, again and again, to the Prime Minister to help them find a compromise, almost any compromise. The spirit of these negotiations is sufficiently illustrated by J. H. Thomas's description to the Conference of Executive Committees of all Trade Unions on the 30th of April, of a meeting the Committee had had that day with Baldwin and other members of the Government. 'My friends,' said Thomas, 'when the verbatim reports are written I suppose my usual critics will say that Thomas was almost grovelling, and it is true. In all my long experience—and I have conducted many negotiations—I have never begged and pleaded like I begged and pleaded all day today, and I pleaded not alone because I believed in the case of the miners, but because I believed in my bones that my duty to the country involved it.'[5] And he added : 'Don't lose your heads. We have striven, we have pleaded, we have begged for peace because we want peace. We still want peace. The nation wants peace. Those who want war must take the responsibility.'[6]

On the same night of April 30th, the Industrial Committee learnt that the King had signed the Proclamation of a State of Emergency under the Emergency Powers Act of 1920, that recruiting posters

[1] Crook, op. cit. p. 337.
[2] ibid, p. 339.
[3] *The Mining Crisis*, op. cit. p. 127. My italics.
[4] See Crook, op. cit. ch. X.
[5] *The Mining Crisis*, op cit. p. 31.
[6] ibid, p. 32. For another, equally revealing account by Thomas of the negotiations, see his speech in the House of Commons on the 3rd of May, below, p. 134.

for O.M.S. were on the printing presses and that local authorities had been instructed to put into operation, so soon as the Emergency Proclamation was issued, the measures previously outlined in Government circulars. Troops, it was officially announced, had been moved to South Wales, Lancashire and Scotland, and arrangements had been made for assistance from the Navy.

Next morning, 1st of May, the General Secretaries of the Unions were asked to vote whether they would place their powers in the hands of the General Council, and whether they approved the proposal that a National Strike should begin at midnight on Monday, the 3rd of May. The voting was 3,653,527 in favour, 49,911 against.[1] On the other hand, the General Council recommended that the Strike should initially apply to a certain number of industries and services only, namely transport, iron and steel, metal and heavy chemicals, the printing trades, and the building trades. Sanitary services were to be continued, as well as food and health services, and Bevin, on behalf of the General Council, offered help in the distribution of foodstuffs. It was also recommended that the supply of power should cease, but there was some hesitation as to how extensive the stoppage should be.[2]

Addressing the delegates, Ernest Bevin emphasized yet again that 'neither the Miners nor we have any quarrel with the people (Cheers). We are not declaring war on the people. War has been declared by the Government, pushed on by sordid capitalism . .' 'I rely,' he concluded 'in the name of the General Council, on every man and woman . . . to fight for the soul of Labour and the salvation of the miners.'[3]

It was Ramsay MacDonald who made the last speech of the day. He too emphasized the responsibility of the Government for the struggle that was about to begin. The unions, he promised, would be supported in the House of Commons. 'We will stand our corner, don't you make any mistake about it. We will perhaps not be dancing about, but we will be by the miners' side, because it is a just side, an honourable side.' But he also indicated that he still hoped for a settlement that would avert the strike. 'I hope, I still hope, I believe, I must believe,' he concluded, 'that something will happen . . . which will enable us to go about our work cheerily and heartily and hopefully during the next week. If not, we are there in the battle with you, taking our share uncomplainingly until the end has come and until right and justice have been done.'[4]

[1] *The Mining Crisis,* op. cit. p. 33.
[2] Crook, op. cit. pp. 413, 599-601.
[3] *The Mining Crisis,* op. cit. p. 35.
[4] ibid, pp. 38-40.

2. the fear of success

The first use to which the General Council put the quasi-unanimous mandate it had received was to reopen negotiations with the Government. On the same evening of the 1st of May, the Negotiating Committee was again in conference with Ministers, and trying to find a 'formula'. The miners' leaders, believing that the final decision had been taken that morning, had by then dispersed. Two tentative formulas were in fact produced. The first, proposed by Baldwin, expressed confidence 'that a settlement can be reached on the lines of the Report within a fortnight', including presumably cuts in the miners' wages. The second formula, elaborated by Lord Birkenhead the following day, made the point explicitly. 'We, the T.U.C.,' it read, 'would urge the miners to authorize us to enter upon discussions with the understanding that they and we accept the Report as a basis of settlement and we approach it with the knowledge that it may involve some reduction in wages.'[1]

The miners' leaders, recalled to London, met the Negotiating Committee later on Sunday evening, 2nd of May. It is certainly possible that, given the chance, the Negotiating Committee would have abandoned the miners that evening and called off the strike there and then.

But they were not given the chance. It was the Government which made an immediate surrender impossible: the would-be negotiators, while they were putting extreme pressure on the miners' leaders, were suddenly asked to see Baldwin who handed them a letter, expressed his regrets and left. The letter contained a demand that the General Council repudiate the 'overt acts (which) have already taken place, including gross interference with the freedom of the press'[2] and that they issue 'an immediate and unconditional withdrawal of the instructions for a General Strike'.[3] After further discussion, the General Council again sent its negotiators to the Prime Minister to repudiate responsibility for the *Daily Mail* incident. They found that the Prime Minister had gone to bed. Those in the Cabinet, like Churchill and Chamberlain, who had long felt that the time for action had arrived, had won the day. Their struggle, it is fair to say, had only been moderately arduous.

With unerring precision, the Government and its supporters concentrated from the start on the one issue which was, above all others, certain to unnerve the Labour leaders: the issue of revolu-

[1] *The Mining Crisis,* op. cit. p. 160.
[2] The machine-men of the *Daily Mail* had refused to print a particularly provocative editorial on the Strike entitled 'For King and Country'.
[3] *The Mining Crisis,* op. cit. p. 67.

tion and unconstitutionality. Concentration on that issue had another immense advantage—it made it unnecessary to discuss the miners' case at all.

On the 3rd of May, a few hours before the strike was due to begin, the Prime Minister, after giving his own account of the negotiations that had taken place, told the House that the Government 'found itself challenged with an alternative Government'; the General Strike was 'threatening the basis of ordered government, and going nearer to proclaiming civil war than we have been for centuries past'; the leaders of the strike had 'created a machine which they cannot control'; there had been signs of economic improvement, yet 'this is the moment which has been chosen to challenge the existing Constitution of the country and to substitute the reign of force for that which now exists'. It was only two years ago, the Prime Minister recalled, that Ramsay MacDonald, writing in the *New Leader,* had reaffirmed his opposition to the sympathetic strike as of no practical value and as only capable of a 'bitter and blinding reaction'. 'I agree with every word of that,' said Mr Baldwin. 'It is not wages that are imperilled; it is the freedom of our very Constitution.'[1] Other Government speakers insistently made the same claim.

Speaking for the Opposition, J. H. Thomas hotly denied that the Constitution was being challenged and recounted how desperate had been the efforts of the General Council to reach a compromise. 'For ten days,' he recalled, 'we said to the Government "You force the coalowners to give us some terms never mind what they are, however bad they are. Let us have something to go upon". They said, "No, it cannot be done".' 'I know the Government's position,' Thomas also said, 'I have never disguised that in a challenge to the Constitution, God help us unless the Government won. That is my view. But this is not only not a revolution. It is not something that says "We want to overthrow everything". It is merely a plain, economic industrial dispute, where the workers say "We want justice".' 'It will be with no light heart,' he concluded, 'that this fight will be entered into. Because I feel in my bones that a last effort ought to be made, I still plead. The die may be cast. The fight may come . . . Do not let us have bitterness, whatever the immediate future may bring."[2]

For his part, MacDonald defended the miners in detail against accusations of obduracy, blamed the Government for its own unwillingness to intervene earlier and more forcefully, and assured the House that 'with the discussion of general strikes and Bolshevism

[1] H. of C. vol. 195, cols. 67-73, 3rd of May, 1926.
[2] ibid, cols. 73-82, 3rd of May.

and all that kind of thing, I have nothing to do at all. I respect the Constitution as much as the right hon. Gentleman the Member for Hillhead.'[1]

Quite naturally, the Government found much in the Labour leaders' attitude to encourage it in its resolve. Reporting the House of Commons debate to the King on the 4th of May, Baldwin wrote that 'the House of Commons rose to its greatest heights yesterday ... So far from there being any disturbance, the atmosphere throughout the debate was grave, solemn and impressive ... The leaders of the Labour Party were sincerely anxious of finding an honourable way out of the position into which they had been led by their own folly.'[2]

So anxious in fact that they had, even on the 3rd of May, continued their efforts to avert the Strike. Indeed, the General Council, in the face of the miners' opposition, had, on that day, agreed to a new 'formula', which implied an acceptance of a reduction in wages. And the Council had accepted that formula with the argument, put forward by Ernest Bevin, that the miners had handed over their powers and must accept the General Council's ruling as final.[3] Little could the miners have expected that the first use the General Council would seek to make of these powers was to accept a settlement which meant their defeat. But the negotiations again failed. The Government no longer wanted formulas: it wanted surrender. There was now no means, on Labour's side, of avoiding the Strike. The leaders might well argue—and did, later—that they were entitled to go to the most extreme lengths in seeking some way of averting a conflict they did not want. But it might be thought that, having been forced into conflict by what they loudly proclaimed to be the obstinacy of the coalowners and the Government, they would now strain every nerve to fight, in Ernest Bevin's words, 'for the soul of Labour and the salvation of the miners'. But this was not the mood in which they entered the conflict. The mood in which they entered it was best expressed by MacDonald, a few hours before the strike began: 'As far as we can see we shall go on. I don't like General Strikes. I haven't changed my opinion. I have

[1] H. of C. vol. 195, cols. 104-16. The Member for Hillhead was Sir Robert Horne, a former Chancellor of the Exchequer, who had said earlier that the constitutional life of the country could not be carried on if 'the extraordinarily powerful machine' which the Trades Unions had created 'is allowed to usurp the place of government and to dictate to the people'. He also believed that the call for a General Strike would 'inevitably lead to the erection of some Soviet of trade unions on which, whether under Parliamentary forms or without them, the really effective control of the economic and political life of the country' would rest. (ibid, col. 103.)

[2] Nicolson, op. cit. p. 417.

[3] Bullock, op. cit. p. 314.

135

said so in the House of Commons. I don't like it; honestly I don't like it; but, honestly, what can be done?"[1]

Anyone in the least inclined to question the political intelligence of Britain's governing class should study very carefully the handling of the General Strike by the Government: it is a classic example of that remarkable skill, no less real for being partially instinctive, which has always made the Tory Party, as the chief representative of that governing class, the most successful of all British political parties.

Under the Emergency Regulations, the Government had extremely wide discretionary powers. These were widely used. The notion that the police spent most of its time during the General Strike playing football with the strikers may be a pleasing one; but it lacks accuracy. Large numbers of arrests were made during the Strike, often on the flimsiest of pretexts, and sentences to short terms of imprisonment were freely handed down by magistrates little disposed to sympathy with those brought before them. There were numerous instances of baton charges by mounted and foot police against strike pickets and gatherings of strikers; and there was also a fair amount of licensed brutality on the part of volunteer special constables. The military too were extensively used for a variety of purposes, not least to intimidate strike pickets and protect strikebreakers, often with the help of armoured cars; in the London docks, an American observer noted, with 'enough artillery to kill every living thing in every street in the neighbourhood of the mills'.[3] On the 7th of May, it was officially announced that any action which the Armed Forces of the Crown might find it necessary to take 'in an honest endeavour to aid the Civil Power' would receive 'both now and afterwards, the full support of His Majesty's Government'.[3]

There were some members of the Government, like Winston Churchill, who, having done their best to make the Strike inevitable, were not only determined to treat it as a revolutionary challenge to constitutional Government (all members of the Government viewed it as such, or said they did), but also to act upon that view, and to give the conflict an even sharper, and more violent, character, be the consequences what they might. Hence the increasingly military terminology of the *British Gazette*,[4] the emergency Government

[1] Arnot, *The Miners: Years of Struggle*, op. cit. p. 430.
[2] Crook, op. cit. p. 419.
[3] R. Page Arnot, *The General Strike* (London, 1926) p. 189.
[4] 'Troops,' it said for instance on the 10th of May, 'had descended on their objective before the enemy had time to realize that they were there.' This to describe the descent of troops and armoured cars on the London docks where, the *Gazette* also said, 'curiously enough there were few expressions

136

bulletin edited by Churchill, the suppression of the appeal for the reopening of negotiations drawn up by Church leaders on the 7th of May, and the warning contained in its 'Official Communiqué', also of the 7th of May, and published on the 8th, that 'an organized attempt is being made to starve the people and to wreck the State' and that 'the legal and constitutional aspects are entering upon a new phase',[1] a sentence which was taken by the General Council to mean, until it was repudiated by Baldwin, that the Government was coming to view the emergency in terms of civil war.

By the week-end, there were rumours that the members of the General Council might be arrested. And preparations were also made to issue an Order in Council for the purpose of prohibiting banks from paying out any money which, in the opinion of a Minister, was to be applied 'for any purpose prejudicial to the public safety or the life of the Community'.[2]

Had men like Churchill and Chamberlain[3] been in control of affairs, they might well, despite the peaceful intentions of the General Council, have forced the conflict into violent channels. But they were not in control: they only represented one of the two permanent facets of Tory strategy—the hard one. Baldwin represented the other. He too was determined upon complete victory, but he also understood that ruthlessness would only stiffen the strikers' resolve and cut off the Labour leaders' avenues of retreat. Also, ruthlessness would alienate a large body of opinion hovering between fear of Labour and dislike of the Government and the coalowners.[4] What was required was to blend a certain amount of force with every appearance of reasonableness and moderation.

This is why word was privately conveyed to the General Council that Winston Churchill's 'Official Communiqué' was unauthorized and did not represent the Prime Minister's views.[5] It is also why Baldwin, though insisting that constitutional government was being attacked and that the General Strike was a 'challenge to Parliament',

of hostility from the crowd and no open demonstration against the soldiers'. (*British Gazette*, 10th of May, 1926.)

[1] Crook, op. cit. p. 415.

[2] Arnot, op. cit. p. 213. According to Harold Nicolson, the King sought to dissuade Baldwin from such a step, on the ground that 'anything done to touch the pockets of those who are now only existing on strike pay might cause exasperation and serious reprisals on the part of the sufferers'. (Nicolson, op. cit. p. 419.) The Order was not promulgated.

[3] The latter confided in his diary at the beginning of the Strike that 'the best and kindest thing now is to strike quickly and hard'. (Feiling, op. cit. p. 158.)

[4] For an assessment of public opinion during the Strike, see K. Martin, *The British Public and the General Strike* (London, 1926).

[5] Crook, op. cit. p. 420.

and 'the road to anarchy and ruin', also continued throughout to express his desire for peace—on his own terms.

Thus, in his broadcast to the nation on the 8th of May, the Prime Minister stressed that 'the General Strike must be called off absolutely and without reserve'; but he also emphasized that 'a solution', by which he meant the acceptance of the Samuel Report, 'is within the grasp of the nation the instant that the Trade Union leaders are willing to abandon the General Strike'. 'I am a man of peace,' Baldwin concluded, 'I am longing and working and praying for peace, but I will not surrender the safety and the security of the British Constitution. You placed me in power 18 months ago by the largest majority accorded to any Party for many years. Have I done anything to forfeit that confidence? Can you not trust me to ensure a square deal, to secure even justice between man and man?'[1] The answer to this last question, at any rate, was soon provided by the manner of the Strike's settlement. But the tone of the broadcast was much more persuasive than Churchill's tanks.

In the battle for public opinion, the Government could also rely on a powerful chorus of Establishmentarians, distinguished and less distinguished, who lent whatever authority they enjoyed to the condemnation of the Strike as unconstitutional.[2] One of the most notable interventions was that of Sir John Simon, one of the Liberal leaders, an eminent advocate, a former Attorney-General and Home Secretary, who told the House of Commons on Thursday, 6th of May, that the General Strike was 'illegal', that every striker in breach of contract was personally liable to be sued in the County Courts for

[1] *British Gazette,* 10th of May, 7926, p. 1.
[2] 'The issue now is not what the wages of miners should be,' said Lord Grey in the *British Gazette,* 'but whether democratic Parliamentary Government is to be overthrown . . . the alternatives are Fascism or Communism.' And Earl Asquith: 'We should have lost all sense of self-respect if we were to allow any section of the community, at its own will and for whatever motives to bring to a standstill the industrial and social life of the whole nation. It would be to acquiesce in the substitution for free Government of a dictatorship.' (Arnot, op. cit. pp. 197-8.) Lord Balfour, for his part, believed that the General Strike was not a strike 'in the proper sense of the term'; it was 'an attempted revolution'. (*British Gazette,* 10th of May, 1926, p. 1). At High Mass in Westminster Cathedral on Sunday, 9th of May, Cardinal Bourne declared that the Strike was a 'sin against the obedience which we owe to God' and that 'all are bound to uphold and assist the Government, which is the lawfully constituted authority of the country, and represents therefore in its own appointed sphere the authority of God Himself'. (Arnot, op. cit. p. 203.)
It is of some minor interest that Mrs Philip Snowden, speaking on the first day of the Strike to the annual conference of the National Federation of Christian Workers among Poor Children, should have said, *inter alia*: 'We must stand quietly behind the Government—any Government, for it would have been the same if a Labour Party had been in power—in all

damages, and that every trade union leader who had advised strike action was 'liable in damages to the uttermost farthing of his personal possessions'.[1]

On the 11th of May, the notion of the illegality of the Strike was given another airing by Mr Justice Astbury, who delivered himself of an *obiter dictum* in the Chancery Division, to the effect that 'the so-called General Strike called by the Trades Union Congress is illegal and contrary to law, and those persons taking part in it are not protected by the Trades Disputes Act of 1906'. Thus fortified, Sir John repeated on the same day that the Strike was illegal and told the House of Commons that 'the proclaiming of this General Strike was a tragic blunder'. 'It is not,' he generously granted, 'that the people who did it were a set of revolutionaries who wanted to break the country to pieces. It is that it has been done under some, I think, confused, but at any rate quite mistaken impression, that this was a lawful exercise of the rights of organized labour. It is nothing of the sort . . .'[2]

As for the B.B.C., it proved, though not yet a public corporation, co-operative with the Government. Its General Manager, John Reith, had successfully resisted Churchill's wish that it should be 'commandeered'. But, as Reith wrote to Baldwin, 'assuming the B.B.C. is for the people and that the Government is for the people, it follows that the B.B.C. must be for the Government in this crisis too'.[3]

To all insistent assertions that it was leading an unconstitutional, illegal and subversive movement, the General Council opposed the no less insistent assurance that the Strike was a purely industrial, limited and respectable affair. The following statement in the

it does to maintain law and order'. (ibid, p. 170.) This curious attitude of the wife of a prominent Labour politician had, in 1958, its equally curious counterpart in Countess Attlee's presence at a Woman of the Year lunch in honour of Mrs. Nancy Waymark, 'the London bus clippie who refused to strike'. 'Grannie Waymark didn't know,' according to the *Daily Mail*, 'that women in high places were watching her during those seven weeks when she reported for duty despite the taunts and jeers of her workmates. She knew yesterday when those same women crowded round to shake her hand and say: "We admire your courage" . . . She knew when she was greeted by Countess Attlee.' (*Daily Mail*, 3rd of October, 1958 in P. Fryer, *The Battle for Socialism* (London, 1959) p. 104.)
[1] H. of C. vol. 195, cols. 584-5, 6th of May. Simon's view was challenged in House on the 10th of May by Sir Henry Slesser, Solicitor-General in the 1924 Labour Government (see H. of C. vol. 195, cols. 787 ff.)
[2] ibid, col. 868, 11th of May.
[3] J. C. W. Reith, *Into the Wind* (London, 1949) p. 108. The two most notable examples of the B.B.C.'s partiality were the refusal to let the Archbishop of Canterbury broadcast the appeal of the Church leaders for negotiations; and the refusal to let Ramsay MacDonald give a broadcast. (ibid, pp. 111-12.)

British Worker, which appeared on the 9th of May, in reply to Baldwin's broadcast of the previous night, is a good example of the General Council's pronouncements: 'The workers,' the statement said, 'must not be misled by Mr Baldwin's renewed attempt last night to represent the present strike as a political issue. The trade unions are fighting for one thing, and one thing only—to protect the miners' standard of life. The General Council never broke off negotiations. This was done by the Cabinet upon an isolated and unauthorized incident at a most promising stage of the discussion. The General Council is prepared at any moment to resume those negotiations where they left off . . . The General Council has never closed any door that might be kept open for negotiation. It has done nothing to imperil the food supplies; on the contrary, its members were instructed to co-operate with the Government in maintaining them. No notice has been taken of this offer. The Prime Minister pleads for peace, but insists that the General Council is challenging the Constitution. That is untrue. The General Council does not challenge one rule, law, or custom of the Constitution; it asks only that the miners be safeguarded . . .'[1]

All this was very true. But just as the Government's insistence that the General Strike was a revolutionary movement carried very little conviction, so, at the other end of the spectrum, did the General Council's attempt to reduce it to the level of an almost routine industrial dispute. By its very nature, and whatever the General Council might say or do, the Strike immediately turned into an unprecedented demonstration of the strength of labour, of its cohesion, of its sense of solidarity.[2]

Organized Labour's response to the call to strike in support of the miners had been unhesitating and well-nigh unanimous, nor did it waver throughout the nine days. Furthermore, opportunities suddenly offered for the release of vast resources of working-class initiative in the organization of a multitude of activities connected with the Strike.[3] Most of these activities, such as the organization

[1] Arnot, op. cit. p. 202.

[2] The Strike was also the occasion of a remarkable demonstration of international labour solidarity. Offers of help and actual donations came from trade union and labour organizations throughout the world, including donations from the All India Trade Union Congress. The All Russia Trade Union Council notified the General Council that it wished to contribute two million roubles, an offer that was hastily rejected. The International Transport and Mining Federations also resolved to prevent the export of coal to Britain and the bunkering of ships.

[3] For a documented account of these activities, see E. Burns, *The General Strike, May, 1926: Trades Councils in Action* (London, 1926), particularly the Reports from Trades Councils in reply to the Questionnaire sent out by the Labour Research Department after the Strike, pp. 99-191.

of pickets, meetings, publicity and information, the issuance of permits, entertainment, socials and sports, the relief of distress, and aid to 'class war prisoners', were undertaken by local Trades Councils. 'For all practical purposes,' Mr Burns notes, 'the Councils were organizations suddenly asked to take on a new and urgent task, without any but the vaguest suggestion of how they should carry it out . . . with very few exceptions indeed the Councils displayed energy and initiative to an extent that astonished all who had known them in the preceding period. Councils which had never had any real existence, Councils which were considered moribund, as well as normally active Councils—all seemed to get a sudden inspiration, developed new forms of organization and activity, drew in numbers of new helpers and for the first time in their history—at any rate in their recent history—became the real expression of the local movement.'[1]

All this was scarcely compatible with the claim that the Strike was a pure industrial dispute. In some areas, Strike Committees were practically sharing control with the authorities in the running of towns and cities.[2] But, though some local committees were more militant than others, the General Council's appeals for good order and discipline were remarkably successful. The following comments from the Dartford Labour Party, written after the end of the Strike, would, on the evidence, seem capable of general application and are worth extensive quotation. 'The men,' it said, 'were not actuated by any revolutionary feelings. They felt they were fighting the Government to get a fair deal for the miners upon the basis of no reduction in wages and no increase in hours. On that issue the men were solid and their enthusiasm was white-heat. But on the revolutionary issue they were cold. (The English are not imaginative enough to produce revolutions.) After the third day of the Strike, if you spoke about the coalowners the audience would listen with polite indifference, but if you attacked the Government, or even mentioned the word, you had the audience with you and that with cheers and wild enthusiasm. The issue was the T.U.C. and the Government; the miners and the owners were secondary to this issue . . . The instructions of the T.U.C. were accepted without question and the faith and confidence of the men in that body was a religion. I should have said the men came out solidly here and they remained so until the end . . .'[3]

The General Council could not in fact have been more faithfully obeyed by the strikers. This it acknowledged in a Message to Trade

[1] Burns, op. cit. p. 111.
[2] See Symons, op. cit. pp. 124 ff.
[3] Burns, op. cit. p. 120.

Union Members which appeared in *The British Worker* on the 10th of May. 'We are,' said the Message, 'entering upon the second week of the general stoppage in support of the mine workers against the attack upon their standard of life by the coalowners.' 'Nothing,' it went on, 'could be more wonderful than the magnificent response of millions of workers to the call of their leaders. From every town and city in the country reports were pouring into the General Council headquarters stating that all ranks are solid, that the working men and women are resolute in their determination to resist the unjust attack upon the mining community.' The General Council then expressed its 'keen appreciation of the loyalty of the Trade Union members to whom the call was issued and by whom such a splendid response has been made', and it especially commended the workers 'on their strict obedience to the instruction to avoid all conflict and to conduct themselves in an orderly manner'. 'Their behaviour during the first week of the stoppage,' it suggested, 'is a great example to the whole world.' And the message ended with an exhortation to the strikers to 'Stand Firm. Be Loyal to Instructions and Trust your Leaders'.[1] That was on the morning of the 10th of May. On the 12th, the Strike was called off—unconditionally.

Notwithstanding the General Council's Message, negotiations to bring the Strike to an end had been resumed almost as soon as it began. On the 6th of May, Sir Herbert Samuel had made contact with J. H. Thomas, and on the 7th began a series of meetings with the Negotiating Committee of the General Council at the house of Sir Abe Bailey, a South African mining magnate who was a close personal friend of Thomas. Sir Herbert Samuel had made it clear that he was acting without any official mandate. The negotiations took place secretly. As Mr Symons notes, 'the essence of any negotiation was secrecy, for the Labour movement was in no mood to hear talks of a settlement, except upon equal terms'.[2] Indeed, after Ramsay MacDonald had stated on the 7th of May that he was 'exerting all efforts to assure that every minute should be utilized in endeavouring to secure a peaceful solution of the conflict and to reach an agreement', the *British Worker* categorically denied that any negotiations, official or unofficial, were taking place, and reaffirmed that any preliminary discussions for a settlement 'must be free from any condition'.[3] Next day, MacDonald told reporters at the House of Commons that 'he was keeping in continual touch with the Government side and was hourly in conference regarding

[1] Arnot, op. cit. p. 205.
[2] Symons, op. cit. p. 188.
[3] Crook, op. cit. p. 417.

settlement of the strike'. This statement was not allowed to appear in the *British Worker* and the General Council, it was said, even sent a 'stern rebuke' to MacDonald.[1]

But negotiations went on all the same. By the 10th of May. J. H. Thomas was telling a public meeting at Hammersmith that he had never been in favour of the principle of a General Strike and that, whatever the outcome, the condition of the nation would be worse than before it. 'The responsibility,' he concluded, 'is indeed a heavy one. But there will be a graver responsibility on whichever side fails to recognize the moment when an honourable settlement can be arrived at. That moment must be accepted and everyone must work to that end.'[2]

In private negotiations of his own, of which the Government was duly kept informed, Thomas had suggested, without any warrant, that the miners' leaders would now accept the Samuel Report 'unconditionally with all its implications'. The Negotiating Committee of the General Council, with no more authority, had also given Samuel, so he wrote to Baldwin, 'the definite assurance that the miners' attitude had changed . . .'[3]

This was entirely untrue, but it is easy to see why the General Council was so desperately eager that it should be true. Negotiations with Sir Herbert Samuel had yielded yet another 'formula', whose acceptance by the Miners would have made it possible for the General Council to give its surrender as least the appearance of a compromise.

Unfortunately for the General Council, the miners' leaders would not play since the new 'formula' did not exclude the possibility of wage reductions, and repeated meetings with the Negotiating Committee and with Sir Herbert Samuel failed to shift them. On Tuesday night, 11th of May, they were presented with a unanimous decision of the General Council that they must accept the Samuel Memorandum (which the Government itself had not endorsed) and the strike brought to an end so that negotiations could proceed. The Miners' Executive refused. Another meeting with a deputation from the General Council on the following morning was equally unsuccessful. The General Council then 'unanimously adhered to the decision arrived at, that in the circumstances they were not justified in continuing the sacrifice and risks of the sympathetic strike'. At noon, the representatives of the General Council made their way to

[1] Crook, p. 427.
[2] Symons, op. cit. p. 196. The *British Gazette*, Mr. Crook also notes, carried that sentence in heavy black type in each successive issue. (Op. cit. p. 429.)
[3] ibid, p. 200.

Downing Street, and brought Baldwin the Council's unconditional surrender. The Samuel 'formula' was not even mentioned.

The calling off of the General Strike without any guarantee of any kind, either for the miners, or against the victimization of other workers, has often been denounced as a terrible act of betrayal. But the notion of betrayal, though accurate, should not be allowed to reduce the episode to the scale of a Victorian melodrama, with the Labour leaders as the gleeful villains, planning and perpetrating an evil deed. The Labour movement *was* betrayed, but not because the Labour leaders were villains, or cowards. It was betrayed because betrayal was the inherent and inescapable consequence of their whole philosophy of politics—and it would be quite foolish to think that their philosophy was the less firmly held for being unsystematically articulated.

Most of these leaders did not really believe that a General Strike could ever be successful and since they did not believe that they could win, their anxiety to put a stop to the drain on their unions' financial resources grew with every day that passed. Nor did the extraordinary response of their followers to the call to strike diminish their anxiety. For that response not only made surrender more difficult: it also roused different anxieties. 'Every day that the strike proceeded,' Charles Duke, of the Municipal Workers, later said, 'the control and the authority of that dispute was passing out of the hands of responsible Executives into the hands of men who had no authority, no control, no responsibility, and was wrecking the movement from one end to the other'.[1] Mr Duke's words express with limpid clarity the trade union leaders' bureaucratic recoil from a movement which, despite its disciplined character, elicited working class initiative outside the established forms of trade union organization. To a growingly bureaucratic and centralized trade union apparatus, this was, almost by definition, equivalent to 'wrecking the movement from one end to the other'.

Most important of all, however, was the belief, common to both industrial and parliamentary leaders, that a challenge to the Government through the assertion of working class strength outside Parliament was *wrong*. Try though they might to persuade themselves and others that they were engaged in a purely industrial dispute, almost a routine strike, they knew that it was more than that, and it was this which made them feel guilty, uneasy, insecure. In fact, they half shared, indeed more than half shared, the Government's view that the General Strike was a politically and morally reprehensible venture. undemocratic, anti-parliamentary, subversive.

[1] *The Mining Crisis,* op. cit. p. 185.

Yet they had, it will be recalled, contemplated something like a General Strike in 1920, for overtly political purposes, and boasted of the fact that they had, with their threats, coerced the Government into peace with Russia. But, in the eyes of the Labour leaders, as was noted earlier, resistance to war with Russia was devoid of any specific class content. As it did not appear to them to bring into question the relation of labour to property, and to the State as the defender of property, they had therefore felt able to claim that they were the authentic agents of the 'national interest', that they spoke for the 'community'.

The General Strike was a movement of an altogether different kind. It did have an unmistakable social content; it did involve the assertion of specific working class claims against property. And it was the prospect of leading such a movement from which the Labour leaders naturally and inevitably flinched. It was the class character of the General Strike which made them behave as if they half believed they *were* guilty men, and which made them seek, with desperate anxiety, to purge themselves of their guilt. Most of them would of course have wanted a settlement that seemed at least honourable. There wasn't one to be had, save from a position of strength they were terrified to occupy. So they chose unconditional surrender.

But this is not all. There was also their view of the Government. The Labour leaders had often said, before and during the Strike, that the Government was the ally of the coalowners. But they could never bring themselves to believe that the alliance was an organic one, and that the Government, or at least some members of it, particularly Baldwin, would not, indeed could not, act as impartial, reasonable, fair. independent, objective arbitrators.

This is well shown by their tone of surprised indignation at the Government's 'bias' during the negotiations which preceded the Strike, and during the Strike itself. It is even better shown in the pleas addressed to Baldwin by men as different as Thomas and Bevin during that last interview in which the General Council announced that it was calling off the Strike. '. . . Whatever may be the view of the merits of the dispute now ending,' Thomas said, 'there is common agreement that assistance from those who were opposing parties ten minutes ago is essential to rectify and make good and start things on the right road again. Your assistance in that is necessary, our assistance is necessary. We intend to give it and in doing that we believe you can help. We want you to help us in that direction. I never liked the word war and I do not want to use it—but we want your help when this dispute is ended. We trust your word as Prime Minister. We ask you to assist in the way you only can assist us by asking employers and all others to make the position as easy and smooth as possible because the one thing we must not have is guerilla warfare. That must be avoided and in that both sides have to contribute immediately. Nothing could be worse than that this great decision which we have taken should be interpreted otherwise than as a general desire to do the right thing in a difficult moment for the industry of the nation.'[1]

Bevin supported Thomas and asked whether Baldwin was prepared 'to make a general request as head of the Government that facilities, etc., ready facilities for reinstatement, and that kind of thing shall be given forthwith . . . We have have a row and it does upset things, but we are quite willing to co-operate with our men to repair the damage just as much as the employers, but the employers are the people who can facilitate that kind of feeling, and I am sure that they would respond to you if you issued that as a statement.'[2]

These pathetic appeals to Baldwin's goodwill on the part of men who had not dared rely on Labour's own strength indicate how little they appreciated the fact that Baldwin, however much he might himself wish for 'moderation', was not a free, independent and impartial arbiter. He had put little enough pressure on the coalowners before the Strike. It was hardly likely that he would do so, indeed that he could do so, at the moment of Labour's defeat, even though that defeat was self-inflicted. In fact, a Government statement issued on that day specifically said that 'His Majesty's Government have no power to compel employers to take back every man who has been on strike, nor have they entered into any obligation of any kind on this matter'.[3]

On the same day, however, Baldwin did ask employers to 'act with generosity' and said that 'the whole British people should not look backwards but forwards'.[4] The King too asked everyone to 'forget whatever elements of bitterness the events of the past few days may have created'.[5] Such appeals, no doubt sincerely meant, usefully served to preserve the appearance of official reasonableness and good will, but they did not affect the harsh reality which the miners and all other strikers confronted, suddenly left as they were

---

[1] Crook, op. cit. p. 606.
[2] ibid, p. 607.
[3] Symons, op. cit. p. 213.
[4] Arnot, op. cit. p. 220. 'I never felt any bitterness in my heart,' Baldwin also said, 'as I realized that sympathy with the miners which we all share was the dominant motive underlying the action of the Trade Unions' (ibid, p. 220).
[5] ibid, p. 118.

face to face with triumphant employers, determined to exploit the advantage they had been accorded.

'In many cases,' Mr Symons notes, 'strikers were offered re-engagement only on the condition that they tore up their union cards and accepted lower wages. In others an attempt was made to single out and punish ring leaders.'[1] There was, in fact, and particularly on the railways, in transport and in the docks, extensive victimization, erosion of trade union rights, reinstatement on lower wages and worse conditions. And the situation would have been even worse had the strikers not held out against their employers: twenty-four hours after the Strike had been called off, the number of strikers had *increased* by 100,000.

The General Council was very indignant at what was happening and issued somewhat belated threats of further struggle if employers and Government failed to respond to its own show of good will. Baldwin himself was sufficiently alarmed by the attitude of the interests he had so ably defended to state in the House of Commons on the 13th of May that he would not 'countenance any attack on the part of any employers to use this present occasion for trying in any way to get reductions in wages below those in force before the strike commenced, or any increase in hours'.[2] Countenance or not, it happened all the same.

Nor was it only private concerns which sought to take advantage of the situation. 'The Board of Admiralty,' to quote Mr Symons again, 'was proposing that strikers should forfeit from two to four years' service for pension purposes. The Army Victualling Department had denied reinstatement to certain men, and was replacing them by volunteers. The London County Council had reduced the wages of some strikers by putting them on different jobs.'[3]

It was the miners, however, who got the rawest deal of all. On the 12th of May, the General Council had stated that it had 'obtained assurances' ('through the magnificent support and solidarity of the Trade Union Movement') 'that a settlement of the Mining problem can be secured which justifies them in bringing the general stoppage to an end'.[4]

It had in fact received no such assurances. The miners stayed out on strike, until they were finally forced into surrender in November. The Government's attitude during those months provides a useful measure of Stanley Baldwin's understanding of the meaning of a 'square deal' and of 'even justice between man and man'. The coal-

[1] Symons, op. cit. p. 213.
[2] H. of C. vol. 195, col. 1048, 13th of May.
[3] Symons, op. cit. p. 214.
[4] Arnot, op. cit. p. 216.

owners would not negotiate at all, unless the miners first agreed to substantial wage reductions. That was also the position of the Government in regard to any proposal for the reorganization of the industry. Meanwhile, the Seven Hour Act of 1919 was repealed, in order to pave the way for the imposition of wage agreements entailing longer hours. More directly, everything that the Government could do to break the strike was done, including the attribution to the Minister of Health by Act of Parliament of powers to suspend Boards of Guardians who refused the Minister's instructions to stop relief and the supply of free milk for babies and free meals for the children of the destitute.

When the miners finally went back, they had to accept district agreements, longer hours and lower wage rates.[1] At the same time, a vast body of miners remained permanently unemployed. The miners' defeat was overwhelming and unqualified.

3. THE CONSEQUENCES OF DEFEAT

The manner of the General Strike's collapse is immensely important in the history of the Labour movement. The miners' plight, the worsened circumstances of other wage-earners, the vindictive Trade Dispute Act of 1927, the loss of members and of financial resources which the Act entailed for the Labour Party and the trade unions[2]—these were some of the consequences of what happened in May 1926. But as important is the fact that the surrender immeasurably advanced the transformation of the workers' movement into a tame, disciplined trade union and electoral interest.

This is not only to say that never again would the trade unions and the Labour Party seek to exercise political influence against the Government of the day by the use of the industrial weapon. It also means that the trade unions would shun militancy over *industrial* issues. As Mr Bullock notes, while the average number of workers involved in strikes and lock-outs in each of the three years 1919-1921 was 2,108,000, in each of the thirteen years 1927-1939 it was 308,100[3]—and not by any means because Labour lacked major

---

[1] Crook, op. cit. p. 481.
[2] The Labour Party's affiliated membership fell from 3,388,000 in 1926 to 2,077,000 two years later; and between 1927 and 1929, it lost a quarter of its total income from affiliation fees. (Cole, *A History of the Labour Party since 1914*, op. cit. p. 185.) Trade union membership fell from 5.5 million before the Strike to well under 5 million in 1927. 'Not until 1934 was the drop in Trade union membership finally arrested' (Bullock, op. cit. p. 353).
[3] ibid, p. 346.

grievances in those years, or achieved notable successes by the use of its parliamentary strength.

It might have been otherwise if defeat, and defeat of this kind and magnitude, had produced a major challenge to Labour's political and industrial leadership. But it did not.

There was, of course, much bitterness, much recrimination, much discontent with the leadership after the General Strike. But when an inquest was finally held in January 1927, the Report of the General Council, which was sharply critical of the intransigence of the miners' leaders, and which concluded with the statement that 'the Council have no excuses to offer and no apologies to make for the conduct of the strike or for its termination',[1] was endorsed by 2,840,000 votes to 1,095,000.

The trade union leaders had no fundamental reason to regret the collapse of the General Strike, since it dealt so crippling a blow to demands for militancy which they had so long opposed. Now that militancy had so clearly 'failed', they were able to plead with a new plausibility an alternative policy of accommodation with employers.

As early as the Annual Conference of the T.U.C. in September 1927, the Chairman, George Hicks, was urging the establishment of 'effective machinery of joint conference between the representative organizations entitled to speak for industry as a whole', so that they might find out 'upon what terms co-operation is possible in a common endeavour to improve the efficiency of industry and raise the workers' standard of life'.[2]

A powerful group of industrialists, headed by Sir Alfred Mond, was, not very surprisingly, found to be in sympathy with these views, and they invited the General Council to meet and discuss the questions they raised. The General Council accepted the invitation and discussions between representatives of each side were soon begun on a wide range of industrial and economic topics.

The proposals which emerged from these discussions included the setting up of a National Industrial Council composed of the General Council and an equal number of employers nominated by the National Confederation of Employers' Organizations and the Federation of British Industries; one of its functions was to be the creation of conciliation boards to which industrial disputes might be referred in order to avoid strikes and lockouts. The two sides also agreed that they should be jointly consulted by the Government on matters affecting industry, and the employers agreed that trade union mem-

[1] *The Mining Crisis*, op. cit. p. 82.
[2] T.U.C. Annual Conference Report, 1927, pp. 7-8.

bership should be encouraged and that Trade Unions should be recognized as bargaining agencies.

In its Report to the 1928 T.U.C. Conference, the General Council set out the three policies which it considered to be the alternatives before the Trade Union movement. They might say frankly that they would 'do everything possible to bring the industrial machine to a standstill, to ensure by all possible means the breakdown of the entire system, in the hope of creating a revolutionary situation on the assumption that this might be turned to the advantage of the workers and the abolition of Capitalism'. That policy, the Council said, the Trade Union movement 'has decisively rejected as futile, certain to fail, and sure to lead to bloodshed and misery'. They could, secondly, refuse co-operation with employers and remain 'purely sectional bodies'. But such a policy would be 'inconsistent with the modern demand for a completely altered status of the workers in industry' and a confession of failure on the part of the unions themselves. The third course, which the General Council supported, was 'for the Trade Union Movement to say boldly that not only is it concerned with the prosperity of industry, but that it is going to have a voice as to the way industry is carried on, so that it can influence the new developments that are taking place'. 'The ultimate policy of the Movement,' the General Council felt, 'can find more use for an efficient industry than for a derelict one, and the Unions can use their power to promote and guide the scientific reorganization of industry as well as to obtain material advantages from the reorganization.'[1]

There was opposition from the Left to policies which so explicitly entailed the acceptance as permanent of a capitalist order of society, in which the trade unions, in return for the hypothetical good will of employers, would assume the obligations of junior—and docile—partners in capitalist industry.[2] But the 1928 Conference did endorse the General Council's Report and its recommendation that the discussions should be continued was carried by 3,075,000 to 566,000.[3]

In the event, the Mond-Turner[4] discussions came to nothing, but only because the employers' interest soon waned while the onset of acute depression put a somewhat discouraging gloss on the hopes of curing the ills of capitalism by a formal system of collaboration

---

[1] T.U.C. Annual Conference Report, 1928, pp. 209 ff.
[2] See e.g. A. J. Cook's speech (T.U.C. Annual Conference Report, 1928, pp. 434-7). But note also Herbert Smith's speech in support of the General Council (ibid, pp. 437-9).
[3] ibid, p. 452.
[4] Ben Turner was the Chairman of the T.U.C. in 1928.

between trade unions and employers. Yet, though the Mond-Turner discussions failed, the impulses which had led the trade union leaders to enter upon them endured, through the depression, through mass unemployment, through the 1931 crisis. These impulses endured because they were an essential part, in fact *the* essential part, of the image the trade union leaders had of Labour's role, of its prospects and future.

As for the political leaders of Labour, they had even less reason than their industrial colleagues to deplore the collapse of the General Strike, since it appeared to confirm the view they had always pressed upon the Labour movement that in Parliament and in Parliament alone lay the workers' salvation.

Beatrice Webb, who had been profoundly hostile to the General Strike throughout[1] (and who had even doubted whether she should send money to the Relief Fund for the Miners when they stayed out alone),[2] had prophesied on the day it began that it would fail, and that it would lead 'to a rehabilitation of political methods and strengthen J.R.M.'s leadership within the Party'.[3] So it did, with remarkable results.

[1] *Beatrice Webb's Diaries*, op. cit. pp. 89 ff.
[2] ibid, p. 103.
[3] ibid, p. 93.

151

CHAPTER VI

THE PRICE OF RESPECTABILITY

'I wonder how far it is possible, without in any
way abandoning any of our party positions, without in any way surrendering any of our party
principles, to consider ourselves more as a
Council of State and less as arrayed regiments
facing each other in battle.'

Ramsay MacDonald, House of Commons,
2nd of July, 1929

1. 'TENTATIVE, DOCTRINELESS SOCIALISM'

Ever since the fall of the first Labour Government, and indeed
before, the I.L.P., and particularly the I.L.P. left, had devoted much
effort to a threefold task: firstly to formulate policies which would,
in its view, be appropriate to a movement which was theoretically
pledged to the establishment of a socialist society in Britain;
secondly, to persuade the Labour Party to incorporate these policies
in its own programme; and thirdly, to compel the Labour leadership
to *act* upon these policies. The first part of that task presented much
less difficulty than the second and the third.

Of all the Reports produced by I.L.P. Policy Commissions, the
one which attracted most attention and aroused most controversy
was that called *Socialism in Our Time*. The most distinctive features
of that Report were its proposals for a legally guaranteed minimum
wage (the 'living wage') and for a State financed system of Family
Allowances. Linked to this were proposals for the planning of economic life, the public ownership of banks and credit institutions,
and of coal, electricity, transport and the land.[1] The Report was
officially endorsed at the 1926 Annual Conference of the I.L.P.

It was not so much the intrinsic merits or demerits of this and
other Reports which concerned the Labour leadership, and particularly MacDonald. What really concerned them was that the Reports
sought to commit a future Labour Government to far more radical
and specific policies than they thought appropriate. What Mac-
Donald objected to, as he put it in March 1926, was 'the sanctifica-

[1] For a full statement of the I.L.P.'s proposals, see H. N. Brailsford, etc.,
The Living Wage (London, 1926).

152

tion of phrases of no definite meaning . . . like "Socialism in Our Time"' and proposals which were, he said, 'millstones for mere show round the neck of the Movement'.[1]

However, simply to reject the I.L.P.'s proposals was not enough. What was required was a programme which was not a millstone round the neck of the Labour movement, yet which would appeal to restive constituency activists. From the end of December 1925, the leadership had watched with angry concern the activities of the Communist-led National Left Wing Movement, whose aim was proclaimed to be 'not to supersede the Labour Party, but to "remould it nearer to the heart's desire" of the rank and file'. A substantial number of constituency Labour Parties had refused to apply the decisions of the 1925 Conference to exclude Communists from membership and, by 1927, the movement had assumed increasingly organized form, with a committee, chairman and secretary. In August, *The Communist* had claimed, with some justification, 'a very marked growth of the organized left-wing opposition within the British Labour Party . . . which is causing the Right-Wing Labour bureaucracy more and more anxiety and alarm'; in September 1927, when the National Left Wing Movement held its second conference, fifty-four local Labour Parties and many other groups were represented.[2]

There was a minority of Communist leaders, notably R. Palme Dutt and Harry Pollitt, who watched the growth of this movement with much unease. For this minority, the way forward lay, not in strengthening the left within the Labour Party, but in building up the Communist Party as an alternative leadership in total opposition to the Labour Party. There must, on this view, be 'no mediator between the Communist Party and the working class', for a 'growing body of workers', R. P. Dutt wrote in February 1928, were 'looking for a new political leadership', and 'expecting to find that political leadership expressed at the election'.[3]

It was only in 1929 that the Communist Party, on instructions from the Comintern,[4] came under the control of the erstwhile minority and adopted the new line of total opposition to *all* non-Communists in the Labour movement. From then until 1933, the C.P. held to a 'revolutionary' policy which isolated it ever more strictly from the Labour movement and brought it to the nadir of its influence.

---

[1] *Socialist Review*, March 1926.
[2] J. Redman, *The Communist Party and the Labour Left 1925-1929* (1957) pp. 8-10.
[3] ibid, p. 12.
[4] For the switch, and the manner in which the minority was turned into a majority, see Redman, ibid, pp. 19 ff. and Pelling op. cit. pp. 47 ff.

From the point of view of the Labour leaders, nothing could have been more welcome than the C.P.'s new line. In 1926 and in 1927, they had found it necessary to disaffiliate a total of 23 Constituency Labour Parties which had refused to accept the ban on Communists.[1] Even so, between 75 and 80 Local Labour Party Left-Wing groups were represented at the annual Conference of the Left Wing Movement in September 1928.[2] The year after, the Movement was suppressed by the C.P. and its weekly newspaper, the *Sunday Worker*, closed down.

As for the new programme which the Labour leaders felt it necessary to give their troops, it was MacDonald himself who had proposed, at the Annual Conference of the Party in 1927, the preparation of such a document, 'setting forth the broad proposals which have from time to time been approved by the Party Conference, and which would constitute a Programme of Legislation and Administrative Action for a Labour Government'.[3] In the discussion of this proposal, there were pleas for a bold socialist programme, and not one, as Ellen Wilkinson put it, 'set up with the idea of persuading the rather more intelligent section of the middle-class to come in with them'.[4] Ernest Bevin, on the other hand, did not want a programme that 'might be over the heads of the people—something they could not understand'; what they needed was a 'short programme of immediate objectives, a programme that could unite all of them, not merely the most advanced. . . .'[5]

Replying to the debate, Ramsay MacDonald answered the pleas of the Left by assuring the delegates that 'the principle in the background of their programme was Socialism . . . as the completion of what was going on and being worked out on the great stage of the House of Commons and of Parliament in general . . . selecting what this item, that item and the other item should be was the work of a Government that had Socialism constantly before its eyes'.[6]

Save for the not very constricting limitation it had imposed upon itself to embody in the programme 'the broad principles which have from time to time been approved by the Party Conference', the Executive was given a free hand. The result was *Labour and the Nation*, whose main author was R. H. Tawney.

In a foreword to the document, Ramsay MacDonald claimed that the Labour Party, 'unlike other Parties, is not concerned with patching the rents in a bad system, but with transforming Capitalism into

[1] Labour Party Annual Conference Report, 1926, p. 19, and 1927, p. 15.
[2] Redman, op. cit. p. 18.
[3] Labour Party Annual Conference Report, 1927, p. 181.
[4] ibid, p. 183.
[5] ibid, pp. 185-6.
[6] ibid, p. 189.

Socialism'. The Labour Party, he also wrote, 'is essentially one of action, and it asks for power both in order to lay the foundations of a new social order and to relieve immediate distress'.[1]

The authors of *Labour and the Nation* stated with similar emphasis that the Labour Party 'is a Socialist Party'. Its aim, they said, was 'the organization of industry, and the administration of the wealth which industry produces, in the interest, not of the small minority (less than 10 per cent. of the population) who own the greater part of the land, the plant and the equipment without access to which their fellow countrymen can neither work nor live, but of all who bring their contribution of useful service to the common stock'.[2]

But the Labour Party's Socialism, they also said, was not 'a sentimental aspiration for an impossible Utopia, nor a blind movement of revolt against poverty and oppression'. It was 'the practical recognition of the familiar commonplace that "morality is in the nature of things", and that men are all, in very truth, members of one another'. And it was also 'a conscious, systematic and unflagging effort to use the weapons forged in the victorious struggle for political democracy to end the capitalist dictatorship in which democracy finds everywhere its most insidious and relentless foe'.[3]

Even more explicitly than *Labour and the New Social Order* of 1918, *Labour and the Nation* equated socialism with a further extension of State intervention in social and economic affairs. It was State intervention alone, the authors of the document said, which had enabled 'industrial civilization' to survive and expand. This trend, which they called 'tentative, doctrineless socialism', had even, they gleefully observed, invaded the political philosophy and practice of their opponents. 'Even those who reject the policy of public ownership,' *Labour and the Nation* said, 'are emphatic as to the necessity of an increasingly stringent public control being applied to all aspects of industrial organization. So, in spite of themselves, are even false prophets induced by the logic of facts to bear tardy testimony on the side of truth!' 'Amid cries of impending ruin from the more thoughtless members of the privileged classes', that truth had found 'tardy recognition in the care of Public Health and Public Education, in Factory Acts and Mines Regulation Acts and Minimum Wage Acts, in the development of Local Government and the extension of municipal enterprise, in the growth of public expenditure upon social services, and in the provision of the financial resources by which such services may be maintained'. What this suggested was that,

[1] *Labour and the Nation*, p. 3.
[2] ibid, p. 5.
[3] ibid, pp. 5-6.

while Tories and Liberals were only reluctant converts to 'tentative, doctrineless socialism', Labour men had always been its eager apostles. They stood, the document said, 'for the deliberate establishment, by experimental methods, without violence or disturbance, with the fullest utilization of scientific knowledge and administrative skill, of a social order in which the resources of the community shall be organized and administered with a single eye to securing for all its members the largest possible measure of economic welfare and personal freedom'.[1]

With regard to concrete proposals for public ownership and control, *Labour and the Nation* stated that the Labour Party ('which believes in democracy in industry as well as in government') intended that 'the great foundation industries' should be 'owned and administered for the common advantage of the whole community'. 'Without haste, but without rest, with careful preparation, with the use of the best technical knowledge and managerial skill, and with due compensation to the persons affected', the Labour Party would vest in the nation the ownership of land, both agricultural and urban, the production and distribution of coal and power, the network of communications and transport, the system of industrial life insurance.

This left out of account the bulk of private industry, and also the joint stock banks which an earlier Party Conference had pledged a Labour Government to nationalize. With regard to the first, the document was content to promise 'stringent control over monopolies and combines' while the way would also be prepared for the 'progressive extension of public enterprise by investigations into the conduct of industry and methods of improving it. . . .'

As for banking, there was envisaged, in a truly splendid passage, 'such changes in the banking and financial systems as will secure that the available supply of credits and of savings shall be used for enterprises of national advantage as distinct from those that are useless or socially injurious', and there would be 'an inquiry into the best method of achieving this purpose'. Furthermore, the Government would encourage the extension of banking facilities to people with small incomes by the spread of Municipal and Co-operative Banks throughout the country; and the Bank of England would be controlled by a public corporation 'containing representatives of such essential factors in the community as the Treasury, the Board of Trade, Industry, Labour and the Co-operative Movement'.[2]

Perhaps more important than all this, in the light of the second Labour Government's history, were the promises made, if the Labour

[1] *Labour and the Nation*, op. cit. p. 6.
[2] ibid, p. 27.

Party was granted power, to repeal the Trade Unions Act of 1927; to establish the forty-eight-hour week; to raise the scale of unemployed benefits; to repeal the Eight Hours Act in the coal industry; to establish and enforce a minimum wage for agricultural workers; and a great deal else that was similarly attractive.[1]

By the time *Labour and the Nation* was presented to the Annual Conference of the Labour Party in October 1928, the left of the I.L.P. had come out into open opposition, not only to the political leadership of the Labour Party, but to the trade union leadership as well. In June 1928, there had appeared the 'Cook-Maxton Manifesto' which complained that 'in recent times' there had been 'a serious departure from the principles and policy which animated the founders'. 'We are now asked to believe,' the authors of the Manifesto wrote, 'that the party is no longer a working-class party, but a party representing all sections of the community. . . . As a result of the new conception that Socialism and Capitalism should sink their differences, much of the energy which should be expended in fighting Capitalism is now expanded in crushing everybody who dares to remain true to the ideals of the Movement. We are convinced that this change is responsible for destroying the fighting spirit of the party, and we now come out openly to challenge it. We can no longer stand by and see thirty years of devoted work destroyed in making peace with Capitalism and compromises with the philosophy of our Capitalist opponents.'

The 'basic principles' of the Labour movement, which had inspired Hardie and the other pioneers who made the Party, said the Manifesto, were firstly 'an unceasing war against poverty and working class servitude', which meant 'an unceasing war against Capitalism'; and, secondly, that 'only by their own efforts can the workers obtain the fullest product of their labour'.

It was therefore proposed, the Manifesto concluded, to organize a series of meetings and conferences throughout the country to give the rank-and-file the opportunity to state 'whether they accept the new outlook, or whether they wish to remain true to the spirit and the ideals which animated the early pioneers'.[2] A campaign was in fact initiated around the Manifesto. It made little impression.

The publication of *Labour and the Nation* was not likely to pacify the left-wing rebels. What they wanted, as Maxton said, was an immediate and mandatory programme which would 'get right into the problem of getting the ownership and control of the essential industries of this country inside the term of the first Labour Govern-

[1] *Labour and the Nation*, pp. 52-55.
[2] J. McNair, *James Maxton, The Beloved Rebel* (London, 1955) pp. 171-2.

ment'. He had, he told the 1928 Conference, taken his stand with those who had 'worked for political power by constitutional methods'; and, 'to workers who were suffering terribly under the Capitalist system, all I could say was "Wait until Labour gets political power"'. They had waited, and now that Labour was on the verge of political power, 'I insist that we are going to redeem the promises that have always been made by MacDonald, Lansbury, Henderson and Snowden'.[1]

Wheatley explained his fears even more pointedly. It was absolutely necessary, he said, to give more definite instructions to the Parliamentary Party as to the policies they should pursue when they were placed in parliamentary power. Otherwise, 'a leader of a Parliamentary Party—possibly the Leader of a Minority Party—will choose the line of least resistance in selecting from these sixty-five items those which are to have immediate Parliamentary sanction, and may I put to your intelligence that it would be easier to select a Liberal programme from these measures than a Socialist programme'.[2]

The rebels got nowhere at all with the Conference. Armed with the crushing power of the trade union vote, the leadership defeated with ease every attempt to give *Labour and the Nation* a more radical bite. However, it is difficult to believe that it would have made much difference if the document *had* been more radical. Nothing in fact could have been more naïve than the belief, so firmly held on the Left, that once the right words were said, and the right resolutions passed, MacDonald and his colleagues would seek, once they came to office, to initiate an advanced socialist programme.[3] Whatever might be said at Conferences, a Labour Government, particularly a minority Government, would find it possible, *because it was in office*, to argue itself out of commitments it had no wish to try and honour. This is exactly what happened after 1929, even on issues, such as the raising of unemployment benefits, which had no socialist connotations. Had the Left then been stronger, it might have made *some* difference to the behaviour of the Government. But it could not, even then, have compelled it to fight for socialist policies of the kind the Left wanted. The *minimum* requirement, if this was to be done, was to get rid of MacDonald but not only of MacDonald, and to wean the party from MacDonaldism. And of achieving either of

[1] Labour Party Annual Conference Report, 1928, pp. 202-3.
[2] ibid, p. 213.
[3] Note, in this connection, that it was the 1929 Annual Conference of the Labour Party which amended Clause 4 of the Party Constitution to include, as part of the Labour Party's objects, the common ownership of the means of distribution and exchange, as well as of production. (See Labour Party Annual Conference Report, 1929, pp. 205-6.)

these aims, the Labour Left had as much chance, in 1929, as of converting Stanley Baldwin to socialism.

2. IN PURSUIT OF THE NATIONAL INTEREST

The Labour Party made very substantial gains in the General Election of May 1929. Its total poll rose from 5,437,000 in 1924 to 8,360,000 in 1929, much of it no doubt accountable to an increase in the electorate from nearly twenty-two million to nearly twenty-nine million. The Conservative Party's poll also rose, from 7.4 million to 8,664,000. Labour was for the first time the largest party in the House of Commons, with 287 seats, as against 260 for the Conservatives and only 59 for the Liberals, who had, however, polled 5,301,000 votes. The Communists lost every one of the twenty-five seats they fought, in most cases very badly.[1] The Labour Party was thirty-eight seats short of an absolute majority.

This time, pleas for a Conservative-Liberal coalition to keep Labour out of office were much less pressing, and fears of a Labour administration much more muted. Baldwin resigned on the 4th of June. MacDonald saw the King on the 5th and agreed to form a Government.

There had, between 1924 and 1929, been some discussion, in the Labour Party, and particularly in the I.L.P., of the need to avoid a repetition of the experience of 1924, when MacDonald had had an almost completely free hand in the selection of his colleagues. According to Snowden, 'there was not a word of enquiry as to the construction of the new Government' at a meeting of the National Executive Committee and the Parliamentary Committee on the 5th of June, the day on which MacDonald began the formation of his Government.[2] However, MacDonald did consult his senior colleagues and was compelled, much against his own inclination, to grant Henderson's demand that he be given the Foreign Secretaryship. Of the nineteen members of the Cabinet, the only one who might have been considered as unorthodox was George Lansbury, and he was made Commissioner of Works. It is not certain that any of the leaders of the I.L.P. would have accepted office if it had been offered them; in any case, it wasn't. MacDonald felt neither the

---

[1] In 1924, when the C.P. had contested six seats, they had polled 41,000 votes. This time, with twenty-five seats contested, they obtained 30,000 votes. At the election, the C.P. advised the workers to abstain from voting where no Communists were standing, and to write 'Communist' across their ballot papers. This was in accordance with the 'New Line', even though the advocates of the 'New Line' were still in a minority on the Central Committee of the C.P. (Redman, op. cit. pp. 17-18).

[2] Snowden, op. cit. II, p. 762.

need, nor certainly the urge, to cover his left flank. Snowden was again Chancellor of the Exchequer; J. H. Thomas was Lord Privy Seal, in charge of the unemployment problem; Clynes was at the Home Office; with MacDonald and Henderson, these formed the inner circle. No need was felt this time to call in outside talent, save for W. A. Jowett, who had been elected to Parliament as a Liberal and became Attorney-General.

The politics of the second Labour Government fall into an easily discernible pattern. On the one hand, it resolutely set its face against any concessions to the Labour left. On the other, it consistently sought the co-operation and goodwill of its Conservative and particularly its Liberal opponents. Nor is this surprising. MacDonald and some of his more influential colleagues found it much easier to agree on crucial aspects of policy with Liberals and even with Conservatives than with Socialists.

MacDonald's most ardent champion to date has recently argued that 'a minority government, however, dependent upon the support of another party or other parties for its necessary majority in the House of Commons, is bound, if it is to endure, to enter into some form of collaboration, some kind of informal coalition. And that, despite its original decision to the contrary, is what happened with the second Labour Government'.[1]

This argument leaves out of account some considerations which are fundamental to any real understanding both of the nature of the second Labour Government and of the crisis of August 1931.

The purpose of a Government, Mr Bassett would seem to suggest, is 'to endure', almost as a metaphysical *Ding an Sich*, regardless of what the purpose of endurance might be. But this, though it undoubtedly represents accurately MacDonald's own view of things, was not what he and his colleagues purported to be their aim.

Labour leaders did not say that they were only charged with the task of seeing to it that the King's government was carried on. They claimed, insistently, that their purpose was to do great things, and no one claimed this more insistently than MacDonald himself. Capitalism, he told the 1930 Annual Conference of the Labour Party in language peculiarly his own, 'has broken down, not only in this little island. It has broken down in Europe, in Asia, in America; it has broken down everywhere, as it was bound to break down'. 'And the cure,' he added, 'the new path, the new idea is organization—organization which will protect life, not property; but protect property in proper relation to life; organization which will see to it that when science discovers and inventors invent, the class that will

[1] R. Bassett, *1931, Political Crisis* (London, 1958) p. 40.

be crushed down by reason of knowledge shall not be the working class, but the loafing class. That is the policy that we are going to pursue slowly, steadily, persistently, with knowledge, and with our minds working upon a plan.' 'And I appeal to you, my friends, today, with all that is going on outside—I appeal to you to go back on to your Socialist faith.' None of them, he concluded, would see the 'fabric' finished. 'But I think it will be your happiness, as it is mine, to go on convinced that the great foundations are being well laid, that the ennobling plan is being conceived, and that by skilled craftsmen, confident in each other's goodwill and sincerity, the temple will rise and rise and rise until at last it is complete, and the genius of humanity will find within it an appropriate resting place.' (Loud cheers.)[1]

This, however cloudy the rhetoric, was hardly the message of a Prime Minister whose purpose was 'to endure'. Nor would Mac-Donald have been so loudly cheered if that *had* been his message.

Furthermore, 'some form of collaboration, some kind of informal coalition' had, in the circumstances of 1929-31, certain definite implications which it does not do to ignore. What it meant, quite simply, was that the Government should do nothing that justified its existence as a *Labour* Government. After all, it was not very likely that the Liberals, not to speak of the Conservatives, would enter into some form of collaboration, some kind of informal coalition to help MacDonald lay 'the great foundations' and 'further the ennobling plan'.

In his first speech to the House of Commons as Prime Minister of the second Labour Government, MacDonald had wondered 'how far it is possible, without in any way abandoning any of our party positions, without in any way surrendering any item of our party principles, to consider ourselves more as a Council of State and less as arrayed regiments facing each other in battle . . . so far as we are concerned, co-operation will be welcomed . . . so that by putting our ideas into a common pool we can bring out from that common pool legislation and administration that will be of substantial benefit for the nation as a whole'.[2]

In saying this, Mr Bassett suggests, MacDonald was merely expressing 'something like a hope that the major problems of the day might be lifted above the party struggle'.[3] But *the* major problem of the day was unemployment. The Labour Party, in its election manifesto, had given an 'unqualified pledge to deal immediately and practically with this question' and had contrasted its own advo-

[1] Labour Party Annual Conference Report, 1930, p. 185.
[2] H. of C. vol. 229, col. 65, 2nd of July, 1929.
[3] Bassett, op. cit. p. 40.

cacy of the claims of the unemployed with 'the opposition and neglect of the Liberal and Tory Parties'.[1] Unemployment could only be 'lifted above the party struggle' on the essential condition that nothing should be done for the unemployed which was repugnant to Conservatives or Liberals and there was practically nothing that *could* be done for the unemployed which, when it came to the point, was not repugnant to the Opposition parties. Lifting the problem above the party struggle was the perfect formula for paralysis. In August 1931 it became the formula for doing something *against* the unemployed.

Nor can it be seriously argued that MacDonald's pleas for co-operation with Liberals and Conservatives were the result of the Government's minority position. 'It is laughable to suppose,' Mr John Strachey has written, 'that in that event (of a majority) Mr MacDonald would have sprung forward, a British Lenin. and begun the gigantic and hazardous task of destroying British capital-ism and replacing it with a socialist economy.'[2] But it is unnecessary to pitch it so high. For it is scarcely more likely that MacDonald and his Government would have done much more about unemploy-ment, let alone the transformation of Britain, if Labour had had a parliamentary majority. MacDonald in 1929 was not a latter-day Prometheus bound, forced into an unnatural political immobility by his minority position. The immobility was implicit in his political philosophy, and in that of his colleagues. As John Paton put it in December 1930: 'We believe the timid policies of the government do not spring from their minority position, but from the adoption of wrong views on policy which would be equally evident if they were a majority. At bottom, their weak policies are an expression of their belief in political gradualism and, therefore, are unaffected by the votes they command in Parliament.'[3] A majority could only have embarrassed them, and made it more difficult for them to with-stand left-wing pressure for action. But there is no reason to suppose they would not have found it possible to cope with the difficulty.

At the time the Government took office, the number of insured workers unemployed in Britain was 1,164,000. There was at first much talk of vast schemes for the creation of work. This came to nothing. By July 1930, the unemployment figures had topped the two million mark. However, the very size of this stagnant pool of deprived humanity was a useful alibi to the Government. Britain, Ministers said, was engulfed in a world-wide 'economic blizzard', for

[1] Labour Party Annual Conference Report, 1929, p. 304.
[2] J. Strachey, *The Coming Struggle for Power* (London, 1932) p. 303.
[3] *New Leader*, 12th of December, 1930.

which the Government was not responsible and which it could not reasonably be expected to control. Indeed, some of them said, the crisis was the most evident sign of the irrationality of capitalism. The crisis could only be resolved by a new, socialist order of society. But since the times, or the electorate, or the parliamentary situation, were not ripe for so fundamental a transformation, there was little that could immediately be done.

It was an argument which was then deemed quite plausible by many people in the Labour movement. In fact, part of the argument, that which posited the virtual irremediability of crisis in a capitalist society, was an intrinsic element of left-wing thinking. Where the left differed from the Government was in its insistence that the latter should introduce socialist measures and, if defeated, go to the country on a socialist programme.

But the alternatives, in 1929 and 1930, were not between socialism and inertia. The idea of stimulating consumer demand by 'pump-priming', which came to be linked with the name of Keynes, had long formed part of the programme not only of the Labour Party, but also of the Liberal Party. Nor did Ministers lack informed advice from friendly sources. *Labour and the Nation* had proposed the establishment of a National Economic Committee, which would be the 'eyes and ears' of the Prime Minister on economic questions 'and keep both him and the country informed as to the economic situation and its tendencies'.[1] The Committee was duly set up, and included Keynes, Bevin, Cole and Tawney. But it also included industrialists, to whom proposals for large-scale schemes of economic development under a national plan for economic expansion appeared, in Mr Bullock's words, 'the raving of wild and irresponsible extremists'.[2] Their view was also shared by the Treasury. What *they* wanted was wage reductions and cuts in the social services and unemployment benefits. And responsible Ministers were at all times more ready to listen to advice from industrialists and Treasury officials than from their own friends.

The controversy reached Cabinet level at the beginning of 1930. When he had formed his Government, MacDonald had made Sir Oswald Mosley, a recent recruit to the Labour Party, Chancellor of the Duchy of Lancaster, and charged him, together with George Lansbury and Tom Johnston, with the task of assisting J. H. Thomas in dealing with the unemployment problem.

In February 1930, Mosley, grown impatient with his chief's lack of interest in his numerous proposals and memoranda, submitted to the Cabinet, in agreement with Lansbury and Johnston, but without

[1] *Labour and the Nation*, p. 21.
[2] Bullock, op. cit. p. 437.

consulting Thomas, a series of proposals which became known as the Mosley Memorandum. This included increased pensions and allowances to induce earlier retirement from industry and to enlarge purchasing power; the protection of home industries through the control of imports, either by tariffs or by direct limitation; bulk purchase agreements with foreign suppliers, but particularly with Dominion and Colonial suppliers; the development of British agriculture; rationalization of industry under public control; and a liberal credit policy, through public control of banking, to finance development.[1]

These proposals, which would have meant the abandonment of Free Trade and orthodox banking policies, as well as substantial government expenditure, were anathema, not only to the Treasury, but also to Snowden, whom it took the crisis of 1931 and his membership as Chancellor of the Exchequer of the 'National' Government to lose something of his quasi-religious devotion to economic and financial principles derived from nineteenth century economic liberalism. Nor was there anybody in the Cabinet to oppose him. Mosley's proposals were rejected and he finally resigned in May 1930. Lansbury and Johnston, both of whom had been concerned with Mosley in the preparation of the Memorandum, didn't. And the Government continued to do nothing.

To do nothing about unemployment was one thing. To do nothing for the unemployed was another. The Labour Party had long adopted the slogan 'work or maintenance'. If, it had argued, the capitalist system could not provide work, it must at least guarantee to the unemployed a minimal standard of living. In their evidence before the Blanesburgh Committee on Unemployment Insurance in 1926, the T.U.C. and the Labour Party had jointly proposed an increased scale of unemployment benefits of twenty shillings a week, with ten shillings for a dependant wife and five shillings for each child, and 'to that scale it adheres', *Labour and the Nation* had said.[2] That these pledges would be fulfilled must have been the expectation of many who had voted for the return of a Labour Government in 1929.

However, when the Government introduced its Unemployment Insurance Bill in November 1929, the Bill was found to leave the unemployment benefit for men at seventeen shillings a week, and the allowance for each child at two shillings; only the allowance of the wife was raised from seven shillings to nine shillings, and the benefits for unemployed juvenile workers were also slightly increased.

[1] Cole, op. cit. p. 237.
[2] 'Though still far from adequate,' the Labour Party and the T.U.C. had said at the time, 'these rates would represent an improvement' (Labour Party Annual Conference Report, 1926, p. 43).

Furthermore, the 'waiting period' of six days, which the Labour Party was pledged to abolish, remained, and, more important, the Bill still required, though less stringently than heretofore, that an applicant for unemployment benefits should prove that he was 'genuinely seeking work'. All that the left could obtain, as a result of fierce pressure, was that this clause should be amended so that it became the sole responsibility of the local official to prove, if an applicant was to be denied benefits, that he had refused reasonable offers of work. Other amendments to raise benefits and allowances to the level promised by the Labour Party at the General Election were resolutely opposed.

The Government was, of course, under heavy fire from the Opposition benches for the Bill's 'extravagance'. And rather than confront the Opposition with the clear responsibility of denying more humane, though still minimal, benefits to the unemployed, even at the risk of parliamentary defeat, the Government much preferred to take the responsibility for that denial itself.

It is not, however, the Government's performance which is the only notable part of Labour's history in the two years in which it held office. After all, there was nothing in that performance which could not have been predicted on the basis of MacDonald and his colleagues' record and pronouncements in the previous years. Even more remarkable is the attitude of their followers, in Parliament and outside.

As in 1924, a Consultative Committee, consisting of twelve members of the Parliamentary Party, had been elected when the Government took office, and Henderson, Clynes and the Chief Whip had been appointed to attend its meetings. Its purpose was 'to act as a medium of communication between the Ministers and the Members'. 'It was felt,' the Parliamentary Report to the 1929 Annual Conference said, 'that it would be of immense benefit to the Government to be kept informed of Party views on particular questions, and that it would be helpful and encouraging to the Members generally to know that their own elected Committee was consulted on proper occasions by responsible Ministers.'[1]

The Prime Minister, however, took an exceedingly limited view of the rôle of the Committee. The day before he took office, he had been told by Lord Stamfordham, the King's Private Secretary, that the King would probably 'speak to him about the (National) Executive Committee, which was popularly supposed to have much control upon the Labour Government when they were in office'. MacDonald had assured him 'that this was not the case: that there were

[1] Labour Party Annual Conference Report, 1929, p. 83.

two of the Cabinet appointed to act as sort of liaison officers between the Party and the Government and he emphasized that the Government were never influenced by, and certainly never followed, the dictates of the Committee, unless their views coincided with those of the Government'.[1]

The left-wing rebels of the I.L.P. had no illusions as to the influence they could wield through the Committee. Rather than seek election to it, they had decided to steer clear of any position that would limit their independence, and to act as a pressure group upon the Government.

But the I.L.P. rebels were not only a small minority within the Parliamentary Party as a whole: they were also a small minority of the 110 Labour parliamentarians who were members of the I.L.P. Group in the House of Commons. Nor were these the least ardent supporters of the Government. When the I.L.P. rebels mounted a full-scale attack on the Unemployment Insurance Bill, in November 1929, and moved a reasoned amendment for its rejection, only thirty-two of their colleagues voted for it, while sixty-six I.L.P. Members published a declaration designed to 'make it clear that recent pronouncements hostile to, or critical of, the Government, and purporting to be made in the name of the I.L.P. Members of Parliament do not represent our views. We refuse to embarrass (the) Ministers in their work'.[2]

The rebels found more support among the I.L.P. activists. At the Annual Conference of the I.L.P. in April 1930, a motion for the reference back of the Report of the Parliamentary Group,[3] was defeated by 357 votes to 53.[4] The same conference laid it down that I.L.P. parliamentarians should give an undertaking that they accepted the policy of the I.L.P. as laid down by the decision of the Annual Conference and as interpreted by the N.A.C. (National Administrative Council).[5] Only eighteen members agreed to give the pledge. These reorganized themselves 'as a compact body, with regular meetings, a small executive committee, and two secretaries, who acted when necessary as "unofficial whips" '.[6]

The rebels thus became a more tightly-knit body. But they also became more isolated from their parliamentary colleagues, who deeply resented their activities. The mass of the parliamentary

[1] Nicolson, op. cit. p. 435.
[2] McKenzie, op. cit. p. 434.
[3] The rebels had gained control of the Executive Committee of the I.L.P. Parliamentary Group in July 1929, at a meeting which only 39 members of the Group attended (I.L.P. Annual Conference Report, 1930, p. 60).
[4] ibid, p. 82.
[5] ibid, p. 79.
[6] Brockway, Inside the Left, op. cit. p. 208.

party, though not very happy with the Government's handling of economic affairs, remained entirely 'loyal' to their leaders.

And it was not only the habitual rebels of the I.L.P. whom their colleagues refused to support. They looked askance at *any* manifestation of rebellion—as was shown by their attitude to Mosley's criticism of the Government.

At a meeting of the Parliamentary Labour Party on the 22nd of May, 1930, Mosley moved a resolution which stated that 'this Party is dissatisfied with the present unemployment policy of the Government and calls for the formulation of an alternative policy more in accordance with the programme and pledges of the Party at the last election'. Not more than 29 Members voted for the resolution; 210 voted against.[1] Sixty members, according to Beatrice Webb, went as far as to sign a demand for the dismissal of J. H. Thomas.[2]

After the crisis of 1931, there was considerable breast-beating about what was then said to have been an excess of loyalty to MacDonald and the Government. Certainly, the fear of embarrassing Ministers played a major part in the parliamentary party's supineness. And Labour backbenchers no doubt also found some compensation for the Government's failings at home in its more assured performance in the field of foreign affairs—notably in Henderson's work at Geneva. But this is not all. For so many Labour parliamentarians found it impossible to resist appeals to 'loyalty', of which there were plenty, not only because they felt compelled to support the Government, but also because, as Mr Scanlon has bitterly but accurately noted, they were 'a mass of good fellows willing to do the right thing, but never quite knowing what was the right thing until told by their leaders'.[3] The appeal to loyalty, in other words, could only have been so effective because so many Labour members shared the 'tentative, doctrineless socialism' of their leaders.

Faced with the hostility of the majority of the Parliamentary Party, there was one other and theoretically higher court to which the critics of the Government could appeal: the Annual Conference of the Labour Party, which met in October 1930. This they did, and evoked a somewhat readier response than they had found among

---

[1] McKenzie, op. cit. pp. 437-8.

[2] *Beatrice Webb's Diaries*, op. cit. p. 244. Thomas himself wished to be relieved of the responsibility for seeking remedies to unemployment. He ceased to be Lord Privy Seal in June 1930 and became Secretary of State for the Dominions and MacDonald himself then assumed responsibility for general policy covering unemployment.

[3] Scanlon, op. cit. p. 127.

their parliamentary colleagues; yet quite insufficient to strengthen their hand against the Government.

On the second day of the Conference, the delegates were treated to a remarkable sample of MacDonald's rhetoric, from which a passage has already been quoted earlier.[1] With his speech ringing in their ears, they then turned to consider a resolution from the National Union of General and Municipal Workers, which actually welcomed 'the efforts made by the Government to deal with Unemployment' but also asked it 'to facilitate schemes of National-ization', the development of more extensive trade with the Common-wealth and other countries, and 'the vigorous application of all other proposals embodied in *Labour and the Nation*'.[2] There was nothing in the resolution which could conceivably have worried the Government. Maxton therefore moved an amendment to it, which attacked the Government for its 'timidity and vacillation' and asked the Conference to instruct it 'to use all its powers towards increasing the purchasing power of the workers, reducing workers' hours, initiating a national housing programme, extending credits to Russia[3] and other countries, and above all, socializing the basic industries and services, using the provision of work or adequate maintenance as its first basic principle and, if necessary, to make an appeal to the people'.[4] The amendment was rejected by 1,803,000 votes to 334,000 and the main resolution was then carried.[5]

But the Conference was also presented with another, less pointed means of expressing any dissatisfaction it felt with the Government's conduct of economic affairs. It had a resolution calling for a full report on the Mosley proposals, which still had the status of an unpublished Cabinet document. Mosley himself put before the Conference a reasoned criticism of the inadequacy of the Govern-ment's plans for dealing with unemployment, described his own

[1] See above, p. 160. The following passage too is a typical example of MacDonald at his best: 'As the result of the most careful examination and testing, and producing of schemes and ideas we have come to the conclusion, that the work of every constructive government must be to put its population upon its land (Hear, hear). There is something permanent. There is a case of planting. There is a case where you take men —I do not mean their bodies only but their minds and their souls—off the pavements which have no roots and no rootable capacity, and put them in the fields, where they will till and they grow and they sow and they harvest. (A Voice: And they starve.)' (Labour Party Annual Conference Report, 1930, p. 183.)

[2] ibid, p. 186.

[3] The Government had resumed diplomatic relations with Russia, broken off in 1927 by the Baldwin Government, in October 1929, and had signed a commercial agreement in April 1930.

[4] ibid, p. 188.

[5] ibid, p. 200.

proposals, and asked that the Party should examine them and improve upon them.[1]

It was George Lansbury who replied for the Executive. and he as good as admitted that the Government could do little more for most of the unemployed than give them 'fair maintenance'. Indeed, it was because he was an old Socialist, Lansbury explained, that he did not believe unemployment could be cured under capitalism. The remedy, he urged the delegates, was to campaign for the creation of a 'Socialist public opinion' which would make it possible to try more radical methods.[2] The resolution was then defeated, though the vote was fairly close.[3] For all practical purposes, the Conference had given the Government a mandate to carry on as it thought best.

3. THE LOGIC OF ENDURANCE

By December 1930, the unemployment figures had risen to 2,500,000; by June 1931, to 2,700,000; a month later, they were up by another 100,000. As the crisis grew, so did pressure on the Government to *reduce* its own expenditure, particularly its expenditure on the unemployed. There was at least one member of the Government, and he no less a person than the Chancellor of the Exchequer, who was firmly convinced that this indeed was the right policy.

As early as February 1931, Snowden had told the House of Commons that 'the national position is so grave that drastic and disagreeable measures will have to be taken if Budget equilibrium is to be maintained and if industrial progress is to be made' The problem, he also said, was one which 'no one party can solve, but the country and the House of Commons must realize the gravity of the position. Instead of party bickering, which we can resume later, we must unite in a common effort to take effective measures to overcome our temporary difficulties and to restore our former prosperity'. What would be required were 'some temporary sacrifices from all, *and those best able to bear them will have to make the largest sacrifices*'.[4]

Snowden's Budget of April 1931 hardly matched the warnings of the previous February. It was what he himself called a 'stop-gap' Budget. It proposed no increase in taxation, save in the petrol tax, and there was also to be a tax on land values some time in the

---

[1] Labour Party Annual Conference Report, 1930, pp. 201-3.
[2] ibid, p. 204.
[3] I.e., 1,046,000 for the resolution, 1,251,000 against (ibid, p. 204).
[4] Bassett, op. cit. p. 45. My italics.

future, when the necessary valuation was completed.[1] There were some very good reasons for the Budget's mildness. As Snowden later explained to the House of Commons, the imposition of drastic measures had to wait upon the Report of the May Committee, since 'the enforcement of economies was such an unpopular thing that they could only be carried through either by a united House of Commons or by a large majority of the House of Commons'.[2]

The May Committee had been appointed in February to recommend ways of 'effecting forthwith all practical and legitimate reductions in the national expenditure consistent with the efficiency of the services'. The proposal to appoint such a Committee, which represented a Liberal amendment to a Tory motion of censure on the Government's policies in regard to public expenditure, was accepted by 468 votes to 21. Both its terms of reference (which were identical to those of the Geddes Economy Committee of 1921) and its composition,[3] made it certain that its recommendations would *not* entail the largest sacrifices from those best able to bear them. In actual fact, the Committee was intended as a weapon which the Chancellor, in his dedicated search for 'economy'. would be able to wield against Labour members insufficiently dedicated to the same cause. It was certainly not the Opposition which needed the Report of the May Committee to persuade them to accept the enforcement of economies. They were persuaded already—and pressing for them. It was the Labour benches and the Labour Party which must, with the help of the report of an 'independent' committee, be made to accept a drastic economy budget, which it was Snowden's intention to introduce in the autumn.[4]

The political crisis of the summer of 1931 was not, in other words, the direct result of the sudden deterioration of Britain's financial and exchange position at that time. That deterioration only added a dramatic quality to it, and provided an additional excuse for the economizers. But the crisis had been in the making ever since the Government came into existence: and it was above all due to the Government's firm determination to endure, even though this meant

[1] 'The Budget on the whole had a favourable reception,' Snowden later recalled; 'that was probably due more to a feeling of relief that I had been able to avoid the imposition of heavy additional taxation than to the merits of the Budget itself. In view of the well-known financial position of the country, a large addition to direct taxation had been generally expected.' (Snowden, op. cit. II, p. 903.)
[2] ibid, p. 48.
[3] I.e. Sir George May, until recently the Secretary of the Prudential Assurance Company, and six others; of these, two represented Labour, and four were nominated by the Conservative and Liberal Parties.
[4] Snowden, op. cit. II, p. 904.

the espousal (in any case eager on the part of Snowden himself) of its opponents' economic orthodoxies.

Even before the May Committee reported, a foretaste of things soon to come was provided by a preliminary attack on the unemployed in July 1931. On the basis of an Interim Report of the Royal Commission on the workings of unemployment insurance, which proposed increased contributions, lower benefits and the remedy of certain abuses in the system, the Government introduced an 'Anomalies' Bill which indicated, more clearly than anything else, the degeneration of that enduring Labour administration. For the Bill so tightened the regulations that it 'opened the door wide to wholesale deprivation of benefits of considerable classes of unemployed workers, especially married women who "could not reasonably expect to obtain employment" in their home areas'.[1] The Bill met with bitter opposition from the left. But most of the Parliamentary Labour Party supported the Government in the lobbies, and, with Liberal and Tory support, ensured its enactment, on the eve of the Government's collapse.

The report of the May Committee[2] presented to the Government at the end of July, was as gloomy as Snowden had anticipated. The gloom was somewhat forced, since the Budget deficit of £120 million which the majority of the Committee forecast for April 1932 was, as Mr Mowat notes, 'chiefly a matter of accounting';[3] the Committee, for instance, simply chose to add the deficit on the Unemployment Insurance Fund to the deficit on the Budget itself and assumed that all unemployment expenditure must be met out of income and not by further borrowing. But having thus presented the worst possible picture of the situation, the Committee went on to recommend new taxation to the derisory amount of £24 million and economies that were anything but derisory amounting to £96 million. Of this total £66.5 million was to be found by a 20 per cent. cut in unemployment benefits, by increased contributions to the Unemployment Insurance Fund and by the imposition of a Means Test on applicants for transitional benefits. And there were also to be cuts in teachers' salaries and grants in aid, in service and police pay, and in public works expenditure.

The May Committee had done its work too well. By the time its Report appeared, foreign fears of British financial weakness, exacerbated by bank failures in Germany and Eastern Europe,

[1] Cole, op. cit. p. 246.
[2] Or rather of its Conservative and Liberal members. The two Labour members issued a dissenting report, which the Government ignored.
[3] Mowat, op. cit. p. 382.

had already produced a substantial run on gold. The publication of the Report served to confirm fears of the weakness of sterling, and provided the appearance of a close link between the stability of sterling and the acceptance of the proposed economies; and the link was further strengthened by the insistence of French and American bankers that requests for further loans (the Bank of England had obtained credits of £25 million each from the Bank of France and the Federal Bank of New York) would only meet with success if the Government balanced the budget by a policy of retrenchment.

The events which followed the publication of the May Report are instructive not only for what they tell of the Labour leaders, but equally for the light they throw on their opponents' *use* of the Labour leaders in a situation which represents the high point of capitalist crisis in Britain between the wars.

MacDonald had, on reception of the May Committee's Report, appointed an Economy Committee of five, composed of himself, Snowden, J. H. Thomas, Arthur Henderson and William Graham, the President of the Board of Trade. The first meeting of the Committee was fixed for the 25th of August. However, in view of the worsening financial position, the Committee held its first meeting on the 12th of August and in a message to Labour Party members, given to the *Daily Herald* in mid-August, MacDonald asked his supporters 'to remember that we are grappling with this situation with all our ideals unchanged. We have not changed our policy. We are simply compelled to devise special measures to meet the temporary difficulties'.[1]

On the 19th of August, the Economy Committee presented to the full Cabinet tentative proposals for economies less drastic than those proposed by the May Committee, yet based upon the latter's recommendations. The cost of unemployment benefits was to be reduced by £48.5 million; of teachers' salaries by £11.4 million; of service pay by £9 million and police pay by half a million; expenditure on roads was to be cut to £7.8 million and other miscellaneous economies amounted to £5,350,000.[2]

These proposals of the Economy Committee were not final, and no recommendation was made to the Cabinet in regard to cuts in the rate of unemployment benefits. But, though Henderson and

---

[1] Bassett, op. cit. p. 68.
[2] Nicolson, op. cit. p. 457. The reduction in the cost of unemployment benefits was mainly to be achieved by increased insurance contributions, the reduction of the period of benefit to 26 weeks, and a reduction in transitional benefits.

Graham later denied that they had agreed to the proposals, Mr Bassett is obviously right to stress that they *were* responsible for agreeing to submit a set of economy proposals to the Cabinet.[1] By so agreeing, they committed themselves, if not to precise and specific proposals, at least to a trend of policy which equated the solution of the crisis with the imposition of further burdens upon the unemployed.[2] Agreement was in fact provisionally reached at the Cabinet meeting of the 19th of August on economies amounting to £56,250,000, but with a minority of Ministers insisting that there must be no cuts in the dole.[3] The figure fell in any case short by a sizeable amount of what Snowden considered necessary, and the Opposition leaders, whose co-operation was now sought more eagerly than ever, also insisted that larger economies, including further cuts in unemployment benefits, would have to be made if 'confidence' was to be restored. Co-operation now meant that the Opposition leaders were in a position to issue what, in Mr Bassett's words, 'amounted to an ultimatum in the every day use of that word'.[4]

However, the Cabinet now came up against resistance from its own side.

On the 20th of August, representatives of the Cabinet Emergency Committee had met the members of the Parliamentary Labour Party's Consultative Committee. This representative sample of back-bench Labour M.P.s came to the unanimous conclusion after the meeting that if the Government attempted to meet the conditions of the Opposition parties, 'it was doubtful', in the words of one member of the Committee, 'if they would get any other votes from our party other than the lawyers'.[5]

On the same day, the members of the Cabinet Economy Committee had attended a joint meeting of the General Council of the T.U.C. and the National Executive Committee of the Labour Party. MacDonald had made a general statement on the situation and, in answer to a demand for more information, Snowden made a statement on the economies that were being considered by the Cabinet. The National Executive Committee and the General Council then met separately to consider the situation.

The National Executive Committee, under the impression that Snowden had said there would be no cuts in unemployment benefits,

[1] Bassett, op. cit. p. 70.
[2] 'That,' Nicolson writes, 'the Big Five, with their immense influence in the Labour Party, should have accepted these sacrifices filled the hearts of Treasury officials with sweet, short-lived joy' (op. cit. p. 456).
[3] Nicolson, op. cit. p. 457.
[4] Bassett, op. cit. p. 117.
[5] ibid, p. 88.

agreed, as was later explained to the 1931 Party Conference, 'to leave matters in the hands of their Ministerial colleagues in the Cabinet'.[1]

The General Council of the T.U.C., on the other hand, was not nearly so pliant. After a four-hour discussion, it appointed a deputation to meet members of the Cabinet Economy Committee in order 'to indicate the Council's complete opposition to the various economy suggestions that had been discussed' and to submit alternative proposals.[2] The General Council wanted the existing unemployment contributions from workers, employers and the State replaced by a graduated levy on profits, incomes and earnings; the imposition of new taxation upon fixed interest securities and other unearned income; and the suspension of the Sinking Fund. The Council also discussed the question of a Revenue Tariff, but took no decision upon it.[3]

The deputation from the Council met the Cabinet Economy Committee on the same evening and, as Snowden wrote later, 'took up the attitude of opposition to practically all the economy proposals which had been explained to them'.[4] The next day, the General Council met again and sent a letter to the Prime Minister, confirming that 'the General Council adhere to their views as expressed to you by the Deputation'.[5] MacDonald replied on the same day. 'Nothing,' he wrote, 'gives me greater regret than to disagree with old industrial friends, but I really personally find it absolutely impossible to overlook dread realities, as I am afraid you are doing.'[6]

This rejection by the General Council, not only of cuts in unemployment benefits, but of all the proposed economy cuts, was, as Mr Bassett notes, 'an event of far-reaching importance in the development of the crisis . . . The members of the Cabinet must all have realized that they now had to meet the determined opposition of the leaders of the industrial side of the Labour Movement, in addition to the inevitably fierce hostility of all Left-Wing elements'.[7] From then onwards, MacDonald and Snowden could have no doubt that to carry through their policy, they would have to separate themselves from the bulk of the Labour movement. On the other hand, the attitude of the General Council undoubtedly stiffened the

[1] Labour Party Annual Conference Report, 1931, pp. 3-4.
[2] ibid, p. 4.
[3] T.U.C. Annual Conference Report, 1931, p. 514.
[4] Snowden, op. cit. 11, p. 942, 'The General Council are pigs,' Beatrice Webb reported Sidney as saying to her, 'they won't agree to any "cuts" of Unemployment Insurance benefits or salaries or wages' (Beatrice Webb's Diaries, op. cit. p. 281).
[5] T.U.C. Annual Conference Report, 1931, p. 515.
[6] ibid, p. 515.
[7] Bassett, op. cit. p. 101.

opposition of the dissenting Ministers, and of the parliamentary party generally, only a handful of whose members ultimately followed MacDonald. This recoil of the General Council and of the parliamentarians was not of course the result of a sudden conversion to the left. What it represented was a last-minute dissociation from the logical outcome of a trend of policy they had, until then, been willing to endorse. But it was the *outcome* of a trend of policy that was being rejected, and not the trend itself. The reappraisal was agonizing, but very partial.

Despite the General Council's attitude, the Cabinet, in answer to warnings and appeals from MacDonald and Snowden, agreed on the 22nd of August that the Opposition parties should be asked whether they would support the Government on the basis of economies amounting to approximately £76 million, including a 10 per cent. cut in the standard rates of unemployment benefit.[1] But the Cabinet as a whole remained uncommitted to these proposals. There was in fact a powerful minority of Ministers opposed to them. As Snowden later noted, 'we were placed in a difficult position in making this suggestion (of further economies), because we had no assurance that if it were accepted by the Opposition leaders the Cabinet would agree to do it'.[2] The position was not only difficult; it was absurd. And it was made absurd by the undecisiveness of the dissenters who opposed further cuts and negotiations and who wanted the Government to resign, yet who were still unwilling to force the issue, even at this late date.

The Opposition leaders were duly consulted and duly gave their somewhat half-hearted assent to the proposals, provided a further American loan could be raised on this basis. After the Opposition leaders, the representatives of the Bank of England were, as MacDonald later told the House of Commons, 'consulted as to whether in their opinion the scheme proposed would produce the loan'.[3] They thought it might and, in their turn, said they would make inquiries in New York. What this sordid tale suggests is that the Labour Government had surrendered all freedom of initiative to the Opposition leaders, to the Treasury officials and, finally, to the goodwill of American finance.

It might seem odd that the Opposition leaders should have been willing to continue support for a Government which they knew to be deeply divided, and therefore incapable of speaking with an authority that might have been deemed essential in conditions which were said to be of catastrophic gravity. In fact, it is not odd at

[1] Bassett, p. 120.
[2] Snowden, op. cit. II, p. 944.
[3] H. of C., vol. 256, col. 19, 8th of September, 1931.

all. The Opposition leaders badly *needed* the Labour Government, or at least MacDonald. 'The Conservatives,' *The Times* had written on the 14th of August, 'recognize that the Government are in an extremely difficult position, largely owing to the campaign which is already being waged in some Labour quarters against the May Report.'[1] This unusual concern for the difficulties of the Government is easily explained by the Opposition's awareness of how desirable it was that *Labour* leaders should be responsible for the introduction of what Snowden called 'unpopular measures'. The Opposition leaders, unassisted by accredited Labour spokesmen, would have found it difficult to persuade the working classes that an attack on the miserable standard of life of the unemployed was essential to 'save the country'. But they could legitimately hope that Labour leaders, invested with the confidence of the Labour movement, claiming that 'we are grappling with this situation with all our ideals unchanged', might, and that the same Labour leaders would also greatly help to blunt and neutralize Labour and left-wing attacks on their policies. 'The critics, like anybody else,' MacDonald had said in the message to the Labour Party quoted earlier, 'will have to face facts and deal honestly with the interests of the country.' Such words sounded more plausible, coming from MacDonald than from Baldwin or Samuel. And MacDonald became even more important to the Opposition when it became clear that the economies upon which it insisted, and which MacDonald and Snowden endorsed, would not be acceptable either to an influential group of Ministers or to the trade union leaders.

Of the three Opposition leaders most closely involved, namely Baldwin, Chamberlain and Samuel, the last two are on record as badly wanting MacDonald to retain the Premiership, even without the support of his party, and their reasons for wanting this are on record too.

MacDonald saw the King on the morning of the 23rd of August, and told him that the Government might have to resign. The King later saw Samuel and then Baldwin. Samuel's advice to the King provides the key to the political crisis then reaching its climax. He told the King that 'in view of the fact that the necessary economies would prove most unpalatable to the working classes, *it would be to the general interest if they could be imposed by a Labour Government.* The best solution would be if Mr Ramsay MacDonald, either with his present, or with a reconstituted Labour Cabinet, could propose the economies required. If he failed to secure the support of a sufficient number of his colleagues, then the best alternative would be a National Government composed of

[1]Bassett, op. cit. p. 67.

176

members of the three parties. *It would be preferable that Mr Mac-Donald should remain Prime Minister in such a National Government.* Sir Herbert made it clear at the same time that such a non-party Government should only be constituted for the single purpose of overcoming the financial crisis'.[1]

George V was not, on the record, a man burdened with a super-abundance of intellectual and political insights. But he was, throughout his reign, guided by the dominant belief that his special rôle was to help blunt the edges of political strife and the sharpness of class tensions. That this made him a pillar of conservatism was not likely to disturb him, not so much because he was, in all essentials, a Conservative, but because conservatism was to him synonymous with the 'national interest'. Once Samuel had explained to him why the 'national interest' required, in this instance, that MacDonald should remain Prime Minister, the King turned himself, as will be seen presently, into a pressing and powerful advocate of that solution.[2]

The King also saw Baldwin that afternoon and asked him whether he would be prepared to serve in a National Government under MacDonald. 'Mr Baldwin answered that he would be ready to do anything to assist the country in the present crisis.'[3] He also added that 'even if Mr MacDonald insisted on resigning', he, Mr Baldwin, would be ready to carry on the Government if he could be assured of the support of the Liberal Party in effecting the necessary economies'.[4] As the leader of the second largest party in the House of Commons, Baldwin could hardly say less, nor could he be easily expected to press the view that his assumption of the Premiership would be an altogether undesirable alternative to Mac-Donald's retention of it. The clear expression of that view to Mac-

[1] Nicholson, op. cit. p. 641. My italics. That same morning, Geoffrey Dawson, the Editor of *The Times,* had, in a telephone conversation with Sir Clive Wigram, the King's Private Secretary, 'respectfully suggested that His Majesty should impress upon Ramsay that it was his business to get the country out of the mess, and to dwell, with any flattery that he liked, upon the opportunity and the responsibility . . . I thought it was everything to get a plan of national economy put out in public by a Labour Government, since it was the only course that would have a permanent effect in reversing a policy of extravagance' (J. E. Wrench, *Geoffrey Dawson and Our Times* (London, 1925) p. 291).
[2] The King was deeply impressed by Samuel's advice. Sir Clive Wigram recorded that 'some time after the crisis, in discussing it with the King, I was impressed by the fact that His Majesty found Sir Herbert Samuel the clearest-minded of the three and put the case for a National Government much clearer than either of the others. It was after the King's interview with Sir Herbert Samuel that His Majesty became convinced of the necessity for the National Government'. (Nicholson, op. cit. p. 461.)
[3] ibid, p. 461.
[4] ibid, pp. 461-2.

Donald himself was left to the King and to Neville Chamberlain.

At the Cabinet meeting of that evening, MacDonald read a telegram from J. P. Morgan, representing the American financial interests from whom the Government hoped to raise credits, which asked whether the programme under consideration 'will have the sincere approval and support of the Bank of England and the City generally and thus go a long way towards restoring internal confidence in Great Britain'.[1] According to Nicolson, MacDonald then 'made a strong appeal to his colleagues to accept the revised schedule of economies though they comprised a 10 per cent. cut in the dole. MacDonald stated that he was all too well aware that to reduce unemployment benefits would cause much resentment in Labour circles and was in fact a denial of much that the Labour movement had always stood for. Yet he was confident that the majority of the Party would support him were he able to lay the whole facts before them. *Moreover, if a scheme that imposed such grave sacrifices on other sections of the community left the unemployed in a privileged position, the Labour Party might lose moral prestige*'.[2]

Even so, eight Ministers made it clear that they would not accept the cuts in unemployment benefits, in addition to all the other economy cuts. MacDonald later saw the King and told him that he had no alternative but to tender the resignation of the Cabinet. The King then pressed MacDonald forcefully, possibly decisively, not to do so. He 'impressed on the Prime Minister that *he was the only man to lead the country through this crisis and hoped he would reconsider the situation.* His Majesty told him that the Conservatives and Liberals would support him in restoring the confidence of foreigners in the financial stability of the country'.[3]

MacDonald then asked the King whether he would confer with Baldwin, Samuel and himself in the morning and the King agreed.

The Prime Minister saw Baldwin, Chamberlain and Samuel the same evening and told them, according to Chamberlain, that 'while a majority (of the Cabinet) supported him, eight Ministers had refused to accept the dole cut'. MacDonald added that he himself 'would help us to get the proposals through, though it meant his death warrant, but it would be of no use for him to join a government . . . would bring odium on us as well as himself'.[4] This was far from Chamberlain's view. 'I then intervened . . . had he considered that, tho' not commanding many votes in the House, he might command much support in the country? And would not a Govern-

---

[1] Bassett, op. cit. p. 135.
[2] Nicolson, op. cit. p. 463. My italics.
[3] ibid, p. 464. My italics.
[4] Feiling, op. cit. p. 193.

ment including members of all parties hold a much stronger position? . . . Finally, I asked him if he had considered the effect on foreign opinion.'[1]

'Foreign opinion', in this context, meant the foreign bankers, whose 'terms', to use MacDonald's own word, a majority of the Cabinet had accepted. But foreign bankers, from whom the Government wanted credits, had no paramount interest in the maintenance in office of a Labour Prime Minister. It is difficult to believe that they would have looked less sympathetically on the kind of Government Baldwin might have formed than on a 'National' Government led by MacDonald, the more so since it was by then obvious that such a Government would not be supported by vast sections of the Labour movement. In truth, it was the Opposition leaders who had a paramount interest in the creation of a 'National' Government headed by MacDonald.

At the Palace meeting on the morning of the 24th of August, MacDonald, in the presence of Baldwin and Samuel, said that 'he had the resignation of his Cabinet in his pocket'.[2] The King again intervened forcibly and said 'that he trusted there was no question of the Prime Minister's resignation: the leaders of the three Parties must get together and come to some arrangement. His Majesty hoped that the Prime Minister, *with the colleagues who remained faithful to him,* would help in the formation of a National Government, which the King was sure would be supported by the Conservatives and the Liberals. The King assured the Prime Minister that, remaining at his post, his position and reputation would be much more enhanced than if he surrendered the government of the country at such a crisis. Baldwin and Samuel said that they were willing to serve under the Prime Minister and render all help possible to carry on the Government as a National Emergency Government until an emergency bill or bills had been passed by Parliament, which would restore once more British credit and the confidence of foreigners.'[3]

The King then left the Party leaders to confer without him. He

[1] Feiling, p. 193.
[2] Nicolson, op. cit. p. 465.
[3] ibid, pp. 465-6. My italics. Nicolson quotes Lord Samuel's *Memoirs* as disposing of the 'legend' that the King went beyond his constitutional powers in urging the leaders of the three Parties to unite in forming a National Government. Lord Samuel wrote that 'the invitation to the Prime Minister to return to office, and to form a new Administration on an all-party basis, was the course advised by them (the spokesmen of the two Opposition parties). So far as I was myself concerned, neither directly nor indirectly, did any expression reach me of any personal opinion or wish of His Majesty.' (Viscount Samuel, *Memoirs* (London, 1945) p. 221.) The record of the Palace Conference, as given by Nicolson, can hardly be said to con-

was later 'requested to return to the Conference, and was glad to hear that they had been able to some extent to come to some arrangement. A Memorandum had been drawn up which Baldwin and Samuel could place before their respective colleagues, but the Prime Minister said that he would not read this out in Cabinet as he should keep it only for those who remained faithful to him. Probably the new National Government would consist of a small Cabinet of twelve. It is quite understood that, up to now, the Cabinet had not resigned. His Majesty congratulated them on the solution of this difficult problem, and pointed out that while France and other countries existed for weeks without a Government, in this country our constitution is so generous that leaders of Parties, after fighting one another for months in the House of Commons, were ready to meet together under the roof of the Sovereign and sink their own differences for a common good and arrange as they had done this morning for a national Government to meet one of the gravest crises that the British Empire had yet been asked to face.'[1]

On this evidence, which he quotes, Mr Bassett's statement that 'although the formation of a National Government had been considered and progress made "to some extent", no final decision had been taken'[2] is rather unconvincing. Mr Bassett also writes that 'it is of course impossible to say' what MacDonald would have done if no Minister had followed him. 'But it is extremely unlikely,' he adds 'that he would have gone forward.'[3] This seems a highly dubious assertion. When he agreed to lead a 'National' Government at the Palace Conference, MacDonald had not made the acceptance of office by *any* of his colleagues a condition of his own acceptance. In fact, MacDonald had spoken in a manner which suggested that the matter was settled. That was the clear understanding of the participants, and certainly of the King. It is not very likely that, had no minister agreed to follow MacDonald, he would have gone back to the King and told him that he had changed his mind. What had still not been decided at the Conference was the actual composition and the detailed programme of the new Government, not the formation of that Government itself. And in any case MacDonald knew that

firm Lord Samuel's assertion; it shows beyond any doubt that the King did very much more than listen to the advice of the Opposition leaders and repeat it to MacDonald. In fact, the evidence shows that the King made very much his own the advice of the Opposition leaders and added his considerable influence to it. Whether, in so doing, he was or was not exceeding his constitutional rôle is of less interest than the fact of his contribution to the particular manner in which the crisis was resolved.

[1] Nicolson, op. cit. p. 466.
[2] Bassett, op. cit. p. 156.
[3] ibid, p. 162.

some Ministers would, in his own phrase, 'remain faithful to him'.

MacDonald met his Cabinet for the last time immediately after the Palace Conference of the 24th of August and announced that he was to lead a 'National' Government. After the meeting, he asked Snowden, Thomas and Lord Sankey to join the new administration and they agreed. How many members of the Cabinet who had supported MacDonald and Snowden on the issue of the reduction in unemployment benefits would have agreed to join the new Government, no one can tell, since it would not appear that MacDonald asked any of them, except Herbert Morrison and, from outside the Cabinet, Emmanuel Shinwell. Both refused, the former, according to Mary Agnes Hamilton, not without much heart-searching, for, as he told her, he had had 'a severe struggle in his mind between loyalty to Mac and loyalty to the Party'.[1]

On the same afternoon, the Prime Minister, in the words of the announcement from the Palace, 'tendered his resignation as Prime Minister of the Labour Government which the King accepted. The King then invited him to form a National Administration. Mr Mac-Donald accepted the offer, and kissed hands on his appointment as the new Prime Minister.' The new Government, it had also been agreed, would not be a Coalition, but 'a co-operation of individuals' and there would be a General Election at the end of the emergency, to be fought not by the 'National' Government as a coalition but 'by each of the three Parties, acting independently'. And it was also agreed that the 'National' Government would impose economies amounting to £70 million, which would include a cut of 10 per cent. in unemployment benefits and increased contributions to the Unemployment Insurance Fund, of about £14 million.[2] Well might the King say that it was a generous Constitution which had made such an end to the second Labour Government possible.

4. AFTER MACDONALD

There was a double postscript to the crisis of August 1931, the first written by Labour, the second by its opponents.

The first official Labour reaction to the 'National' Government was a joint manifesto of the T.U.C. General Council, the National Executive Committee of the Labour Party and the Consultative Committee of the Parliamentary Party. The manifesto, issued on the 27th of

[1] M. A. Hamilton, *Remembering My Good Friends* (London, 1944) p. 247.
[2] Nicolson, op. cit. p. 467. It was the day after the Government was formed that MacDonald, in reply to Snowden's observation that he would now find himself very popular in strange quarters, was reputed to have made the famous remark: 'Yes, tomorrow every Duchess in London will be wanting to kiss me' (Snowden, op. cit. II, p. 957).

August, denounced the new Government as a 'Government of persons acting without authority from the people' and noted that the phrase 'equality of sacrifice' had been invoked as a justification for cuts in social expenditure, but that 'no comparable sacrifice has so far been demanded from the wealthier sections of the community'. £4,000 million, it pointed out, were invested abroad; Britain was still one of the greatest creditor countries; she was still adding to her capital assets; 'the taxable capacity of the country has not been exhausted' and the immediate difficulties could be met, 'if the will were present', by mobilizing the country's foreign investments, by a temporary suspension of the Sinking Fund, by the taxation of fixed income securities and other unearned income which had benefited by the fall in prices, and by measures to reduce the burden of War debts.

Great Britain, the manifesto warned, was under pressure from national and international financial interests to take the lead in 'a process of world wide degradation' of working class standards of living : 'the effective resistance of the Labour movement' could alone avert this calamity. Though the forces of Labour were vitally concerned with the national interest, the Manifesto also said, they emphatically rejected the view that the national interest could only be secured by the impoverishment of the workers and Labour therefore called 'upon the mass of the people and all men and women of good will to stand firmly against the new Government and to rally to the aid of the Labour movement in its defence of true national interests and its constructive efforts towards a new social order'.[1]

In the light of the circumstances in which Labour had suddenly found itself expelled from office, and of the measures which the new Government had been formed to carry through, the Manifesto was a remarkably restrained document;[2] and, though it asserted that 'the effective resistance of the Labour movement' could alone avert a calamitous degradation of working class standards of life, it had nothing to say on the practical steps that might be taken to evoke and organize that 'effective resistance'.

This restraint is only partly to be explained by the fact that former

[1] Labour Party Annual Conference Report, 1931, pp. 5-6.
[2] This, however, was not the view of people like Sir Herbert Samuel, who told the Liberal Party meeting on the 28th of August that 'taking up a partisan and class attitude, they (the Labour Party) would fall into a great error of judgment, the same mistake which the T.U.C. Council made when they plunged the country into the general strike . . . The typical British working man knew quite well when it was necessary to adopt a national rather than a class attitude' (Bassett, op. cit. p. 202). The *Manchester Guardian* was also worried about the attitude of the Labour Party and pleaded with

ministers carried the heavy burden of their previous endorsement, however tentative, of many of the economy proposals which the Government was about to incorporate in its programme. After all, they did speak, after their resignation, as if they had been altogether opposed to the general tendency of MacDonald and Snowden's policies. More fundamental was their automatic acceptance of the notion that their opposition must remain confined within strictly parliamentary channels, coupled with and related to their defensive fear that the organization of any other kind of opposition, particularly before a General Election, would expose them to the accusation of wilful disregard of the 'national interest'. They were in any case accused of that in the following days and weeks. And so they had the worst of both worlds: they went into opposition; and the manner in which they went into opposition condemned them to ineffectualness.

There were many prominent Labour men who suffered from other inhibitions, not least in regard to MacDonald and those of the Labour Party associated with him. Initial reactions of some of MacDonald's former colleagues to his alliance with Labour's political opponents were characterized by a magnanimity which would have been more admirable if it had not betokened partial agreement with his policies, whatever disagreement they might have with the way in which he chose to implement them. As Mr Bassett notes, references to MacDonald and Snowden immediately after the formation of the 'National' Government were 'often strikingly complimentary'[1] and much stress was laid on their sincerity and high motives.

Henderson himself, who had been elected leader of the Party on the 28th of August, was exceedingly mild about his former colleagues when Parliament reassembled on the 8th of September. 'By the change that has taken place,' he told the Commons, 'we have lost three if not four of those who have been in the very forefront of the battle, and who especially in two cases, have been associated with the building-up of the movement . . . I want to say this, that *whether the withdrawal of our colleagues be long or short, whether it is temporary or permanent,* it is a direct loss to the Labour movement.'[2]

Two days later, addressing the T.U.C. Annual Conference as the

it to show 'restrained Parliamentary conduct', and to provide 'a large measure of courageous co-operation with the Government in putting through its principal financial measures'. Above all, there must be avoided 'an appeal to the country on the crudest and most inflammatory grounds'. 'From that,' the paper said, 'only the Labour Party can save us.' (ibid, p. 200.)

[1] For instances, see Bassett, ibid, pp. 196-7.
[2] H. of C. vol. 256, col. 25. My italics.

Labour Party's fraternal delegate, Henderson recalled that, on his return from a visit to Paris some weeks before the break-up of the Government, he had been informed that 'the question of a National Government had been the subject of conversation'. Someone in the audience cried 'Shame' and Henderson went on: 'I am not so sure that there was very much shame in it, because as I have said before, if this situation is all that we have been told, if in its magnitude, if in its possible consequences, if in its urgency, it was such as has been described, I have no hesitation in saying that I would have preferred that the idea of a National Government had been seriously considered and approached in the proper way . . .', by which he meant that the Parliamentary Labour Party and a specially convened Labour Conference should have been consulted and asked to endorse such a step.[1]

Henderson's attitude held no promise of vigorous and uncompromising resistance, inside Parliament or outside, to the Government's policies. In fact, his election to the leadership of the Parliamentary Labour Party was a good indication that there would be no real departure from previous Labour policies and postures. Everything about Henderson's personality and character was utterly different from MacDonald's, and Henderson's total devotion to the Labour Party made him incapable of the kind of self-deception which had caused MacDonald to betray it. But there was little, in ideological terms, which separated him from MacDonald. If anything, Henderson was the more consistent representative of a Labourism not substantially different, on most counts, from progressive liberalism. Now that MacDonald was gone, and gone in such circumstances, Henderson, whose stolidity provided a reassuring contrast to what was now denounced as the tinsel glamour of MacDonald, emerged as the symbol of Labour's capacity to endure in the face of disaster. And the influence he had was used to help restrain the Party from too violent a recoil from MacDonaldism, and to guide it in the paths of cautious moderation.

On the 10th of September, Snowden introduced his emergency budget proposals. Direct taxes were to be increased by £51½ million in a full year, by raising income tax from 4s. 6d. to 5s. in the pound, by a reduction of exemptions and children's allowances. and by an increase in surtax payments by 10 per cent. Proposed increases in indirect taxation to the amount of £24 million involved higher duties on beer, tobacco, petrol and entertainments. In addition, a National Economy Bill proposed cuts in the unemployment benefit rates by an average of 10 per cent.: for men from 17s. weekly to 15s. 3d.; for women from 15s. to 13s. 6d.; and for adult dependants

[1] T.U.C. Annual Conference Report, 1931, p. 400.

from 9s. to 8s. Contributions were also to be increased, the benefit period limited to 26 weeks, and a means test provided for transitional benefits. Teachers' salaries were to be reduced by 15 per cent. and lesser cuts were proposed in the pay of the police and the armed services, as well as in the salaries of ministers, judges and Members of Parliament. The Bill also empowered the Government to give statutory effect to the proposed changes by Orders-in-Council.

On the 21st of September, the 'National' Government took Britain off the gold standard. Even though credits amounting to £80 million had been obtained from New York and Paris on the 28th of August, the drain on the Bank of England's gold reserves had continued. By the middle of September the credits were almost exhausted. What had earlier been deemed the end of civilization, to be avoided by economy cuts and a 'National' Government, was now accepted as the inevitable command of common sense, and, as Mr Mowat notes, 'hardly a leaf stirred'.[1]

Given the fact that Britain was in 1931 one of the richest countries in the world, and blessed with one of the richest ruling classes in the world, it is surely amazing that there were actually found rational men to argue that the saving of a few million pounds a year on the miserable pittance allowed to unemployed men and women and their children was the essential condition of British solvency; even less credible that two men, exalted by the Labour movement and owing what they were to the faithful support of millions of working men and women, should have been the main actors in this obscene charade.

The Budget and economy proposals roused bitter indignation on the Labour benches and caused some members to issue threats of extra-parliamentary action that can have been scarcely more welcome to the Labour Front Bench than they were to the Government's supporters.[2] There was in fact no attempt on the part either of the Labour Party, or of the General Council of the T.U.C., to organize that 'effective resistance' of which they had spoken on the 27th of August.

The T.U.C. Conference, which met at Bristol on the 7th of September, was mainly notable for the reaffirmation by the trade union leadership of the principles which had determined its policies over the previous years. On the 8th of September, the Conference was asked by P. H. Collick, of the Locomotive Engineers and Firemen,

[1] Mowat, op. cit. p. 404.
[2] See, e.g. Fenner Brockway's speech on the 11th of September, H. of C. vol. 256, cols. 458 ff., and Aneurin Bevan's, ibid, cols. 1214 ff., on the 18th.

to reject the section of the General Council's report which referred to the latter's negotiations and discussions with employers' organizations on such subjects as rationalization in industry. What Mr Collick really wanted was an explicit repudiation of the spirit which had moved the General Council when it began the Mond-Turner discussions and which had moved it ever since. For the General Council, C. T. Cramp argued that 'there is no collaboration in the ordinary set understanding of that term whereby we and the employers are marching forward and pulling together', and Ernest Bevin agreed that circumstances had changed; but, he added, 'my complaint is not against the Mond-Turner Report, but that the Movement did not grasp the recommendations contained in the Mond-Turner Report and try to apply them'.[1] The reference back was rejected by 2,818,000 votes to 160,000.[2]

On the 10th of September, A. Pugh introduced on behalf of the General Council a resolution which curiously welcomed 'the present tendency towards a planned and regulated economy in our national life' and which proposed that the General Council should 'boldly' advance this policy both nationally and internationally.[3] In the debate which followed, P. H. Collick again introduced a jarring note into the proceedings. '. . . You cannot naturally plan in this country,' he said, 'because you have not real power, and the problem which this Congress ought to face, if you are going to have national planning, is how best you can get that real power. . . . If it is going to be done by the Parliamentary machine, certainly we have to follow a very different line of policy to that which has been followed in the last two years. . . . I will go so far as to say that you will never solve it wholly and solely by the Parliamentary machine. You have had a classic example. When the history of the last three weeks comes to be written, it will be shown that extra-constitutional means have been used by the financial classes to exert their will; and if we face the ugly truth in all its nakedness, unashamed of our position, we have to recognize the probability that it may be necessary for this Movement to use extra-constitutional means to achieve its aims If we imagine we are going to do this job with the consent of those who control finance, we have missed the goal towards which we aim; and, instead of warning our movement, instead of preparing our people, instead of doing all the things that are necessary to that end, we fritter away our time passing pious resolutions which will make no difference to the real position.'[4]

[1] T.U.C. Annual Conference Report, 1931, p. 363.
[2] ibid, p. 364.
[3] ibid, p. 406.
[4] ibid, p. 415.

A delegate of the Miners' Federation, G. Lumley, was equally critical of the resolution which did not, he said, meet the present-day crisis. They had been told that it was their duty to stand firm against any attack. But 'if we have got to stand firm against any attacks, particularly the attacks that are going to be made immediately on the unemployed,' he told the Conference, 'then we must recognize that our simple belief in the Parliamentary vote is not going to help the workers to defeat this attack. . . . There is only one way, in my opinion, to do this, and that is not the way by which the General Council is proceeding, but along the lines of organizing the workers outside Parliament to take extra-constitutional action. . . . There is only one thing to be done, and that is for the General Council this week immediately to organize and prepare for a stoppage of the whole of the wheels of industry . . . so far as Parliamentary action is concerned, either with a majority or a minority Government, the fact remains that it is only a smoke screen that enables the financier to have a policy, hidden in the name of democracy . . . we must be immediately prepared as representatives of the workers who are organized in this country to put the financiers and the capitalist group of this country in greater difficulties than they have ever been in before.'[1]

This was not at all how the General Council viewed matters.

Replying to the debate, A. Pugh suggested that the implication of the views expressed by Messrs Collick and Lumley was that, having stopped the whole industries of the country and made it impossible for the industrialists to carry on, 'then, without any previous conception of what we are to do, with no plan of our own, we have got to do what Russia has had to do—step in and build from the bottom in a manner which must inevitably increase the sufferings of our people'. 'That,' he went on, 'has not been the method of the British Trades Union Movement. Whether it is on the political or on the industrial side, the British Trades Union Movement throughout the whole of the struggles of the past century has been gradually building, building and building. On its political side it built until it was able to put a Labour Government in the House of Commons. In the same way it must build up industry. We must go into these economic and financial questions, we must have research and investigation, we must make our own plan if we are to make the future of our political movement effective, and that is what this resolution is designed to do.'[2] The resolution was passed by 2,8660,000 against 749,000, a sizeable minority.[3]

[1] ibid, p. 419.
[2] ibid, p. 425.
[3] ibid, p. 425.

While the T.U.C. was thus quietly going about its business, there was rising, throughout the country, a considerable movement of protest against the Government's economy measures, with unemployed marches, demonstrations and petitions.[1] Nor was it only the unemployed who protested. So did teachers, civil servants, postal workers, even policemen, and, most startling of all, sailors of the Atlantic Fleet, 12,000 of whom staged the 'Invergordon Mutiny' on the 15th of September by refusing to muster, in protest against the cuts in their pay. On the 21st, the Government announced that no reductions would exceed 10 per cent. in the pay of either servicemen or of the police, and the teachers were similarly placated.

No such concession was made to the unemployed and their agitation continued. From that agitation, the General Council held disapprovingly aloof, not only because much of it was led by the Communist-led National Union of Unemployed Workers, but also because it was altogether opposed to this kind of resistance.

So was the Labour Party, whose Annual Conference was even more placid than that of the T.U.C. The Conference met at Scarborough on the 5th of October, a day before the announcement that a General Election would be held on the 27th. Six weeks had passed since the collapse of the Labour Government, but there was no debate on the events which had brought about its collapse.

The Executive Committee's Report to the Conference was confined to a brief review of the events which had led to the crisis, added to which was a tribute to MacDonald for his services to the Party and 'their deep regret that events should have arisen to give occasion to his separation from the great Movement he has been so powerful an influence in founding and inspiring'. 'Years of close co-operation and joint endeavour,' the Report added, 'have been brought to a most lamentable conclusion, *but a high sense of duty to the more unfortunate section of the nation, the unemployed men and women of the country whose welfare has ever been the special care and mission of the Labour Movement, gave the Party no other option but to oppose the policy of the new Government, no matter by whom it may be led or by whom it may be supported.*'[2]

But all that the Conference did was to pass a resolution, moved by Sir Stafford Cripps, which reaffirmed Labour's belief that proper provision for the unemployed was a social duty, protested against the recent Government measures, promised that it would reverse these measures, and called for the immediate cancellation of the cuts in unemployment benefits.[3] Even an amendment moved by David

[1] For this movement of protest through September and October, 1931, see Hutt, op. cit. ch. IX and Hannington, op. cit. ch. XIII.

[2] Labour Party Annual Conference Report, 1931. p. 176. My italics.

[3] ibid, p. 204.

Kirkwood, pledging the Labour Party 'to raise the benefits to the scale endorsed by the Party before the last election and to abolish the means test for those on transitional benefit',[1] was defeated, after Tom Johnston had told Conference, in words almost identical to those Ramsay MacDonald had used at the 1928 Conference, that, when the time came, 'it would be better not to be fettered by precise figures, but that whoever are your representatives should be left free to interpret the spirit of this resolution, which, we believe, covers all the possibilities that may have to be faced'.[2]

Even if account is taken of the General Elections of 1918 and 1924, there can be no good ground for disagreement with the *Manchester Guardian*'s view, voiced at the time, that the campaign of 1931 was 'the most fraudulent campaign of modern times'.[3] Given the manner in which the 'National' Government was formed, its composition and programme, it had to be.

It was the Conservatives who, with the co-operation of Mac-Donald, dictated the timing and nature of the appeal to the country. The Conservatives wanted an early General Election, while the crisis was still fresh; they wanted it to be fought on a platform which included Protection; and they also wanted it to be fought in the closest association with MacDonald.

The reason for this latter wish is not difficult to fathom. Even more after the formation of the 'National' Government than before, MacDonald was indispensable to the Tories precisely because he had been the leader of the Labour Party and was still closely identified with it. Nothing could be more certain to introduce an essential element of confusion in the campaign, and to work to the detriment of the Labour Party, than to have a former Labour Prime Minister lead an anti-Labour coalition. As the Parliamentary Correspondent of *The Times* noted on the 17th of September, 'one of the great assets of the present National Government is the faith which large masses of electors who voted for Labour candidates at the last election have in Mr MacDonald, Mr Snowden and Mr Thomas'.[4] How great an asset only became fully evident in the course of the campaign itself.

There were some difficulties in the way of Conservative wishes to have an early General Election, under a 'national' label, but with a protectionist programme. For one thing, the Liberals did not want an early election, and they were deeply opposed to Protection, as

[1] Labour Party Annual Conference Report, 1931, p. 206.
[2] ibid, p. 208.
[3] Mcwat, op. cit. p. 411.
[4] Bassett, op. cit. p. 254.

was Snowden. For another, the Government, it had been said at the time, had been specifically formed to overcome the emergency; only then would there be a General Election; and MacDonald had explicitly stated that it would not be a 'coupon' election. Either the emergency was still on, and there must therefore be no election: this was MacDonald's view on the 20th of September, the day on which Britain went off the gold standard, when he wrote to Samuel that 'obviously there is not even a theoretical justification for an Election now';[1] or the emergency was over, in which case there was no justification for fighting an election on a 'national' ticket. And there was also the fact, as Sir Clive Wigram wrote to the King on the 28th of September, that MacDonald did 'not like the idea of smashing up the Labour Party at the head of a Conservative association'.[2]

MacDonald's expulsion from the Labour Party, decided on by the National Executive on that day, was, Mr Bassett suggests, 'a contributory factor in his subsequent decisions'.[3]

In actual fact, whatever the Labour Party might or might not have done (and it could hardly have been expected *not* to expel MacDonald),[4] the Prime Minister was not the master of his decisions. Having gone so far, he had no option but to fall in with the wishes of his Conservative associates. The only thing that was required was to find a 'formula' which would serve to conceal his surrender.

At a meeting of the Cabinet on the 5th of October, it was agreed that each party (i.e. the Conservatives and the Liberals) should issue its own electoral manifesto, but that there should also be a general manifesto, signed by the Prime Minister himself, though in terms to be approved by Baldwin and Samuel.[5] In the Manifesto, the Prime Minister conveniently argued that 'as it is impossible to foresee in the changing conditions of today what may arise, no one can set out a programme of detail on which specific pledges can be given. The Government must therefore be free to consider every proposal likely to help, such as tariffs, expansion of exports and contraction of imports, commercial treaties and mutual economic arrangements with the Dominions'. Soon after, MacDonald was appealing for a 'doctors' mandate'.

The words mattered little, save for the purpose of confusion. For figures show better than anything else that the election, though it

[1] Samuel, op. cit. p. 209.
[2] Nicolson, op. cit. p. 493.
[3] Bassett, op. cit. p. 267.
[4] Indeed, the remarkable thing is that the Executive should have waited until then to expel MacDonald and his associates. According to M. A. Hamilton, Henderson alone voted against the decision. (M. A. Hamilton, *Arthur Henderson*, op. cit. p. 399.)
[5] Samuel, op. cit. p. 211.

190

was claimed to be a contest between the 'National' Government and the Labour Opposition, was in fact fought between the Conservative Party and the Labour Party. The former contested 519 seats and the latter 513. The next largest grouping, the Liberals, fought 121 seats; the National Liberals had 39 candidates and 'National Labour' 21.[1] There were also 25 Communists in the field and 23 candidates of Mosley's New Party. In asking for the return of candidates pledged to support the 'National' Government, MacDonald was *in fact* asking most of the electorate to vote Conservative.

Nor was the election fought on the basis of programmes and doctrines. 'As the campaign proceeded,' Mr Bassett notes, 'it resolved itself more and more into a contest between the Labour Ministers[2] and the Labour Party.' And he adds that these Ministers 'constituted the chief obstacle to the attempt on the Labour side to make Socialism the great Election issue. They stood in the way of a clear cut campaign for and against "the Tories". . . .'[3] This, of course, was precisely their main use to the Tories. Nor could the latter help being the beneficiaries of the ex-Labour Ministers' attacks on the Labour Party, culminating in Snowden's broadcast warning that Labour's programme was 'not Socialism' but 'Bolshevism run mad', and bound, 'were it taken seriously', to 'destroy every vestige of confidence and plunge the country into irretrievable ruin'. MacDonald was less verbally spectacular; he only 'implored' the electors, if they cared for their country, and did not want to see it go to the dogs, to vote for the candidates who supported the 'National' Government.[4] However, he also waved for the benefit of election audiences German marks from the days of the runaway inflation, 'to illustrate the perils of inflation', Mr Bassett explains, somewhat charitably. And both MacDonald and Snowden went a long way towards lending their authority to the scare that Post Office Savings would not be safe if the 'National' Government was not returned.[5]

Labour's voice had been muffled throughout the crisis and it remained hesitant and defensive during the campaign. The Labour Ministers had been too deeply implicated in the policies of MacDonald and Snowden for their efforts at dissociation from them to carry conviction. Indeed, the Labour Party's electoral manifesto was lavish in its praise for the endeavours and achievements of the Labour Government, carried through, it said, despite 'the intolerable restrictions of its minority position in the House of Commons',

[1] Of these, 13 were former Labour M.P.s who had chosen to follow MacDonald out of the Labour Party.
[2] I.e. the ex-Labour ministers.
[3] Bassett, op. cit. p. 293.
[4] ibid, p. 324.
[5] ibid, pp. 326-7.

'political intrigues', 'the class-conscious hostility of the House of Lords' and the undermining of its efforts 'by the organized pressure of business interests'. A new Labour Government, it warned, would 'tolerate no opposition from the House of Lords to the considered mandate of the People'; and it would 'seek such emergency powers as are necessary to the full attainment of its objectives'. One of these objectives was 'to reverse immediately the harsh policy of the present Government'. At the same time, Labour's programme marked a substantial advance on 1929. A Labour Government, it said, would bring the banking and credit system under public ownership and control, and it would also reorganize the most important basic industries as public services, owned and controlled in the national interest.[1]

There was much talk during the campaign of the urgent need to subordinate party interests to the 'national interest'. But it can hardly be claimed that the Conservative Party was faced with, and accepted, any great subordination of *its* interests in the election of 1931. In fact, it never fought an election under more favourable circumstances: nor did it ever win a more resounding victory. When the poll was declared, it was found to have 471 out of 615 seats; in 1929, it had had 260. Its rule was assured for the remainder of the decade. The National Liberals returned 35 candidates, the Liberals 33, and 'National Labour' 13. In all, Government supporters won 556 seats.

On the other hand Labour, with 289 seats at the dissolution, came back with fifty-two members, including five I.L.P.'ers and one Independent Labour. Communist candidates were everywhere defeated, and in most cases did extremely badly. All Cabinet Ministers in the Labour Government who stood lost their seats, except Lansbury. Labour's defeat was overwhelming, but much more so in parliamentary terms than in terms of its popular support. Labour's total poll in 1929 had been 8,360,000, an increase over 1924 partly due, as has been noted earlier, to a major increase in the electorate. The Labour Party now lost much that it had gained between 1924 and 1929. In 1924, just under 5.5 million people had voted for it. In 1931, 6.6 million did. Though powerless in Parliament, Labour had retained massive support in the country, most of it, obviously, from within the ranks of the organized working class. The Labour leadership could, in the following months and years, have chosen to mobilize that support for effective opposition to the Government's policies, at home and abroad. The history of that terrible decade might have been different, perhaps decisively different, but for its deliberate refusal to do so.

[1] For full text, the Manifesto, see Labour Party Annual Conference Report, 1932, pp. 319-22.

CHAPTER VII

MACDONALDISM WITHOUT MACDONALD

'My view of the situation is that nothing has happened either to the Party or to our electoral position to warrant any scrapping of our programme or policy or the revolutionizing of our methods.'

Arthur Henderson,
Labour Party Annual Conference, 1932

1. THE LURE OF WORDS

It is today commonly believed, inside the Labour movement and outside, that the Labour Party underwent a kind of socialist renaissance after 1931. Having rid itself of its evil genius and been purged in the fire of electoral disaster, the Labour Party, so the story would have it, now faced the future with a new resolution, and found in mass unemployment and the threat of Fascism 'causes' which both strengthened it in its radical beliefs and also gave these beliefs a new edge and a new bite. Indeed, people now say, the Labour Party, given the circumstances of the thirties, had it easy then: would that there were 'causes' so evidently compelling today!

The evidence shows all this to be very dubious history. The experience of 1931 did not cause any major transformations in the Labour Party. Nor did mass unemployment. Nor did Fascism. Certainly, the circumstances of the thirties moved many more people than ever before to the adoption of more sharply defined socialist views. But the impact of 1931 and of the thirties on the *leaders* of the Labour movement was, all things considered, very limited. Nor is this really surprising. Most of them were the same men who, through the twenties, had found acceptable the particular version of socialism propagated by MacDonald, whatever reservations some of them might have had about MacDonald himself. On the morrow of electoral defeat, they were willing to accept, though not without a good deal of pressure, a long-term *programme* for Labour more advanced than earlier programmes had been. But when it came to *doing* anything, here and now, about the evils they denounced, they showed the same inhibitions they had always shown before. Throughout that decade, they never swerved from the belief that opposition meant opposition in Parliament and that Labour could achieve little, and must not attempt much, until it had been returned to office as a majority Government. Meanwhile, as the Executive Report to the 1932 Annual Conference of the Labour Party said, they must create 'by education and organization', a mighty force of Socialist faith, which would carry Labour to victory, 'with effective authority to proceed boldly and speedily with its programme of Constructive Socialism'.[1]

This was also the view of those among the trade union leaders who thought of themselves as Socialists. 'We must,' Ernest Bevin had told his Executive Council in November 1931, 'consider the taking of steps by literature, by meetings and by the spread of knowledge in every possible way in order to get the principles of socialism more deeply rooted in the hearts of the people . . . there is nothing for it but grim, determined effort and intensive and continuous educational work.'[2]

That was very well, but it was hardly likely to worry the 'National' Government, or help the unemployed, or put new heart into Labour's supporters, let alone win new ones. The emphasis on education and propaganda was in fact a new form of *attentisme*, which was to be characteristic of the Labour leadership throughout the thirties.

In contrast, the experience of 1931 served to convince the I.L.P., as the Statement of Policy adopted by its Annual Conference at Easter 1932 said, that 'the class struggle which is the dynamic force in social change is nearing its decisive moment . . . there is no time now for slow processes of gradual change. The imperative need is for Socialism *now*'.[3] Futhermore, the Statement said, 'the possessing classes will not lightly abandon the political and economic power on which depends its privileges and vested interests . . . the struggle to dispossess it will call for a new militancy of spirit from the working class'. The I.L.P. had 'always recognized that the approach to Socialism could not be made by Parliamentary methods only . . . the critical circumstances demand that Socialists must be prepared to organize mass industrial action as an additional means to the attainment of their objectives and realize that the development of a capitalist dictatorship may compel the resort to extra-constitutional methods'.[4]

These formulations sufficiently indicate that the I.L.P.'s continuing

[1] Labour Party Annual Conference Report, 1932, p. 4.
[2] Bullock, op. cit. p. 503.
[3] I.L.P. Annual Conference Report, March 1932, p. 59. Italics in text.
[4] ibid, p. 60.

dispute with the Labour Party, though ostensibly concerned with internal party discipline, was about weightier matters. In discussing the conflict with Fenner Brockway, Henderson had brushed aside organizational problems and raised a question of a different order: 'He had gathered that the I.L.P. believed that ultimately the transition from Capitalism to Socialism would be made not through Parliament but by a direct struggle for power between the working class and the possessing class. Did this mean that the I.L.P. stood for socialism by revolution?'[1]

It was not a question which most leaders of the I.L.P. would, even then, have found it at all easy to answer. But they had no difficulty in condemning the lack of urgency they detected in their Labour colleagues. At the I.L.P. Conference of Easter 1932, a substantial body of delegates, led by Maxton, urged disaffiliation from the Labour Party, while another section favoured continued affiliation. A third group, which temporarily carried the day, was in favour of affiliation on condition that the Parliamentary Labour Party Standing Orders be amended. This the P.L.P. would not do. A final attempt at negotiation was unsuccessful and a special conference of the I.L.P. in July 1932 resolved on disaffiliation, by 241 votes to 142.[2]

Whatever influence the I.L.P. might have wielded within the Labour Party, it could hardly have been less effective than it was outside it. After it had left the parent body, it went into an irreversible decline.[3] Nothing better illustrates the fact that, even in the circumstances of the time, there was room in the Labour movement for two quite separate political parties, and for no more than two. There was a very small amount of room (and there was, in the following years, to be a little more) for a party as distinctive as the Communist Party. The rest was taken up by the Labour Party. There was no room at all for a socialist party independent of either.

This was very hard on men and women who did feel that they had a contribution to make of a kind different from that of the Labour Party or the Communist Party. But it was part of a situation which had not, in this context, been materially altered by the crisis of 1931. This, of course, is where the disaffiliationists erred. They believed that British politics had now entered an altogether new phase and that, therefore, old alignments must be replaced by new ones, in which a party such as the I.L.P. could play a significant rôle. It was a bad estimate, which had its origins in an apocalyptic view, increasingly current on the left, of the likelihood of capitalism's

[1] J. McNair, op. cit. p. 210.
[2] Cole, op. cit. p. 277.
[3] The I.L.P. had 16,773 members in 1932, 11,092 in 1933, 7,166 in 1934 and 4,392 in 1935 (Pelling, op. cit. p. 77, ft. 1).

economic 'collapse'. Ernest Bevin had a better appreciation of the prospects of British capitalism. It was not true, he told his Union in his presidential address in May 1932, that capitalism was breaking down; it was in fact adjusting itself far more rapidly than many people in the Labour movement imagined.[1] But this view did not lead to a new insistence on the need for a militant assertion of Labour's claims; on the contrary, its corollary was taken to be that Labour's only possible strategy was a defensive one, based on conciliation and the discouragement of militancy.

The departure of the I.L.P. left a void in the Labour Party which the Socialist League sought to fill.

The League, which held its inaugural meeting on the eve of the 1932 Labour Party Conference, was an amalgam of many tendencies, the most important of which was that of former members of the I.L.P., who had left that organization, not because they dissented from its general political analysis, but because they would not cut themselves off from the Labour Party. Others, like Sir Stafford Cripps, who was the dominant figure in the League after Frank Wise, its first Chairman, died in 1933, saw the League as the spearhead of much-needed Socialist agitation within the Labour Party. And there were also those who came into it from the Society of Socialist Information and Propaganda, when that body decided to amalgamate with the League.[2]

The League's Executive Committee encompassed every shade and nuance of the left, from barely left of centre to near Communist. Besides Frank Wise[3] and Cripps, it included William Mellor and H. N. Brailsford, C. R. Attlee and Sir Charles Trevelyan, Aneurin

[1] Bullock, op. cit. p. 504.

[2] The S.S.I.P. had been formed in the winter of 1930-31, while the second Labour Government was still in office, with Ernest Bevin as its Chairman and G. D. H. Cole as its Vice-Chairman. The S.S.I.P. was closely linked with the New Fabian Research Bureau, of which Clement Attlee was the Chairman and Cole the Secretary. The N.F.R.B. was primarily intended as a research organization for the 'development of a constructive Socialist programme' (Cole, op. cit. p. 282). The S.S.I.P. was intended to be its secular arm and to 'devote itself to the diffusion of this research' (ibid, p. 282). Furthermore, it was 'an essential part of the plan on which both S.S.I.P. and N.F.R.B. were founded that neither should take any direct part in parliamentary politics, or seek formal affiliation to the Labour Party' (ibid, p. 282-3). The S.S.I.P., Bevin wrote in May 1931, 'is not a ginger group to the Party or anything of that kind; it is an attempt to work out problems and to give the new generation something to grip' (Bullock, op. cit. p. 501).

[3] The representatives of the S.S.I.P. had wanted Bevin to be Chairman of the League. The ex-I.L.P. members were not only determined to have Frank Wise as Chairman, but refused to accept Bevin in any office at all. To prevent the negotiations from breaking down, the S.S.I.P. representatives agreed. Bevin bitterly resented the rebuff.

Bevan and D. N. Pritt, Ellen Wilkinson and G. R. Mitchison; there were also the three leading academic figures of the Labour Party, G. D. H. Cole, Harold Laski and R. H. Tawney; and trade unionists like Harold Clay, of the Transport and General Workers' Union, and H. L. Elvin, of the National Union of Clerks and Administrative Workers.

Some of the members of the Executive had long been Marxists, or at least *marxisant*. But there were others who had, until 1931, dwelt fairly comfortably within different traditions, either Christian Socialist or Secular Fabian. Some of these now came to question their earlier assumptions concerning the inevitability of parliamentary gradualism. In specifically political terms, this questioning took the form both of a demand and of a warning: of a demand that a future Labour Government should embark, as soon as it assumed office, on a programme of nationalization far more extensive than the Labour Party had ever put forward;[1] and of a warning that a Labour Government, intent on the carrying out of such a programme, must expect fierce and, quite likely, unconstitutional resistance on the part of its opponents.

Thus in 1932, Harold Laski was asking whether 'evolutionary socialism (had) deceived itself in believing that it can establish itself by peaceful means within the ambit of the capitalist system', and reflected that 'the road to power is far harder than Labour has, so far, been led to imagine'.[2] And Tawney, writing in the summer of that year, now insisted that the implementation of a socialist programme would be 'a pretty desperate business': that it would immediately provoke 'determined resistance' was, he held, 'as certain as political facts can be'.[3] The privileged classes, if their position was seriously threatened, would, he wrote, 'use every piece on the board, political and economic—the House of Lords, the Crown, the Press, disaffection in the army, financial crisis, international difficulties and even, as newspaper attacks on the pound in 1931 showed, the émigré trick of injuring one's country to protect one's pocket—in the honest conviction that they are saving civilization'.[4] Even more emphatically, Sir Stafford Cripps expressed the same opinion, in speeches and in writing. In a pamphlet significantly entitled *Can Socialism Come by Constitutional Means?* he warned that 'the ruling class will go to almost any length to defeat Parliamentary action if

[1] The Socialist League's programme included a demand for 'the immediate nationalization of the banks, land, the mines, power, transport, iron and steel, cotton, and control of foreign trade', with 'restricted compensation'.
[2] *The Crisis and the Constitution* (London, 1932) p. 9.
[3] 'The Choice Before the Labour Party', *The Political Quarterly*, July-September 1932, p. 327.
[4] ibid, p. 337.

the issue is the direct issue as to the continuance of their financial and political control'.[1]

These doubts as to the possibility of a smooth transition from a capitalist to a socialist society by normal constitutional and parliamentary means is an important facet of the intellectual and ideological stirrings of the thirties. For the first time in the history of the Labour movement in the twentieth century, the notion that a parliamentary majority might not be enough to ensure a socialist transformation of society gained some currency outside the small circle of Marxists and near-Marxists who had always assumed that it would not be enough. Even during the lifetime of the Labour Government, Shaw, in a new Preface to the Fabian Essays, had recalled that 'when the greatest Socialist of that day, the poet and craftsman William Morris, told the workers that there was no hope for them save in revolution, we said that if that were true, there was no hope at all for them, and urged them to save themselves through Parliament, the municipalities and the franchise'. 'It is not so certain today as it seemed in the 'eighties,' Shaw wrote, 'that Morris was not right.'[2] It seemed even less certain in the aftermath of 1931.

These ideological stirrings could not be confined to a questioning of the assumptions underlying parliamentary gradualism. The doubts were bound to produce, at the very least, a markedly more sympathetic view of Marxism, in many cases an espousal of Marxian doctrine, or what was taken to be Marxian doctrine. And so it was, most notably with a new generation, which, unencumbered by the Fabianism of its elders, and coming to political consciousness in an age of crisis, found it easy to reject gradualist assumptions.

Nor was it only Marxism which gained a new attraction. From 1932 onwards, Soviet Russia entered into the consciousness of the non-Communist left as never before, not only because its official ideology was Marxism, nor even because it was the land of the workers' revolution, but because it was now viewed as the country of planning, of the rational and scientific utilization of resources, of full employment; and, certainly no less important than all these, because it seemed, particularly to many progressive people for whom the worst abomination of capitalism was its moral degeneration, to be moved by a moral purpose which capitalism was altogether unable to generate. 'It seems,' as Beatrice Webb wrote in January 1932, 'to provide the spiritual power.'[3]

There were, however, some definite limits to these doubts as to the validity of parliamentary gradualism. Laski, though he averred that

[1] *Can Socialism Come By Constitutional Means?* (London, n.d.) p. 2.
[2] G. B. Shaw Ed., *Fabian Essays in Socialism* (London, 1931) p. ix.
[3] *Beatrice Webb's Diaries*, op. cit. p. 298.

a Socialist Government would meet fierce challenge, also suggested that the consequences need not necessarily be revolutionary ('though it is, of course, tempting to think in communist terms and make them so'). What might, he felt, yet make 'all the difference' and cause the Conservative forces to bow to the inevitable was the power of the trade union movement, on condition that the trade union movement should be moved by a much more coherently socialist outlook than had ever been the case. And, he added, though what had happened in 1931 'makes one pause before accepting the traditional hypothesis that a mere conquest of a majority is a sure road to a Socialist victory', it remained 'a necessary road to follow'.[1]

Tawney, for his part, wrote that a majority Labour Government, even one armed with wide discretionary powers, would need to be supported, on the example of Russia, by a body 'at once dynamic and antiseptic, the energumens, the zealots, the Puritans, the religious orders, the Communist Party—call it what you please—which possesses, not merely opinions, but convictions, and acts as it believes. . . . Till something analogous to it develops in England, Labour will be plaintive, not formidable and its business will not march'.[2] But he did not define what this body should actually *do* and he was also careful to add that the existence of the kind of body he had in mind did not 'depend on political forms; it is as compatible with Parliamentary, as with any other machinery'.[3]

It was Sir Stafford Cripps, then the most prominent Labour Front-bencher after George Lansbury, who came to be identified with the advocacy of far-reaching constitutional changes. Not only did he insist that a majority Labour Government would require wide emer-gency powers as soon as it took office; he also assumed that it would soon face a situation of extreme constitutional crisis. In the pamphlet mentioned earlier, which is fairly typical of his thinking at this time, he envisaged an early conflict with the House of Lords and then launched out on free speculation. Faced with a hostile House of Lords, the Government would ask the Crown to create peers. Should this be refused, the Labour Government would either resign or continue in office unconstitutionally. The latter alternative would lead to civil war. It would therefore be better to choose the former and allow Labour's opponents to form a minority govern-ment, which would have to fight a General Election, which Labour would win. On the other hand, Cripps reflected, the Conserva-tives might not go to the country but choose to govern with the support of the Armed Forces by means of a military dictatorship.

[1] *The Crisis and the Constitution*, op. cit. p. 56.
[2] *The Choice Before the Labour Party*, op. cit. p. 340.
[3] ibid, p. 340.

'If the Socialist Government came to the conclusion,' he then added, 'that there was any real danger of such a step being taken, it would probably be better and more conducive to the general peace and welfare of the country for the Socialist Government to make itself temporarily into a dictatorship until matters could again be put to the test at the polls.'[1] And this, he also wrote, might have to be delayed beyond the normal duration of Parliament, 'unless during the first five years so great a degree of change has been accomplished as to deprive Capitalism of its power'.[2]

Cripps undoubtedly meant all this very seriously. On the other hand, he neither was nor saw himself as a revolutionary, as he was at pains to point out in March 1932 in correspondence with the Attorney-General who had accused him of having become the advocate of violent revolution. 'I have stated,' he wrote, 'that I believed in a very rapid change of the present system by the method of Parliamentary Democracy. You may term that a "revolutionary" change in the same sense as one speaks of a "revolutionary" change in fiscal policy, but I am sure you must appreciate the difference between this use of the term revolutionary and the use you made of it by adding the qualification—"in the manner of the Russian revolution".'[3] Cripps not only believed that a Labour Government would only come to power on the basis of an electoral majority; he also insisted that such a Government would only have a chance at all if that majority was 'in favour of an active policy of socialism'.[4] It was, in 1932, an eventuality sufficiently remote to reduce the consideration of the desperate expedients a Socialist Government might have to take to the level of a parlour-game. The issues which Cripps raised, and which Laski in particular explored throughout the thirties,[5] were of fundamental importance—nor have they ceased to be important. But the question confronting the Labour movement in 1932 was not what a socialist government would do after it had won a General Election. It was rather what kind of challenge a Labour Opposition would offer to the 'National' Government. And on this question, the Labour Left was rather weak.

The Labour Left's main endeavour at the 1932 Annual Conference of the Labour Party (held at Leicester) was to commit the Party to a programme much more far-reaching than was thought appropriate

[1] *Can Socialism Come by Constitutional Means?* op. cit. p. 5.
[2] ibid, p. 2.
[3] Estorick, op. cit. p. 123.
[4] *Can Socialism Come by Constitutional Means?* op. cit. p. 2.
[5] See, e.g., his *The State in Theory and Practice* (1935) and his *Parliamentary Government in England* (1938).

by Labour's controllers. The Executive's Report to the Conference had promised, in language that was highly ambiguous, that 'a Labour Government, equipped with adequate power, would turn its immediate attention to the reorganization of banking and finance as a public service, to the transference of the land to the nation, and to the development under public auspices of the power and transport services'. 'Banking and finance, land, mines, power and transport and iron and steel,' it also said, 'are basic resources and services on which the whole economic system, and indeed the national life, in the last resort depend.'[1] But, it also warned, 'it is not possible . . . to specify exactly in advance the order in which a majority Labour Government would proceed with its measures of economic reorganization'.[2]

The delegates were in a mood for something bolder.[3] They passed without discussion a resolution which declared that 'the main objective of the Labour Party is the establishment of socialism', and that 'the common ownership of the means of production and distribution is the only means by which the producers by hand and brain will be able to secure the full fruits of their industry'.[4] And they also endorsed a resolution, moved by Sir Charles Trevelyan, asking that 'on assuming office, either with or without power, definite Socialist legislation must be immediately promulgated, and that the Party shall stand or fall in the House of Commons on the principles in which it has faith'.[5] 'Let us lay down in some such resolution as this,' said Trevelyan, 'the unshakable mandate that they (i.e. a Labour Government) are to introduce at once, before attempting remedial measures of any other kind, great Socialist measures, or some general measure empowering them to nationalize the key industries of the country.'[6]

Henderson, then about to resign as leader of the Party,[7] opposed the resolution because, he said, it would tie their hands. His intervention was badly received, so much so that the Chairman had to ask the delegates to hear him out.[8] Among those who spoke for the

[1] Labour Party Annual Conference Report, 1932, p. 4.
[2] ibid, p. 4.
[3] Hugh Dalton thought the delegates 'irritable' and attributed their irritability to the fact that the Conference was not held at the seaside (H. Dalton, *The Fateful Years, Memoirs 1931-1945* (London, 1957) p. 30).
[4] Labour Party Annual Conference Report, 1932, p. 202.
[5] ibid, p. 204.
[6] ibid, p. 204.
[7] Henderson continued, despite the fall of the Labour Government, as Chairman of the Disarmament Conference at Geneva and was replaced as Leader of the Opposition by George Lansbury.
[8] 'It is unusual for you to behave in this way when he is speaking,' the Chairman remarked (ibid, p. 204).

resolution was C. R. Attlee. 'The events of last year,' he said, 'have shown that no further progress can be made in seeking to get crumbs from the rich man's table . . . in the present condition of the world we are bound in duty to those whom we represent to tell them quite clearly that they cannot get Socialism without tears, that whenever we try to do anything we will be opposed by every vested interest, financial, political and social, and I think we have got to face the fact that, even if we are returned with a majority, we shall have to fight all the way, that we shall have another crisis at once, and that we have got to have a thought-out plan to deal with that crisis; that we have got to put first things first, and that we have not got to wait until our mandate has been exhausted and frittered away, but, as Sir Charles Trevelyan says, we have got to strike while the iron is hot.'[1] The resolution was carried without a vote.

This was not the only success which the Left registered at the 1932 Conference: it also won a narrow majority for the nationalization of the joint-stock banks.

At the 1931 Conference, a general policy resolution had been passed which explicitly envisaged the public ownership of the banking and credit system. But, in 1932, a resolution introduced by Hugh Dalton on behalf of the Executive only promised the nationalization of the Bank of England and the creation of a National Investment Board. In addition, it warned that 'all necessary emergency powers' would be taken 'to deal with any attempt by private persons or institutions to obstruct the Government, damage national credit, or create a financial panic'.[2] This provoked an amendment, moved by Frank Wise and supported by Sir Stafford Cripps, asking that the joint-stock banks should also be nationalized, and that power should be taken to nationalize or control the finance, acceptance and banking houses.[3]

The amendment met with a good deal of opposition, notably from Ernest Bevin, who seemed to argue simultaneously that the proposal could not be implemented, and that it was in any case unnecessary to the purposes of a Labour Government.[4] For the Executive, Dalton pleaded with the delegates to allow 'a further period for intensive study', following which 'definite proposals' would be submitted to the next Labour Party Conference.[5] But the amendment was carried,

[1] Labour Party Annual Conference Report, 1932, p. 205.
[2] ibid, p. 182.
[3] ibid, p. 188.
[4] ibid, p. 190. At the 1919 T.U.C. Conference, it was Bevin who had moved a resolution (which was carried) demanding the nationalization of the whole banking system (T.U.C. Annual Conference Report, 1919, p. 277).
[5] ibid, p. 194.

by 1,141,000 votes to 984,000.[1] For the Left, it was an encouraging vote, at least on paper.

Beside a Report on Currency, Banking and Finance, the Conference was also presented with three Reports, prepared by the Policy Committee set up in December 1931 to restate Party policy. These dealt with agriculture, transport and electricity supply. More Reports, 'covering a considerable range of policy', were promised for the 1933 Conference.

The three reports envisaged the public ownership of agricultural land, of transport, and of electricity generation and distribution. In each case, the accent was heavily on the need for planning, co-ordination and efficiency, to be secured by public corporations under ministerial control, members of the boards being appointed 'on appropriate grounds of ability'.

Despite Herbert Morrison's ardent commendation of this particular approach to 'constructive socialism', the demand was raised that provision should be made for consultation with the appropriate trade unions on the appointment of certain of the members of the boards. This, which amounted in effect to a demand for trade union representation on the boards, was embodied in an amendment moved by Harold Clay, of the Transport and General Workers' Union, and supported by Ernest Bevin. The same issue had been raised at the Trade Union Congress the previous month and referred to the separate unions for further consideration. Indeed, the divergence of views expressed at the Conference was only an echo of the conflict which had opposed Morrison to Bevin during the lifetime of the second Labour Government, when Morrison, as Minister of Transport, had been in charge of the London Passenger Transport Bill, and had adamantly opposed direct labour representation on the proposed London Passenger Transport Board.

In moving his amendment, Clay complained that the plan for the nationalization of transport 'stratifies industrial society' and left the workers under the 'perpetual control' of an 'efficient bureaucracy'.[2] Against this, Morrison argued that trade union representation would leave the way open to claims for representation by a multitude of special interests inimical to Labour.[3] At the other extreme, a number of speakers opposed the amendment on the ground, as C. T. Cramp, of the National Union of Railwaymen, put it, that 'getting a few friends on these Boards, Socialism is not going to be advanced'.[4] In the end, the issue was referred to

[1] Labour Party Annual Conference Report, 1932, p. 194.
[2] ibid, p. 214.
[3] ibid, p. 211.
[4] ibid, p. 222.

further discussion between the Labour Party and the T.U.C.

A year later, the National Executive presented to the Party Conference a Memorandum on the subject, agreed to by the General Council of the T.U.C. and endorsed, by a small majority, at the Trades Union Congress. The Memorandum cautiously acknowledged the right of Trade Unions to nominate 'competent and suitable persons' for appointment to the Boards of publicly-owned industries, but distinguished carefully between the control and direction exercised by such Boards, and day-to-day administration, which would have to be undertaken by 'trained business administrators'.[1]

In sharp contrast, a resolution moved at the 1933 Conference demanded that 'wage earners of all grades and occupations' should have the right, acknowledged by law, 'to an effective share in the control and direction of socialized industries which their labour sustains', and also asked that the Trade Unions should be directly represented, not only on the board of direction and control, but on 'other administrative bodies in the industry or service'.[2]

These divergent formulations reflected crucially important differences of approach to nationalization. In the Morrisonian concept endorsed by the National Executive and the General Council, nationalization was no more than a piece of administrative machinery, designed to improve the performance of some particular industry or service, and to be run by managers on strict business lines, though under the ultimate control of a Minister.[3] The resolution moved at the 1933 Conference, on the other hand, harked back to an older concept of socialization, in which new forms of industrial organization were to be created on the basis of the wage earners' 'effective share in the control and direction of socialized industries'. The Morrisonian concept was pregnant with bureaucratic paternalism; the resolution at least showed some desire to grapple with the problem of industrial democracy. At the 1933 Conference, it was Morrison's opponents who narrowly prevailed, by 1,223,000 votes to 1,083,000.[4] But when it came to the point, much later, it was Herbert Morrison who won.

The Labour Left after 1931 was not only concerned to persuade the

[1] Labour Party Annual Conference Report, 1933, p. 14.
[2] ibid, p. 205.
[3] For an exposition of Morrison's conception of nationalization, see his *Socialisation and Transport* (London, 1933). For a useful dissection of the debate, see R. A. Dahl, 'Workers' Control of Industry and the British Labour Party', in *American Political Science Review*, XLI, No. 5 (October 1947) pp. 875-900.
[4] Labour Party Annual Conference Report, 1933, p. 205.

Labour Party to adopt a more radical programme; it was also concerned, as has already been noted, with what a Labour Government should do in order to implement such a programme. That concern was naturally much enhanced by the Nazis' overthrow of the Weimar Republic at the beginning of 1933. For the Labour Left, the Nazis' triumph soon came to provide additional ground for pessimism as to the viability of capitalist democracy in an age of crisis, and greatly increased doubts as to the possibility of a peaceful and parliamentary transition to socialism, in Britain as anywhere else. Whatever its specific national variant, Fascism, it appeared to them, held a fatal attraction to ruling classes everywhere, the more so if those ruling classes came to find it impossible to defeat a challenge to their power and privileges within the framework of representative government. Thus, they argued with renewed emphasis, a Labour Government must expect and anticipate bitter resistance if it seriously sought to bring about a socialist transformation of society.

At the 1933 Labour Party Conference, Sir Stafford Cripps asked that the Executive should be instructed 'to specify the means to be adopted by the next Labour Government for a rapid and complete conversion of the Capitalist into the Socialist system'; and those means should include, his resolution stated, the immediate abolition of the House of Lords, the immediate passing of an Emergency Powers Act, the revision of the procedure of the House of Commons and the machinery of Government, 'so that a rapid transition to Socialism may be carried through constitutionally, and dictatorship avoided'; and 'an Economic Plan for Industry, Finance and Foreign Trade designed rapidly to end the present system and thus to abolish unemployment and poverty'.[1]

The Executive did not oppose Sir Stafford's resolution outright. Instead, it promised to consider the points he had raised and to report to the next Conference. But Cripps and his friends came in for some severe criticism, notably from Ernest Bevin.

This, Mr Bullock notes, 'was the first of many encounters in which Bevin and Cripps were to find themselves on opposite sides during the next few years', and the contrast between the two men, he goes on to add, 'could hardly have been more strongly marked, Cripps slender and ascetic, the passionate doctrinaire to whom ideas were more real than human beings, Bevin thick set and earthy with a critical power of judgment tempered by long experience of men'.[2] Bevin himself was at pains to underline the contrast between his point of view 'as a Trade Unionist who has to deal every day

[1] Labour Party Annual Conference Report, 1933, p. 159.
[2] Bullock, op. cit. p. 530.

205

with the masses of the people' and that of 'a good many who have now joined with the Labour Party'. 'Our work,' said Bevin, 'is eminently practical, and it is to deliver the goods to our members, and we know, as leaders, the absolute folly of putting up programmes that are not likely to be realized . . .'[1]

Despite its plausibility, the suggestion that the opposition was simply between a practical trade unionist and a doctrinaire intellectual conceals more than it reveals. Cripps had many ideas, but to call him an intellectual doctrinaire is to overlook the fact that he was exceedingly weak on doctrine; nor was Bevin by any means as crassly empirical as his own antitheses, then and later, were intended to suggest. On the contrary, Bevin, in many ways, had a much more organized theory of the rôle of Labour than Cripps on the Left, and than his trade union colleagues on the Right. At the core of that theory lay the notion of institutionalized co-operation between the trade unions, management and the State, to be supplemented by the parliamentary pressure of the Labour Party for legislation beneficial to the working classes. For all the claims of realism that were made for it, it was not a strategy likely to have much effect on the Government.

The 1933 Conference was also presented with a Report on *Labour and Government*,[2] whose recommendations, obviously inspired by the experience and character of the second Labour Government, were designed to provide a lesser measure of independence to a future Labour administration. Among the main proposals of the Sub-Committee was a recommendation that, after a General Election which had resulted in the possibility of a Labour Government, the National Joint Council should meet and record its opinions 'as to the advisability or otherwise of the Labour Party taking office'; on the other hand, if the Party only found itself in a position to take office as a Minority Government, a special Conference of affiliated organizations should be summoned. In neither eventuality, however, was it suggested that any body other than the Parliamentary Party should make the final decision: the P.L.P. was only to receive and consider the recommendations of the outside bodies.

The sub-committee agreed that final responsibility for the selection of Ministers must rest with the Prime Minister; but it suggested that three members of the Parliamentary Party, elected by the P.L.P.,

[1] Labour Party Annual Conference Report, 1933, p. 161.
[2] ibid, pp. 8-10. The Report was the work of a Constitutional Policy Sub-Committee whose Chairman was J. R. Clynes and whose members included George Lansbury, C. R. Attlee, H. J. Laski, H. B. Lees-Smith and Walter Citrine.

should, together with the Secretary of the Party, 'advise and consult the leader'. The Prime Minister, it was also proposed, should be subject to majority decisions of the Cabinet, and 'he should only recommend the Dissolution of Parliament on the decision of the Cabinet confirmed by a Parliamentary Party meeting'.

It was essential, the sub-committee said, that the Government and the P.L.P. should keep in close contact with the Labour Movement as a whole and the National Joint Council, it felt, provided effective machinery for the purpose: three members of the Cabinet were to be selected, one or more of whom should attend meetings of the National Joint Council in a consultative capacity.

It was no less essential, the Report stated, that 'the closest possible relations' should exist between the Government and the P.L.P. To that purpose, a Minister was to be given responsibility to act, both as a means of contact between the Prime Minister and his colleagues on the one hand, and the Parliamentary Party on the other. He would attend meetings of the Consultative Committee of the Parliamentary Party, and other Cabinet Ministers should when occasion required be available for attendance at the Consultative Committee, whose meetings would in any case be attended by the Chief Whip.

Furthermore, the policy to be pursued by the Labour Government 'would be that laid down in Resolutions of the Annual Conference and embodied in the General Election Manifesto . . . the King's Speech would, from year to year, announce the instalments of the Party's policy with which the Government proposed to deal'; and, where questions arose for decision on which Party policy had not been declared, 'they would be dealt with by discussion with the appropriate bodies'. Not least, it was proposed that the General Council of the T.U.C. 'should be fully consulted with regard to proposed legislation in which it is directly concerned'.

There was one amendment to the Report, moved at the Conference by the Barrow Labour Party; it asked that 'the selection of men and women to hold Cabinet rank or other Governmental posts shall be made by a Joint Committee of the National Joint Council and the Co-operative Party'. This was defeated by 519,000 votes to 1,579,000, and the Report was endorsed by Conference.[1] None of its recommendations became relevant until 1945, by which time they could be ignored.

In July 1934, the National Executive issued *For Socialism and Peace*, the third major programmatic statement in the Labour Party's history and much the most radical it has ever adopted. The statement summarized the policy decisions of the previous three years and committed itself to the proposition that in regard to 'banking and

[1] Labour Party Annual Conference Report, 1933, p. 167.

credit, transport, water, coal, electricity, gas, agriculture, iron and steel, shipping, shipbuilding, engineering, textiles, chemicals, insurance', the time had come for drastic reorganization', and that 'for the most part nothing short of immediate public ownership and control will be effective'. Furthermore, the programme promised that 'public ownership of industries and services will be marked not only by the introduction of a new purpose, but by a new spirit in relation to the workers engaged therein . . . the employees in a socialized industry have a right, which should be acknowledged by law, to an effective share in control and direction of the industry'.[1]

As to the question of means, *For Socialism and Peace* stated that 'no party in Great Britain today can seriously embark upon the task of Socialist reconstruction without adapting the machine of government to its purpose'. The defects of the present regime, it said, were the existence of an hereditary Chamber and the old-fashioned procedure of the House of Commons, which facilitated obstruction and delay. 'A Labour Government meeting with sabotage from the House of Lords,' the document said, 'would take immediate steps to overcome it; and would, in any event, during its term of office pass legislation abolishing the House of Lords as a legislative chamber'. In regard to parliamentary procedure, *For Socialism and Peace* declared that the Labour Party was 'not less jealous than any other Party in the State' for the historic rights of an Opposition, but proposed a number of minor reforms designed to speed up the consideration of legislation in the House of Commons.[2] None of the other proposals that were put forward represented more than an extension of existing constitutional tendencies or of long-standing suggestions for political and administrative reform. A Labour Government would make greater use of delegated legislation and 'would seek to make Parliament the place where principles and legislative structure, and not details, are debated and decided'; electoral reform, including the abolition of plural voting, was overdue; an 'efficient democracy' needed to revise 'the foundations of its whole administrative system'; the Labour Party believed in the need to reconstruct the Cabinet, to regroup departmental functions, and to reorganize the machinery and methods of local government.[3]

The National Executive had also something to say on the subject of emergency powers. A Labour Government, faced with an emergency situation for which the normal powers of government should

[1] *For Socialism and Peace*, p. 15.
[2] For details, see Labour Party Annual Conference Report, 1934, Appendix VIII, Parliamentary Problems and Procedure, pp. 261-3.
[3] *For Socialism and Peace*, pp. 31-2.

prove inadequate, 'would seek for the necessary emergency powers from Parliament to deal with the position'. This, it was carefully recalled, had been the course adopted by Governments in 1914, 1926 and 1931; but a Labour Government would 'ask for such powers, and such powers only, as the nature of the emergency required'; their use would be for the periods of the emergency only, and for the problems which it raised; and the Orders and Regulations issued under the Emergency Act would be subject to discussion in, and approval by, the Houses of Parliament; finally, the powers taken would have a definite and clear relationship to the character of the emergency created, and they would be operated with a view to the most rapid return possible to the processes of normal government.

Regard for constitutional propriety could not have gone much further and, in any case, the Executive, increasingly worried and embarrassed by the tone of the speeches and writings of members of the Socialist League,[1] had repeatedly stressed the Labour Party's devotion to parliamentary democracy. 'The Labour Party,' the Executive had said on the 4th of January, 1934, 'stands for Parliamentary Democracy. It is firmly opposed to individual or Group Dictatorship, whether from the Right or from the Left. It holds that the best, and indeed the only tolerable, form of Government for this country is Democratic Government, with a free electoral system and an active and efficient Parliamentary machine for reaching effective decisions, after reasonable opportunities for discussion and criticism.' And the statement concluded, 'in so far as any statements which are at variance with the declared policy of the Party on this question have been or may be made by individuals, these are hereby definitely repudiated by the National Executive'.[2] Two days after the statement had been issued, Cripps, speaking at Nottingham on the theme of resistance to the purposes of a Labour Government, had said that 'we shall have to overcome opposition from Buckingham Palace and other places as well'.[3] This, his biographer notes, 'provoked immediate disclaimers from other Labour leaders . . .'[4] and Cripps himself precipitately retreated; he was, he explained, 'most certainly not referring to the Crown'; he had used the words Buckingham

[1] 'If the Socialist League point of view were approved by the Party,' Herbert Morrison wrote in September 1933, 'it would drive us to defend ourselves for the greater part of our time against Tory allegations of Bolshevism and dictatorship' (*New Clarion*, 30th of September,' 1933, in J. Jupp, *The Left in Britain, 1931 to 1941*, unpublished thesis for the M.Sc. Econ. degree of the University of London, p. 172).
[2] Labour Party Annual Conference Report, 1934, p. 9.
[3] C. Cooke, *The Life of Richard Stafford Cripps* (London, 1957), p. 159.
[4] ibid, p. 161.

Palace as 'a well-known expression used to describe Court Circles and the officials and other people who surround the King'. Some days later, he was assuring an audience in Glasgow that he was in favour of constitutional monarchy.[1]

At the 1934 Labour Party Conference the Socialist League mounted a major attack on *For Socialism and Peace*—no less than 75 amendments to the document were put down, including the deletion of the draft's statement of aims and substitution of a five-point Programme of Action, stating that the Party would ask for a mandate 'to act with the speed called for by the situation at home and abroad in a decisive advance within five years towards a Socialist Britain'. The amendment was defeated by 2,146,000 votes to 206,000[2] and the Socialist League was no more successful in its other attempts to have *For Socialism and Peace* amended. The League was by no means a spent force. Indeed, it had, by December 1934, come to see itself as 'a disciplined organization founded on a common policy and working as part of the Labour movement . . . we have passed out of the realm of programme making into the realm of action'.[3] But the League, though not a parliamentary body, faced problems scarcely less severe than those which the I.L.P. had encountered in its attempts to act as a pressure group within the Labour Party. It is quite likely that *For Socialism and Peace* would not have gone nearly so far had it not been for the League's pressure. In this sense, and despite the fact that its membership never exceeded more than a few thousand members, it fulfilled one of the main tasks which the Labour Left had always fulfilled in the Labour Party, and it is a task whose importance should not be underestimated. But the partial response of the Executive to its pressure itself served to neutralize the League and diminish, as the Executive intended, its appeal to the rank and file.[4] Nor had the Executive reason to regret Cripps's election to it in 1934—there could have been no better way of containing him than by saddling him with the burdens of collective responsibility.

2. LABOUR AND THE UNEMPLOYED

While Labour Right and Left were debating what a future Labour Government should do some time in the future, there remained the

[1] Cooke, op. cit. p. 160.
[2] Labour Party Annual Conference Report, 1934, p. 165.
[3] *Socialist Leaguer*, December 1934, in Jupp, op. cit. p. 173.
[4] No doubt the leadership was also helped by the fact that 1934 had, electorally, been a fairly good year for the Labour Party. In March, it had, for the first time, captured a clear majority of seats on the London County Council; and it had also made considerable gains in other local government elections.

unemployed, nearly three million of them, and their families, living on a reduced dole, in the shadow of the Means Test.[1]

The operation of the Means Test, which had begun in November 1931, had given a sharper edge to the anger provoked by the 'National' Government's economy measures. Though one would scarcely guess it from reading the reports of the Labour Party or the T.U.C. Annual Conferences, 1932 was a year of widespread unemployed agitation, with meetings, demonstrations, marches, pitched battles with the police, baton charges, arrests and prison sentences.[2]

The national organization of this unemployed agitation continued to be provided by the National Unemployed Workers' Movement. This, Mr Pelling notes, 'was the one body which agitated fiercely on behalf of the unemployed as such'.[3] And, as before, the General Council would have nothing to do with the N.U.W.M. because of its Communist leadership.

Of course, the General Council had the alternative of itself leading a movement of protest on behalf of the unemployed and of helping to organize that 'effective resistance' to the Government's policies which it had, in August 1931, declared to be of essential importance. But this the Trade Union leaders had no thought of doing. Their strategy was an altogether different one and Walter Citrine explained its character with remarkable candour at the 1932 T.U.C. Conference, when the General Council was challenged for having submitted, with the Federation of British Industries, a joint statement to the Government on the subject of the Imperial Conference at Ottawa.[4] 'Time after time,' said Citrine, 'we are told from this rostrum that the all-important body which dictates the policy of the British Government at the present time is the employers'

---

[1] From August 1931 until January 1933, just under three million insured workers were unemployed in Britain. The total was still over two million at the beginning of 1936, and well over one and a half million in 1938. (Mowat, op. cit. pp. 432-3.) As Mr Mowat notes, these figures seriously underestimate the true position if account is taken of the unemployed who were not insured.

[2] See Hutt, op. cit. ch. IX and Hannington, op. cit. chs. XIV and XV. From the formation of the 'National' Government up to the end of 1932, there had been over one hundred baton charges on mass demonstrations, more than 1,300 people had been arrested for alleged offences in connection with their political activities, and of these 421 had been sentenced to imprisonment, in some cases to two years' hard labour or three years' penal servitude (Hutt, op. cit. p. 237.)

[3] Pelling, op. cit. p. 64.

[4] For the statement, which was, the General Council reported, the result of discussions in which 'it was found that there was a certain measure of agreement' with the F.B.I., see T.U.C. Annual Conference Report, 1932, p. 220.

organization—that the Government is merely the mouthpiece, that the Federation of British Industries cracks the whip and the Government obeys. *Surely if there is something which the General Council desire to get done it cannot be a bad thing to get the support of the people who crack the whip. Everything depends on whether the "something" is a right "something".*[1]

The General Council did recommend to local Trades Councils that Unemployed Associations should be formed under their auspices, if they saw fit. The Associations were designed 'further to cater to the needs of the unemployed'; and they should also, in the view of the Council, become 'organizing auxiliaries of the Trade Union Movement'.[2] They were certainly not intended as instruments of unemployed agitation.

In addition the General Council was also ready to support and even to sponsor resolutions on unemployment which 'emphatically protested' and 'strongly demanded'. But it did not feel it could do much more; and it did what it could to stifle action on the part of those who felt otherwise.

As for the Labour Party, there were some isolated voices raised at the 1932 Annual Conference for a more resolute defence of the unemployed. Ben Tillett urged the 'arm-chair revolutionist' and the 'high-brow academic' to 'get on the street corners', and he proposed a 'national organized drive' against the Means Test.[3] Emmanuel Shinwell asked more specifically 'whether the time had not arrived when the Movement as a whole should refuse to undertake any longer the administration of the Means Test'.[4] This was rejected by George Lansbury—the former apostle of Poplarism. Speaking for the Executive, Lansbury told the Conference that 'while it is true that when you are in a hopeless minority you cannot do much, you can do a little to soften the business'[5] (i.e. the administration of the Means Test). And, he also told the Conference, 'it is no use imagining that with the people who are in control of finance and industry generally they will allow you to do what ought to be done with the unemployed or the victims of unemployment'. Much though he and his colleagues in the Parliamentary Party might try, they were 'absolutely helpless'. All that could be done was to 'go out and preach the gospel that capitalism will not provide a decent standard of life either for the workers who are at work or those who are not allowed to work'. That, he concluded, 'is the message

[1] T.U.C. Annual Conference Report, 1932, p. 407. My italics.
[2] ibid, p. 122.
[3] Labour Party Annual Conference Report, 1932, p. 174.
[4] ibid, p. 175.
[5] ibid, p. 177.

of the Executive to this Conference today'.[1] Upon which the Conference unanimously passed a resolution recording its 'emphatic protest' at the Means Test, demanding its 'immediate withdrawal' and reaffirming support of the principle of work or full maintenance for the unemployed, 'as laid down in *Labour and the Nation*'.

It is notable that no spokesman of the Labour Left challenged the Executive's admission of near impotence, the more notable when one recalls how much the Labour Left insisted that a socialist government would, on the morrow of its election, face the gravest dangers and require, at the minimum, the devoted support of the working classes. If this was so, the need was surely all the greater to begin evoking that support by a more resolute defence of working class interests than was entailed by the passage of resolutions of protest.

Unemployment relief did continue to be administered by the Public Assistance Committees of the local authorities and 'the system worked smoothly'.[2] During the first year of the Means Test, 'ten or a dozen Labour Public Assistance Committees, out of a total of over 200 in Great Britain, made trouble over administering the Poor Law principles laid down for them'; only in two cases, Rotherham and Durham, was it found necessary to supersede the P.A.C.s by commissioners appointed by the Ministry of Labour.[3]

The Labour Party's Annual Conference had taken place in the first week in October. Three weeks later, on the occasion of the attempted presentation to the House of Commons of a National Petition on the grievances of the unemployed, there occurred in London some of the largest demonstrations and some of the fiercest encounters with the police so far seen in the history of the unemployed agitation.[4] Amongst those arrested, Wal Hannington received a three months sentence of imprisonment, and Sid Elias, the chairman of the N.U.W.M., was sentenced to two years' imprisonment on a charge of disaffection. On the 17th of December, 1932, Tom Mann, the national treasurer of the N.U.W.M., and Emrhys Llewellyn, its secretary, were arrested under an Act of Edward III and the Seditious Meetings Act of 1817. No charge was preferred against them; it was, the magistrate said, 'merely a preventive measure', and, as they refused to be bound over on condition that they desist from further activity on behalf of the unemployed, they were both sent to jail for two months. George Lansbury, his biographer notes, visited Tom Mann after his release, and was

[1] Labour Party Annual Conference Report, 1932, p. 178.
[2] Mowat, op. cit. p. 470.
[3] R. C. Davison, *British Unemployment Policy* (London, 1938) p. 22.
[4] Hannington, op. cit. pp. 247 ff.

'deeply discontented with himself because he was not in prison too'. And, Mr Postgate adds, Lansbury 'told the friend who helped him up the hill (he was seventy-three and tired) that if he had had Tom's courage he would have been where Tom was, instead of being a sentimental windbag'.[1] It was a hard judgment, made by a troubled old man. His colleagues, genuine though their compassion was for the unemployed, managed to be less sentimental.

At the beginning of 1934, the National Unemployed Workers Movement mounted a new campaign on behalf of the unemployed. A new Hunger March started from Glasgow in January and arrived in London on the 24th and 25th of February where a 'Congress of Action' also met. 'In the organizing of hunger marches,' Wal Hannington notes, 'we had now become experts, knowing every detail that was required in the preparation and the carrying through of the march.'[2] Better than anything else could have done, the March served to publicize the continuing plight of the unemployed, while the expressed hostility of the Government and the conduct of the police also helped to rally much non-Labour support. On the 26th of February, John McGovern, M.P., presented a petition from the marchers to the House of Commons and on the 27th, a deputation, which included both McGovern and James Maxton, tried to see the Prime Minister.[3] MacDonald's refusal to see the deputation led to a sharp clash in the House of Commons, with Attlee and Herbert Samuel, the leader of the Liberal Opposition, supporting the marchers' request to interview the Prime Minister.[4] By March, the Government was under pressure from a wide variety of sources to restore the cuts in benefits and to bestir itself a little more on behalf of the unemployed.[5] In April, Neville Chamberlain, the Chancellor of the Exchequer, announced in introducing his Budget that the cuts in the scales of unemployment benefits, imposed in 1931, would be restored. The Means Test, however, remained.

The Government was then piloting through the House of Commons a major piece of legislation, the Unemployment Bill, which became law in May 1934. The Unemployment Act radically reshaped the whole system of unemployment relief;[6] it centralized and unified its administration under a new Unemployment Assis-

[1] Postgate, op. cit. p. 282.
[2] Hannington, op. cit. p. 278.
[3] A letter which had been sent to the Prime Minister, and which asked him to receive the deputation, included the signature of one Labour M.P., Aneurin Bevan.
[4] H. of C. vol. 286, cols. 1058 ff.
[5] Hannington, op. cit. pp. 295-6.
[6] For details, see Davison, op. cit. ch. II; also Hannington, op. cit. pp. 298 ff.

tance Board (U.A.B.), with its own offices and staff throughout the country; and it created a new Unemployment Assistance Fund, provided by the Treasury, but with a contribution from local authorities; to keep a watch over the Fund and to advise on administrative changes, the Government also appointed an Unemployment Insurance Statutory Committee, to consist of a Chairman and not more than five other members, two of whom were to represent employers' organizations and two to represent the trade unions.

The Act widened eligibility for relief; one of its provisions was that applicants for relief should accept, where required, training in either residential or non-residential centres; the Act also introduced a modified and uniform 'Needs Test'. But when the U.A.B. published the new regulations for uniform scales of relief in December 1934, it was found that, while many workers would gain, many would also incur serious losses, not least in the most heavily depressed areas. In South Wales, the operation of the new scheme would have meant a cut in relief payments of £1,000,000.

The new regulations produced a storm of protest greater than any since September 1931, when the economy measures had been introduced by the 'National' Government. 'In three weeks,' one writer not notably sympathetic to such protests notes, 'the industrial towns of England, Wales and Scotland were in an uproar. There were protest meetings, marches, and deputations from outraged local P.A.C.'s. Members of Parliament of all parties reproached the Government. A serious political crisis threatened.'[1] Much of the popular protest was again led by the N.U.W.M.; some of it was of local and spontaneous origin. Officially, neither the Labour Party nor the T.U.C. had any share in that agitation. Some Trade Union leaders and Labour members of Parliament addressed demonstrations; Lansbury, Attlee, Bevin and Citrine accompanied a deputation from South Wales to the Minister of Labour; Labour Members protested in Parliament. Finally, on the 1st of February, the National Council of Labour published an 'Appeal to the Public Conscience' addressed to 'all leaders of public opinion, to Parliament, Press and Pulpit' and urging 'in no partisan spirit' that cognizance be taken of the 'new and terrible hardship' produced by the new regulations.[2] The leadership of the Labour movement followed the agitation—it did not lead it; and it does not seem unreasonable to suggest that, had the unemployed solely relied on the efforts of that leadership, the Government would not have been quite so ready to withdraw the regulation, which it did on the 5th of February.

[1] Davison, op. cit. p. 66; for details, see W. Hannington, op. cit. pp. 306 ff.
[2] Labour Party Annual Conference Report, 1935, p. 13.

Nor, it may be, would the Government have found it so easy to do so little for the depressed areas had the Labour Party and the T.U.C. applied greater pressure upon it. Under the Depressed Areas (Development and Improvement) Bill, introduced in November 1934 (and renamed the Special Areas Bill in the House of Lords), the Government allowed £2,000,000 for the 'economic development and social improvement of the depressed areas' in England, Wales and Scotland.[1] It was a ludicrous sum, whose inadequacy was much criticized from all quarters: in 1937, the rate of unemployment in these areas was still double that for the whole country, and in some parts much higher. Ernest Bevin's biographer, noting the fact, also notes that Bevin, 'refusing to make a political issue of the Special Areas', offered the Government the full co-operation of the T.U.C., if it would promise a grant of £20,000,000 and give the newly-appointed Commission on the Special Areas the power to co-ordinate schemes between different departments. The offer was ignored and, says Mr Bullock, 'as a member of a party out of office there was no more Bevin could do'.[2] Labour's tragedy, and the tragedy of the unemployed, was that Labour leaders did believe that there was little they could do to force the Government out of its ways. The same belief was later a material contributory factor to Labour's paralysis over matters of even larger import, and with consequences even more grim.

3. LABOUR AND FASCISM

With the Nazis' conquest of power in Germany at the beginning of 1933, the spectre which ever more insistently came to haunt the Labour movement was the spectre of Fascism, and of Fascist aggression. But Fascism did not reconcile the divergent elements within the Labour movement. On the contrary, it accentuated and deepened the divisions between them. The first issue which Fascism raised was that of the Labour Party's relations with the Communist Party; the second was defence.

Ever since 1929, the Communist Party had stuck to the 'New line', and had habitually come to denounce the Labour leaders as 'social fascists', from whose treachery the Communist Party alone could

---

[1] The percentage of insured workers unemployed in Jarrow was 67.8; in Gateshead, 44.2; in Workington, 36.3; in Maryport, 57; in Abertillery, 49.6; in Merthyr, 61.9; in Greenock, 36.3; in Motherwell, 37.4. (Mowat, op. cit. p. 465.)

[2] Bullock, op. cit. p. 543. Two pages earlier, however, Mr. Bullock notes that the withdrawal of the U.A.B. regulations showed 'that organised public protest by the Labour movement could still make an impression on the Government'. (ibid, p. 541.)

save the working classes. This line, it will be recalled, involved un-qualified denunciation not only of the orthodox Labour leaders, but of the Labour Left as well. As late as April 1932, Harry Pollitt, in a debate with Fenner Brockway, was insisting that 'this is not a debate between parties differing on minor points but united on fundamentals. The I.L.P. and the C.P. have nothing in common. It is war to the death.'[1]

The net result of this sectarianism, grotesque in Britain and catastrophic in Germany, had been the steady isolation of the Communist Party and a constant diminution of its influence in the trade union movement. Nor even was it able to canalize the discontent of the unemployed. Of the tens of thousands of men and women who were drawn, under the impulse of the N.U.W.M., into the agitation of 1932, only a fraction actually joined that organization. Even fewer joined the C.P. itself. In November 1932, after a year of strenuous activity, the C.P. had 5,400 members, 60 per cent. of whom were unemployed.[2]

With the Nazis' triumph, the Comintern's policy began to change and, again in accordance with its directives, the Communist Party now made new overtures to the Labour Party. Together with the I.L.P.,[3] it proposed on the 21st of March, 1933, the formation of a 'United Front' with the Labour Party. The proposals were promptly rejected and, on the 24th of March, the National Joint Council, representing the National Executive Committee of the Labour Party, the General Council of the T.U.C. and the Executive of the Parliamentary Labour Party, issued a manifesto, *Democracy and Dictatorship*, in which it set out its collective view of the lessons to be drawn from the spread of Fascism.[4]

The most notable feature of that document was its rejection, with equal vehemence, of the 'iron Dictatorship of Capitalism and Nationalism' on the one hand, and of 'the Dictatorship of the Working-Class' on the other. Instead, it fervently reaffirmed its authors' faith in 'Democracy and Socialism' and the belief that 'a United Working-Class Movement, founded and conducted on the broadest democratic principles, can establish a Socialist Society so soon as the workers are sufficiently advanced in political wisdom as to place their own Movement in the seat of Government, armed with all the power of the Democratic State'. 'British labour,' the document said, 'has led the world in its claim for Industrial

[1] *Forward*, 23rd of April, 1932.
[2] Report of the Battersea Congress, November 1932, p. 42.
[3] The C.P. and the I.L.P. had reached agreement on a 'United Front' on the 17th of March, 1933.
[4] For full text, see Labour Party Annual Conference Report, pp. 277-8.

Democracy and its demand for Political Democracy. Its historic task today is to uphold the principles of Social Democracy ... If the British Working-Class ... hesitate now between majority and minority rule and toy with the idea of Dictatorship, Fascist or Communist, they will go down to servitude such as they have never suffered.'

Democracy and Dictatorship had suggested that the more pacific, constitutional and democratically minded Labour showed itself to be, the less would be the danger of ruling class resistance to its purposes. The point was underlined at the 1933 Conference by Herbert Morrison, speaking on behalf of the Executive. 'The real point about the Manifesto,' he said, 'is that we condemn dictatorship as such, whether the dictatorship is a dictatorship of the Left or of the Right ... we cannot hunt with the hounds and run with the hare. If we are opposed to dictatorship, we must be open about it and say so. If we ourselves flirt with a dictatorship of the Left or with a dictatorship of our own (sic), and if some of our people use the word "dictatorship" in a sense that they ought not to ... we are preparing a political psychology which, if we justify one form of dictatorship, gives an equally moral justification for a dictatorship of the other side.'[1]

In immediate practical terms, what followed from these affirmations was an ever greater determination than in the past to warn members of the Labour Party against any form of collaboration with Communists as, for instance, in anti-Fascist organizations under Communist influence or control.[2]

In February 1934, the I.L.P. and the C.P. again proposed to the National Executive of the Labour Party the formation of a 'United Front' to assist their foreign comrades and to resist the advances of Fascism in Britain. This was again rejected, and the Executive, in its reply to the Communist Party, once again stated its conviction that the Communists did not believe in Parliamentary democracy, that Communist parties 'were allowed by the Third International to enter Parliament not for the purpose of organic work, but in order to destroy Parliament "from within" ', and that the Communist Party's real aim was 'to destroy the Labour Party's influence and to disrupt its membership'[3]

[1] Labour Party Annual Conference Report, 1933, p. 219.
[2] See, e.g. *The Communist Solar System*, published by the Labour Party in 1933, and designed to expose the Communist use of 'front' organizations.
[3] Labour Party Annual Conference Report, 1934, p. 11. In October 1934, the General Council of the T.U.C. issued two circulars, one to Trades Councils and the other to its affiliated unions, the first warning them that 'recognition' would be withdrawn from any council which accepted 'delegates connected in any way with either Communist or Fascist organizations or any of their

But the Executive did more than reject proposals for a United Front or than lengthen the list of organizations to which members of the Labour Party must not belong. It also declared (in May 1934) that 'united action with the Communist Party or organizations ancillary or subsidiary thereto' was incompatible with membership of the Labour Party, and it announced that it would seek 'full disciplinary powers' from the 1934 Conference 'to deal with any case or cases that may arise'. 'Loose association with the Communist Party,' it explained, 'is just as dangerous to the interests of the Labour Party as is Communist membership itself.'[1] Cases of 'loose association' were in fact arising, and the Executive might well fear that, under the impact of events, at home and abroad, there might soon be more.

Since the previous Party Conference, the Nazis had further consolidated their power, and were making ruthless use of that power to suppress all opposition, as well as to persecute Jews. In Austria, the Socialist opposition had, in February 1934, been crushed in blood. In the same month, Fascist riots in Paris, followed by the fall of the Government and the formation of a Ministry further to the right, suggested that the cancer was rapidly spreading, as did the instoration of a military dictatorship in Bulgaria in May. In Britain itself, Fascism, in 1934, was more militant and better organized than ever before: the British Union of Fascists had some 400 branches established throughout the country, with a total membership estimated at some 20,000. The famous mass meeting at Olympia in June 1934, when hecklers had been savagely assaulted by Fascist stewards, was only the climax of a series of huge meetings in the provinces.

Nor was it only Fascism of Mosley's particular brand which then seemed to many people on the Left to constitute the only, or even the main, danger of Fascism in Britain. The overt sympathy which Mussolini and Hitler evoked among many people of influence and wealth; the markedly different treatment accorded by the police to Fascists and anti-Fascists, or to unemployed demonstrators; and, in connection with the last, the authorities' much less than punctilious regard for civil liberties[2] and the Government's desire to arm itself on a permanent basis with extraordinary police powers, as shown in the original draft of the Incitement to Disaffection Bill

ancillary bodies,' and the second asking the unions to do 'all in their power' to debar persons associated with 'disruptive organizations' from any official positions, either in the unions or the Trade Councils (T.U.C. Annual Conference Report, 1935, pp. 110 ff).

[1] Labour Party Annual Conference Report, 1934, p. 13.

[2] See R. Kidd, *British Liberty in Danger* (London, 1940), especially Chapter V.

of 1934;[1] all this fed the fears of many people on the Left that Britain too might slide into its own form of what Cripps called 'country gentleman's Fascism'.[2]

In France, Socialists and Communists had agreed on a United Front in July. In Spain, a similar agreement was concluded in September, and, in October, the two rival French Trade Union organizations, the Socialist C.G.T. and its Communist-controlled equivalent, also agreed to unite. Though circumstances might be different in Britain (as Labour leaders never failed to point out), it was inevitable that the Communist campaign for a United Front, pursued with tireless insistence throughout 1934, should, for many socialists in the Labour Party, have acquired a new degree of plausibility—the more so since the Communist Party, despite its minute membership, undeniably had an *élan* and a spirit of militancy which seemed more than ever appropriate to the times. It was the Communists who were responsible for the organization of the big Hunger Marches of 1934; and it was the Communists who not only denounced Fascism most loudly, but who were also in the vanguard of opposition to the Fascists—and who got arrested by the police.

However, the partisans of a United Front 'for Britain were still a sufficiently small minority to give no trouble at all to the Executive. It was not until later that the Socialist League came out in full support of the United Front. An attempt at the 1934 Labour Party Conference to move the reference back of the sections of the Executive's Report dealing with the issue was 'overwhelmingly defeated'.[3] Another challenge, to the Executive's decision to include 'The Relief Committee for the Victims of German and Austrian Fascism' among proscribed organizations, was defeated by 1,347,000 votes to 195,000.[4] A third attempt to deny the Executive the 'full disciplinary powers' it sought was defeated by an even larger majority.

It was in 1934 that the Labour Party and the T.U.C. began, in the light of the emergence of Fascism, to reappraise Labour's policies on defence. In 1933, the Labour Party Conference had unanimously passed a resolution moved by Sir Charles Trevelyan which expressed an 'uncompromising attitude to war preparations

[1] See Kidd, pp. 58-68. The Bill, which provoked widespread protest, was substantially amended during its passage through the House of Commons. But the Act still included 'provisions of so wide and general a character that under it almost any pacifist and anti-war activity' could be proved an offence (ibid, p. 68).

[2] See S. Cripps, *'National' Fascism in Britain* (London, 1935).

[3] Labour Party Annual Conference Report, 1934, p. 136.

[4] ibid, p. 136.

and which pledged the Conference 'to take no part in war and to resist it with the whole force of the Labour movement . . . including a general strike'.[1] By 1934, after further consultations with the T.U.C., the Executive had moved substantially from this position, which some of its members and members of the General Council had considered unrealistic from the start.[2] Both *For Socialism and Peace* and a separate document on *War and Peace* reaffirmed the Labour movement's dedication to 'all round disarmament' and its attachment to collective security through the League of Nations (which the Soviet Union joined in September 1934). It was also agreed that the British Government should 'settle its disputes by peaceful means and eschew force' and that, in the event of Britain being condemned as an aggressor by the League, it would be necessary to 'refuse to serve or support our Government'.

On the issue of a General Strike, however, *War and Peace* bluntly stated that 'the responsibility for stopping War ought not to be placed upon the Trade Union Movement alone' and that 'every citizen who wants Peace, and every other section of the Labour Movement must share the responsibility of any organized action that might be taken to prevent war'. All that the General Council would undertake to do, in a situation in which war threatened, was, in accordance with its Standing Orders, to call a special Conference to decide on industrial action. But, the statement suggested, the call for a General Strike to prevent an outbreak of war would not be effective in such countries as Germany, Italy or Japan, though it was 'quite possible that aggressive action might come from some of these countries'. There might therefore be circumstances, in which 'the Government of Great Britain might have to use its military and naval forces in support of the League to restrain an aggressor nation'. And in those circumstances, it would be necessary 'unflinchingly (to) support our Government in all the risks and consequences of fulfilling its duty to take part in collective action against a peacebreaker, making sure at the same time that such action is inspired by a sincere determination to enforce the rule of international law'.

Arthur Henderson, in introducing *War and Peace* to the 1934 Conference, told the delegates that the Executive was not putting forward a new policy.[3] But there could be no question, as Hugh

[1] Labour Party Annual Conference Report, 1933, p. 185. A similar resolution had been remitted to the General Council by the T.U.C. the previous month (T.U.C. Annual Conference Report, p. 407) and a resolution also recommending a General Strike in case of war had been passed at the International Trade Union Congress in Brussels in July-August 1933 (ibid, p. 436).
[2] See, e.g., Dalton, op. cit. p. 44; also, for Bevin's attitude, see Bullock, op. cit. p. 550.
[3] Labour Party Annual Conference Report, 1934, p. 152.

Dalton wrote later, that the Executive 'had moved a long way in twelve months',[1] and its policies came under attack from pacifists, who were easily defeated, and from the spokesmen of the Socialist League, whose opposition was based on different grounds.

The Socialist League took a much more critical view of the League of Nations than the Labour leadership. The League's impotence, demonstrated by its failure to check Japanese aggression against China in 1932, and the more recent failure of its Economic and Disarmament Conferences were, the spokesmen of the Socialist League argued, the inevitable result of the crisis of capitalism. 'The League of Nations,' they said, 'cannot end War. To rely blindly upon it is to endanger Peace.'[2]

Nor was the Socialist League prepared to support a British Government whose purposes it absolutely distrusted in any military venture of any kind. The Labour Party, it said, should declare that it did not intend 'that the workers of this country shall be called upon to pay for the anarchy of capitalism with their lives', and that it should warn the Government 'that it will use all its power to strengthen and make effective the determination of the workers not to participate in any War in which this Government may involve this country', for, the Socialist League's amendment to the Executive's resolution explained, 'it is impossible to allocate the blame for War, which is inherent in the system, springs from contradictions, and brings to the workers added misery and exploitation'. The Labour Party, it was therefore proposed, should call upon the workers in all capitalist countries to make every effort to prepare resistance to War declared by their own Governments, and should undertake 'to resist a War entered into by this Government by every means in its power, including a General Strike'.[3]

This was a remarkably unrealistic approach to the problem of potential (and, before long, actual) Fascist aggression: for it clearly made nonsense of any armed resistance to such aggression; and it could only have been logically (though not more realistically) sustained on the basis of traditional pacifism, which the Socialist League never endorsed, or on the basis of a Leninist kind of revolutionary defeatism, whose implications were altogether alien to its modes of thought. The Executive had a comfortable majority, 1,519,000 against 673,000.[4] The debate, however, had only begun; it was resumed, under more dramatic circumstances, at the 1935 Conference.

[1] Dalton, op. cit. p. 54.
[2] Labour Party Annual Conference Report, 1934, p. 175.
[3] ibid, p. 176.
[4] ibid, p. 178.

Though pledged to the support of the League of Nations and collective security to the point of support of war against an aggressor, the Labour Party in 1934 was also committed to 'all-round disarmament'. More important in concrete political terms, it was also opposed to British rearmament which had, very tentatively, begun in 1934. At the time, however, the contradiction between the desire to resist aggression and opposition to armaments was not nearly so marked as it later became: it was then still possible to argue that the aggressor (in 1935, Italy) could be deterred, and if necessary, militarily checked under the auspices of the League of Nations by concerted action with existing military forces. Though much has since been made of pacifism in Britain in the thirties, not least as an apologia for appeasement, the major objection of most so-called pacifists was not to any kind of military action as such, but to military action by Britain for any purpose other than the defence of collective security, under the auspices of the League of Nations.[1] This 'pacifism' had its roots in a profound distrust, which extended far outside the Labour movement, of the motives of the British Government, and in the fear that, left to its own devices, the only purposes that Government would be willing to serve would be evil ones. In contrast, the League then seemed to millions of people the only guarantee of collective security against aggression and imperialism, from any quarter.

In June 1935, the results of the Peace Ballot conducted by an *ad hoc* National Declaration Committee, closely associated with the League of Nations Union, and strongly supported by the Labour Party and the Trade Unions, not only showed overwhelming support for combined economic and non-military measures against an aggressor (more than ten million against less than 640,000); it also showed a smaller, but still very substantial, majority for *military* measures (6,784,368 against 2,351,981).[2] As Winston Churchill wrote later, the Peace Ballot was 'regarded in many quarters as part of the Pacifist campaign'; 'on the contrary, Clause 5 (referring to sanctions) affirmed a positive and courageous policy which could, at this time, have been followed with an overwhelming measure of national support'.[3]

[1] For a useful discussion, see *The Role of the Peace Movements in the 1930's* (University Group on Defence Policy, Pamphlet No. 1, 1959).
[2] The Peace Ballot also indicated an enormous measure of support (among those who took part in it) for British membership of the League; for an all round reduction of armaments by international agreement; for the abolition by international agreement of all national air forces, and for the prohibition by international agreement of the private manufacture and sale of arms.
[3] W. Churchill. *The Second World War* (London, 1948) I, *The Gathering Storm*, p. 132.

Certainly the Labour movement was then overwhelmingly in favour of such a policy.

At the beginning of September 1935, when it became clear that an Italian aggression against Abyssinia, which had threatened throughout the year, was now imminent, the T.U.C. passed a resolution which pledged 'firm support of any action consistent with the principles and statutes of the League to restrain the Italian Government and to uphold the authority of the League in enforcing peace'. The voting was 2,962,000 for the resolution and 177,000 against.[1]

On the 11th of September the Foreign Secretary, Sir Samuel Hoare, spoke before the Assembly of the League of Nations and, with all the appearance of deep conviction, also pledged Britain's support 'for steady and collective resistance to all acts of unprovoked aggression'. 'The attitude of the British nation in the last few weeks,' he told the Assembly, 'has clearly demonstrated the fact that this is no variable and unreliable sentiment, but a principle of international conduct to which they and their Government hold with firm, enduring and universal persistence.'[2]

The Annual Conference of the Labour Party met at Brighton on the 30th of September and began debating the crisis of the 1st of October, two days before Mussolini actually attacked Abyssinia.

The Conference had before it an Executive resolution which, like the resolution passed at the T.U.C., pledged 'firm support of any action consistent with the principles and statutes of the League to restrain the Italian Government and to uphold the authority of the League in enforcing peace'.[3] Moving the resolution, Hugh Dalton denied that sanctions against Italy necessarily meant war: the threat of sanctions might be enough to prevent war, and if not, the use of sanctions, economic and financial, without military or naval action, might be sufficient to re-establish peace. But, he added, '*if not—face all the facts—it is hard even now to believe it, but if Mussolini be so lunatic as to resist the united League of Nations by force, then so be it. He will order the firing of the first shot, and he will take the consequences of that order*'.[4]

The issue, after the vote at the T.U.C., was never in doubt (the vote in favour of the resolution was *2,168,000 against 102,000*),[5] and the dramatic nature of the occasion was heightened by the opposition expressed to the resolution by George Lansbury, the Leader of

[1] T.U.C. Annual Conference Report, 1935, pp. 346, 371.
[2] Survey of International Affairs, 1935, II, p. 187.
[3] Labour Party Annual Conference Report, 1935, p. 153.
[4] ibid, p. 155. My italics.
[5] ibid, p. 193.

the Party, the final repudiation of whose pacifism by the Conference led to his immediate resignation from the leadership.[1]

It was not from pacifist quarters that came the fiercest opposition to the Executive's resolution. It was from Sir Stafford Cripps and some other leading members of the Socialist League. Cripps, rather than support the Executive on the issue of sanctions, had resigned from it before the Conference met. His opposition, he told the delegates, stemmed from his utter distrust of the 'National' Government and his conviction that it would misuse the military power that was granted to it for its own imperialist purposes. 'Had we a workers' Government in this country, as they have in Russia,' he said, 'the whole situation would be completely different. Then, with a Socialist Government, there would be no risk of imperialist and capitalist aims being pursued, as today it is certain they are being, and will be, pursued . . . then, so far as we are concerned, we could prevent the misuse of war and could see to it that it was not merely the cloak for imperialist bargainings and wranglings.' In the existing circumstances, however, and with the existing Government, it was 'unfortunate, tragic, but inescapably true, that the British workers cannot at this moment be effective in the international political field'. If the Labour movement felt 'a desperate urge to do something at all costs in the present situation', it must fall back 'on the attempt to use working-class sanctions'. Best of all, however, would be to turn out the 'National' Government and replace it by a British Socialist Government.[2]

The whole argument was typical of an artificial kind of 'leftism' which did immense harm to the credit of the Labour Left in the Labour movement. Starting from the premise that only a Socialist Government could pursue policies geared to the right purposes, the argument ended with the conviction that there was nothing the Labour movement could do here and now to inflect in the desired directions the policies of a Conservative Government. The argument

[1] This was the famous occasion on which Bevin, speaking immediately after Lansbury, said that 'it is placing the Executive and the Movement in an absolutely wrong position to be taking your conscience round from body to body asking to be told what to do with it'. ibid, p. 178. To those who reproached him for his brutality, Bevin is reputed to have said: 'Lansbury has been going about dressed in saint's clothes for years waiting for martyrdom. I set fire to the faggots.' (F. Williams, *Ernest Bevin, Portrait of a Great Englishman* (London, 1952), p. 196.)
[2] Labour Party Annual Conference Report, 1935, p. 158. See also the intervention of William Mellor, who supported Cripps, and who concluded his speech by saying that 'there are times when it is well to remember that the positive action of fighting your enemy at home is greater in value than the negative disaster of defending your home enemy abroad'. 'Our enemy is here.' (ibid, p. 172.)

225

was not only a catastrophic counsel of paralysis; there was also embedded in it a fundamental contradiction. For, if it was true that Labour was strong enough to elect a 'Socialist Government', it must be equally true that its influence in the country was such as to prevent the Government from pursuing imperialist ventures under the cloak of collective security. And if Labour was *not* strong enough to elect a Socialist Government, the need to exercise what influence it had (and it was a considerable influence) for the policies it deemed right was all the greater.

The leadership did not, in 1935, actually seek to mount a campaign in support of its policies. But it did insist that Labour was not powerless and that pressure upon the Government could be effective. Thus, so moderate and orthodox a member of the Executive as H. B. Lees-Smith insisted that there was a 'profound difference' between the capitalist democracies and the Fascist States, and one of those profound differences was that the former could be influenced by vigorous opposition, while the latter could not.[1] Indeed, Attlee claimed that it was not Labour which was following the lead of the Government but that it was the Government that was now 'tardily and very doubtfully beginning to do what they had been demanding for the past four years'.[2] But it was Dalton who, in introducing the Executive's resolution, was most emphatic as to the opportunities which existed for influencing the Government. Why, he asked, had the British Government changed its tune at Geneva? 'Largely because of the Peace Ballot; because, *although the British Labour Party is today negligible in members of Parliament, the force behind the Labour movement in the country is great and growing, and the Peace Ballot showed it. We took our part in that work, and no piece of political work that we have done in this Parliament was more worthwhile than the work we did for the Peace Ballot. It was worth more than a hundred speeches in the House of Commons. I say that great popular mandate on behalf of the Labour Party's foreign policy given through the Peace Ballot—I say that is one reason, and a very important reason, why the British Government has changed its tune.*'[3]

Had the Labour Party made this its text in the years of appeasement, and acted upon the fact that there were opportunities for effective opposition *outside Parliament*, the history of those years might have been vastly different.

[1] Labour Party Annual Conference' Report, 1935, p. 161.
[2] ibid, p. 173.
[3] ibid, p. 156. My italics.

226

On the 23rd of October, 1935, Stanley Baldwin, who had become Prime Minister in place of Ramsay MacDonald the previous June,[1] announced that there would be a General Election on the 14th of November. Theoretically, this should have been very good news for the Labour Party. It had had four years in which to prepare its electoral revenge for what it had never ceased to denounce as the fraud and deceit of the previous Election, and those four years, moreover, had been years of depression, mass unemployment and mass deprivation.

As against this, the Labour Party had just lost its parliamentary leader, and could be taxed, as indeed it was, with internal divisions at a time of international crisis. And, by choosing this particular time to have an Election, Stanley Baldwin had made sure that foreign affairs would compete for attention with the Government's record at home. He had furthermore appropriated slogans—the League of Nations, collective security—which the Labour Party felt, quite rightly, to be its own. Even at home, the Government could point to, and did not hesitate to claim the credit for, Britain's emergence from the depths of the depression.

Yet, these factors do not begin properly to explain why Labour, after more than four years of the 'National' Government, did not even poll as well as it had done in 1929. Lansbury was not a towering Labour figure, as MacDonald had been, nor were the divisions of the Labour Party such as to prevent it from presenting policies to the electorate which had received the overwhelming endorsement of the T.U.C. and Labour Party Conferences. And, if contradictory statements on the subject of armaments could be quoted against prominent Labour politicians, there were, to counter these, innumerable sins of omission and commission, in foreign no less than in home affairs, which could be (and were) quoted against the Government.

An explanation in terms of economic recovery is no more convincing. For what recovery there was could not conceal the fact, about which the Government had tried to do so pitifully little, that Britain, in 1935, was still a country of mass unemployment, and of great poverty, by no means confined to the 'depressed areas', a land of neglected health and starved opportunities for education, of malnutrition and monstrous rates of infantile mortality—all in the midst of enormous wealth and parasitical appropriation.

The temptation therefore is to fall back on the catch-all formula of the electorate's conservatism, including working-class conservatism, and to see in the results of the election of 1935 another

---

[1] MacDonald, however, did not leave the Government. He became Lord President of the Council.

expression of a deep-rooted popular preference for government by representatives of England's traditional ruling classes.

The temptation should not be too easily indulged. If by popular conservatism is meant that there was nothing resembling a revolutionary temper in Britain in the year 1935, the point need hardly be disputed. Had there been, the Communist Party, notwithstanding its desire to show how much it cared for Unity with the Labour Party, would not have been content to put up two candidates at the General Election.[1] Nor would the Government have been able, in May 1935, to stage with such success the celebrations of the King's Silver Jubilee. It is of course possible to exaggerate the significance of the many expressions of popular affection and 'loyalty' that were shown to George V and his Consort on that occasion; and the scale of the celebrations no doubt owed much to the Government's hope that they would also serve to strengthen feelings of patriotism and national identification from which it might hope to benefit. But even if popular acclaim for the ageing monarch and his wife are taken to indicate a profound attachment to traditional forms and images, that attachment could hardly, in 1935, have had much influence on the Labour Party's electoral fortunes.

For not only did the Labour Party ardently disclaim any revolutionary intentions; there were also far fewer people in 1935 disposed to question the disclaimer; indeed its respectability was given explicit recognition by its opponents with the inclusion, in the Birthday Honours List of the 3rd of June, 1935, of Charles Edwards, the Labour Party's Chief Whip, and two prominent trade union leaders, Walter Citrine and Arthur Pugh, all three of whom were knighted. Attlee himself, the Deputy Leader of the Labour Party, appeared in the Birthday Honours List: he was made a Privy Councillor.[2]

---

[1] One of them, William Gallacher, was elected for West Fife; the other, Harry Pollitt, standing in Rhondda East, polled 13,655 votes to 22,088 for his Labour opponent. The I.L.P. put forward seventeen candidates, eleven of them in Scotland, and it won four seats, all in Glasgow.

[2] For a classic attack on the acceptance of honours by members of the Labour Party, see R. H. Tawney's letter to the *New Statesman and Nation,* 22nd of June, 1935. At the 1935 Labour Party Conference in October, a resolution was moved deprecating the acceptance by members of the Party of titles and honours 'other than those which a Labour Government finds necessary for the furtherance of its own business in Parliament' (Labour Party Annual Conference Report, 1935, p. 238); an amendment, while expressing the conviction that Ceremonial Functions and Honours were means by which 'the decaying capitalist system seeks to maintain its prestige and its influence over immature minds', also stated that participations in such Functions and the acceptance of Honours were justified only 'in exceptional circumstances for the express purpose of frustrating the propaganda of the capitalist parties', and the National Executive was asked to report on the subject (ibid,

True, Labour's electoral programme was more advanced than it had ever been before, with 'schemes of public ownership for the efficient conduct, in the national interest, of banking, coal and its products, transport, electricity, iron and steel, and cotton'. Labour, the programme said, had 'also declared for the public ownership of land'; it would deal with the problem of the Distressed Areas as part of a 'vigorous policy of national planning'; it would 'sweep away the humiliating Means Test . . . provide adequately for the unemployed . . . reabsorb idle workers into productive employment by far reaching schemes of national development'; it would initiate a big move forward in education, including the raising of the school-leaving age with adequate maintenance allowances; it would 'vigorously develop' the health services; it would increase the amount of old-age pensions and lower the qualifying age; and 'go ahead with the provision of healthy homes for the people at reasonable rents, until the needs of the nation are fully met'. But it would do all this, the manifesto was careful to point out, 'by constitutional and democratic means', and, 'with this end in view', wanted power to 'abolish the House of Lords and improve the procedure of the House of Commons'.[1]

Had it not been for the fact that much of the election campaign was devoted to international affairs, the Conservatives might have tried a much more vigorous scare campaign against Labour. As it is, they were content with routine cries of 'Chaos and Crisis', with warnings of 'Your House to Go! Your Building Society Too! If Socialism Comes!', with adjurations to the electorate to 'Guard Your Savings', with references to 'Leaders at Loggerheads' and with prophecies that 'The Socialist Policy Means War'.[2] By previous standards, the election of 1935 was not a scare election. And it is unlikely that these warnings were sufficient to keep many potential Labour voters from supporting Labour, or that Labour's proposals, in themselves, were sufficient to confirm these voters' conservative, as well as Conservative, leanings.

It is not, in fact, in the specific circumstances of the election that the answer must be sought to Labour's inability to break down the resistance to its appeal. The answer must be sought in its perfor-

p. 238). The Report of the Executive to the 1936 Conference stated that 'it would be impossible for the Labour Government to lay down a binding rule which would bar individuals from accepting Honours' (Labour Party Annual Conference Report, 1936, p. 293). The reference back, moved at the Conference, was narrowly defeated on a show of hands—185 to 174 (ibid, p. 257).

[1] General Election Manifesto, *The Times*, 26th of October, 1935.

[2] These were all titles of Conservative Election leaflets (D. E. McHenry, *The Labour Party in Transition* (London, 1938) p. 186).

mance over the four previous years. For it had entirely failed, in those years, to act as if it really meant to create that 'mighty force of Socialist faith' which it had declared to be its aim in 1932. It had produced programmes. Its accent, after the defeat of 1931, had been on 'education and organization'. But it had deliberately refused to further that education by the organization, outside Parliament, of a militant movement in defence of working-class interests. To erase the stigma of the Labour Government's performance in 1931, it would have had to embark, after 1931, on something like a permanent crusade, in deed as well as in words, as a result of which it might have hoped, come an election, to do substantially better than ever before. But instead of the massive effort of which there had been so much talk after the catastrophe of 1931, there had only been the routine of speeches and of meetings, of eminently reasonable wage negotiations and of an equally reasonable conciliation of employers and of the Government, of polite parliamentary debates and of equally polite representations to Ministers, with the occasional rally or demonstration, all suggesting that Labour had good intentions and even remedies—much less that it had an angry cause.

So it was that Labour, with 8,326,000 votes (as against 6,648,000 in 1931 and 8,380,000 in 1929) won 154 seats, as against 52 in 1931 and 288 in 1929). The Conservatives alone had 387 seats with nearly 10.5 million votes; with the National Liberals, they commanded 420 seats. The Liberals had 21 seats, with a poll of under 1.5 million votes. Once again, the Conservatives had an impregnable majority in the House of Commons. It was a remarkable achievement. It would have been an even more remarkable achievement if Labour's postures in the previous years had not so greatly favoured its opponents.

CHAPTER VIII

THE CHALLENGE OF APPEASEMENT

> 'If this country is ever to be secure
> again, this Government must go, and
> it is our job to shift it.'
> Hugh Dalton, Labour Party Annual
> Conference, 1936.

1. PARLIAMENTARY OPPOSITION

THE Conservative victory at the General Election of 1935 meant that Labour would not, in the normal course of events, have the remotest chance of office for at least some years to come; and the size of the Conservative majority in the House of Commons also meant that parliamentary opposition, by itself, would achieve very little. This, from Labour's point of view, would have been bad enough had these been normal times. But the coming years, it was widely believed in the Labour movement, would be years of acute international danger; and it was no less generally agreed that the Government could not be trusted to fulfil the pledges of support for the League of Nations and of resistance to aggression which it had made before and during the Election.

What doubts there might have been in the matter were soon dispelled by the Government's handling of the Abyssinian crisis. The Government had intended from the first that the imposition of sanctions on Italy should under no circumstances involve any risk of war, which meant that sanctions would be so limited as to make next to no difference to the Italian aggressor. From the middle of October 1935 onwards, the Foreign Office, in conjunction with its French counterpart, had been actively pressing a 'settlement' upon Abyssinia. As embodied in the Hoare-Laval proposals, this came to entail the outright cession of a slice of Abyssinia to Italy, and the virtual cession of much of the rest.

Press publication of the proposals at the beginning of December roused a storm of protest in the country, which caused Baldwin to sacrifice his Foreign Secretary. Speaking in the House of Commons on the 19th of December, immediately after Sir Samuel Hoare's resignation, Baldwin made one of his famous admissions: 'I was not expecting,' he said, 'that deeper feeling which was manifested by many of my hon. Friends and friends—in many parts of the country on what I may call the ground of conscience and honour . . . I felt that there could not be that volume of popular opinion which it is necessary to have in a democracy behind the Government in a matter so important as this . . . It is perfectly obvious now that the (Hoare-Laval) proposals are absolutely and completely dead. This Government is certainly going to make no attempt to resurrect them.'[1]

However, the policy which underlay the Hoare-Laval proposals was not modified. Nothing that mattered was done to check Italian aggression: on the 9th of May, 1936, Mussolini was able to proclaim Italy's annexation of Abyssinia. By then, another thread had been woven in the Fascist pattern of conquest: in March, Hitler had reoccupied the demilitarized zone in the Rhineland, the British Government having previously made it clear to the French Government that it would not support any counter-action.

From then until the outbreak of war, all Labour leaders, whatever else they might disagree on, had in common a profound conviction that British foreign policy was utterly wrong, not only in detailed execution but also in general conception. They had said so, again and again, since 1932. But they now said it with ever greater insistence as the Conservative Government, first under Baldwin and, after 1937, under Neville Chamberlain, trod the path that led to what Winston Churchill has called 'the unnecessary war'. There was then no 'bipartisanship' over foreign policy: at no time in this century have Labour leaders been as insistent as they were in the late thirties that a British Government was leading Britain and helping to lead the world to a disaster of unparalleled magnitude.

And yet, no historian has found it necessary to dwell at any length on Labour's impact in those years, when so much was at stake, or to attribute to the Labour Party any significant (or indeed any minor) shift in the Government's foreign policy. This is no oversight due to faulty historiography: it is an accurate reflection of Labour's ineffectiveness in this period.

One familiar answer is that Labour was crippled by its own confusions over rearmament. It is not a good answer. There *were* confusions, ambiguities and hesitations. But these, as we shall see, did not prevent the Labour Party and the T.U.C. from reaching appropriate and realistic policy decisions in the face of Fascist aggression and British appeasement. Over a whole series of crucial issues, the Labour leaders, certainly by 1937, knew what ought to have been

[1] H. of C. vol. 307, cols. 2034-5.

done. And both the Labour Party and the Trade Union leaders continued to enjoy, throughout these years, the overwhelming support of their Annual Conferences.

There is, secondly, the argument that the Labour Party, even if it had tried to do more than it did, would have broken against the solid wall of popular acquiescence in the Government's policies. 'It was a stagnant period,' George Orwell wrote of the thirties in 1941, 'and its natural leaders were mediocrities. In spite of the campaigns of a few thousand left-wingers it is fairly certain that the bulk of the English people were behind Chamberlain's foreign policy.'[1]

This, like the argument based on the notion of popular conservatism, is very glib. The bulk of the English people deeply wanted peace. But this does not mean that the bulk of the English people could not have been moved to support any foreign policy other than appeasement. Millions of them, Liberals and Conservatives as well as Labour, had voted for collective security in 1935. There is no good reason to think that they could not have been moved to respond to different policies than those pursued by Baldwin and Chamberlain. And after 1935, it was the Labour leaders and only the Labour leaders who could have organized effective resistance to the Government.

But what, it may be asked, could the Labour leaders have done? What *can* an Opposition do when it is persuaded that the policies of the Government of the day are likely to end in utter disaster? The Labour leaders, it must be stressed again, were so persuaded. Nor could they find much comfort in the thought that all would in the end be well. There was nothing to suggest that it would: Dunkirk, in those years, was no more than a small, unattractive port, and Stalingrad only a large industrial city.

There were many things the Labour leaders could have done. They could, to begin with, have embarked on an unremitting campaign of meetings, demonstrations, marches, rallies and petitions, all designed to mobilize a body of public opinion sufficiently strong to force the Government on to different courses, or to force changes in its leadership, or to sweep it out of office. Secondly, they could have used, indeed abused, their parliamentary opportunities to harass the Government, to obstruct its business, to refuse to participate in that sedate parliamentary minuet which was the Government's best guarantee against effective challenge. They could, thirdly, have sought to mobilize their industrial strength and used that strength as a means of pressure upon the Government, for instance

[1] G. Orwell, 'England, Your England', in *England, Your England and Other Essays* (London, 1953) p. 207.

on the issue of the official embargo of arms for Republican Spain. And they could also have sought to bring about a grand alliance of all those who opposed the Government so as to break the frozen political mould in which Britain was imprisoned.

Of course, all this might have failed. The point is that the attempt was not made. There were parliamentary debates; there were manifestos, declarations, pamphlets, meetings and even half-hearted 'campaigns'. There was, in other words, little more than the traditional routine of Labour politics.

There were many people on the Left who passionately urged upon the Labour leaders the view that the politics of the late thirties required immeasurably more. Their efforts were resisted by the Labour leadership with a fierce energy and a dedicated ingenuity it altogether failed to display against the Government; and, greatly helped by the Left's own confusions and blunders, it won endorsement, without much difficulty, for the politics of paralysis.

There are, in effect, four main reasons to explain why the Labour leaders acted as they did.

The first is that, while clear as to the need to resist aggression, they feared to appear bent on war-like courses.

Secondly, there was the encouragement to irresolution which French social-democracy and Léon Blum's Popular Front Government provided to the Labour leaders—who in turn enhanced the irresolution of the French. At a crucial period of history, the two major social-democratic parties in Western Europe greatly accentuated each other's weaknesses.

Thirdly, there was the fear of anything resembling alliance with non-Labour and anti-Labour elements. To adapt Miss Dorothy Parker's phrase, the sky was then dark with the shadow of chickens coming home to roost—until it grew dark with the shadow of bombing planes. Whatever the Labour leaders had not learnt from 1931, they had learnt that never again must any Labour leader propose any kind of collaboration with Labour's opponents, least of all with such opponents as Churchill. Now it was that Churchill (and Britain) paid for his part in Russian intervention, for the military rhodomontades of the General Strike, for the stark imperialism which opposed any concessions to Indian nationhood.[1] And now

---

[1] At the end of 1936, Churchill led a campaign for 'Arms and the Covenant', based upon rearmament and support for the League of Nations. The campaign evoked support from a number of trade union leaders, including Walter Citrine. (See W. Churchill, op. cit. p. 170.) Though Churchill believed that 'we were on the threshold of not only gaining respect for our views, but of making them dominant', and that these hopes were dashed by the diversion of the King's abdication, there is no evidence that the campaign could have prospered without the full support of the Labour

it was too that the Liberals who had helped to save the 'national interest' in 1931 found that they were not wanted to save the national interest in the late thirties.

But by far and away the most important reason why the Labour leaders did none of the things that might have turned the scales was that doing these things corresponded even less to the view they took of politics than it had before 1935.

As a result of the General Election, the Labour Front Bench had come to be much better staffed than in the previous years. Besides Attlee, who became Leader after the Election, there was Hugh Dalton, Herbert Morrison, Arthur Greenwood, and a number of other influential figures who had returned from the exile of 1931. It was a much more professional team, a much more assured official Opposition than had ever existed before, also a much more 'responsible' one. Indeed, in 1937, its responsibility was given explicit recognition in the granting, under the Ministers of the Crown Act of that year, of a salary to the Leader of the Opposition.

This Official Opposition was deeply immersed in the conventions of parliamentary politics, which it easily took for the whole of politics, certainly for the most important part of it by far. It was an Opposition which quite deliberately narrowed its field of political action, and which was content, for the most part, to go through the motions of parliamentary battle. To have done more would have been to upset conventions to which the Labour leaders were as deeply wedded as their opponents. It would have meant a reversal of the habits of decades. It would not have been 'democratic'.[1] So it was not done: much more reasonable to wait for another chance of office which must, at the latest, come in 1940. Meanwhile, there was the Spanish Civil War, Japanese aggression in China, the German annexation of Austria, the German conquest of Czechoslovakia, the Italian annexation of Albania—and finally war.

The parliamentary leaders' view of politics was entirely shared

Party, and there was no chance of that support being obtained for it under Churchill's leadership.

[1] 'The Labour Party,' Attlee wrote in 1937, 'opposes Government policy, and seeks to convert the country to its point of view, but it does not carry on a campaign of resistance, passive or active, to hinder the ordinary functions of Government being carried on. It accepts the will of the majority, which has decided that the country shall be governed by a Capitalist Government, and it expects its opponents to do the same when it is returned to power.' Yet, he also said, not very consistently, it might be thought, that 'when the Government is disregarding its obligations under the League of Nations, and is acting aggressively, it is the duty of all those who support League loyalty as against national loyalty to oppose the Government by every means in its power.' (*The Labour Party in Perspective* (London, 1937) p. 219.)

by their industrial allies. More and more, as the thirties unfolded, the trade union leaders assumed the status of an official Industrial Opposition, as closely involved in playing the game in the industrial field as their parliamentary colleagues were in the political field. More and more, the trade union leaders spoke and acted as the responsible heads of vast, highly centralized concerns, engaged, by means of well-tested and routinized processes of bargaining and compromise, in the hiring out of their members' labour, and deeply concerned to avoid any disturbance of industrial discipline. As Ernest Bevin told his Executive Council in December 1936 with reference to the 1920's: 'Those were the days of advocacy. Ours is the day of administration.'[1] And as he also said to the 1937 Labour Party Conference: 'The industrial policy of your opponents has changed. Do not be under any delusion. The old bitter hostility which made the Trade Unions fight on the basis of the Taff Vale Judgment, and similar things, has gone. It is a new technique which is being introduced.'[2]

Nor was it only in private industry that the 'new technique' was being introduced. As the danger of war grew, so did trade union leaders again find the Government anxious for their co-operation and advice—though not in regard to foreign policy.

The trade union leaders were, and felt themselves to be, the living proof of the higher status of Labour within a capitalist system. They had no liking for the Conservative Government, and were genuinely opposed to most of its policies, at home and abroad; and they had no more illusions (some had less) than their parliamentary colleagues as to the threat of Fascist aggression and the dangers of appeasement. But they were not the men to press more militant political postures upon their parliamentary friends. At no time in those years did the industrial leadership of the Labour movement consider the use of industrial action for political purposes. As far as all Labour leaders were concerned, such action belonged to the distant and dismal past. They too were content to wait for the election of 1940, and to make, with the massive power they wielded at Party Conferences, a decisive contribution to the defeat of those who were not so content.

2. THE WASTED YEARS

The Spanish Civil War began in July 1936. From the start, there was passionate sympathy throughout the Labour movement, as

[1] Bullock, op. cit. p. 600.
[2] Labour Party Annual Conference Report, 1937, p. 140.

indeed far outside it, for the Republican cause, just as there was much active sympathy for Franco on the Right. Nor was there any doubt in the Labour movement that the conflict had vast international implications: a victory for Franco, helped as he was by Germany and Italy, must mean a major defeat for all opponents of Fascism everywhere in Europe.

The British Government had a policy towards the Spanish Civil War: it wanted to do nothing, and it also wanted that others should do nothing. Léon Blum, the head of a French Popular Front Government formed in June 1936, was at first inclined to give help to the Republican Government. Faced with a divided Cabinet and much internal right-wing opposition to intervention on the one hand, and with Communist pressure for aid to Spain on the other, he opted for non-intervention, much encouraged in that policy by the British Government's rejection of any kind of involvement in Spain.

When the War started, the international Labour movement had also had a policy. On the 28th of July, the General Council of the International Federation of Trade Unions and the Executive Committee of the Labour and Socialist International had stated that 'in accordance with the existing rules of international law the legal Government of Spain should be permitted to obtain the necessary means for its own defence'.[1] On the 18th of August, a Labour deputation had interviewed Anthony Eden, the Foreign Secretary, and pressed upon him the view, as Walter Citrine told the T.U.C. Conference on the 10th of September, that non-intervention 'while on paper preventing the Fascist Powers from supplying munitions, was in fact being held up in such a way as to give those Governments all the opportunities they needed for supplying arms . . . all the evidence proved that you could not trust the word of Mussolini or of Hitler, irrespective of what they signed or promised'.[2]

Yet, the National Council of Labour had, by then, come to support the Non-Intervention agreement signed by Britain, Russia, Germany, Italy and other concurring powers. In a statement on the 28th of August, it had expressed regret 'that it should have been thought expedient, on the ground of the dangers of war inherent in this situation, to conclude agreements among the European Powers laying an embargo upon the supply of arms and munitions of war to Spain, by which the rebel forces and the democratically elected and recognized Government of Spain are placed on the same footing'; but it also agreed that the non-intervention agreement might lessen international tension, provided it was scrupulously

[1] Labour Party Annual Conference Report, 1936, p. 29.
[2] T.U.C. Annual Conference Report, 1936, p. 362.

observed on all sides,[1] a pious hope which no one could seriously expect to see fulfilled.[2]

In accepting non-intervention, the Labour leaders had been deeply influenced by the fact that Léon Blum had made it his own policy, and had pressed it upon his British comrades as the only policy which the French internal situation allowed him.[3] However, at the T.U.C. Annual Conference in September 1936, both Walter Citrine and Ernest Bevin sought to defend the National Council's position on its own merits. 'We do not accept the gibe,' said Citrine, 'that we are following the British Government. We are not even taking our policy from the Socialist-led Government of France, which was the initiator of this. We decided our policy, unpopular though it may be with large masses of our own people who do not understand perhaps the niceties (sic) of the question, because we believe that policy is right, however distasteful, and the policy which your wisdom will commend.'[4] Bevin too emphasized that 'our decision was a British decision'; but he agreed that 'we have not ignored the French situation'.[5] In fact, the French Government's difficulties and Blum's support for non-intervention played a major part in Bevin's presentation of a case made more difficult by his own stated conviction, earlier in the debate, that 'the time has come when the whole of the Democratic Powers have to say to Hitler and Mussolini "Do not take us too cheaply" ':[6]

An amendment was moved to the General Council's resolution; it deplored the withholding of supplies from the Spanish Government and asked the General Council 'to call upon the International Federation of Trade Unions and the Labour and Socialist International to launch a great international campaign to force the democratic countries to abandon the deceptive policy of neutrality, which the Fascist dictators are not observing, so as to enable the Spanish Government to get the arms that will enable it to strike a blow for European peace and democracy'. This was defeated by 3,029,000 votes to 51,000,[7] a majority the size of which undoubtedly

[1] Labour Party Annual Conference Report, 1936, p. 29.
[2] On the 7th of October, Russia complained of violations of the agreement to the Non-Intervention Committee and, on the 23rd, announced that help would be sent to the Spanish Government.
[3] See, e.g. Hugh Dalton's account of discussions with Blum in Paris at the beginning of September (op. cit. p. 95). Dalton had gone to Paris as a member of a deputation of three from the National Council of Labour to discuss the Spanish situation with Blum and other Socialist leaders.
[4] T.U.C. Annual Conference Report, 1936, pp. 366-7.
[5] ibid, pp. 385-7.
[6] ibid, p. 369.
[7] ibid, p. 390.

owed much to Bevin's insistence that a policy other than non-intervention would lead to war. In any case, Bevin had also argued, no one could imagine that even if it was thought desirable, which he did not think it was, 'the British Government is going to release arms to the Spanish Government ad. lib.'[1] What this implied was that the Labour movement could not, even if it had wanted to try, move the British Government to adopt different courses. Yet, it was also Bevin who told the Conference, almost in the same breath, that 'the Government may have their hundreds of majority, but they cannot neglect the opinion of the National Council of Labour and its organized expression in the Labour Party and the Trades Union Congress'; and, he also said, 'it is not a question of calling men out on strike and paying them strike pay, when the worst you have to face is defeat and loss of membership—it is an issue of life and death, an issue of the road that humanity is going to take for the next hundred years'.[2]

The delegates to the T.U.C. had hardly returned home when evidence accumulated of Fascist breaches of the non-intervention agreement. By the 28th of September, the General Council of the I.F.T.U. and the Executive Committee of the Labour and Socialist International were asking the British and French Governments to examine the charges of Fascist intervention.[3] The same plea was addressed to the British Government by the National Council of Labour on the 30th of September.[4]

By the time the Labour Party Conference met on the 5th of October, it had become a great deal more difficult to claim that non-intervention meant anything, save the eventual doom of the Republican Government. The best that Arthur Greenwood could say for it, when he opened the Conference debate on Spain, was that 'it was felt by all those who have considered this matter, sad though they were about it, that in the circumstances of the time, there was no alternative but this very, very bad second best of non-intervention'. Nor did he now offer any possible alternative to it : its repudiation would not change Government policy; it would increase the difficulties of the Blum Government[5] and most likely bring it down; and, though the members of the National Council of Labour were

[1] T.U.C. Annual Conference Report, 1936, p. 388.
[2] ibid, p. 388.
[3] Labour Party Annual Conference Report, 1936, p. 31.
[4] ibid, p. 31.
[5] This was a point also made with considerable emphasis by Ernest Bevin (ibid, p. 174).

not 'people who would lightheartedly let our Movement down'. neither were they 'men and women who are prepared to head this country into war'.[1]

There were angry speeches against the Executive's position. 'You are beggared of policy at this moment,' said Sir Charles Trevelyan; 'we cannot now save or mar Spain, but what I am thinking of is this. When the last great war that is looming comes, and when Germany and Japan crash in to destroy Soviet Russia, I hope then that the Labour Party will have some other policy to offer than their sympathy accompanied by bandages and cigarettes.'[2] A dreadful picture, said Aneurin Bevan, had been painted of what would be the consequences if free trade in arms took place. But, he asked, 'is it not obvious to everyone that if the arms continue to pour into the rebels in Spain, our Spanish comrades will be slaughtered by hundreds of thousands? Has Mr Bevin and the National Council considered the fate of the Blum Government if a Fascist Government is established in Spain? How long will French democracy stand against Fascism in Germany, Fascism in Italy, Fascism in Spain, and Fascism in Portugal?. . . If the Popular Front French Government is destroyed and democracy in France is destroyed, then the Franco-Soviet Pact will soon be denounced,[3] and democracy in Europe will soon be in ruins. This is the consequence of this policy. And what is going to be the effect upon the vitality of Socialism throughout the world if our comrades in Spain are slaughtered and democracy in Europe is on its back as a consequence of our acquiescence of neutrality in Great Britain?'[4]

It was Attlee who wound up the debate, and his main argument in defence of the National Council's policy was different from the arguments put up by Greenwood and Bevan. It was that there was so far insufficiently conclusive proof of Fascist intervention in Spain. 'You must,' he said, 'give the Government the right to see what the evidence is . . . we demand that our Government and the other Governments who have put their hands to this International Agreement should see that it is being fully carried out.'[5]

The Executive's policy was endorsed by 1,836,000 votes to

---

[1] Labour Party Annual Conference Report, 1936, pp. 169-71.

[2] ibid, p. 173.

[3] A treaty of mutual assistance had been signed between Russia and France in May 1935.

[4] Labour Party Annual Conference Report, 1936, p. 177.

[5] ibid, p. 180. Earlier in the debate, Charles Duke, of the National Union of General and Municipal Workers, had also insisted, much more emphatically, that they had no evidence whatever of help being sent to the rebels since the Non-Intervention Agreement had been signed (ibid, p. 176).

519,000.[1] Next day, however, two Spanish delegates deeply stirred the Conference with an urgent appeal for help. One of them was Isabel de Palencia, whose speech, delivered in English (she was, she reminded the delegates, Scottish on her mother's side), concluded with the words 'Do not tarry. Now you know the truth. Now you know what the situation is in Spain. Come and help us. Come and help us. Scotsmen, ye ken noo!' To this, the Conference rose 'and sang enthusiastically "The Red Flag" '.[2]

That same afternoon, Hugh Dalton announced that the National Council of Labour had met during the adjournment to consider the statements made by the Spanish delegates, and had decided that the speeches should be published in pamphlet form; and the Council had also agreed to send Attlee and Greenwood on a deputation to the acting Prime Minister, Neville Chamberlain, to discuss the situation in Spain.[3] On the last day of the Conference, the Executive, having heard their report, presented another statement. It now asked that allegations of breaches of the Non-Intervention agreement 'should be pressed forward with the utmost speed' and that, if it was found that the agreement was ineffective or had been violated, 'the French and British Governments being responsible for the initiation of the Non-Intervention policy should take steps forthwith to restore to the Spanish Government their right to purchase the arms necessary to maintain the authority of the Constitutional Government in Spain and to re-establish law and order in her territory'. Should this be done, Attlee warned the delegates, they must be prepared to accept the possible consequences and risks, and, though the word was not mentioned, he obviously meant the risk of war.[4] Sir Stafford Cripps asked that the Conference should also express its conviction that the Fascist Powers had broken their pledges. Attlee accepted this and, so amended, the statement was unanimously approved.[5] The initiative was thus left to the National Council of Labour. How it fulfilled its responsibility will be dealt with below.[6] It is now necessary to turn to two other issues which came up at the 1936 Conference: one concerned the Communists and the 'United Front'; the other was rearmament.

At the end of November 1935, yet another application from the Communist Party for affiliation to the Labour Party was received

[1] Labour Party Annual Conference Report, 1936, p. 181.
[2] ibid, pp. 213-15.
[3] ibid, p. 215.
[4] ibid, p. 258.
[5] ibid, p. 262.
[6] see below, p. 254 ff.

by the National Executive. The application stressed the need for united action by the Labour movement for 'the immediate fight against the National Government, against Fascism and imperialist war'; it also stated that the Communists were 'prepared to work honestly and sincerely for the strengthening of the working-class movement and the winning of a majority of working-class representatives on all local bodies and in Parliament'. On the other hand, it reaffirmed that 'the Communist Party has always stated its revolutionary standpoint and will continue to do so'; and it would also 'maintain its international connections with working-class parties in other countries which are based on the revolutionary point of view'.[1]

There could never have been any doubt that the application would be rejected by the Executive: at the end of January, the Secretary of the Labour Party wrote to Harry Pollitt that, as had been stated in 1922, 'the fundamental difference between the democratic policy and practice of the Labour Party and the policy of dictatorship which the Communist Party had been created to promote was irreconcilable' and that affiliation was being sought, 'not for the purpose of promoting the Labour Party's declared Policy and Programme, but, on the contrary, to utilize Party facilities on the platform, in public conference, and in the Party press, to displace their essential democratic and Socialist character and substitute a Policy and Programme based upon Communist Party principles'. Affiliation would also imply, the Executive said, a weakening in the Labour Party's defence of political democracy which would 'inevitably assist the forces of reaction, would endanger our existing liberties, and would retard the achievement of Socialism in this country'.[2] This was endorsed at the 1936 Conference by 1,728,000 votes to 592,000.[3]

The relatively high vote in favour of Communist affiliation is partly explained by the fact that the Mineworkers' Federation had supported it. But it was also a token of the strong radical current running through the Labour movement in response to the events of the previous twelve months. Abroad, there had been the Italian conquest of Abyssinia, the German reoccupation of the Rhineland and, traumatic in its impact on the Left, the Spanish conflict. In face of these events, British appeasement had assumed clearly identifiable form and was regarded on the Left as being principally due to Conservative sympathy for right wing authoritarianism. The British Union of Fascists had again been much in evidence in 1936 and the

[1] Labour Party Annual Conference Report, 1936, p. 50.
[2] ibid, p. 51.
[3] ibid, p. 211.

police had not become more tender in its handling of counter-demonstrators. On the 4th of October, Mosley's Blackshirts had tried to march through the East End of London, under police escort, and had confronted a massive concentration of men and women, drawn from all over London, whom repeated baton charges had failed to disperse. The Public Order Bill, introduced soon after by the Government, had banned the wearing of political uniforms; it had also further extended the powers of the police.[1] The Left felt no confidence that these powers were not at least as much intended to impede its own activities as those of Fascists.

And the Left *was* very active in 1936: more meetings, more protests, more demonstrations, including, in the autumn. an Unemployed March larger than any of its predecessors in protest against the Unemployment Assistance Regulations and the Means Test.[2]

In May 1936, there had been launched the Left Book Club, whose monthly offerings, selected by Victor Gollancz, Harold Laski and John Strachey, met and in turn enhanced a quite unprecedented demand for a new, committed political literature, much of which was inspired by Marxism, and all of which was fiercely anti-Fascist. The Club greatly prospered: by April 1939 it had achieved a peak membership of nearly 60,000 and had some 1,200 local discussion groups, linked by a monthly bulletin, *Left News*. In addition, there were functional groups for scientists, doctors, engineers, lawyers, teachers, civil servants, poets, writers, artists, musicians and actors; and the Club was also responsible for the arrangement of rallies, meetings, lectures, weekend and vacation schools.[3] In the late thirties, it provided the one forum in which activists of different tendencies, and of diverse social origin, were able to meet and engage in common political activity.[4]

But the temper of the Left was not only fashioned by books, anti-Fascist meetings or demonstrations. It also, and certainly no less, drew strength from the blood that was spilt on Spanish battlefields, by Spaniards, but also by members of the International Brigade, including its British volunteers, whose dead gave urgent proof of the bitter reality of the struggle against Fascism.

In all the activities of the Left, it was, now more than ever, the

---

[1] Kidd, op. cit. pp. 68-78.

[2] Hutt, op. cit. p. 282.

[3] N. Wood, *Communism and British Intellectuals* (London, 1959) p. 61.

[4] By March 1939, the Labour leadership was sufficiently worried about this for the Labour Party's National Agent to write to local Labour Parties and warn them against engaging in political activities with the local Clubs, 'especially when these are in the direction of a so-called "Popular Front" with any other political party' (Jupp, op. cit. p. 184).

Communists who were busiest, organizing, demonstrating, protesting and also fighting in Spain.[1] And, inevitably, the Communists also derived some benefit from the increased popularity which the Soviet Union enjoyed on the Left, as the only positively and actively anti-Fascist Power. There is a whole *Zeitgeist* suggested in the fact that the question mark in the Webbs' *Soviet Communism: A New Civilization?*, first published in 1935, should have disappeared in the second edition, published in 1937. There were, of course, many more people in the Labour movement who remained as critical of Russia after 1936 as they had been before; and whose hostility fed on such episodes as the great Soviet purges and trials of the late thirties. But, in expressing hostility to Russia, they did now find it more difficult to resist the charge of guilt by dissociation.

There are two other facts which need stressing, if the temper of the period is to be accurately gauged. The first is that, though there was a powerful ideological current to the Left among intellectuals, the Fabian tradition was even then very far from submerged. If one part of a new generation of intellectuals was deeply influenced by the writings of men like John Strachey and Harold Laski, another part of the same generation found even more attractive books like Hugh Dalton's *Practical Socialism for Britain,* which was a prime example of 'tentative, doctrineless socialism'.[2] It is just as well to remember that it was in those years that a new generation of Fabian academics, like Evan Durbin, Hugh Gaitskell and Douglas Jay, embraced Keynes and 'practical socialism' with as much eagerness as their counterparts on the Left embraced Marx, historical materialism , and the class struggle.

The second point is that, though many more people than ever before came to think (and to speak) of the Communist Party as 'the Party', to be influenced by it and to support its policies, a remarkably small number actually joined it. In May 1937 its membership was 12,250, and 15,570 in September 1938. In the first eight months of 1939, the membership fluctuated around 18,000.[3] In comparison with earlier figures, these gains were substantial; but they were, in

[1] About one half of the 543 British volunteers killed in Spain were members of the Communist Party or the Young Communist League (Wood, op. cit. p. 56).

[2] Dalton himself recalls that the book was greatly praised by Evan Durbin as conveying 'in every chapter the sense of a mind acquainted with the detail of legislative and administrative action—aware of its possibilities and its limitations'. (Dalton, op. cit. p. 59.) Dalton also notes that Roy Jenkins, twenty years after the publication of *Practical Socialism for Britain,* described it as 'the first swallow of the post-1935 summer' and as marking 'the beginning of the return of self-confidence', evidently meaning confidence in Fabian gradualism.

[3] Pelling, op. cit. p. 104.

the circumstances, less than spectacular. What compensated for this was the fact that both the new recruits and many of those who came to support the Communist Party without joining it were extremely gifted and articulate people, whose contribution to the cultural climate of the period made it appear much more red than it really was.

To many left-wing members of the Labour Party, it seemed increasingly obvious that events, at home and abroad, rendered less and less defensible the treatment of Communists as pariahs. In fact, meetings of representatives of the Socialist League, the C.P. and the I.L.P. had begun to be held soon after the General Election of 1935 for the discussion of co-operation in a Unity Campaign.

The Labour leaders, for their part, were firmly opposed to the formation either of a 'United Front' with the Communists,[1] or of a 'People's Front' including anybody opposed to the Government's policies, which was also then being considered.[2]

At the 1936 Labour Conference, the official attitude was overwhelmingly endorsed: a United Front resolution, moved by a delegate of the Amalgamated Engineering Union, was defeated by 1,805,000 votes to 435,000.[3] An amendment to the resolution which asked that the National Executive should 'take all practicable steps to mobilize the support of all peace-loving and democratic citizens in the struggle for peace and fight against Fascism' was turned down by 1,933,000 votes to 190,000:[4] the delegates then unanimously agreed to a resolution which declared that they were 'irrevocably opposed to any attempt to "liberalize" the Labour Party by "watering down" its policy in order to increase its membership'.[5]

It was only the following year that the Executive was given occasion to stamp down on left-wing dissidents. But it had already found occasion to do so in regard to the Labour League of Youth, which had grown increasingly critical of the leadership's lack of drive, and had passed a resolution in favour of a 'United Front' of all Working-Class Youth organizations. The Executive was not prepared to grant the League any right to register opinion on the policy of the Party, least of all left wing opinion. In its view, as it stressed in a Report to the 1936 Conference, 'the real object of the League is to enrol large numbers of young people, and by a social life of its own, provide opportunities for young people to study Party Policy and to give

[1] See the National Executive's Report, *British Labour and Communism*, issued in July 1936 (Labour Party Annual Conference Report, 1956, pp. 296-300).
[2] See J. T. Murphy, *New Horizons* (London, 1941) p. 319.
[3] Labour Party Annual Conference Report, 1936, p. 257.
[4] ibid, p. 257.
[5] ibid, p. 257.

loyal support to the Party of which they are members'.[1] The members of the League, on the other hand, wanted not only to study but to discuss and criticize party policy. The Executive therefore proposed that the age limit on membership of the League should be lowered from twenty-five to twenty-one; it was also decided to disband and then reconstitute the League's National Advisory Committee; not to convene the Annual Conference of the League the following Easter, and to suspend publication of the League's paper, *The New Nation*.[2] These decisions were endorsed at the 1936 Conference by 1,909,000 votes to 214,000.[3] The League was subsequently brought under much closer Executive control and the 1937 Conference agreed to the proposal that it should be deprived of representation on the Executive.[4] There was, however, more trouble to come. For the Labour League of Youth ardently espoused the 1938 campaign for a Popular Front. In 1939, the National Advisory Committee was again disbanded and the League's Annual Conference again cancelled.[5]

On the issue of rearmament, there were, in 1936, no less than four distinct currents of thought in the Labour movement. The first, by then of marginal importance, was the straightforward pacifist view; the second, which was still the majority view, was a waning, but still powerful, belief in Labour's traditional programme of disarmament by international agreement coupled with an increasingly inconsistent acceptance of the obligation of collective action in defence of Labour's principles, and support for the League of Nations.[6] In March, Labour had opposed in the House of Commons the Government's new programme of rearmament, as laid out in the White Paper on Defence; and it also voted against the Service Estimates.[7] A third view, rapidly gaining in strength and of which Hugh Dalton and Ernest Bevin were the main advocates, was that Labour had no option but to support British rearmament. The fourth view was that of the Labour Left, the most 'ideological' of the four, which entailed both an ardent demand for resistance to Fascist aggression, and a no less ardent refusal of support for the Government's programme, on

[1] Labour Party Annual Conference Report, 1936, pp. 73-4.
[2] ibid, p. 75.
[3] ibid, p. 247.
[4] Labour Party Annual Conference Report, 1937, p. 155. The vote was 2,056,000 to 423,000.
[5] Labour Party Annual Conference Report, 1939, p. 8.
[6] *Labour and the Defence of Peace* (published in May 1936 by the National Council of Labour).
[7] The decision to oppose, when challenged by Dalton in the Parliamentary Labour Party, was endorsed by 57 votes to 39 (Bullock, op. cit. p. 582).

the ground that the British Government could under no circumstances be trusted to use arms for any but its own reactionary purposes. The corollary of this view was that the Government must be swept out of office as an essential condition for the prosecution of a vigorous policy of resistance to aggression.

The resolution which the National Executive presented to the 1936 Labour Party Conference was an uneasy and ambiguous compromise between the second and the third of these views It declared that 'the armed strength of the countries loyal to the League of Nations must be conditioned by the armed strength of the potential aggressors' and it therefore stated that the Labour Party's policy was to 'maintain such defence forces as are consistent with our country's responsibility as a Member of the League of Nations, the preservation of the people's rights and liberties, the continuance of democratic institutions, and the observance of International Law'; on the other hand, given 'the deplorable record of the Government', the Labour Party declined 'to accept responsibility for a purely competitive armament policy' and reserved 'full liberty to criticize the rearmament programme of the present Government'. And the resolution concluded by pledging the Labour Party to 'unceasing efforts, both by exposing the present Government's record of incompetence and betrayal of its Peace pledges and by expounding our own positive International Policy, to secure the return of a Labour Government to power'.[1]

In the debate, different members of the Executive stressed whichever aspect of the resolution appeared to accord with their own views. Hugh Dalton, who introduced it, said that the Labour Party could not logically support 'unilateral non-rearmament in a world where all are increasing their armaments', and insisted that a Labour Government, in the existing world situation, 'would be compelled to provide an increase in British armaments'.[2] Morrison, on the other hand, emphasized that the Labour Party was opposed to 'unilateral competitive national rearmament' and continued to rely on 'pooled, collective security', and that the resolution indicated continued opposition to the Government's rearmament programme.[3] Attlee, who wound up the debate, also promised that there would be no support for the Government in its rearmament policy; but he also said that this did not necessarily mean 'that the arms you have got now or the arms you had last year are the exact amount required'.[4]

[1] Labour Party Annual Conference Report, 1936, p. 182.
[2] ibid, p. 184.
[3] ibid, p. 193.
[4] ibid, pp. 205-6.

The Executive's evident inability to make up its mind on the issue was fiercely criticized by Bevin, who said that if he was asked 'to face the question of arming this country, I am prepared to face it'; prophetically, he warned that Czechoslovakia, 'one of the most glorious little democratic countries, hedged in all round, is in danger of being sacrificed tomorrow'. What he wanted, he said, was to 'drive this Government to defend democracy, even against its will, if I can'.[1] What he did *not* say was how this was to be done. Dalton, who was very anxious not to convey the impression that his acceptance of rearmament meant support for the Government, went even further. 'If this country is ever to be secure again,' he said, 'this Government must go, and it is our job to shift it.'[2] But he was no more specific than Bevin as to the strategy required to achieve an objective which, his own formulation suggested, was of the greatest urgency.

On the other hand, the Labour Left, which did want a much more vigorous opposition to the Government's foreign policy, and a national campaign to drive it out of office, was as confused and incapable of giving a lead as was the Executive. A composite amendment from a number of Constituency Parties to the Executive's resolution stated that confidence in the 'existing' League of Nations was misplaced, 'as the League continues to be used by the Great Powers for their own imperialist purposes rather than in the interest of world peace'; it then declared that co-operation of the Labour Movement in the Government's rearmament plans, 'in any conditions, would be fatal and destroy resistance to war'; and the Executive was asked to campaign against military and industrial conscription; 'to establish on a local and national basis a powerful movement of resistance . . . for the carrying out of such a campaign, and for the defeat of the Government's policy'; and, thirdly, 'to re-establish international working-class unity in active resistance to capitalist and imperialist war and war preparations'.[3]

Retrospective wisdom is easy, and it is certainly true that the Left in 1936 faced agonizing dilemmas. But the evaluation of the problem reflected in the resolution was, on any count, gravely amiss. For it failed to discriminate between the British Government and the Fascist Powers and to appreciate that salvation lay, not in the denial of arms to the Government, but in compelling it to pursue a foreign policy which would either make it unnecessary for arms to be used or, if they were to be used, that they should be used for appropriate

[1] Labour Party Annual Conference Report, 1936, pp. 203-4.
[2] ibid, p. 183.
[3] ibid, p. 96. The resolution was defeated on a show of hands (ibid, p. 207).

purposes. The determination to sweep the Government out of office was fine. But meanwhile?

Cripps, who moved the reference back of the Executive's resolution, was, on that occasion, a little more *nuancé*. He did not object, he said, to armaments which could be controlled by 'the working-class of the world', though he did object 'to putting power into the hands of those people whom we have uniformly accused of being responsible for the present world conditions and for the new exploitation of the workers'. However, he immediately added, 'it may be that in some circumstances one is driven to seek even the most doubtful ally' and the problem they had to settle was the problem 'of whether we are prepared to seek the British imperialist Government as an ally against the possible aggression of a Fascist Germany'. It was not a problem to which he had an answer. Instead, he asked that the Executive should produce another document 'which will decisively say whether we are for or against rearmament in the hands of the British National Government'.[1] It was not an inspiring call, and the reference back was defeated by 1,438,000 to 652,000. The Executive's resolution was then endorsed by 1,738,000 votes to 657,000.[2]

The 1936 Conference, it was agreed on all sides, was a bad Conference, and it left everyone, Right and Left, deeply frustrated and dissatisfied.[3] But the Conference was also a turning point. By 1937, the Labour Party and the T.U.C. had acquired a much more consistent policy on defence and foreign policy. What they still lacked, and never acquired, was the will to fight for these policies.

Despite the fact that the 1936 Conference had given massive endorsement to the Executive's opposition to the United Front, the Socialist League pressed more vigorously than ever for its creation.[4] On the 16th and 17th of January, a special delegate Conference of the Socialist League approved by fifty-six votes to thirty-eight, with

[1] Labour Party Annual Conference Report, 1936, p. 201. This should not be taken to mean, however, that Cripps was not then fiercely opposed to rearmament by the existing Government. A few weeks after the Conference, he said in a speech that the Labour Party should not support rearmament under the National Government, even at the risk of defeat in war. (Cooke, op. cit. p. 187.)

[2] ibid, p. 207.

[3] For a wide range of expressions of that dissatisfaction, see Hutt, op. cit. pp. 300 ff. Hugh Dalton recalls that he found the Conference 'a most unhappy experience' (Dalton, op. cit. p. 97) and Ernest Bevin, Mr. Bullock notes, 'came as near to despairing of the Labour Party after the Edinburgh Conference as he ever did' (Bullock, op. cit. p. 588).

[4] In January 1937 it also acquired a weekly paper, *Tribune*, for the propagation of its views.

twenty-three abstentions, the launching of a Unity Campaign with the Communist Party and the I.L.P. By then, the National Executive, aware of the preparations for the Campaign, had already issued an *Appeal for Party Loyalty,* which had yet again reiterated the Executive's opposition to the venture.[1] However, on the 18th of January, the three bodies announced their agreement to launch a unity campaign 'for action, for attack, for the ending of retreat, for the building of the strength, unity and power of the working-class movement'. In a Unity Manifesto, the first and last such joint production of representatives of the British Left, the parties to the agreement[2] called for 'unity of all sections of the working-class movement . . . in the struggle against Fascism, reaction and War, and against the National Government . . . in the struggle for immediate demands, and the return of a Labour Government as the next stage in the advance to working-class power'. The Manifesto also proclaimed 'implacable opposition to the rearmament and recruiting programme of the National Government'; the fight for peace, it was stated, 'demands unbending hostility to a National Government that can in no circumstances be trusted to use armaments in the international interests of the working-class, of the peoples, or of peace'; such armaments, on the contrary, would be used 'only in support of Fascism, of Imperialist War, of Reaction, and of Colonial Suppression'. The workers must be mobilized 'for the maintenance of peace, for the defence of the Soviet Union and its fight for Peace, and for a pact between Great Britain, the Soviet Union, France, and all other states in which the working-class have political freedom'. Nor should the movement wait for General Elections; the workers 'should wage incessant struggle, political and industrial alike', for the satisfaction of immediate demands, such as the abolition of the Means Test, for a forty-hour week, paid holidays for all workers, higher wages, non-contributory pensions of £1 at sixty, nationalization of the mines, 'effective control' of the banks and the stock market, and 'making the rich pay for social ameliorization'.[3]

The Executive's reaction to the publication of the Manifesto was predictable and it was also prompt. The Unity Campaign was officially launched at a mass meeting in the Free Trade Hall in Manchester on the 24th of January. On the 27th, the Socialist League was disaffiliated from the Labour Party and its members

[1] Labour Party Annual Conference Report, 1937, p. 26.
[2] Cripps, Mellor and G. R. Mitchinson signed the Manifesto for the Socialist League, Pollitt, Dutt and Gallacher for the C.P., and Maxton, Jowett and Brockway for the I.L.P. Other signatories included Bevan, Laski, Brailsford, Strachey, Tom Mann and Arthur Horner.
[3] For full text, see *Tribune,* 22nd of January, 1937.

were urged 'to continue their work for Socialism through the Labour Party'.[1] The same point was again made, and the Campaign vigorously denounced, in another circular, *The Labour Party and the So-Called 'Unity Campaign'*.[2]

This was no bar to the continuation of the Campaign, and many United Front meetings were held all over the country in the following weeks. On the 24th of March, however, the Executive went much further and declared that membership of the League would be incompatible with membership of the Labour Party as from the 1st of June.

This was the first time that proscription had been applied against a *bona fide* organization of the Labour Left, and it proved extremely effective. The Labour Party members who had sponsored the Unity Campaign had no wish to leave the Labour Party, or to be thrown out of it, and the Whitsuntide Conference of the Socialist League therefore decided to dissolve the organization. On the other hand, the Unity campaigners also agreed to continue with their meetings and propaganda,[3] but in an 'individual capacity'; and there was formed a 'Committee of Party Members sympathetic to Unity', which organized a separate campaign of its own.

This was still too much for the Executive. On the 26th of May it appealed to all members of the Party 'to refrain from any further joint activities with the Communist Party and the I.L.P.', and to 'concentrate on Labour's constructive proposals,[4] which are now commanding widespread public attention, and are about to be brought before every elector in the country through an organized campaign, with a view to achieving a great Labour victory at the next General Election'.[5] Finally, the Executive, on the 28th of July, further announced that no committee or body within the Party had any authority to 'prosecute unity between the Communist Party, the I.L.P. and the Labour Party' and that 'anything in the nature of a public campaign for this purpose could not be entertained'.[6]

[1] Labour Party Annual Conference Report, 1937, p. 27.
[2] ibid, pp. 268-70.
[3] Cripps tried to organize a United Front meeting at the Albert Hall at the beginning of April but was refused the use of the auditorium by the trustees. He then tried to bring political pressure to bear upon them on the issue of freedom of speech and wrote for support (a delightfully English touch, this) to Stanley Baldwin, Sir John Simon, Ramsay MacDonald, Winston Churchill, Lloyd George, Archibald Sinclair and Attlee. The last three of these did in fact support Cripps's right to speak in the Albert Hall (Estorick. op. cit. p. 156; Cook, op. cit. p. 190).
[4] This was a reference to *Labour's Immediate Programme*, which was published in March 1937.
[5] Labour Party Annual Conference Report, 1937, p. 27.
[6] ibid, p. 28.

At the 1937 Party Conference, Cripps, Laski and G. R. Strauss sought to persuade the delegates to vote for the reference back of the section of the Executive's Report dealing with the Socialist League and the Unity Campaigners. They failed—by 1,730,000 votes to 373,000.[1]

However, the Executive mixed sternness with encouragement. *Labour's Immediate Programme* had been intended, in Dalton's words, 'to arouse interest, to maintain self-confidence, and to blanket and discredit the disloyalists'.[2] The document in fact marked a retreat from *For Socialism and Peace*[3] and brought the Labour Party right back, even in programmatic terms, to marginal collectivism. But it promised enough to satisfy most Labour Party followers. Indeed it was adopted unanimously by the 1937 Conference[4] and, over the next two years, the Executive was able to insist that the acceptance of the Programme by the electorate, and the return of a majority Labour Government pledged to its realization, should be the sole aim towards which loyal Labour Party members should strive.

There was also a consolation prize the Executive was willing to offer the activists in the constituencies: it agreed to amend the Party Constitution to increase the number of representatives of the Constituency Parties on the Executive from five to seven and to provide for their election, not by the whole Conference, which really meant by the Trade Unions, but by the Constituency delegates only. A number of trade union leaders felt very dubious about these concessions;[5] others, like Bevin,[6] felt them to be appropriate. The trade union leaders had nothing to fear. The change still left them with a decisive majority on the Executive. Nor indeed did the constituency delegates immediately use their new freedom to return the representatives of the Left. They did elect Laski, Cripps and D. N. Pritt, all three prominent Unity campaigners. But they also elected Herbert Morrison and Hugh Dalton, who had strongly opposed the cam-

[1] Labour Party Annual Conference Report, p. 164.
[2] Dalton, op. cit. p. 125.
[3] Its nationalization proposals, e.g., were confined to the Bank of England, the mines, the electricity and gas supply industries, the railways, 'and such other Transport Services as are suitable for transfer to Public Ownership'. In addition, it also said, 'the land should belong to the people' but only proposed that a Labour Government and other public authorities should be enabled 'to acquire such land as they needed for any purpose without delay and at a reasonable price'. Labour Party Annual Conference Report, 1937, p. 186.
[4] Labour Party Annual Conference Report, 1937, p. 186.
[5] See, e.g., the speech of Charles Duke, of the National Union of General and Municipal Workers, ibid, pp. 143-4.
[6] ibid, pp. 145-7.

paign, as well as Philip Noel-Baker and George Dallas, who were certainly not identified with the Left.

On the question of rearmament, *Labour's Immediate Programme* had declared that a Labour Government would 'unhesitatingly maintain such armed forces as are necessary to defend our country and to fulfil our obligations as a member of the British Commonwealth and of the League of Nations'. In the same month, Ernest Bevin, then Chairman of the T.U.C., told the Executive Council of his Union that 'from the day Hitler came to power, I have felt that the democratic countries would have to face war. . . . I cannot see any way of stopping Hitler and the other dictators except by force'.[1] In July, the Parliamentary Labour Party, in contrast to its attitude the previous year, did not vote against the Service Estimates, but merely abstained. The issue was carried a step further in *International Policy and Defence,* issued by the National Council of Labour.

This document expressed the National Council of Labour's conviction that war could be prevented, the arms race stopped, and the League of Nations made strong again 'provided that a British Government soon comes to power which will base its policy on the declarations of the British Labour Movement'. Such a Government would have to be 'strongly equipped to defend this country, to play its full part in Collective Security, and to resist any intimidation by the Fascist Powers designed to frustrate the fulfilment of our obligations'; and such a Government, the Statement also said, would not, until there had been a change in the international situation, be able 'to reverse the present programme of Rearmament'.[2]

Though the statement did not make the point explicitly, the delegates at both the T.U.C. and the Labour Party Conferences were left in no doubt that their leaders had now abandoned their opposition to the Government's own rearmament programme. At the T.U.C. in September, their position was endorsed by 3,544,000 votes to 224,000,[3] and at the Labour Party Conference in October, by 2,169,000 to 262,000.[4]

The major weakness in the Executive's statement was its emphasis on what a *future* Labour Government would do. Save for their acceptance of the need for rearmament by the present Government, the Labour leaders had nothing to say as to how they proposed at least to influence affairs in the interval. This is the more striking, in the light of their strong condemnation of Conservative foreign policy

[1] Bullock, op. cit. p. 592.
[2] *International Policy and Defence,* p. 7.
[3] T.U.C. Annual Conference Report, 1937, p. 42.
[4] Labour Party Annual Conference Report, 1937, p. 212.

and purposes. As for the Labour Left, it continued to hold that rearmament must be opposed until the Tories had been displaced. The Labour Left was blinkered on this issue. But it was a great deal more alive than the Executive to the urgency of another issue—the issue of aid to Republican Spain.

Almost immediately after the Labour Party Conference at the beginning of October 1936, the Socialist International and the International Federation of Trade Unions had met in Paris at the request of the National Council of Labour. The thirty-three delegates from twelve different countries had then recognized the failure of the Non-Intervention policy, and agreed that it was 'the common duty of the Working-class of all countries, organized politically and industrially, to secure by their influence upon public opinion and upon their respective Governments the conclusion of an international agreement—for which the French and British Governments should take the initiative—restoring complete commercial liberty to Republican Spain'.[1]

From then onwards, Hugh Dalton notes, 'we stood on the simple slogan "Arms for Spain" '.[2] There could, however, be no hope that this would ever become more than a 'simple slogan' unless the Labour leaders were prepared to initiate the kind of national campaign which was being urged upon them by the Left. This they were not prepared to do.

In November 1936, a delegation of representatives of the French Popular Front had come to London, with Léon Blum's approval, to discover what British support there would be for a French denunciation of the Non-Intervention Pact. They received no encouragement from their Labour colleagues. The latter, as Cole notes, 'held off, because they could not assure the French of British support, and were hesitant about invoking the war danger which stronger pressure, if it had been successful, would have involved'.[3]

It would be unprofitable as well as tedious to list the succession of international Labour meetings which were held in the following months to consider the Spanish situation,[4] or to enumerate the resolutions of protest and support which were regularly produced by its delegates. The main feature of both meetings and resolutions was that they carefully avoided any kind of commitment to more than routine protests against violations of non-intervention and inef-

[1] Labour Party Annual Conference Report, 1937, p. 7.
[2] Dalton, op. cit. p. 105.
[3] Cole, op. cit. p. 329.
[4] For the dates and decisions of these meetings, see Labour Party Annual Conference Report, 1937, pp. 6-14.

fectual demands for help to Republican Spain. British Labour was only one of the groupings in the Socialist International which refused to commit itself to more positive action; but neither was it by any means the least paralytic of them. Perhaps the most pathetic Labour document issued over Spain was the Manifesto it published after the mass bombing of Guernica. This, after protesting at the outrage and calling attention to evidence that it had been perpetrated by German airmen using German aircraft, also 'called upon the British Government to take the initiative, through the League of Nations, for an examination of the whole problem of the bombing in warfare of open towns and the indiscriminate slaughter of the non-combatant population'. And, the Manifesto also appealed for further contributions to the International Solidarity Fund for Spain.[1]

At the Labour Party Conference in October 1937, Sir Charles Trevelyan moved a composite resolution, which instructed the National Executive 'to launch forthwith a nation-wide campaign' to compel the Government to abandon Non-Intervention and to restore to the Republican Government its right to purchase arms. This last demand, Trevelyan noted, had been 'vigorously' pressed in Parliament, but, he added, 'something more formidable is needed in the way of public opinion here'. They would be foolish, he felt, if they believed that the Government would 'ever concede to the Spanish people their rights unless they are driven by an irresistible wave of opinion here'.[2]

On behalf of the Executive, George Latham assured the Conference that everything that could be done 'in the direction suggested by the mover and seconder of the resolution' would be done. He only had one qualification to make: a nation-wide campaign would have to be considered by the National Council of Labour; and, he reminded the delegates, they had another campaign in view (i.e, on behalf of *Labour's Immediate Programme*); however, 'whatever may happen in regard to a specific campaign, you may be sure that we shall not relax our efforts to secure justice for our comrades who are fighting in Spain'.[3] The resolution was then unanimously adopted.

A 'Spain Campaign Committee' was in fact appointed by the Executive after the Conference and it did organize a number of meetings, demonstrations and collections of relief funds, culminating in a demonstration at the Albert Hall in December 1937.[4] After that,

[1] Labour Party Annual Conference Report, 1937, p. 11.
[2] ibid, p. 212.
[3] ibid, p. 215.
[4] Interim Report of the National Executive Committee, October 1937 to July 1938, pp. 19-20. It was also in December 1937 that Attlee, with some of

the initiative, save in the matter of relief, was mainly left to local parties and organizations. At the end of April 1938, the Mineworkers' Federation arranged a special delegate conference in London to discuss Spain and asked the T.U.C. to call a conference of affiliated unions 'to examine ways and means of giving practical assistance to the Spanish Government and to secure the reversal of the present policy of the National Government'. This was refused; organized Labour, said Walter Citrine, was doing everything in its legal power to influence public opinion against the Government's policy in Spain.[1] The scarcely veiled implication was that 'direct action' was more or less illegal. By then, there was in any case very little demand for such action, save on the part of the Communist Party. A proposal for industrial action against the Government's foreign policy was made in private session at the T.U.C. Conference early in September 1938, and defeated.[2]

At the next Labour Party Conference, which only met in May 1939,[3] there was bitter criticism of the Executive's failure to do more.[4] By then, Republican Spain had been crushed.

3. WAITING FOR WAR

Within six months of the Labour Party Conference in October 1937, the international situation had grown very much worse. In Spain, the Republicans steadily lost ground. Austria was occupied by German troops in March 1938, and then incorporated into Germany. Immediately after, Czechoslovakia came under threat from the Nazis, and under pressure from Britain and France to make concessions to the Nazis' demands. After Anthony Eden's resignation as Foreign Secretary in February 1938, Neville Chamberlain

---

his colleagues, visited Republican Spain, and was, uncharacteristically, responsible for providing the thirties with one of its lasting images by returning the salute of the Spanish forces with the clenched fist sign. For this, Attlee recalls, he was criticized on his return to England 'on the ground that I was thereby approving of Communism'. But, he explains, 'at that time the salute was commonly used by all supporters of the Republic whether they were Liberals, Socialists, Communists or anarchists' (C. R. Attlee, *As It Happened* (London, 1954) p. 95).

[1] S. Davies, *The British Labour Party and British Foreign Policy, 1933-1939* (unpublished Ph.D. Thesis, University of London, 1950) p. 657.

[2] Cole, op. cit. p. 356.

[3] The 1937 Conference had agreed that future Conferences should be held at Whitsuntide, and left the Executive to decide whether there should be a Conference at Whitsuntide 1938. The Executive, though pressed to convene an Emergency Conference in the spring of 1938, preferred, for obvious reasons, to wait until 1939.

[4] See Labour Party Annual Conference Report, 1939, pp. 258 ff.

was in full control of British foreign policy, and unswervingly bent on appeasement.

By then, the idea of a Popular Front, or a United Peace Alliance, was again being canvassed. What was now proposed was a wide-ranging coalition of groupings and individuals from Communists to Liberals and even Conservatives, designed to exercise all possible pressure to reverse Chamberlain's policies, if possible to drive him from office, and to base British foreign policy on the restraint of aggression by an alliance between Britain, France and the Soviet Union. Support for such a campaign came from a variety of sources: from Constituency Labour Parties, 120 of whom declared themselves in favour of a People's Front at a Conference called to campaign for aid to Spain; from *Reynolds' News,* whose manifesto for a United Peace Alliance was endorsed at the Easter Congress of the Co-operative Party by 2,343,000 votes to 1,947,000; from the Liberal *News Chronicle*; from the Communist Party, and from a variety of other bodies.[1] It is a token of the desperation which the Government's foreign policy engendered among quite moderate people that R. H. Tawney should have suggested, in a letter to the *Manchester Guardian* in late March, that if the Labour and Liberal Parties could not prevail upon the Government to reverse its policies, they should withdraw from Parliament and carry on agitation in the country.[2]

However, the pressure for a Popular Front, as G. D. H. Cole notes, lacked 'either a definite organizing centre or a single focus'.[3] The only political formation which could have given it a focus, as well as a chance of success, was the Labour Party—and the Labour leaders were uncompromisingly hostile to it from the start.

On the 12th of April, the National Executive had issued a circular recalling previous Conference decisions 'against the weakening of Party policy to accommodate other political elements'. Movements such as the proposed United Peace Alliance were, the Executive also said, 'bound to weaken the Party's organization and electoral power by association with other political bodies that do not share the Party's policy or its determination to achieve its democratic Socialist objectives'; affiliated organizations were reminded, with dubious relevance, that 'in the Parliament of 1929 Labour was only nineteen seats short of a bare majority' and that, ever since 1931, it had been 'the open and avowed aim of successive National Executive Committees to work strenuously and without ceasing to secure a Labour Government with a majority in Parliament and adequate support in the Constituencies'. This remained the objective: 'with the exercise

[1] Cole, op. cit. pp. 352-3; Murphy, op. cit. pp. 326-7.
[2] See Davies, op. cit. p. 632.
[3] Cole, op. cit. p. 313.

of disciplined loyalty, thorough organization, and widespread propaganda, the capture of power can be achieved . . . the Party membership throughout the country is called on at this crucial moment to stand by our Party, its policy and its principles, to join with the National Executive Committee in redoubling our efforts, and definitely to plan for Labour Victory'.[1]

Despite this appeal, the Executive's Interim Report noted, 'a number of Constituency Parties initiated action in their areas to form local Councils of Action, based on "Popular Front" principles'; they were 'either prevailed upon to liquidate the new organizations, or where occasion warranted, the Parties were disaffiliated and new Parties created upon the lines laid down in the Party Constitution'.[2]

The Executive's exclusive concern with an election of which there was no sign, and which might not, in the normal course of events, be held for at least eighteen months, was made even more emphatic in a further statement, *The Labour Party and the Popular Front*, which was issued in May.

The statement consistently refused to discuss the Popular Front in terms of its prime function, which was, in Cole's words, 'to stop the policy of appeasement at once, and not to wait until the Conservatives saw fit to dissolve Parliament'.[3] Instead, the Executive went into an elaborate discussion of the electoral disadvantages a Popular Front would have for the Labour Party. There was only one qualification to the Executive's rejection of a wider alliance, namely if there should be any evidence of an internal crisis in the Conservative Party. 'If any considerable number of Members of Parliament now supporting the Government were to rebel against the Prime Minister's authority,' then, 'a new situation might arise'. But there was no such evidence, the statement also noted, that many Conservative members did think of revolt. And that, therefore, was that. Until the Government did see fit to dissolve Parliament, the Labour leadership was content to make speeches in the House of Commons (on the occasion of a debate on Air Defence, Dalton recalls, 'I knew I made a pretty powerful speech'[4]), to go on deputations to the Prime Minister, to write indignant articles, to address meetings on behalf of Spain, China, Austria and Czechoslovakia, even to appeal for a boycott of Japanese goods. This exhausted the ritual they knew. The Government did the rest.

There were a few members of the Executive who did favour a

[1] Interim Report of the National Executive Committee, October 1937 to July 1938, p. 4.
[2] ibid, p. 4.
[3] Cole, op. cit. p. 354.
[4] Dalton, op. cit. p. 166.

Popular Front. On the 5th of May, Cripps, Laski, Ellen Wilkinson and D. N. Pritt presented the Executive with a memorandum on the subject; it was turned down by seventeen votes to four. The Executive was more narrowly divided on the question of calling a Special Conference of the Party to consider Spain and the international situation; but a majority was found against that too.

In the face of the Labour Party's determined disapproval, the campaign for a Popular Front rapidly lost momentum. In June, a resolution in favour of the United Peace Alliance, sponsored by the Co-operative Party, was defeated at the Annual Co-operative Congress—by 4,492,000 votes to 2,382,000; it was similarly turned down by the National Conference of Labour Women, and the Conference of the National Union of Railwaymen also voted against it the same month, by sixty-two votes to eighteen.[1] A few months later came Munich.

As the Czech crisis broke at the beginning of September 1938, the National Council of Labour submitted to the Trades Union Congress a statement on the International Situation[2] in which it plainly said that the world now stood on the brink of war and that a heavy responsibility for this situation rested upon the 'indecisive and misdirected policy of the British Government in these last seven years'. German demands, the Statement also said, were 'incompatible with the integrity and independence of Czechoslovakia . . . British Labour emphatically repudiates the right of the British or any other Government to use diplomatic or other pressure to compel an acceptance of such an humiliation'. The National Council did not exclude mediation, but the facts, 'grim as they are', must be faced: if mediation failed, 'a relentless and inevitable chain of events will drag the whole world into war . . . British interests are too closely involved, as declarations of the British Government have affirmed, for this country to be able to stand aside'. The time had come, the Statement went on to say, 'for a positive and unmistakable lead for collective defence against aggression and to safeguard peace. The British Government must leave no doubt in the mind of the German Government that they will unite with the French and Soviet Governments to resist any attack upon Czechoslovakia. The Labour movement urges the British Government to give this lead, confident that such a policy would have the solid support of the British people.' After all this, however, the statement ended, somewhat lamely, with a demand for the immediate summoning of Parliament: 'it is in that historic assembly of our

[1] Cole, op. cit. p. 355.
[2] T.U.C. Annual Conference Report, 1938, Appendix G, pp. 474-5.

democratic State that these principles should be reaffirmed with the utmost energy and determination. Whatever the risks involved, Great Britain must make its stand against aggression. There is now no room for doubt or hesitation.'

In the short debate which occurred at the T.U.C. on this statement, there were some few voices raised against the commitment it entailed, but the reference back was lost by an 'overwhelming majority' on a show of hands.[1]

This was on the 8th of September. On the 13th, Chamberlain, with a telegram to Hitler offering to go and visit him to find a 'peaceful solution', initiated the series of events which led to the final betrayal of Czechoslovakia at Munich on the 30th of September.

In the fortnight between the 13th and the 28th of September, when Chamberlain announced to a hastily summoned Parliament that Hitler had invited him to Munich with Daladier, the French Prime Minister, and Mussolini, all seemed to point to war; by Tuesday night, the 27th of September, Mr Mowat notes, 'almost everyone in Great Britain expected that the country would be at war next day, or at least by the week-end'.[2]

Within that fortnight, there was considerable Labour activity. There were interviews with Chamberlain and Halifax; at one of these, on the 21st of September, Attlee, on being told the details of plans for the dismemberment of Czechoslovakia, reported telling Chamberlain: 'You have abandoned these people completely. You have made an absolute surrender. All Eastern Europe will now fall under Hitler's sway. We are full of the most profound disgust. This is one of the biggest disasters in British history.'[3] On the same evening, another deputation from the National Council of Labour told Lord Halifax, the Foreign Secretary, of the 'sense of shame, humiliation and disgust at what was taking place and at the British Government's part in it'.[4] There were also further statements against the betrayal of Czechoslovakia,[5] and demands for the summoning of Parliament. And, at the week-end of the 23rd of September, 'all sections of the Movement were urged to use all opportunities for demonstrations and meetings in support of Czechoslovakian integrity'.[6]

It was, however, much too late to influence the Government, or, in

[1] T.U.C. Annual Conference Report, 1938, p. 386.
[2] Mowat, op. cit. p. 615.
[3] Dalton, op. cit. p. 188.
[4] ibid, p. 188. At one point of the interview, one member of the deputation, George Dallas, told Halifax: 'Lord Halifax, listening to you, we are ashamed to be Britishers' (ibid, p. 189).
[5] Labour Party Annual Conference Report, 1939, pp. 15, 17.
[6] ibid, p. 16.

the midst of a crisis which threatened war, to compel it by the force of a public opinion now powerfully encouraged, from a multitude of sources, to look upon Chamberlain as the saviour of peace.[1] The time to launch a campaign against Chamberlain's appeasement of Hitler over Czechoslovakia was in May, when the Labour Party refused to do so, even though it knew then that Czechoslovakia was in danger, both from the Nazis and from Chamberlain's well settled policy of peace at any price.

After Munich, the National Council of Labour placed on record, as the Executive Committee's Report to the 1939 Conference put it, 'the mingled feelings of the British Labour Movement upon the preservation of world peace, through the betrayal of the Czechoslovakian Government and the Czech people'.[2] The statement it issued noted that through the 'painful sacrifices made by the Czechoslovak nation' an immediate outbreak of war had been averted: 'British Labour shares in the fullest measure the relief which the whole world felt when the imminent risk of war passed'; but, the National Council also said, 'it is now the inescapable duty of the Governments which sanction the cession of territory, and allow it to be occupied by Germany's armed forces, to protect the Czechoslovak people against acts of tyranny, spoliation and injustice'; effective help must be given for the economic rehabilitation of Czechoslovakia, full provision made to compensate those compelled to leave the occupied territories in fear of reprisals; hostages in German prisons must be released, and refugees helped.[3]

In actual fact, appeasement over Czechoslovakia did not cease with the Munich 'settlement': the Czechs were given no support by the British or French Governments in the working out of the agreement, and suffered accordingly at the hands of the Germans and the Italians.[4]

Whatever their feelings of relief after Munich, the Labour leaders had no illusion as to the continuing threat of further Fascist aggression, nor had they any doubt that Chamberlain, while proceeding with a lethargic and inadequate rearmament programme, would also continue to appease the dictators. The replacement of his Government by a Labour Government, the Labour Party said in yet another Manifesto (*Labour's Claim to Government*), published soon after

[1] Note, in this connection, Attlee's welcome for Chamberlain's announcement in the House of Commons on the 28th of September that he was going to Munich (H. of C., vol. 339, col. 26) and contrast with W. Gallacher's protest 'against the dismemberment of Czechoslovakia' (ibid, col. 28).
[2] Labour Party Annual Conference Report, 1939, p. 19.
[3] ibid, p. 19.
[4] See J. Wheeler-Bennett, *Munich* (London, 1948) pp. 192-4 and 314-18.

261

Munich, was an urgent necessity if Britain's resources were to be mobilized against aggression.

It was still a Tory rebellion which seemed to some few Labour leaders the only hope of getting rid of Chamberlain. On the 3rd of October, Dalton had had a meeting with a number of anti-Chamberlain Tories, among them Churchill, Eden and Macmillan, to discuss parliamentary tactics in the debate on Munich that had begun on that day.[1] On the 6th, Cripps, who had since July been on holiday in Jamaica and who had only returned to England on the 2nd of October,[2] urged upon Dalton, as the latter recalls, the need to 'make common cause with the anti-Chamberlain Tories' and thought that agreement could be reached on a programme 'to preserve our democratic liberties, to rebuild collective security, and for national control of our economic life'; 'he would put Socialism aside for the present . . . the Labour Party alone could never win. He regarded the old Popular Front idea as dead, but this move had much bigger possibilities'. On this last point, Dalton agreed with Cripps: 'to split the Tory Party,' he thought, 'would be real big politics.'[3]

Both Attlee, 'rather eagerly', and Morrison, more hesitantly, agreed to Dalton's suggestion that talks with the rebel Tories might, in Attlee's words, 'be very useful'. Further talks were held between Dalton and some of the rebels. The latter, however, differed as to how far they would carry their dissidence. (Macmillan, again according to Dalton, wanted 'to see a "1931 in reverse"—an influential breakaway from the Conservative Party and a union of Labour and Liberals with Tory dissentients to form a new "National Government" '.[4] Churchill was equally resolute. Eden, on the other hand, was caution itself—and commanded then a much larger following than Churchill.) The talks came to nothing.

There were those, however, who were not content to wait for a problematic Tory rebellion and who, after Munich, found the idea of a Popular Front more compelling than ever and again campaigned for it. At a by-election at Oxford in October, the Oxford City Labour Party, against the advice of the National Executive, set aside its prospective candidate, Patrick Gordon-Walker, in favour of A. D. Lindsay, the Master of Balliol, who, though a member of the Labour Party, ran as an Independent Progressive on a Popular

[1] Dalton, op. cit. p. 199.
[2] Bevin too was away in Australia throughout the Czech crisis, attending an unofficial Commonwealth Conference under the sponsorship of the Royal Institute of International Affairs. (Bullock, op. cit. pp. 617, 629.)
[3] Dalton, op. cit. p. 200. Cripps also said that he wished to see Attlee shifted from the leadership and replaced by Morrison; Dalton did not believe this could be done. (ibid, p. 201.)
[4] ibid, pp. 201-2.

Front programme, against the Conservative Quentin Hogg. Lindsay, who received a letter of good wishes from thirty-nine Labour M.P.s, was defeated, but reduced the Conservative majority from 6,645 to 3,434.[1] At Bridgwater in November, the local Labour Party similarly gave its support to Vernon Bartlett, of the *News Chronicle,* who also stood as an Independent Progressive and actually won the seat from the Government in a straight fight.

These results, though they gave some encouragement to the supporters of the Popular Front, entirely failed to move the Executive Committee of the Labour Party, which firmly stuck to its previously expressed views on the subject. Only 'a big Tory breakaway', Dalton recalls, would have invalidated the arguments put forward against the Popular Front in May, 'and it would not be useful to say this publicly now'.[2] But, he also notes, 'by the New Year the Tories had settled down again'.[3]

Then came the Cripps Memorandum. In that Memorandum, considered by the Executive on the 13th of January, 1939, Cripps now argued for something like a Popular Front, but mainly in terms of winning by-elections and the next General Election.[4] The 'National' Government, he suggested, could not, within the next eighteen months in which an election was bound to be held, be defeated by the Labour Party alone. On the other hand, a combination of all Opposition parties could, he had calculated, return some 331 Members of Parliament, which would provide an alternative Government with a working majority. Cripps wanted a special Conference of the Labour Party to be called forthwith, a manifesto to be issued inviting the co-operation of every genuine anti-Government party on a suggested outline of policy; and the Labour Party should also publicly state that it was willing to enter into arrangements in constituencies with co-operating groups.[5]

The programme outlined by the Memorandum was based on two principal objectives: the first was 'the effective protection of the democratic rights, liberties and freedom of the British people from internal and external attack'; the second was a 'positive policy of peace, by collective action with France, Russia, the United States of America and other democratic countries for the strengthening of

[1] Cole, op. cit. p. 355.
[2] Dalton, op. cit. p. 207.
[3] ibid, p. 210.
[4] 'Cripps,' Cole notes, 'laid himself open to attack by arguing with the Labour Party Executive on the ground which it had chosen, as if the Popular Front were mainly a device for winning the next General Election, when it came, rather than for mobilizing public opinion at once against the Government's foreign policy.' (Cole, op. cit. p. 358.)
[5] Cooke, op. cit. p. 231.

democracy against aggression, and a world economic reconstruction based upon justice to the people of all classes and nations'. And, in addition, Cripps also mentioned planning and control, better education, and vigorous help to the areas of unemployment. There was no mention of nationalization or Socialism.[1]

The Executive turned down the Memorandum by seventeen votes to three.[2] Cripps then immediately sent off his document to all Labour M.P.s and parliamentary candidates, and the secretaries of all affiliated organizations, with a printed and stamped postcard addressed to himself, indicating approval of his proposals, and which the recipients were asked to return. Summoned by the Executive to 'reaffirm his allegiance to the Labour Party within the meaning of the Constitution, Programme, Principles and Policy of the Party' and to withdraw his Memorandum 'by circular to the persons and organizations' to whom it had been addressed, Cripps refused, whereupon the Executive expelled him from the Party, by seventeen votes to one.[3]

Undeterred, Cripps then began a country-wide 'National Petition' Campaign for presentation to the next Labour Party Conference, and calling for a union of anti-Government parties 'to act together and at once for the sake of peace and civilization'.[4]

The campaign attracted a fair measure of support, both inside the Labour movement and outside,[5] and the Executive felt compelled to move again. In two statements, *Unity: True or Sham,* and *Socialism and Surrender,* it again argued that nothing must be done to jeopardize the Labour Party's chances of winning the next election as an independent political entity and condemned Cripps for his political defeatism; in addition, it now emphasized its attachment to the socialist content of its policies and made great play of the fact that Cripps, who had earlier insisted on an advanced socialist programme, was now willing to advocate a non-socialist one.[6] At the end of March, it also expelled from the Party Aneurin Bevan, G. R. Strauss, Sir Charles Trevelyan, and a number of other members who had refused to withdraw their support for Cripps's

[1] Cooke, op. cit. p. 232.
[2] The three were Cripps himself, Ellen Wilkinson and D. N. Pritt.
[3] Dalton, op. cit. pp. 211-12. The one dissentient was Ellen Wilkinson. Pritt was absent, ill with rheumatism in the feet, but wrote to say that he would have voted against expulsion. He also thought, he added, that some people had rheumatism higher up. (ibid, p. 212.)
[4] Cooke, op. cit. p. 236.
[5] ibid, pp. 236-7.
[6] It will be recalled, however, that Attlee, Dalton and Morrison, all of whom wrote and spoke against Cripps and his campaign, had been willing to consider a non-socialist combination with dissident Tories after Munich. (See above, p. 261.)

campaign. Others, like Will Lawther, the President of the Miners' Federation, did withdraw.[1]

By the time the Labour Party Conference met at Southport on the 29th of May, war had come perceptibly nearer. On the 15th of March, German troops had marched into Prague; six days later, Poland was summoned to cede to Germany the Free City of Danzig and to accept a revision of the Polish Corridor; one day later, the port of Memel was ceded by Lithuania to Germany, under the threat of immediate occupation; and Rumania too was under pressure to grant trade concessions in oil and grain to Germany. On Good Friday, the 7th of April, Italian troops invaded Albania, which was annexed to Italy.

The German occupation of the whole of Czechoslovakia at last placed the appeasers on the defensive, and Chamberlain, who had at first appeared unwilling to make much of that episode, was compelled to announce that if Hitler's intention was to dominate the world by force, he must realize that Britain would 'take part to the uttermost of its power in resisting such a challenge'.[2] On the 30th of March, he announced that the Government, in the event of any action which threatened Poland's independence, would lend her all support in its power; similar guarantees were given to Rumania and Greece in April, and there was an Anglo-Turkish declaration in May to the effect that the two countries would take joint action against any aggression in the Mediterranean.

The new diplomacy, as was pointed out by many critics, by no means all on the Left, made little sense, particularly in regard to Poland, without a corresponding will to close alliance and co-operation with Russia. The will was altogether lacking. Nor did the critics of Chamberlain feel, on this and on many other scores, that the Government's handling of affairs was now much more reassuring than it had been in the past. Indeed, if war was to come, and this now seemed a virtual certainty in the near future, the need for new, less tarnished, more vigorous and competent leadership, seemed more essential than ever.

This was very strongly felt throughout the Labour movement, and found a profoundly mistaken expression in the fierce opposition aroused by the Government's decision, announced at the end of April, to introduce military conscription. The measure, Labour

[1] Cooke, op. cit. p. 237.
[2] Wheeler-Bennett, op. cit. pp. 356-8. Cripps recorded a talk with Churchill on the 22nd of June, in which the latter said that 'but for Chamberlain's switch on foreign policy after Prague's occupation the Popular Front movement would have swept the country' and, Cripps added, 'I gathered he would have supported it' (Cooke, op. cit. p. 242).

argued, was unnecessary, since the Government's purpose, which involved no more than the calling up of all men aged 20 and 21 for six months' training, could be equally served by voluntary recruitment, which Labour was willing to encourage. Furthermore, it was generally feared that military conscription would be the forerunner of industrial conscription, to which Labour was even more strongly opposed.[1] But military conscription would not have aroused the same feelings had there not been so deep a distrust of the motives and purposes of men who, as Bevin amongst others argued, were so deeply compromised by their record, as much at home as abroad.[2]

It is in the light of this distrust, in times so grave, that the debates at the 1939 Conference on the expulsion of Cripps and his friends, and on the Popular Front, must be read.

Constitutionally, Cripps had no right to appear before the Conference. However, a motion that the Constitution and the Standing Orders be suspended so that he might speak was carried by 1,227,000 to 1,083,000.[3] Cripps deliberately confined himself to a defence of his right to circulate his Memorandum, and argued that in no other way could he have started an urgently necessary discussion as to the best means of getting rid of the Government.[4] For the Executive, Dalton concentrated on the issue of minority acceptance of majority decisions.[5] For the reference back of the sections of the Executive Report dealing with Cripps, there were 402,000 votes—against 2,100,000.[6]

On the issue of the Popular Front, the Executive had an even easier victory. Those who advocated a broad progressive coalition argued from their belief that Labour could not, alone, win a General Election,[7] and that consequently, as J. T. Murphy said, 'the immediate choice before the people in this Party is not that of Capitalism *versus* Socialism' but 'a choice between the continued existence of the pro-Fascist Chamberlain Government and the advance towards

---

[1] However, there was active support by the Trade Unions and the Labour Party for the Government's schemes for the organization of industry and communications in the event of war (Cole, op. cit. pp. 362-3; Bullock, op. cit. pp. 634-6).

[2] Bullock, op. cit. pp. 637-8.

[3] Labour Party Annual Conference Report, 1939, p. 220.

[4] ibid, pp. 226-9.

[5] ibid, pp. 229-32.

[6] ibid, p. 236.

[7] J. T. Murphy, who put the case for the Popular Front, pointed out that, in order to win, the Party would not only have had to retain all the 154 seats it had won in 1935, but to win another 164 seats, which meant capturing every seat in which the Tory Party had had up to a 6,000 majority. (Labour Party Annual Conference Report, 1939, p. 293.)

Socialism through the preservation of Democracy, of peace and of our liberty'.[1] The first point could plausibly (at least to many loyal Labour Party delegates) be dubbed 'defeatist', and the second, with its apparent overtones of 'class collaboration', made many purists uneasy. If the issue was an electoral one, most delegates found much more attractive Herbert Morrison's picture of what he called a 'Popular Front electorate behind a Labour Party that knows its mind, behind a Labour Party that commands the confidence of the country for its capacity for government, and its belief in our capacity for decision in government'.[2] Against the Popular Front, and for such a Government, they voted by 2,360,000 to 248,000.[3]

But it was all the same under Chamberlain that Labour waited helplessly to be led into war. Even Cripps had now formally abandoned his 'Popular Front' campaign[4] and gave up the struggle altogether after conversations with Churchill and a number of other Conservatives on the possibility of bringing about an 'All-In Government' came to nothing.[5] As to the Executive Committee of the Labour Party, the most notable event to record in regard to it between May and the end of August 1939 (it is of course fair to recall that these were summer months) was its decisive suppression of an indecisive intrigue to get rid of Attlee as leader of the Party.[6]

However, at the end of August 1939, with a German invasion of Poland imminent, Labour did add its voice to those that were urging the Government to stand firm against any further compromise. Indeed, after the Prime Minister's inconclusive speech in the House of Commons on the 2nd of September, the day after Poland had been attacked, it was to Arthur Greenwood, the acting Leader of the Opposition, that the Conservative opponents of Chamberlain turned, in L. S. Amery's memorable call, to 'Speak for England', a call matched on Greenwood's own side with calls to 'Speak for Britain' and 'Speak for the Workers'. Much that had then come to pass might have been avoided if Labour, in the previous years, when there was still time, had not only spoken but acted as an Opposition conscious of the responsibility which, given the policies and personnel of the Government, devolved upon it.

[1] Labour Party Annual Conference Report, p. 293.
[2] ibid, p. 299.
[3] ibid, p. 299.
[4] Cripps and his fellow expellees reapplied in June for membership of the Labour Party. The Executive was in no hurry. It was only at the end of September 1939 that it replied to Cripps by asking him to sign a declaration expressing regret for his actions and undertaking to refrain from any campaign in opposition to Party policy. Cripps refused. (Cooke, op. cit. p. 240.)
[5] ibid, p. 241.
[6] Dalton, op. cit. pp. 222-5.

4. WAR

Between September 1939 and May 1940, the Labour Party, like the rest of Britain, settled into a state of suspended animation, certain in the belief that war must be waged, uncertain as to its conduct.

The Labour leaders had no more confidence in Chamberlain as a war leader than they had had in him as the saviour of peace.[1] They declined (as did the Liberal leaders) the Prime Minister's invitation to join his Government, which now included Churchill as First Lord of the Admiralty and Eden as Dominions Secretary. However, a semi-formal liaison system was arranged between members of Labour's Parliamentary Executive and leading Ministers. Pledged to full support of the war effort, Labour reserved 'the right to criticize, both publicly and privately, in the national interest'. 'We should,' Dalton said at the time, 'be patriotic gadflies to Ministers.'[2] This, with minor qualifications, entailed agreement to the Government's measures of military and industrial mobilization, and trade union co-operation, willingly given. It also entailed an Electoral Truce for the duration of the war, under which the Conservative, Labour and Liberal parties agreed not to contest each other's parliamentary vacancies.

A remarkable feature of the Labour leaders' attitude, once war had been declared, was their unwillingness to apply all possible pressure for a radical reorganization of the Government. 'On our Parliamentary Executive as early as September 19th,' Dalton notes, 'there was a rising growl, led by Morrison, against Chamberlain and his cronies, and on the need to kick them out if the war was to be more than, as Shinwell put it, "a silly escapade".' The Government, Dalton argued, 'could be changed only if there was a serious defection among their supporters who, after all, had a large majority in the House. We must, I said, break down the morale of the Ministerial mass.'[3] Yet, though there was some criticism, both public and private, and ever growing doubts of the Government's competence and even of its determination, Labour's pressure upon the Government never amounted to much until the great crisis of April-May 1940. A party more boldly led, and less inhibited in its political strategy, might well have exacted, as the price of its indispensible co-operation and support, major changes in the political direction of the war.

The second other notable contribution which Labour made to

---

[1] '. . . In the ranks of Labour there was no confidence in Chamberlain and his immediate associates.' (Attlee, op. cit. p. 105.) See also Bullock, op. cit. pp. 644-5 for Bevin's attitude.

[2] Dalton, op. cit. p. 272.

[3] ibid, p. 282.

the history of the 'phoney war' was its ardent support for British and French assistance to Finland, with whom Russia went to war on the 30th of November, after the Finns' refusal to cede territory the Russians claimed for the strengthening of their defences.

The Nazi-Soviet Pact of the 23rd of August, 1939, had already been a profound shock to the Labour movement, to many on the Left a traumatic shock with agonized and intransigent reappraisals of Russian policies and intentions. Russia's entry into Poland from the East, after the Germans had attacked it from the West, and Russian occupation of Polish territory, further helped to strengthen anti-Russian sentiments. Nor certainly was the Russian case helped by the support of the Communist Party, then more generally suspect than ever on account of its switch from support of the war to opposition.[1] On the 7th of December, the National Council of Labour vehemently condemned the Russian action, as a result of which, it said, 'Soviet Imperialism has thus revealed itself as using the same methods as the Nazi power against which the British Working-Class is united in the War now raging'.[2] Even more notable was Labour's call upon 'the free nations of the world to give every practical aid to the Finnish nation in its struggle to preserve its own institutions of Civilization and Democracy'.[3]

The Statement's reference to the 'war now raging' was little more than a hyperbole. Far from raging, the war, after the conquest of Poland, had practically come to a standstill, with both the British and particularly the French Government involved in a new

---

[1] The Communist Party, it will be recalled, had expressed wholehearted support for the War at its outbreak. On the 29th of September, a joint Soviet-German declaration urged the Western Powers to make peace. On the 4th of October, after, in Palme Dutt's words, 'the sharpest and most intense debate in the history of the Party' (Pelling, op. cit. p. 111), a resolution adopted by the Central Committee of the Communist Party now declared that 'the struggle of the British people against the Chamberlains and Churchills is the best help to the struggle of the German people against Hitler'. (ibid, p. 112.) On the 12th of October, the *Daily Worker* described the war as 'unjust and imperialist'. Neither the political changes of May 1940, nor Britain's mortal peril in that summer, lessened the Party's active opposition to the war. On the contrary, it mounted a major campaign in support of the 'People's Convention', which met in London on the 12th of January, 1941, and was attended by some 2,000 'delegates', who claimed to represent more than a million workers. Among the six points of the Convention's programme was a demand for 'a people's government truly representative of the whole people and able to inspire the confidence of the working people of the world', and for 'a people's peace that gets rid of the causes of the war'. (ibid, p. 113.) On the 21st of January, Herbert Morrison, as Home Secretary, banned the *Daily Worker*.

[2] Labour Party Annual Conference Report, 1940, p. 13.

[3] ibid, p. 13.

kind of appeasement of Germany. On the other hand, aircraft were sent to Finland and both Governments agreed, in early February, to prepare for an expedition to Finland and to send supplies and reinforcements. On the 2nd of March, the French Government decided to send 50,000 volunteers and a hundred bombers. The British Government, more cautious, agreed to send fifty bombers. On the 12th, however, the Finns signed an armistice. Thus this project, fraught with so many disastrous implications, came to naught.

Labour's leaders were, from the start, deeply committed to help for Finland. In France, Léon Blum 'was for helping the Finns to the utmost and at all costs, even though this led to war with Russia'.[1] British Labour did not go quite so far. Philip Noel-Baker, who had led an official Labour delegation to Finland,[2] 'told Labour M.P.s that, if only we would send the Finns a few more aircraft, they would win the war'.[3] The delegation's Report, issued after the Russo-Finnish armistice, glowed with praise for Finland's 'free and democratic State in which personal liberty and civil rights are the foundation of national life'; it also insisted that Finland had been entitled 'under the Covenant of the League' to British assistance and that 'they could have continued the struggle much longer had they received more adequate supplies of modern armaments and greater numbers of volunteers'.[4]

The Report 'indignantly' repudiated the suggestion that 'to ask for help for Finland was to work for war with Russia'; and its authors expressed the view that 'war between this country and Russia would be a grave misfortune'.[5] Yet, had the struggle continued much longer, and had it been possible for the British and French Governments to send an expedition to Finland, it is difficult to see how the Labour leaders, on the strength of their own pronouncements, could have opposed it. Unlike some of the loudest advocates in Britain and France of intervention on behalf of Finland, the Labour leaders were certainly not 'working for war with Russia'. But neither was it their fault that those who did not think of such a war as a 'grave misfortune' made no greater headway.

In the end, it was Hitler who proved the main agent of Chamberlain's fall. At last, with the disastrous fiasco of the Norwegian campaign, the Conservative ranks broke: on the 8th of May, at

[1] Dalton, op. cit. p. 292.
[2] Its other members were Sir Walter Citrine, representing the T.U.C., and John Downie, for the Co-operative movement.
[3] Dalton, op. cit. p. 293.
[4] Labour Party Annual Conference Report, 1940, p. 14.
[5] ibid, p. 14.

the end of that most dramatic of debates in the House of Commons on the conduct of the war, thirty-three Government supporters voted with Labour[1] and about double that number abstained. The Government still had a majority, but it had shrunk from some 240 to 81. Though Chamberlain sought to hang on, at the price of reconstructing his Government, he found this impossible; the main factor which made it impossible was Labour's refusal to serve in a coalition under him; and the Tory rebels would not join or support a Government which did not include members of the Labour and Liberal parties. But the question of the succession remained open. Some Labour parliamentarians even thought (as did the King[2]) 'that there was much to be said for Halifax'.[3] Dalton, who was one of them, felt that, though 'many would now think of Churchill as Prime Minister . . . in my view he would be best occupied in concentrating, as Minister of Defence and with very great authority, on directing and winning the war'.[4]

The issue was settled on the 10th of May, the day on which the German armies struck at France and the Low Countries, and it was settled without Labour intervention. At a meeting between Chamberlain, Churchill and Halifax that morning, Halifax intimated that he could not lead the Government from the House of Lords; on the same evening, Churchill assumed the Premiership. The War Cabinet of five included Attlee, as Lord Privy Seal and Deputy Leader of the House of Commons, and Arthur Greenwood. There were four other Labour Ministers in the Government: Bevin at the Ministry of Labour and National Service, Morrison as Minister of Supply (later Home Secretary), Dalton who was Minister of Economic Warfare, and A. V. Alexander at the Admiralty; and there was also a due proportion of lesser Labour appointments. So ended one of the most disgraceful periods in British history.

The Conservatives' derelictions in that period have been sufficiently documented for the verdict passed on the guilty men not to be reversed by history. But the Labour leaders of those years have been fortunate that Conservative guilt was as great as it was. For it has helped to obscure their own share of the guilt and their own contribution to the politics of appeasement through the immunity from effective challenge they provided to the actual culprits.

[1] There was some doubt in the Parliamentary Executive and in the Parliamentary Party whether Labour should in fact press a vote in the House of Commons, for fear of consolidating the Government majority (Dalton, op. cit. p. 305).
[2] Wheeler-Bennett. *King George VI, His Life and Reign,* op. cit. p. 443.
[3] Dalton, op. cit. p. 307.
[4] ibid, p. 307.

CHAPTER IX

THE CLIMAX OF LABOURISM

'During the Coalition the Labour
members had learnt a great deal from
the Conservatives in how to govern.'
Herbert Morrison to King George VI,
November 1945.

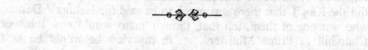

1. THE IMPACT OF WAR

July 1945, when the first majority Labour Government came to
office, is generally regarded as marking the beginning of a new era
in British history. In fact, the new era did not begin in 1945, but
in 1940, and in the years of war. These years are not the prologue
to the history of the Labour Government. They are an essential
part of it. Without them, neither July 1945 nor what followed from
it can be properly understood. For it was the experience of war which
caused the emergence in Britain of a new popular radicalism, more
widespread than at any time in the previous hundred years. It was
of that popular radicalism that the Labour Party was, in 1945 the
electoral beneficiary. And it was also the war which was responsible
for the setting in place of an elaborate system of State intervention
and control, which was of immeasurable help to the Labour Government in its first years of office after 1945.

In the first phase of the War, the new popular radicalism was
submerged in the will to national survival, and in an intense national
pride in Britain's lone struggle against the Axis Powers. But once
survival seemed assured, the men who had imperilled that survival
were remembered, as well as the class to which they belonged, and
the Party whose label they wore. True, Churchill himself belonged
to the same class and the same party, and his own prestige at the
end of the War was no doubt worth many votes to the Conservative
Party, but not enough to prevent the popular repudiation of Tory
rule. The war leader was easily distinguished from the Conservative
politician.

The rhetoric of war was itself an important element in the fashioning of popular radicalism. That the conflict was not only against
Germany, or Italy or Japan, but against Fascism, gave it powerful

ideological overtones, with an emphasis on democratic values and a celebration of the 'common man' which entailed an implicit (and often explicit) condemnation of the manner in which Tory Governments had treated him, and his family, in the inter-war years. With the entry of Russia in the war, and with the manner of her resistance to the German onslaught, these ideological overtones acquired an even sharper edge: to admiration for Russia, there was coupled an entirely new interest in the social and economic system under which the Russian war effort was organized. And it was not forgotten that pre-war Conservatism had been as eager to appease the Fascist aggressor as it had been loath to seek co-operation and alliance with Russia.

Nor was America's entry into the war a counter-balancing factor. On the contrary, America too helped to feed the growth of popular radicalism. For the American message during the war was the message of freedom rather than of free enterprise, of democracy and of opportunity, of the New Deal and of social equality: to millions of people, the embodiment of the promise which victory held was not Winston Churchill, or Clement Attlee, or Joseph Stalin, but Franklin Roosevelt.

As important was the fact that the war constituted an enormous exercise not only in military but also in social and economic planning; and that it was a very successful exercise. Because of the demands of war, Britain's rulers were forced to give a convincing demonstration that economic planning and State intervention on a massive and, for Britain, quite unprecedented scale, not only worked. but were the indispensable conditions of victory. Because of State intervention and control, millions of people found themselves better fed in wartime than they had been in peace time; and. through the agency of the State, they found their needs the object of more solicitude than any Government had ever before thought appropriate. Well before the war had come to an end, they had been officially assured that the State. which had been deemed capable of so little in the inter-war years, would, when peace came, guarantee them employment, welfare. security and greater opportunities for education. Nor were the millions of men and women who were winning the war disposed to regard these promises with the gratitude of the humble poor. With a new consciousness of their collective strength, and with a new confidence in their own worth, they regarded a new deal as a right which dare not be denied them.

In the political articulation of the experience of war, left-wing activists played a considerable part. In barracks and mess decks, in factories and air-raid shelters, in organized and even more in unorganized discussions and debates, the anti-Fascists of Popular

Front days now found an audience receptive as never before to the message of socialist change.

Despite the Party Truce, there were already clear political signs of this groundswell in the later stages of the war. Indeed the continuation of the Party Truce itself was strongly disliked by the constituency activists, and the policy of giving Labour support to Government candidates of other parties was only endorsed at the 1942 Labour Party Annual Conference by 1,275,000 votes to 1,209,000.[1] From early 1943 onwards, a new Party of the Left, Commonwealth, founded by a convert from the Liberal Party, Sir Richard Acland, had begun to contest by-elections in Conservative seats, and actually won two of them. As was later noted, 'the long series of Government rebuffs in the latter part of the war was a portent to which observers were curiously blind. Commonwealth candidates, Radical Independents, Scottish Nationalists, Independent Labour Party men, all sorts of political enthusiasts, had only to present themselves and they would either poll extremely well, or even win the seat'.[2]

The Communist Party was prevented from sharing in these successes by its own ardent support for the Coalition after Russia's entry into the war. But neither this, nor its appeals for higher productivity and no strikes, prevented it from active political propaganda, or from campaigning for members—with conspicuous success. From around 12,000 in June 1941, membership leapt up to nearly 23,000 at the end of that year, and to nearly 60,000 by the end of 1942. This was a peak. But the Party's membership at the end of the war still stood at some 45,000,[3] while its influence in the trade union movement was now greater than at any time since the Party was founded.

All this is not to suggest that the popular radicalism of war-time Britain was, for the most part, a formed socialist ideology, let alone a revolutionary one. But, in its mixture of bitter memories and positive hopes, in its antagonism to a mean past, in its recoil from Conservative rule, in its impatience of a traditional class structure, in its hostility to the claims of property and privilege, in its determination not to be robbed again of the fruits of victory, in its expectations of social justice, it was a radicalism eager for major, even fundamental, changes in British society after the war.

The Labour leaders also thought and spoke of the new social order that must follow the ordeals of war. But the impact of war upon

---

[1] Labour Party Annual Conference Report, 1942, p. 150.
[2] R. B. McCallum and A. Redman, *The British General Election of 1945* (London, 1947) p. 268.
[3] Pelling, op. cit. pp. 120, 192.

them was very different from the impact it had on their supporters.

Most of the major figures of the post-war Labour Government (Aneurin Bevan was the only important exception) held high office in the Churchill Coalition. For five years, they were deeply immersed in the business of government, and they acquired in those years an even more 'responsible' view of affairs than they had had in opposition. And they also forged in those years close and personal links with Conservative colleagues, with high civil servants and high-ranking officers, collaboration with whom was also much more conducive to caution than to radicalism. 'I have,' Attlee later recalled, 'very pleasant memories of working with my colleagues in the Government. It was very seldom that any Party issue arose to divide us, until the last stage, when I think they were designedly fomented by certain persons. Usually applying our minds to the actual problems which faced us, we came to an agreement as to what was the best course.' And, he adds, in a significant phrase, 'quite naturally, in war, when the public good must take precedence over private interests, the solutions had a strong socialist flavour'.[1]

Differences of course remained, but there was also much common ground between Labour Ministers and their Conservative colleagues on the shape of the post-war settlement, the more so since the latter agreed, at least in principle, that post-war reconstruction would have to be geared to a 'high level of employment', and to extended provision for welfare and social security. Even on the issue of controls over the economy, most Conservative leaders agreed, before the end of the war, that many controls would have to be retained for some time after it. The difference was that Conservatives naturally laid the main emphasis upon a speedy restoration of a system of 'private enterprise', in which State intervention, though not wholly discarded, would play a marginal and mainly indirect rôle, while the Labour leaders wanted much more than this. The war had greatly reinforced their already strong interventionist bias and, haunted by the memory of what had happened at the end of the First World War, they were determined to see maintained in peace time the web of controls over the economy which they deemed essential to post-war reconstruction and full employment.

On the other hand, the now prevalent notion that they thought, at the end of the war, of a fundamental transformation of the social

[1] Attlee, op. cit. p. 140. One of the most significant transformations brought about by the war was that of Cripps. 'He had worked,' Sir Stafford's biographer notes, 'with men of other political beliefs than his own, he counted them among his personal friends . . . he appreciated the high principles and personal qualities of his Conservative friends'; however, Mr. Cooke also notes, 'their politics were not his, and their ideas of post-war government were *not enough* for him'. (Cooke, op. cit. p. 326. My italics.)

order on the basis of common ownership is quite inaccurate, as is shown in the debates on a future Labour Government's programme in 1944.

By the time the Annual Conference of the Labour Party met in December 1944, the war with Germany was evidently drawing to a close, and a General Election, if not imminent, was at least in sight. In the previous two years, the Executive's Reconstruction Committee had issued a number of Reports, and those dealing with coal, transport, gas and electricity had recommended nationalization. However, the main economic resolution which the Executive presented to the Conference (under the rubric *Economic Controls, Public Ownership and Full Employment*) made no mention whatever of public ownership. It said that 'Full Employment and a high standard of living for those who work by hand and brain can only be secured within a planned economy, through the maintenance and adaptation of appropriate economic controls after the war, *and above all by the transfer to the State of power to direct the policy* of our main industries, services and financial institutions'.[1] In particular, the resolution said, a Labour Government, in order to sustain a high and steadily rising level of purchasing power. would find it necessary '*to control* the Bank of England, and the lending policy of the Joint Stock Banks, and to set up a National Investment Board'; secondly, it would be 'essential for the State to control the location of Industry' in order to prevent the re-emergence of local unemployment and depressed areas; and, thirdly, it would also be necessary, in order to encourage foreign trade and establish a more prosperous and secure economic system throughout the world, to enter into International Agreements with the Dominions, Russia, the United States and other friendly nations'.[2]

It was Emmanuel Shinwell who introduced this resolution on behalf of the Executive. 'The Socialist policy of the Labour Party,' he claimed, 'remains unchanged . . . we stand, as always, for the abolition of a vicious competitive system and for the establishment of the highest possible standard of living based on collective organization and the ownership of indispensable national industries and services.' But 'naturally', he added, anticipating later re-thinkers, 'we have to bring our policy up to date and adapt ourselves to an ever-changing situation; that is a scientific procedure and in the nature of the case inevitable'. And in any case, he told the delegates, the resolution did not indicate a long term policy; 'it is a short term policy designed, and rightly designed, for those years in which a Labour Government will have assumed full power in this country'.

[1] Labour Party Annual Conference Report, 1944, p. 161. My italics.
[2] ibid, p. 161. My italics.

However, he promised the delegates that 'if (sic) a monopolistic undertaking has reached that economic position when the commodity it produces or over which it has power is indispensable to the life of the community, that monopolistic undertaking must be taken over by the State in the interests of the community'.[1]

On the basis of these remarkable formulations and, more important, of the Executive's resolution, it is evident that, after five years of war and twenty-six years after the Labour Party's adoption of its common ownership clause, not to speak of its inter-war programmes and resolutions, most members of the Executive would have been content to present to the electorate a programme altogether free from any commitment to the nationalization of anything at all, save for the half-nationalization of the Bank of England.[2] Not, as Shinwell had explained, that they were *opposed* to some few measures of nationalization; they merely did not think nationalization essential to the immediate purpose at hand, namely a post-war 'reconstruction' which did not entail major structural transformations in the economy. Nor in any case were they in the least convinced that the electorate was now ready for such a transformation.

The activists, both in the constituencies and in the trade unions, had very different ideas. Resolution after resolution on the agenda of the Conference demanded an extensive programme of common ownership. One of these came from the Transport and General Workers' Union and it asked that 'all vital services, Land, Banking, Coal and Power, Steel, Chemicals, and Transport (including Road, Rail, Shipping and Civil Aviation) shall be brought under a system of Public Ownership and Control'.[3]

A composite resolution, moved by Ian Mikardo, asked the Executive to include in its programme 'the transfer to public ownership of the land, large-scale building, heavy industry, and all forms of banking, transport and fuel and power'; and to say that 'appropriate legislation' would be passed to ensure that publicly owned enterprises would be 'democratically controlled and operated in the

[1] Labour Party Annual Conference Report, 1944, pp. 161-3.
[2] The Bank of England, the Executive's Report on *Full Employment and Financial Policy* (1944) noted, was already 'no more than a section of the Treasury, subject to the direction of the Chancellor of the Exchequer and the Cabinet'. This, the Report said, would have to be made permanent; the responsibility of appointing the Governor of the Bank should be made to rest with the Chancellor of the Exchequer, whose approval should also be required for the appointment of members of the Court of the Bank; as to the joint-stock banks, the Report said, they must be 'required' to behave as a Public Service and to act in the interests of the community. (*Full Employment and Financial Policy*, p. 3.)
[3] Supplementary Report and Special Final Agenda, Labour Party Annual Conference, 1944, p. 36.

277

national interest, with representation of the workers engaged therein and of consumers'.[1]

For the Executive, Philip Noel-Baker asked that the resolution should not be pressed to a vote. 'Of course,' he said, 'we are in general agreement with it' but, he added, in a phrase which expressed well the leadership's hesitations, 'we think that the resolution should be neither accepted nor rejected today.' What they would undertake to do was to examine the various points of the resolution 'with great care'.[2] But the resolution was pressed, and carried without a card vote,[3] and some, but only some, of its provisions were embodied in *Let Us Face the Future,* the Programme on which the Labour Party went to the country in July 1945.

Let Us Face the Future was published in April 1945, by which time it was certain that the days of the war-time coalition were numbered. Though Labour's spectacular electoral victory some months later, and developments since, have invested it with a quasi-revolutionary aura, it was, in its concrete proposals, a mild and circumspect document, which marked no advance on *Labour's Immediate Programme* of 1937. The Labour Party, it said once again, 'is a Socialist Party, and proud of it. Its ultimate purpose at home is the establishment of the Socialist Commonwealth of Great Britain—free, democratic, efficient, progressive, public-spirited, its material resources organized in the service of the British people'. But, it also warned, 'Socialism cannot come overnight, as the product of a week-end revolution. The members of the Labour Party, like the British people, are practical-minded men and women'.

In regard to industry, a careful distinction was made between 'basic industries ripe and over-ripe for public ownership and management in the direct service of the nation',[4] and 'big industries not yet ripe for public ownership'; these, however, would be required 'by constructive supervision' to further the nation's needs. And there were, thirdly, 'many smaller businesses rendering good service which can be left to go on with their useful work'.

What this meant of course was that the largest part by far of

[1] Labour Party Annual Conference Report, 1944, p. 163.
[2] ibid, p. 167.
[3] ibid, p. 168.
[4] I.e., coal, gas, electricity, inland transport, and iron and steel, as well as the Bank of England, but not the banks. The document also said that Labour believed in land nationalization and would work towards it, but it was only proposed to give to the State and to local authorities wider and speedier powers to acquire land for public purposes wherever the public interest so required.

British industry and finance[1] would in fact remain in private hands, indefinitely, though subject, or so at least the intention was, to State direction and control. Furthermore, so 'ripe and over-ripe' for public ownership were the industries and services it was proposed to nationalize that this had in fact already been recommended, as Professor Brady has noted, 'by Conservative dominated fact-finding and special investigating committees'.[2] Save for iron and steel, of which more later, they had long ceased to occupy a strategic place in the system of capitalist power, and this, as later debates showed, was quite clear to Conservatives, more so than it was to most Labour supporters. This did not make their nationalization less necessary or desirable; it only made it a rather less revolutionary enterprise than was later claimed. The document itself made no such claim. It noted that, as a result of nationalization, other industries would benefit, that 'fair compensation' would be paid, and its emphasis was overwhelmingly on efficiency rather than power. Indeed, it is remarkable, in retrospect, how defensive some of the most prominent Labour leaders were even about these minimal proposals. Thus, Herbert Morrison, introducing the debate on *Let Us Face the Future* at the 1945 Conference,[3] insisted that the case for nationalization must be argued out 'industry by industry on the merits of each case . . . in our electoral arguments it is no good saying that we are going to socialize electricity, fuel and power because it is in accordance with Labour Party principles so to do . . . you must spend substantial time in arguing the case for the socialization of these industries on the merits of their specific cases. That is how the British mind works. It does not work in a vacuum or in abstract theories.'[4]

The implication was that the case for nationalization must not be argued as part of a *general* socialist case against capitalist enterprise but in terms of a specific remedy for particular situations and applicable in purely functional and technical terms to particular industries and services. It is, however, doubtful whether Morrison's advice was much heeded by Labour candidates and speakers in the election of 1945.

Directly related to Morrison's view of nationalization was the Executive's refusal to commit itself to any kind of experiment in industrial democracy. At the 1944 Conference, Philip Noel-Baker had

[1] The operations of the Banks, *Let Us Face the Future* said, would be 'harmonized with industrial needs.'
[2] R. A. Brady, *Crisis in Britain, Plans and Achievements of the Labour Government* (London, 1950) p. 41.
[3] The Conference met from the 21st to the 25th of May. The Coalition came to an end on the 23rd.
[4] Labour Party Annual Conference Report, 1945, p. 90.

279

assured the delegates that 'we are all for the participation of workers in control' and that discussions were proceeding with the Trade Unions as to the methods for workers' participation in control and management'.[1] *Let Us Face the Future* merely said that the workers should have 'proper status and conditions' in the nationalized industries. At the 1945 Conference, one composite resolution (later withdrawn) demanded a far more extensive programme of nationalization and also asked the Party to pledge itself 'to secure the democratic control and operation of these (nationalized) institutions by the workers and technicians'.[2] This latter demand, Morrison said, did not 'demonstrate good socialization in its method of administration and management'.[3] For his part, Shinwell, replying to the debate, agreed that 'of course workers have a right to participate in industry', and so had technicians; 'but as to the form of participation, that is a matter that has to be worked out'.[4] Much the same had repeatedly been said since 1918.

The nationalization proposals of *Let Us Face the Future* represented the least the Executive could present to the 1945 Conference without causing acute dissension in the Party. The Left was given a great deal less than it wanted (and less indeed than had been agreed by the 1944 Conference). But the Left, though more powerful at the end of the War than for many a year, was not an organized and coherent pressure group. Nor, given what they had been able to obtain, were left wing delegates disposed, on the eve of an election, to challenge the leadership. The latter's proposals, on nationalization, on economic policy, and on social reform[5] were all unanimously endorsed. Outwardly, *Let Us Face the Future* united the Party as no document had ever done. In reality, the divisions within the Party were as profound as they had ever been,[6] in some ways more;

---

[1] Labour Party Annual Conference Report, 1944, p. 167.

[2] Labour Party Annual Conference Report, 1945, p. 134.

[3] ibid, p. 90.

[4] ibid, p. 137.

[5] *Let Us Face the Future* promised that Labour would initiate a housing programme 'with the maximum practical speed'; that it would put the 1944 Education Act into effect and raise the school-leaving age to 16 'at the earliest possible moment'; that a National Health Service would be established and social insurance greatly extended. 'Labour,' the document said, 'led the fight against the mean and shoddy treatment which was the lot of millions while Conservative Governments were in power over long years.'

[6] 'There was,' two outsiders later wrote about the Conference debates, 'a striking difference of tone betwen the speeches of the leaders and the rank and file of the party. The leaders tended to restrain, while their followers urged them to go farther in their policy of socialism' (McCallum and Redman, op. cit. p. 129).

but they were, in 1945, sufficiently blurred to suggest a common purpose.

This was even more true in relation to foreign affairs, about which *Let Us Face the Future* said little, and said it in unexceptionable generalities. The main point it made was that it would be necessary, when peace came, to consolidate the war-time association between the British Commonwealth, the U.S.A. and the U.S.S.R.;[1] and the British Labour movement, it claimed, came to the task of international organization 'with one great asset: it has a common bond with the working peoples of all countries, who have achieved a new dignity and influence through their long struggles against Nazi tyranny'.

At the 1945 Conference, both Attlee and Bevin, speaking for the Executive, only referred in very vague terms to the strains and stresses which the shape of the post-war settlement had already produced between Russia and her Anglo-American partners, and they both managed to convey the impression that Britain under a Labour Government would act as a bridge between the United States and the U.S.S.R. 'We have,' said Attlee, 'to have our own line and our own judgment as Socialists.'[2]

The delegates were even less prepared to press their leaders on foreign affairs than on home policy. But Denis Healey was certainly speaking for many of them when he insisted that 'the Labour Party should have a clear foreign policy of its own, which is completely distinct from that of the Tory Party'. The Socialist revolution, he said, had already begun in Europe and was already established in many countries in Eastern and Southern Europe; 'the crucial principle of our foreign policy,' he proposed, 'should be to protect, assist, encourage and aid in every way that Socialist revolution wherever it appears . . . The upper classes in every country are selfish, depraved, dissolute and decadent. These upper classes look to the British Army and the British people to protect them against the just wrath of the people who have been fighting underground against them for the past four years. We must see that that does not happen.'[3]

When he came to reply to the discussion, Ernest Bevin, in a long, rambling speech, made it obvious that, whatever other principles might inspire a Labour Government's foreign policy, help to socialist revolutions in Europe was not one of them. By 1945, both he and

---

[1] 'Let it not be forgotten,' the document urged, 'that in the years leading up to the war the Tories were so scared of Russia that they missed the chance to establish a partnership which might well have prevented war.'
[2] Labour Party Annual Conference Report, 1945, p. 108.
[3] ibid, p. 108.

Attlee, as members of the Cabinet, had shared responsibility for policy decisions which, as for example in the case of Greece,[1] were designed to achieve the precise opposite. As to relations with Russia, Bevin said that it would be the duty of the Labour Party, if returned to power, to remove the mutual·fears and suspicions that existed between the Soviet Union and the 'Western Powers'. 'We have no bad past to live down,' he claimed, 'we never sent the Director of the Bank of England to deal with the enemies of Soviet Russia. We opposed it. We fought all the machinations. If we had been in power in 1939 we would have sent the Foreign Secretary to Moscow, and not just an official.'[2]

However, fears that a Labour Government would be committed to foreign policies neither of its own making nor of its own inspiration remained, and were enhanced by Churchill's invitation to Attlee to accompany him to the Potsdam Conference due to begin the day after the Election.[3] On the 14th of June, Churchill told the House of Commons that in the last few years, he and Attlee had 'always thought alike on the foreign situation', and that Attlee's attendance would show that '. . . although Governments may change and parties may quarrel, yet on some of the main essentials of foreign affairs we stand together'.[4]

It was precisely this suggestion of bi-partnership that Laski, the Chairman of the Party, was concerned to dispel in a statement he issued on the 15th of June. Neither Attlee nor Labour, the statement said, should accept responsibility for agreements concluded by Churchill and which had not been debated either in the Party Executive or at meetings of the Parliamentary Labour Party. 'Labour,' it asserted, 'has a foreign policy which in many respects will not be continuous with that of a Tory-dominated Coalition. It

[1] At the previous Party Conference, in December 1944, Bevin had, against strong attacks from the floor, vigorously defended the British Government's intervention in the Greek Civil War on the side of the Government. 'If we win at the next General Election, as I hope we shall,' he had said then, 'we shall find that we cannot govern this world by emotionalism . . .' (Labour Party Annual Conference Report, 1944, p. 145). And he had also told the delegates that 'the British Empire cannot abandon its position in the Mediterranean' (ibid, p. 147).

[2] Labour Party Annual Conference Report, 1945, p. 118. It was in the course of that speech that Bevin made his famous remark about Left understanding Left. But the reference was to France, not Russia. 'France,' he said, 'will recover, she will come back and confidence between her and ourselves will be re-established. Then, again, France was going Left, and Left understands Left; but Right does not' (ibid, p. 119).

[3] The results of the election were only due to be declared three weeks after polling day, on the 27th of July.

[4] H. of C., vol. 411, col. 1788.

has in fact a far sounder Foreign Policy.'[1]

Conservative leaders expressed deep alarm at this threat of Labour independence in foreign affairs. 'We believed,' one leading Conservative spokesman said in a broadcast, 'that there was a broad measure of agreement between the Socialist Party and the National Government in carrying forward to a conclusion the policy of the great Churchill coalition . . . We are now advised in plain terms that a continuing foreign policy is something we can no longer take for granted.'[2] They need not have feared. As James Byrnes, then the American Secretary of State, later noted, 'Britain's stand on the issues before the (Potsdam) Conference was not altered in the slightest, so far as we could discern, by the replacement of Mr Churchill and Mr Eden by Mr Attlee and Mr Bevin. This continuity of Britain's foreign policy impressed me.'[3] Indeed, Bevin's manner towards the Russians was 'so aggressive' that 'both the President and I wondered how we would get along with this new Foreign Minister'.[4]

This, however, was for later. Before the Election, the Conservatives not only professed alarm at the possibility that Labour might pursue a distinctive foreign policy; they expressed equal alarm, from Churchill downwards, at the possibility which Laski's statement was alleged to imply, that the election of a Labour Government would mean rule by a Party caucus, and the Government's subjection to its commands. Immediately upon the publication of the statement, Churchill wrote to Attlee to ask whether he proposed 'merely to come (to Potsdam) as a mute observer', which would, he suggested, 'be derogatory to your position as leader of your party'.[5] In reply, Attlee wrote that 'there never was any suggestion that I should go as a mere observer', and added that he did not anticipate 'that we shall differ on the main lines of policy, which we have discussed together so often'.[6] At the end of the campaign, Churchill again wrote to Attlee to say that 'the constitution (of the Labour Party) would apparently enable the Executive Committee to call upon a Labour Prime Minister to appear before them and criticize his conduct of the peace negotiations'. This, said Churchill, must entail the disclosure of confidential information and he asked for a statement 'signed jointly by yourself and the Chairman of the Executive

[1] K. Martin, *Harold Laski, 1893-1950* (London, 1953) p. 169.
[2] McCallum and Redman, op. cit. p. 145.
[3] J. Byrnes, *Speaking Frankly* (London, 1947) p. 79.
[4] ibid, p. 79.
[5] Martin, op. cit. p. 171.
[6] ibid, p. 171.

Committee' clarifying the position.[1] Attlee replied that the Executive had 'a right to be consulted' but denied that it had 'power to challenge (the actions) and conduct of a Labour Prime Minister'.[2]

These last exchanges were only the dim echoes of a Conservative scare campaign with Laski cast as the main villain, and designed to convince the voters that, in the event of a Labour victory, Attlee, as some Conservative candidates put it, would be no more than 'a ventriloquist's dummy sitting on Laski's knee'.[3] In the event, the image was found to have lacked force. As a bogey, 'Gauleiter Laski', about to play Lenin to Attlee's Kerensky, proved a poor successor to Zinoviev and Post Office Savings.[4] Times had changed. Potential Labour voters refused to be scared off by Conservative assertions that Labour had irresistible propensities to totalitarianism, and that a Labour victory would result in the creation of a 'Police State'. These charges, dismissed by Labour as typical Conservative stunts, only strengthened the view, fatal to Conservative electoral fortunes, that the Tories had learnt nothing and forgotten nothing. So did the latter's deliberate enlargement of the progammatic differences between the two parties.

At the end of the 1945 Labour Party Annual Conference, Laski had described the coming General Election as a 'straight fight . . . a fight between private enterprise now expressed as monopoly capitalism, and socialism that realizes that the new age is born and that only through the establishment of a Socialist Commonwealth can we realize the purposes for which we have been fighting this war'.[5] At the time this had been said, neither Labour's programme, nor certainly the pronouncements of most Labour leaders, remotely suggested that this was the issue of the election. Nor, in reality, did it ever become the issue of the election. But it was made to appear the issue, not by the Labour leaders, but by the Tories. It was they who, from the start of the campaign, insisted that the electorate *was* confronted with a choice between 'free enterprise' and socialism, and it was also they who sought to create an image of the Labour leaders as red-blooded socialists, determined upon the strangulation of British capitalism, and much else besides. In the mood of that

[1] Labour Party Annual Conference Report, 1946, p. 5.
[2] McKenzie, op. cit. p. 331.
[3] McCallum and Redman, op. cit. p. 148.
[4] Laski was also accused on the 20th of June of having said that if Labour could not achieve its aims by consent, it would do so by violence. A writ of libel which he immediately issued against the *Daily Express* and other newspapers prevented further comment. For the libel action, which Laski lost, see Laski v. Newark Advertiser Co. Ltd. and Parlby (published by *Daily Express*, 1947).
[5] Labour Party Annual Conference Report, 1945, p. 108.

summer, the Tories could not have adopted a strategy more likely to enhance Labour's electoral chances.

After so many years of disappointments and defeats, a Labour victory, resulting in the first majority Labour Government, held an element of real drama. The victory was made the more dramatic by coming at the end of the war, and after a campaign in which socialism had been proclaimed to be the issue. But what made it most dramatic of all was the size of Labour's parliamentary majority. When the votes had been counted, it was found that 393 Labour candidates had been returned, and that Labour would have a majority of 146 over all other parties. The Conservatives had lost 172 seats and, with their allies, would number 213 in the new House of Commons. It may be incongruous that Sir Hartley Shaw-cross should have been the one to say 'We are the masters now.' But this was the feeling of countless men and women in the Labour movement who found in Labour's victory the vindication of their faith and the fulfilment of their hopes, and who believed that now at last was to begin the transformation of Britain into a socialist commonwealth. Nor was there now anyone to prevent the Parliamentary Labour Party from singing the *Red Flag* when the new House of Commons assembled.

In terms of votes cast, as opponents were quick to point out, the majority was less spectacular. Nearly 12,000,000 people (48.3 per cent. of the votes cast) had voted for the Labour Party; the Conservatives and their allies had polled less than 10,000,000 votes (39.8 per cent.) and the Liberals, who won twelve seats, polled 2,239,668 votes. The Communist Party, which put forward twenty-one candidates, increased its parliamentary representation from one to two, and polled 102,760 votes. The Commonwealth Party had twenty-three candidates, one of whom was elected, and it polled 110,634 votes. The I.L.P., with five candidates (three elected), polled 46,679. Taking the poll as a whole (76 per cent. of the electorate, on an antiquated register) there was, as Cole notes, 'very little in it'[1] as between Right and Left. Nevertheless, no one denied that Labour had scored a remarkable victory.

2. LABOUR'S SOCIALISM

In the first flush of victory, the hesitations and inhibitions of Labour's leadership in the year preceding the Election were easily overlooked. And indeed, the leaders themselves, as a result of a

[1] Cole, op. cit. p. 432.

victory so great and so unexpected,[1] found a measure of confidence they had previously lacked. They too now spoke of the social revolution they were about to initiate.

The mood was sufficiently strong to carry the Government forward to the achievement, in its first three years of office, of much that had been promised at the Election. By 1948, it had ensured an orderly transition from war-time mobilization to peace-time reconstruction. It had placed on the Statute Book the nationalization proposals of *Let Us Face the Future*—except for the nationalization of iron and steel. And it had brought into being a National Health Service and a new comprehensive system of social insurance. In housing, in education, in welfare, it could well boast to have done more than any Government had done before—and to have done it in the midst of acute economic difficulties. In a different context, it could also point to its ready recognition of the fact that there was no alternative to India's political independence, with which went the political independence of Burma and Ceylon.

These achievements were real, and of permanent importance, but even in those first years of social and economic reform, the Government's impact upon post-war Britain was profoundly ambiguous.

Of course, the very fact that a Labour Government had come to power, with an assured majority, was sufficient to give bourgeois England, and all those who-identified themselves with bourgeois England without being part of it, a genuine sense of outrage at what was taken to be the country's capture from its traditional rulers, and at the proletarian threat which Labour's assumption of office was deemed to entail. Mr Evelyn Waugh may have been straining for effect when he wrote in 1959 that he had 'bitter memories of the Attlee-Cripps regime when the kingdom seemed to be under enemy occupation'.[2] But there was a vast and socially heterogeneous host which did then feel that the Government. if not the kingdom, was in enemy hands, and whose hostility fed as much on post-war scarcities and restrictions, for which the Government was held to be responsible, as on the welfare and nationalization measures of those years.

Yet, with the hostility went the realization that things could have been much worse. As *The Economist* wrote in November 1945,

[1] The King, Attlee later recalled, always used to say 'that I looked very surprised, as indeed I certainly was, at the extent of our success'. (Attlee, op. cit. p. 148.) Most of Attlee's colleagues were not only surprised at the extent of Labour's victory, but that they had won at all.
[2] *The Spectator,* 2nd of October, 1959.

after the Government had announced its nationalization proposals,[1] 'an avowedly Socialist Government, with a clear Parliamentary majority, might well have been expected to go several steps further . . . If there is to be a Labour Government, the programme now stated is the least it could do without violating its election pledges'.[2] The sentiments were apposite in regard to much more than nationalization. For if the social advances of the post-war years were substantial in comparison wih the pace of earlier years, they were also modest by any more humane criterion. And if the Government further enhanced the sense of confidence and strength of the working classes, it also made it its business to moderate and discipline both their claims and their expectations.

As far as the trade unions were concerned, the coming to office of a Labour Government did not entail any substantial departure from a pattern of consultation on economic and social matters which the war itself had done much to enhance. The unions could of course rely on a sympathetic hearing from a Government, more than one third of whose members were trade union sponsored M.P.s, and one of the Government's first acts was to repeal the Trades Disputes and Trade Union Act of 1927. But in return, the Government expected, and received, from the trade unions a measure of co-operation in the maintenance of industrial discipline which was of inestimable benefit to it.[3] And when industrial discipline did break down, the Government's interventions, as V. L. Allen notes, 'were not markedly dissimilar from interventions before 1926. Troops who moved food supplies were employed in the interests of the community, but in fact they were blacklegs who reduced the effectiveness of the strikes . . . Whatever the motives of the Government, troops invariably

---

[1] By then, the Bill for the nationalization of the Bank of England was already on its way through the House of Commons.

[2] *The Economist,* November 1945, p. 139 in A. A. Rogow, with the assistance of Peter Shore, *The Labour Government and British Industry 1945-1951* (London, 1955) p. 156. The Government proposals, it may be noted, did not include the nationalization of iron and steel: the Government was awaiting, it said, the report which the Coalition Government had invited the industry to submit 'before taking its final decision' (Labour Party Annual Conference Report, 1946, p. 59). In a different context, see Churchill's view, as expressed in March 1946 to James Forrestal, the American Secretary of Defense. He said 'there was considerable consolation in the victory of Bevin, because Bevin was able to talk more firmly and clearly to Russia than he could have, by virtue of being a Labour Government.' (*The Forrestal Diaries,* Ed. W. Millis (New York, 1951) p. 144).

[3] In the six years after the war, the number of man days lost through strikes and lockouts amounted to 12,740,000. In the equivalent period after the First World War, the figure had been 187,580,000. It is of course unlikely that even if a Conservative Government had been elected after 1945, there would have

appeared as strike-breakers and as protectors of the interests of employers."[1]

In regard to nationalization, there was no ambiguity at all. From the beginning, the nationalization proposals of the Government were designed to achieve the sole purpose of improving the efficiency of a capitalist economy, not as marking the beginning of its wholesale transformation, and this was an aim to which many Tories, whatever they might say in the House of Commons, were easily reconciled, and which some even approved—with the exception of iron and steel.[2]

By 1945, what really mattered about the nationalization measures of the Government was compensation and control. As to the first, the interests affected found the Government forthcoming and, as in the case of coal, for instance, did considerably better out of nationalization than they could conceivably have done had the industry remained in private ownership. In fact, one consequence of the Government's compensation policies was to release vast financial resources for profitable investment in the 'private sector'; another was to saddle the nationalized industries with a burden of debt which materially contributed to difficulties that were later ascribed to the immanent character of public ownership.

As for the effective control of the nationalized industries, the Conservatives found the Government much more than half way in their own camp. Though ultimate control was vested in the Minister and provision made for a measure of parliamentary accountability more formal than real, the Government's conception of public ownership ensured the predominance on the boards of the nationalized corporations of men who had been, or who still were, closely associated with private finance and industry,[3] and who could hardly be expected to regard the nationalized industries as designed to achieve any purpose other than the more efficient servicing of the 'private sector'.

Most people in the Labour movement believed that the nationalized industries should be examples of a new socialist spirit in industry, islands of socialist virtue in a sea of capitalist greed. This would in any case have been difficult enough to achieve in a pre-

---

been anything resembling the industrial strife which followed 1918. But it is equally unlikely that industrial discipline would have been as great as it was.

[1] Allen, op. cit. p. 127.

[2] 'There was not much real opposition to our nationalization proposals, only Iron and Steel roused much feeling' (Attlee, op. cit. p. 165).

[3] For detailed documentation on the preponderance on the boards of men associated with business and finance, see C. Jenkins, *Power at the Top* (London, 1959) *passim*.

dominantly capitalist economy.[1] But the Government's conception of the nature of public ownership did not even induce it to try. In fact, had the Government been determined that nationalization should make little appeal to the voters, it could not easily have managed the business better.

The T.U.C.'s Interim Report on Post-War Reconstruction had stated as 'fundamental to any plan for the organization of a public service that the workpeople have the right to a voice in the determination of its policy'.[2] But when it came to concrete applications, both the Government and most trade union leaders gave no sign that they wished to see brought about major changes in the pattern of 'industrial relations' in the nationalized industries. There was at hand a system of joint consultation, which had been extensively used during the war. The Government was entirely willing to extend this further and to make joint consultation compulsory in the public sector. But joint consultation was always confined to a narrow range of subjects.

In a famous speech in October 1946, Sir Stafford Cripps declared that 'there is not yet a very large number of workers in Britain capable of taking over large enterprises . . . until there has been more experience by the workers of the managerial side of industry. I think it would be almost impossible to have worker-controlled industry in Britain, *even if it were on the whole desirable*'.[3] The doubt was certainly not unique to Cripps. But even those Ministers who expressed their fervent belief in industrial democracy[4] agreed that the difficulties were overwhelming and that much time would have to pass before anything could be done to overcome them. What is more notable is how little the Government tried to do to overcome them. It did introduce limited training and promotion schemes in the nationalized industries; like the trade union leaders, it wanted to encourage promising youngsters from the working classes to 'rise to the top', in industry as in other walks of life.[5]

---

[1] For an excellent analysis of the limitations, from a socialist point of view, of marginal public enterprise, see J. Hughes, *Nationalized Industries in the Mixed Economy* (London, 1960).

[2] T.U.C. Annual Conference Report, 1944, p. 409.

[3] *The Times*, 28th of October, 1946. My italics.

[4] See e.g. James Griffiths at the 1948 Labour Party Conference, Labour Party Annual Conference Report, 1948, pp. 170-2.

[5] Thus E. Shinwell at the 1946 Annual Conference of the Labour Party on the importance of providing that 'every boy who enters the pit or who enters any other nationalized industry, shall have the possibility of a Manager's Certificate or of working in a technical, expert or administrative capacity, which will enable him to attain access to the highest possible posts in the industries concerned' (Labour Party Annual Conference Report, 1946, p. 140).

But their rise to the top could hardly be said to bring any nearer that 'best obtainable system of popular administration and control of each industry and service' which the Constitution of the Labour Party had enshrined as one of the Party's major aims.

The prime concern of the Labour leaders, it has been noted earlier, was not to nationalize British industry, but to control it and to bend it to the Government's purposes. As has also been noted, the Government, when it came to office, found at hand a ready-made system of war-time controls, operated in close consultation with the industrial interests concerned—indeed, largely operated *by* representatives of these interests. These arrangements had been strongly criticized in the Labour movement during the war. The Government, however, relied at least as much as its predecessors upon the advice of private industry and finance and gave their representatives a major share in the operation of controls:[1] if there was no workers' participation in those years, there was at least employers' participation.

This partnership between Government and private enterprise would no doubt have been much less easy had the Government sought to apply controls in a manner and for purposes irreconcilable with the purposes and profits of business. But the Government had no such wish, and it thus enjoyed the co-operation of private industry. Or, more accurately, private industry enjoyed the co-operation of the Government. And where co-operation did not suit industry, exhortations, appeals, inducements, and occasional muttered threats fell on very deaf ears.

There was of course Labour's much reiterated belief in planning. But the Government, when it finally came, early in 1947, to announce what it meant to do about it, drew a sharp distinction between 'totalitarian' and 'democratic' planning. The former, the *Economic Survey for 1947* said, 'subordinates all individual desires and preferences to the demands of the State'; a democratic government, on the other hand, must plan 'in a manner which preserves the maximum possible freedom of choice to the individual citizen'.[2] This entailed much more freedom of choice than planning, particularly freedom of choice for private enterprise. 'Had shortages not existed,' Mr Rogow notes, 'planning under the Labour Government would have been largely confined to the compilation of economic information and of forecasts by the expert agencies in the Economic Section, the Central Statistical Office, and the Economic Planning Staff—with the use of a small number of key controls to guide

[1] Rogow, op. cit. pp. 62-3.
[2] *Economic Survey for 1947*, Cmd. 7046, p. 5.

resources into the right places. In other words, the decisions as to the quantity and kind of industrial output required would have been left substantially to market forces.' And indeed, he adds, 'it was towards this goal of essentially liberal planning that the Labour Government was moving throughout its period of office and with considerable speed between 1948 and 1950'.[1]

Government intervention in economic affairs, though in some aspects irksome to private industry and finance, presented no serious challenge to the power of the men who continued to control the country's economic resources, the more so since they themselves played so large a rôle, directly or indirectly, in determining the nature and applications of Government intervention. This situation had its parallel in the field of politics and administration generally. If Labour's rule did not signify any notable diminution in private economic power and influence, neither did it represent nearly so striking a diminution in the power and influence of political Conservatism as the existence of a Labour Government was widely believed to entail. For the Conservatives, though expelled from the centre of the political stage, namely the Government, yet remained an important part of the play—and could always rely on the support of a noisy claque, led by a Conservative press eager to exploit every opportunity of damaging the Government.

There was, to begin with, the House of Commons itself. The Government was entirely safe from defeat, but it was also deeply concerned to placate the Opposition. Nor did the Conservatives in Parliament behave like a defeated party, expecting little and therefore receiving little. They could not hope to prevent the Government from enacting its main proposals. But they could hope, by unremitting pressure, to limit the import of those proposals. Seldom if ever has the House of Commons been so effectively used as in those years of Conservative opposition to denounce the Government and to erode its morale. 'I have not forgotten,' one of the least timid of junior Labour Ministers has recalled, 'the tension of rising to answer questions or conduct a debate under the cold, implacable eyes of that row of well-tailored tycoons, who hated the Labour Government with a passion and fear which made them dedicated men in their determination to get it out of office and to limit the damage it could do to the world which they saw as theirs by right.'[2]

There was also the House of Lords. *Let Us Face the Future* had done no more, despite earlier pledges of reform and even abolition, than 'give clear notice that we will not tolerate obstruction

[1] Rogow, op. cit. p. 25.
[2] J. Freeman, 'The Old Look', *New Statesman*, 14th of November, 1959.

of the people's will by the House of Lords', and, at the 1945 Labour Party Conference, Herbert Morrison had also given 'their lordships notice that if we have any serious nonsense from them, they will have some serious nonsense from us—and we mean that'.[1] That the House of Lords avoided any 'serious nonsense' in the first years of the Government's life, when the operation of the Parliament Act would in any case have overcome its opposition, is more often remembered than the steady pressure it exercised upon the Government. 'Though it almost never coerced the Government,' Dr P. M. Bromhead writes, 'it persistently obliged the Government to justify its decisions, and it sometimes persuaded the Government to be accommodating on matters with regard to which it had been adamant in the Commons.'[2] And when it came to the nationalization of iron and steel, by which time the provisions of the Parliament Act of 1911 had been amended to reduce the Lords' powers of delay from two years to one, the House of Lords fought a very different kind of battle than it had fought over earlier measures of nationalization.[3]

But in their struggle to 'limit the damage' and to induce the Government to 'moderation', the Conservatives were not only able to rely on their political resources, inside and outside Parliament, or on the hostility to the Government of powerful industrial and economic interests. There were other more diffuse but no less persuasive influences also directed to the purpose of enhancing the Government's already well developed tendencies to 'moderation'.

One of these influences, which should neither be exaggerated nor too lightly discounted, was that of the King. The King, in the advice he gave to the Prime Minister, undoubtedly felt that he was doing no more than fulfilling his constitutional duty and that he was, indeed, helping the Government. But the fact remains, on the available evidence, 'that his advice was not calculated to stiffen the Government's boldness. 'On the subject of strikes,' Mr Wheeler-Bennett notes, the King 'was emphatic with his Prime Minister'.[4] As to nationalization, the King, as early as November 1945,

[1] Labour Party Annual Conference Report, 1945, p. 133.

[2] P. M. Bromhead, *The House of Lords and Contemporary Politics, 1911-1957* (London, 1958) p. 176. In 1952, Lord Jowett, the Lord Chancellor in the Attlee Government, recalled that he had, in the conditions of 1945-51, been 'forced to be reasonable'. 'As many of your lordships well remember,' he said, 'I used to get them round to my room and we would thrash out our problems frankly and in the most friendly way. Very often I used to be able to meet them on all sorts of topics . . . If I could not, I explained why . . . Sometimes I used to go round to Ministers to try to get them to give way. The net result of all this was very satisfactory' (ibid, p. 159).

[3] See below, p. 300.

[4] Wheeler-Bennett, op. cit. p. 652.

expressed the view to Herbert Morrison that 'he was going too fast in the new nationalizing legislation'.[1] 'I told Attlee,' he wrote in his Diary on the 20th of November, 1945, 'that he must give the people here some confidence that the Government was not going to stifle all private enterprise. Everyone wanted to help in re-habilitating the country but they were not allowed to'.[2] In January 1947, he wrote again that 'I was doing my best to warn them that they were going too fast in their legislation and were offending every class of people who were trying to help them if they were asked to, but were swept aside by regulations, etc.'[3]

It is hardly likely that the King, had he tried to do so, would have been able to deflect the Government's course on any major issue. But it is a naïve mistake, particularly in regard to the operation of so subtle an instrument as the British Constitution, only to look for the dramatic and, not finding it, to conclude that this exhausts the range of possibilities. As Mr Wheeler-Bennett notes, the King 'was aware that in his talks with Ministers he was not infrequently successful in presenting arguments which caused them to reconsider decisions at which they had already arrived',[4] and it would seem reasonable to suppose that the reconsideration was not in the direction of greater radicalism.

Mr Wheeler-Bennett's words might equally be taken to describe the Labour Government's relations with its professional Civil Service advisers. Lord Attlee has recalled that, when he returned to Potsdam, this time as Prime Minister, 'our American friends were surprised to find that there was no change in our official advisers and that I had even taken over, as my Principal Private Secretary, Leslie Rowan, who had been serving Churchill in the same capacity'.[5] This pattern was substantially reproduced throughout the whole administration. The Government gratefully inherited from the war-time coalition, and from previous Conservative govern-ments, a body of officials who, by social provenance, education and professional disposition, were bound to conceive it as one of their prime tasks to warn their Ministers against too radical a de-parture from traditional departmental policies. No doubt, the experience of war had taught them to view with far less distaste than in the past the enlargement of State intervention and control and they were, at the end of the war, quite ready to serve the purposes of a Government pledged to positive State action. But

[1] Wheeler-Bennett, p. 653.
[2] ibid, p. 651.
[3] ibid, p. 662.
[4] ibid, p. 653.
[5] Attlee, op. cit. p. 149.

they were equally ready to try and convince their political masters of the dangers of innovation. This did not involve the kind of administrative sabotage which the Left had feared likely in the thirties. What it entailed was the active discouragement of bold experimentation. Of course, Ministers usually had the last word. But the last word was likely to be greatly influenced by the cautious words that had gone before. Mr Shinwell notes that many of his officials at the Ministry of Fuel and Power were 'apathetic or antagonistic to nationalization'.[1] This would not prevent his leading advisers from executing the policy laid down for them; but neither would it dispose them to search for unconventional solutions to the problems it raised, or to press upon their Minister plans and ideas unhallowed by the routines and usages they knew.

Labour Ministers have often paid generous tributes to the loyalty and co-operation of their official advisers. This, however, may be less a comment on the conversion of those advisers to socialist principles than on the Government's failure to act upon these principles. It would have been odd indeed if Foreign Office officials had not given their wholehearted support to a Foreign Secretary whose views accorded so largely with their own, and with those of the Conservative Opposition; or if the Service Chiefs had refused to co-operate with a Ministry whose approach to military matters differed little from their own; and, in this last instance at any rate, Lord Montgomery has said enough[2] to show that, where differences did arise between Ministers and their military advisers (colleagues would be a better word), it was not the Service Chiefs who had the worst of the encounter. The point is not that the Government's advisers *should* have pressed socialist policies upon their Ministers; the point is that they provided an additional and powerful reinforcement to all the forces in the land whose purpose it was to 'limit the damage' they feared even so moderate a Labour Government might do.

As against these pressures, but by no means of equal weight, there were the contrary pressures on the Government from within the Labour movement. These were not only incomparably weaker, less persistent and less organized, but Ministers, heavy with the responsibilities of office and invested with a new authority and prestige, were also better equipped to resist them, and much more determined to do so.

[1] Shinwell, op. cit. p. 174.
[2] See Field-Marshal Viscount Montgomery of Alamein, *Memoirs* (London, 1958) chs. 29 and 30. On the basis of his experience as Secretary of State for War and Minister of Defence, Mr. Shinwell did come to think that there was 'one facet of Army life which deserved changing. While it may be important to maintain the traditions of the various regiments, I query whether

Although there was much in the Government's handling of affairs at home which worried the Labour Left, its greatest unease was with foreign policy. In its attempts to defend traditional imperial interests in the Middle East, the Government resolutely pursued the policies inherited from its predecessors. And in the developing conflict between East and West, it had also shown, even before the Cold War was properly under way, that it would unhesitatingly take its place as the most senior of the junior partners of the United States. Given its belief in a Russian military threat, and its economic dependance upon the United States, there never was any question that it would explore any 'third way'.

British foreign policy after 1945 was soon under fire from the Labour Left, over specific issues such as Bevin's handling of the Palestine question, but also in regard to its general drift. At the 1946 Labour Party Annual Conference, the Government was attacked for, as one resolution put it, the 'apparent continuance of a traditionally Conservative Party policy of power politics abroad', and it was urged to return 'to the Labour Party foreign policy of support of Socialist and anti-Imperialist forces throughout the world'.[1] Another resolution called upon the Government to 'maintain and foster an attitude of sympathy, friendship and understanding towards the Soviet Union' and to 'repudiate Mr Churchill's defeatist proposal to make the British Commonwealth a mere satellite of American monopoly capitalism, which will inevitably lead to our being aligned in a partnership of hostility to Russia'.[2] A third also asked the Government 'to undertake a drastic revision of existing methods of recruitment to the Foreign Service' and to entrust the execution of a Socialist foreign policy 'to men who believe in it, rather than to those whose whole background and tradition have rendered them incapable of understanding the first principles of such a policy'.[3] The first of these resolutions was withdrawn after Ernest Bevin had said he considered it a vote of censure upon him, and the other two were lost on a show of hands. But the unease they reflected endured: one of its expressions was an Amendment to the Address tabled by fifty-three Labour M.P.s in November 1946;[4]

so much ceremonial both in public and within the messes is wholly necessary'. (Shinwell, op. cit. pp. 194-5.)

[1] Labour Party Annual Conference Report, 1946, p. 157.
[2] ibid, p. 157.
[3] ibid, p. 157.
[4] The Amendment expressed the 'urgent hope' that the Government would 'review and recast its conduct of International Affairs' and provide 'a democratic and constructive Socialist alternative to an otherwise inevitable conflict between American Capitalism and Soviet Communism' (H. of C., vol. 430, col. 526, 18th of November, 1926). Its sponsors did not press the Amendment to a vote.

another was *Keep Left,* the manifesto of a number of Members of Parliament, which appeared in April 1947. This document, though paying tribute to the Government's achievement, urged greater boldness upon it at home, denounced 'the fallacy of collective security against Communism', and repudiated the argument that 'the only way to stop Communism spreading is to organize the world against Russia'. 'It would be a betrayal of British and European Socialism,' said the document, 'if we meekly accepted Communist leadership. But it would be equally fatal to accept American leadership in exchange for dollars.'

However, the *Keep Left* group was never more than a fairly loose group of M.P.s, without any hard centre. Never in fact had the Labour Left so entirely lacked coherence and organization as it did after 1945. Nor did it now have any leader of any prominence : its standard bearer of the war years, Aneurin Bevan, was now safely busy, as Minister of Health, with the creation of the National Health Service.

As for the Parliamentary Party as a whole, it was not the body to deny loyal support to the Government, at meetings of the Parliamentary Party as well as in the division lobbies of the House of Commons. The Standing Orders of the Parliamentary Party were suspended throughout the lifetime of the Labour Government. But this was without prejudice to the right of the Party to withdraw the Whip from Members should occasion arise. And there was never any occasion when a decisive majority was not to be found for whatever policy the Government might decide, even though, as R. T. McKenzie notes, 'there was no question of the Government revealing in detail its parliamentary proposals or seeking formal approval for them in advance of their presentation to Parliament'.[1] From the first, the Government had easily established its supremacy. Even the earlier pattern of consultation with backbench M.P.s was now discarded. This time, there was created a Liaison Committee, composed of a Chairman and Vice-Chairman (a second Vice-Chairman was later added) elected by the Parliamentary Party, a Labour Peer the Leader of the House of Commons, the Chief Whip and the Secretary of the Parliamentary Party, who was not an M.P.; but this body was much more a watchdog for the Government than a lever of pressure upon it.

Of course, backbench pressure was exercised upon Ministers either informally, or at the fortnightly meetings of the P.L.P., or through the latter's standing committees, and Ministers, as Mr McKenzie also notes, 'tended to take party feeling into account before attempting to make a case for a particular line of policy at

[1] McKenzie, op. cit. p. 447.

the party meeting'; but, he adds, 'when an issue *was* forced to a vote (in the P.L.P.) the Government could rely on a solid block of votes composed of approximately seventy members of the ministry. In addition, of course, those who hoped to win promotion into the Government tended to take care not to carry any misgivings they might have concerning the Government's policies to the point of voting against them. And in any case the party's strong sense of loyalty to its leaders and its internal cohesion almost invariably sustained the Government'.[1]

Most of the rebellions which did occur in the course of the Government's existence[2] only involved a small minority of Members. One issue which provoked a sizeable Labour backbench rebellion and forced the Government to a retreat which proved temporary was the length of conscription. When the National Service Bill, which proposed a period of conscription of eighteen months, was introduced in the House of Commons in March 1947, eighty Labour backbenchers signed an amendment asking the House to reject it, and seventy-two later voted against it. The Government then agreed to reduce the conscription period from eighteen to twelve months. The Bill was due to come into operation on the 1st of January, 1949. In October 1948, by which time the international situation had greatly worsened, Lord Montgomery, the Chief of the Imperial General Staff, 'assembled the Military Members of the Army Council . . . and asked them if they were all prepared to resign in a body, led by me, if anything less than eighteen months National Service with the Colours was decided upon by the Government. They all agreed.'[3] The Government gave way in November,[4] without serious parliamentary opposition,[5] and later extended National Service to two years.

What, in the present context, is notable about the relationship of the Government to its backbenchers is not only the Government's

---

[1] McKenzie, op. cit. p. 447.

[2] See J. M. Burns, 'The Parliamentary Labour Party in Great Britain', in *The American Political Science Review*, vol. XLIV (December 1950), pp. 855-87.

[3] Montgomery, op. cit. p. 479.

[4] On the 12th of November, James Forrestal recorded that 'Attlee said (presumably in relation to the possibility of armed conflict breaking out as a result of the Berlin blockade) that there was no division in the British public mind about the use of the atomic bomb—they were for its use. Even the Church in recent days had publicly taken this position' (*The Forrestal Diaries*, op. cit. p. 523).

[5] 'When all is said and done,' Lord Montgomery also writes, 'one must pay tribute to the courage of the Labour Government in introducing National Service in peace-time in the face of great opposition with its own party. Attlee and Bevin pushed it through for us' (Montgomery, op. cit. p. 480).

strength, but also the fact that its use of that strength was mainly devoted to the neutralization of one current of thought: that of the Left.

This was also true of the Government's relation to the Labour rank and file. The former's insistence on its prior constitutional responsibility to Parliament, and its concern that the Parliamentary Party (which meant the parliamentary leaders) should be free from Conference 'dictation' proceeded much less from some abstract model of parliamentary government, or from some preconceived notion of the desirability or otherwise of 'inner-party democracy' than from a desire to escape from the *radical* pressure of the rank and file. The debate on these issues, then and later, was firmly rooted in the ideological divisions between leaders and activists, and is only meaningful with reference to these divisions.

3. 'CONSOLIDATION'

By 1948, as Herbert Morrison pointed out to the Labour Party Conference of that year, the Government had, save for the nationalization of iron and steel, passed into legislation all the major nationalization proposals contained in *Let Us Face the Future*. In a crucial sense, the Labour Party had now, at long last, reached its moment of truth. What had now to be decided was whether it would go forward with a nationalization programme which, by eating really deep into capitalist enterprise, would be immeasurably more significant than the previous one, or whether it would stop at bankrupt industries and public utilities. The Government's predictable answer, though wrapped up in a vague promise of further public ownership, was that the time had now come for 'consolidation'.

'Whilst in the next programme,' Morrison told the delegates, 'it will be right—and I can promise you that the Executive will do it—to give proper consideration to further propositions for public ownership, do not ignore the need, not merely for considering further public ownership, but for allowing Ministers adequate time to consolidate, to develop, to make efficient the industries which have been socialized in the present Parliament . . . we must make the programme as attractive as we can to ourselves, but we must make it attractive also to public opinion . . . *you must expect the new programme to be of a somewhat different character and a somewhat different tempo from the last . . .*'[1]

[1] Labour Party Annual Conference Report, 1948, p. 122. My italics.

The speech of the constituency delegate who followed Morrison[1] is worth quoting at some length, since it so clearly shows the gulf that divided most of the leadership from some at least of its following, and is also a succinct statement of the latter's case, then and ever since. Referring to Morrison's insistence on the need to make Labour's election programme not only attractive to themselves but also to 'public opinion', the delegate argued that 'the programme will be attractive to the public, not if it is something very wishy-washy and watered down but if it is bold and challenging. I want to see in the forefront of our General Election programme a declaration of faith in Socialism—not the approach the Liberal has to nationalization, that when two or three Royal Commissions have decided that in a particular case, for empirical reasons, an industry ought to be nationalized, then we will nationalize it. I want us to say we believe, as economic scientists and on the grounds of social justice, that the large resources of production in this country ought to belong to the common people. When Churchill says, "You Labour people are doing it for doctrinaire reasons", I want him to be quite right. I want us to be doing it from principle and doctrine . . . When the present programme of the Labour Government has been completed some twenty per cent. of the industrial and economic life of this country will be publicly owned. At this speed it will take us twenty-five years to get to the stage when Socialism predominates. I want to see the present tempo maintained. I am not very happy about the suggestion that there is going to be some slackening off in speed. I do not feel that anybody can say that we are going too fast. Many of us think we are going too slow . . . I would say that there are two ideas as to the next step. One is to increase the degree of public control, the other is to extend the area of publicly-owned industry. I do not believe that it is feasible, as a permanent basis, for a Socialist Government to control privately-owned industry. Ownership gives control. The only way in which we can get control is by getting ownership. So I want it to be made quite clear in our programme that we stand for control through common ownership.'[2]

He was destined to be greatly disappointed. The Labour Party's Policy Statement, *Labour Believes in Britain,* published in April 1949, and endorsed by Annual Conference in June, proposed for nationalization industrial life assurance, sugar, cement, meat wholesaling and slaughtering, water and 'all suitable minerals'. In addition, if private enterprise should fail 'to act in the public interest', the Government would, 'wherever the need is clearly shown', start upon

[1] Hugh Lawson, of Rushcliffe Divisional Labour Party.
[2] Labour Party Annual Conference Report, 1948, p. 122.

new public enterprises;[1] secondly, the existing power to take over concerns 'which are woefully failing the nation' would be continued; and, thirdly, the Government should be prepared 'to acquire suitable existing concerns where these are willingly offered for sale'.[2]

Herbert Morrison, in commending the document to the delegates, had said that each nationalization proposal was 'carefully chosen and fitted into the pattern'. But the programme, whatever its specific merits, quite failed to conceal the fact (save to many devoted Labour supporters) that Labour's leadership, should it be returned to power at the next election, was entirely prepared to postpone indefinitely any further attempt at the structural transformation of a predominantly capitalist economy, now increasingly and euphemistically labelled 'the mixed economy'.[3] *Labour Believes in Britain* in fact inaugurated a pattern that was to acquire ever more precise shape in the following years. Proposals for nationalization were not entirely eliminated; but neither were the proposals which appeared in Labour's programmes intended to make more than marginal inroads into the 'private sector'. They neither satisfied the activists nor made any marked impression on the electorate. But they also failed to pacify Labour's enemies or to attract that middle-class vote, whose seduction had become a major obsession with Labour's electoral strategists.

'Consolidation' was intended to define the strategy and purpose of the next Labour Government; but it was already a reality when Herbert Morrison spoke of it at the 1948 Labour Party Conference. By then, the Government's reforming zeal was all but exhausted. Doubts had even arisen in the Cabinet about the wisdom of proceeding with the outright nationalization of iron and steel and an attempt to find an alternative in greater State control only foundered because the proposals came up against strong opposition from some members of the Cabinet,[4] including, so

[1] 'We introduce a new application of Socialism and of Socialist doctrine. It is called Competitive Public Enterprise. This we shall push into new fields and revitalize private enterprise with its own techniques of competition, and, if I may say so, it will not be a bad thing for private enterprise that that should be.' (Herbert Morrison, Labour Party Annual Conference Report, 1949, p. 155.)

[2] *Labour Believes in Britain,* London, 1949, p.

[3] 'We shall,' Herbert Morrison told the delegates to the 1949 Conference, 'be living in a mixed economy for a good long time to come. Part of it will be socialized, part of it will be private enterprise; all of it will be required to fit in with the general requirements of economic planning in the public interest of the people as a whole' (Labour Party Annual Conference Report, 1949, p. 155).

[4] Lord Morrison of Lambeth, *An Autobiography* (London, 1960) p. 296.

it was said, a threat of resignation from Aneurin Bevan.

Of all the Labour Government's nationalization measures, the nationalization of iron and steel was the only one which entailed a serious threat to the 'private sector'. Had the Government differently conceived its task in 1945, iron and steel, instead of being left last, would have been among the first to be taken over, at a time when opposition was likely to be least effective. And, had the Government differently conceived its task in 1949, it would have reacted with greater vigour to the pressure and threats of the steel interests, and made fewer concessions to them.

Neither these interests nor the Opposition could prevent the passage of the Bill through the House of Commons. But they could rely on the obduracy of the House of Lords. Under the procedure of the Parliament Act of 1949, the Government could have rejected the Lords' amendments and carried the nationalization Bill through all its parliamentary stages by the beginning of 1950. Instead, it agreed, in return for the House of Lords' withdrawal of its amendments to the Bill, not to make any appointments to the Iron and Steel Corporation until the 1st of October, 1950, and not to transfer properties to the Corporation until the 1st of January, 1951. This delay was of course intended to ensure that another General Election would intervene before nationalization could come into operation. In the meantime, the steelmasters, while preparing to defeat the eventual application of the Act,[1] also embarked on a massive campaign in the country to persuade the electors that nationalization was unnecessary and fraught with disastrous consequences to the nation.

Their efforts were only part of a more general offensive by business and financial interests, now confident that they had the full measure of the Government, to discredit not only nationalization but also bulk buying, municipal trading, Government intervention and control. In the two years preceding the General Election, enormous resources, in money, skill and ingenuity,[2] were deployed to sell 'free enterprise' and anti-Labour propaganda to the public. The most lavish of these campaigns were undertaken by Tate and Lyle, the sugar refiners,[3] and by the insurance interests; by Septem-

---

[1] See J. Hughes, *Steel Nationalization and Political Power* (London, 1958).
[2] See H. H. Wilson, 'Techniques of Pressure—Anti-Nationalization Propaganda in Britain', in *Public Opinion Quarterly* (Summer, 1951) pp. 225-42; also Rogow, op. cit. pp. 139 ff.
[3] 'Mr. Cube, a cartoon-style figure sugar lump proclaiming anti-nationalization slogans, appeared each day on more than two million sugar packages, on 100,000 ration book holders distributed free to housewives by Tate and Lyle, and on all Tate and Lyle delivery trucks. Propaganda was inserted into material on the sugar refining industry sent out to 4,500 schools. Six

ber 1949, the latter 'had set up 400 anti-nationalization committees up and down the country on which 4,000 employees were working after office hours to publicize their objections to the Labour Party's proposals. Insurance agents also constituted a ready-made army of canvassers, the great majority of them in favour of the preservation of the status quo.'[1]

Neither in resources, nor, it may be added, in energy and determination, was the Labour Party a match for the business interests and their public relations experts. What is even more notable, however, is that the Government itself was no match for them either. Its own information services were perpetually attacked in Parliament and in the Press as wasteful, costly and partisan. In actual fact, most Government information was deliberately and carefully 'neutral'; much of it was also couched in language both repellent and partly incomprehensible to the audiences to which it was addressed. This was not what the Opposition disliked: it simply wanted to reduce the Government's information to the public to the barest minimum. And, by October 1948, the Government was sufficiently defensive to appoint an official committee to make recommendations 'as to any direction in which economies may be desirable or the organization (of information services) could be improved'. The Committee reported that it regarded the expenditure as 'too high', and its recommendations for reductions were duly accepted—at a time when business expenditure against the Government was soaring.

From the end of 1949, with an election in the offing, Ministers did go as far as to warn business interests that the expense of their propaganda campaigns might well come to be added to the election expenses of Conservative candidates, how and with what effect was

mobile vans toured the entire United Kingdom, and more than three thousand speeches and lectures were delivered to factory and working men's clubs, youth and university organizations, women's clubs, schools and even groups of soldiers in His Majesty's Forces. Stories or news items concerned with sugar and sponsored by Aims (i.e. Aims of Industry, the public relation firms founded to promote business interests and employed by Tate and Lyle) filled 15,000 column inches in 400 newspapers, approximately £200,000 worth of space' (Rogow, ibid, p. 142). This was by no means all. Besides advertising in more than 100 newspapers adverse comments on the nationalization of sugar by W. A. Bustamente, the head of the Jamaican Industrial Trades Union, the services of Richard Dimbleby were also engaged to record interviews with 'contented Tate and Lyle employees'; and in September 1950, a profit-sharing agreement was negotiated with the National Union of General and Municipal Workers, representing Tate and Lyle employees, which 'served to support the contention that labour relations at Tate and Lyle could hardly be improved by nationalization which, of course, would destroy the profit-sharing scheme' (ibid, pp. 142-3).

[1] Nicholas, op. cit. p. 72.

not made clear. The interests concerned replied that they were not attacking the Labour Party, but the threat of nationalization as such, and that they had an elementary right to defend themselves.[1] Lord Woolton, the Chairman of the Conservative Party, was even more bland. 'Throughout these industrial campaigns,' he said after the date of the election had been announced, 'Conservatives have been completely dissociated from them . . . The only thing I do suggest to these gentlemen is that to avoid confusion they should desist as soon as Parliament is dissolved . . . At the General Election we shall fight nationalization tooth and nail and we want the ring clear for the politicians to fight.'[2] There spoke the voice of the true parliamentary democrat—of course after whatever damage could be done had been done.

The parliamentary battles over the Iron and Steel Bill and the business campaigns against the modest nationalization proposals of *Labour Believes in Britain* had their uses to the Government. For they helped to obscure the fact that, over the wider range of policy, there existed an ever more substantial measure of agreement between the Labour leadership and its Conservative counterpart, and most of all in regard to foreign policy. This bipartisanship was not due to any Conservative shift to a distinctive Labour foreign policy. There was no such policy. Winston Churchill was not vainly boasting when he said, as he often did, that the Government had consistently followed his own recommendations and proposals.[3] With the setting-up of NATO, of which Ernest Bevin was one of the main architects, agreement between the two front benches had become sufficiently explicit to cause serious embarrassment to the Foreign Secretary.[4] With NATO, and for the first time in twentieth-century British

[1] Nicholas, op. cit. p. 73.

[2] ibid, p. 79.

[3] See e.g. his speech in the House of Commons in 1952: 'The policy which I outlined at Fulton five years ago (sic) has since been effectively adopted both by the United States and by the Socialist Party. Two years later by the Brussels Pact and in the following year by the North Atlantic Treaty, the whole substance and purpose of what I said was adopted and enforced by the Socialist Government, and today we all respect the foresight and wise courage of the late Ernest Bevin in helping to bring those great changes about' (H. of C., vol. 496, col. 966. 27th of February, 1952).

[4] 'Though my handling of some events would have been different from his' (i.e. Bevin's), Sir Anthony Eden recalls, 'I was in agreement with the aims of his foreign policy and with most that he did, and we met quite frequently. He would invite me to his room in the House of Commons where we discussed events informally. In Parliament I usually followed him in debate *and I would publicly have agreed with him more, if I had not been anxious to embarrass him less.*' (Sir Anthony Eden, *Memoirs. Full Circle* (London, 1960) p. 5.) My italics.

politics save in time of war, the most important factor in foreign policy was now agreed to be above and beyond 'partisan' debate.

Nor, from the time Labour had taken office in 1945, had there been any serious disagreement over the management of the Colonial Empire. All that *Let Us Face the Future* had said on the subject was that the Labour Party would seek to promote 'the planned progress of our Colonial Dependencies'. Both parties were agreed on the need for 'Colonial Development' and Labour Ministers made no bones about the fact that the purpose of such development was to help alleviate Britain's economic and financial difficulties. As John Strachey, then Minister of Food, put it in 1948, to obtain, 'by one means or another, by hook or by crook, the development of primary production of all sorts', everywhere in and outside the Empire was 'a life and death matter for the economy of this country'; 'we certainly do not want to score any party points,' he also said, 'about which is the best of these forms of development . . . our national position is really too grave to warrant any indulgence'.[1] As to this, the Opposition concurred wholeheartedly, which is not very surprising since, as Conservatives were delighted to point out, the Government's plans were quite in tune with traditional Conservative colonial policy, however different the colonial rhetoric of each party might be.

Over most of the Colonial Empire, there were national leaders who did indulge in particular opinions on the methods of overseas development. The Government's response to the anti-colonial challenge it faced was a mixture of minimal constitutional reforms on the one hand, and of repression on the other, including, as part of the defence of the 'free world' against Communism, the waging of a fierce colonial war in Malaya.

Even at home, there was, after 1947, less and less about the Government's economic policy that was really distinctive. With the rapid dwindling of the American Loan, the Government had faced a major balance of payments crisis.[2] This, to an appreciable extent, was the result of the Government's failure in effective planning and control.[3] Yet, no sooner had the immediate crisis passed than the Government initiated a substantial reduction in physical controls

[1] Brady, op. cit. p. 601; H. of C., vol. 446, cols. 140-1, 20th of January, 1948.
[2] The deficit on the balance of payments in 1947 was £443 million.
[3] In 1953, the Labour Party's Policy Statement, *Challenge to Britain,* claimed that 'of £645 million of private capital which left Britain during 1947-9 only £300 million represented genuine investment in new projects. Some £350 million was "hot" money quitting Britain because its owners disliked the Labour Government's policy of fair shares or were engaged in currency speculation' (*Challenge to Britain,* 1953, p. 6).

and moved rapidly from 'democratic planning' to an even more democratic reliance upon appeals, particularly to wage earners, to produce more without seeking to earn more. In 1948, the policy of 'restraint' both on wage claims and dividend payments had found official expression in the Government's *Statement on Personal Incomes, Costs and Prices*. From then onwards, the Government was mainly concerned to preach 'austerity' to its supporters, who might have responded with greater enthusiasm had austerity been less obviously reserved for wage earners. The 'wage freeze' had been accepted by both the T.U.C. and the Labour Party Conferences in 1948.[1] In 1949, the Government was again caught in a financial crisis and devalued the pound. In September 1950, the policy of wage restraint was rejected by the T.U.C. Conference, against the advice of the General Council.[2] By then, the Government, returned in February with a majority of six, had given up the pretence that it was in control of economic policy. As *The Economist* wrote, the *Economic Survey* for 1950 was a 'humble document, meek almost to the point of being meaningless. There is nothing here of the notions of "democratic economic planning" as proclaimed in earlier *Surveys*, which presented a working pattern for the year's economic effort and left all men of good will to work for it. Indeed, the perplexing thing about the *Survey* for 1950 is its lack of plan.'[3]

It was not only the Government which was in retreat in the latter part of its period of office. The Labour Left was too. On the evidence of its first years of office, the Government would have retreated in any case. What above all caused the retreat of the Labour Left was the exacerbation of the Cold War, which, as *Keeping Left*, published in January 1950, made clear, greatly affected its attitude to a policy of alignment with the United States. The Labour Left only accepted that alignment with reluctance, with reservations, with the hope that the Labour Government would use its membership of the alliance to 'restrain' its American partners, and with the even greater hope that the time would soon arrive when Britain would become the leader of a 'third force' of democratic socialism. But it accepted the alliance all the same, and found much in Russian foreign policy which made any general challenge to Government policy much more difficult to sustain.

[1] At the 1948 Labour Party Conference, a resolution welcoming the Government's 'initiative' was moved by Arthur Deakin and seconded by C. A. R. Crosland, and was carried after a prolonged debate. (See Labour Party Annual Conference Report, 1948, pp. 141 ff.)
[2] T.U.C. Annual Conference Report, 1950, p. 473. The voting was 3,949,000 to 3,727,000.
[3] *The Economist*, 1st of April, 1950.

Root and branch opposition had in any case become a risky enterprise, particularly for the Labour parliamentarians. For the Cold War, and the anti-Communist climate it engendered, exposed the Government's critics to the now dread charge of 'fellow-travelling', and to threats of punishment commensurate with the offence.

In this respect, the turning-point in the taming of the Government's parliamentary critics was the leadership's reaction to the telegram of good wishes for success in the Italian General Election which a number of M.P.s sent, in April 1948, to what the Parliamentary Report of that year called the 'Communist-dominated Nenni-Socialists'.[1] Twenty-one of the signatories were summoned by the Executive to undertake individually that they would cease 'acting as a group in organized opposition to Party policy', failing which they would be expelled from the Party. The assurances were given. This episode, and the subsequent expulsion from the Labour Party of a few M.P.s, notably Konni Zilliacus,[2] were sufficient to discourage the expression of dissent on the fundamentals, as distinct from the specific applications, of the Government's foreign policy.

Even on home policy, the Labour Left's message was now uncertain. By 1950, there were many who found plausible the view that first attention should now be given to something like the consolidation of what had been achieved in the previous years. *Labour Believes in Britain* would have raised greater opposition had this not been the case. In 1947, the authors of *Keep Left* had insisted that Labour would have to proceed with more measures of large-scale nationalization. In 1950, *Keeping Left* was 'less concerned about who owns a factory and more about who manages it and how, and whether it is working according to socialist plans . . . the next steps are not so obvious or so simple'. Indeed, *Keeping Left* now expressed the belief that *Labour Believes in Britain*, 'with its new proposal of flexible, multi-purpose competitive public enterprise, opens up a whole new field for national ownership'. This of course entirely missed the drift of the Government's proposals; and the insistence of the authors of *Keeping Left* that they still believed in an extension of public ownership, coupled with appeals

[1] Labour Party Annual Conference Report, 1948, p. 17.
[2] For a full account of the episode, see K. Zilliacus, *Why I was Expelled* (London, 1949). His case, and that of another expellee, L. J. Solley, were debated at the 1949 Annual Conference and the Executive's action endorsed by 4,721,000 votes to 714,000 (Labour Party Annual Conference Report, 1949, p. 127). Subsequently, Zilliacus's constituency party, Gateshead, was 'reformed' and adopted a candidate of which the National Executive approved. Zilliacus stood as an Independent Labour Candidate in the Election of 1950 and was badly defeated.

to the Government to show greater boldness and imagination, was hardly likely to worry the consolidators.

It is very unlikely that, in July 1945, any Labour activist would have thought it possible for the next General Election to be called 'demure', as Winston Churchill called the General Election of February 1950. Any such Labour activist would have argued, in 1945, that, on the contrary, this election would be the most fiercely contested ever, since the Government, having by then negotiated the outworks of British capitalism, would be asking the electors to return it to power so that it might begin the investment of the citadel. No doubt, he would also have said, the leaders would need to be kept up to the mark by the Left; but he would have been confident that, under pressure, there would be further and more significant advances towards the socialist society.

The fatal flaw in the argument was the assumption that the differences between the activist and most of his leaders were differences of degree when they were in fact differences in kind. For the activist saw the Welfare State and the nationalization measures of 1945-8 as the beginning of the social revolution to which he believed the Labour Party was dedicated; while his leaders took these achievements to *be* the social revolution. Of course, they would readily agree that there was still much to be done to consolidate that social revolution. But, as far as they were concerned, the bigger part of the task had, by 1950, been completed.[1] And they therefore were genuinely impatient with the argument that there remained a citadel to be conquered. They believed it to be already occupied. It is this, rather than economic difficulties, or the international situation, which explains why Labour's election programme was so barren and the campaign 'demure'.[2]

[1] 'Had Parliament re-assembled after the Christmas recess,' Mr. Nicholas notes, 'there would certainly have been difficulty in devising profitable employment for it' (op. cit. p. 76). Note however that in 1960, Hugh Gaitskell claimed that 'even if we were to be elected on a wholesale nationalization programme we could never carry it out in one Parliament. Most of us who were in the 1945-50 Parliament know that we just about had as much as we could conceivably digest in those five years' (Labour Party Annual Conference Report, 1960, p. 221).

[2] How demure is perhaps best suggested by the fact that, for the first time in British political history, as Mr. Nicholas notes, the campaign began with a 'service of prayer and dedication before the General Election' at St. Paul's Cathedral, attended by the leaders of the Conservative, Labour and Liberal parties, with their wives and many of their colleagues. Similar services were held in a number of cities outside London. In his sermon, the Archbishop of Canterbury reminded his audience that 'it is the proper business of politicians in a General Election to urge their views upon the people with confidence, with

307

Since it had few positive proposals to make, and was not very sure about those it had, particularly in regard to nationalization,[1] the Labour Party was almost exclusively concerned to stress how much the Government had achieved since 1945, and how much these achievements, and particularly full employment, would be threatened if the Tories were returned. Conversely, the Conservatives dwelt on the miseries and shortages attendant, as they would have it, upon 'socialism', and stressed their own devotion to welfare and full employment—and also quoted authoritative Labour spokesmen to suggest that, without American aid, there would have been mass unemployment in Britain. One of the main items in this titanic confrontation between the two parties was a broad Conservative hint that the abolition of petrol rationing might well follow the return of a Conservative Government, which Labour spokesmen denounced as a cheap bribe to the electorate.[2]

The two parties would have found it even more difficult to find points of substantial disagreement over foreign affairs. And, over relations with Russia, there was an ironical demonstration of how the wheel had come full circle since 1945 in Labour's reaction to Churchill's cautious suggestion (coupled with a complaint that Britain did not yet have her own atomic bomb) of 'another talk with Soviet Russia upon the highest level'; 'the idea', said Churchill, 'appeals to me of a supreme effort to bridge the gulf between the two worlds, so that each can live their life, if not in friendship, at least without the hatreds and manoeuvres of the cold war'.[3] This was instantly dismissed by Labour Ministers as an election stunt. If it was, it is perhaps a pity that they had not thought of it themselves. Instead, Ernest Bevin was content to recapitulate his difficulties in negotiating with the Russians, and Herbert Morrison to note that 'these things would need careful preparation between

vigour, even with passion, out of the sincerity of their own honest thinking and convictions, and yet never to forget that God is greater than us all in truth, in righteousness, in purpose and in love'. He then went on, Mr. Nicholas writes, 'to set the amicable conflict of the election in the shadow of the deeper world conflict of Christianity and materialism', and to exhort the Party leaders to 'be ready to learn from one another even in opposing one another' (op. cit. p. 90).

[1] See *Let Us Win Through Together*, the Labour Party's Election Manifesto.
[2] One Labour spokesman, however, and he no less than Hugh Gaitskell, the Minister of Fuel and Power, did not disdain to engage in competition with the Conservatives on this issue. He, too, held out hopes that 'if, as I hope, it (the dollar position) improves steadily, then the prospects are not bad. At this very moment discussions are going on in Washington with the Americans to see if we can find some way of getting extra petrol without spending dollars.' (ibid, p. 96.)
[3] ibid, p. 103.

us and the Soviet Union', that 'the United States would be involved', and that 'it could cause unnecessary friction if we suddenly took the issue out of the hands of the United Nations, for delicate discussions are taking place'.[1]

Defensive and hesitant though Labour was throughout the campaign, its achievements were sufficient for it to receive well over 13 million votes as compared with nearly 12 million in 1945, on a poll of nearly 84 per cent. However, the Conservatives, with a poll of 12.5 million votes, did substantially better than in 1945; their percentage of the votes cast had risen from 39.8 per cent. to 43.5 per cent.; that of Labour had declined from 48.3 per cent. to 46.1 per cent.[2] What made the election results appear much more dramatic than they were was the virtual disappearance of Labour's parliamentary majority. With 315 seats, Labour had an overall majority of six.[3]

Labour's opponents immediately chose to interpret the result as a decisive rejection by 'the electorate' of nationalization, particularly of the nationalization of steel. Nor had Labour's leaders any great wish to rebut the interpretation. After all, they themselves, while very willing to defend *past* measures of nationalization, had appeared almost apologetic about future ones. Indeed, such an interpretation had its use to the consolidators: for it made it appear that it was 'the electorate', rather than the leadership, which was satiated with reform.

In the same sense, Labour's tiny majority usefully served to hide

---

[1] Nicholas, op. cit. p. 105. Churchill's reply to Labour accusations that he was engaged in stunt or soapbox diplomacy included questions which might have been thought more natural for a Labour Prime Minister or a Labour Foreign Secretary. 'Why should it be wrong,' he asked, 'for the British nation to think about these supreme questions of life and death, perhaps for the whole world, at a time when there is a General Election? Is that not the one time of all others when they should think about them? What a reflection it would be upon our national dignity and moral elevation, and indeed upon the whole status of British democracy, if at this time of choice, this turning point in world history, we found nothing to talk about but material issues and nice calculations about personal gain or loss . . .

'The only time when the people really have a chance to influence and, in fact, decide events is at a General Election. Why should they be restricted to the vote catching or vote snatching game? Why should they be told that it is a "stunt" or "soap-box" diplomacy to speak to them of the great world issues upon which our survival and salvation may well depend?' (ibid, p. 105).

[2] The Liberals polled over 2.5 million votes, a little more than in 1945, and the Communists received 91,684 votes, a little less. But they also lost their two Members of Parliament.

[3] The Conservatives came back with 298 members, the Liberals with nine; the Irish Nationalists had two.

the fact that, on the evidence of the two previous years, the Government would have been seriously embarrassed with a larger one. For it would then have had to justify itself as a radical, reforming administration. And neither its programme, nor its mood,[1] would have made this at all easy.

4. FROM CONSOLIDATION TO DEFEAT

What a Government returned to office with a majority of six could do to improve its chances of obtaining a more satisfactory result at the next election is, in the present context, a rather academic question. *This* Government, exhausted politically and ideologically long before it entered its second term, could only endure, to no distinctive purpose, and, by the manner of its endurance, improve the chances of its opponents.

The first casualty of the election was the nationalization proposals of *Let Us Win through Together*. The King's Speech of the first session of the new Parliament in March 1950 spoke tentatively of the possibility of legislation affecting water supplies but, for the rest, victory was implicitly conceded to the anti-nationalizers. Still, the Government's legislative programme did include such proposals as the breaking-up of roads by public-utility undertakings, changes in the constitution of the General Medical Council and the Central Midwives Board, and the placing of cattle grids along certain highways.[2]

On the other hand, the Government had inherited one embarrassing legacy from its previous term of office, namely the nationalization of iron and steel, the vesting date for which was the 15th of February, 1951. In the intervening year, an unequal battle was fought out between a demoralized Government and steel

---

[1] A good illustration of that mood is Herbert Morrison's complaint after the election that 'over the months past' the Conservatives had 'done their very best to make this an election of an acute class character'. (Nicholas, op. cit. p. 294.)

[2] In the following session of Parliament, 'the most important passages of the Speech', the Parliamentary Report to the 1951 Annual Conference of the Party grotesquely noted, 'were the measures to put on a permanent basis the controls which in the past have been carried by the Annual Supplies and Services Act; the intention of the Government to take over the privately owned share capital of the Beet Sugar Corporation; the introduction of a Bill on leaseholds which would protect those householders and shopkeepers whose leases have lately fallen in, or are due to expire shortly, from eviction and allowing them to continue in occupation at existing ground rents; and a Bill to amend the Restoration of Pre-war Trade Practices Act, 1942' (Labour Party Annual Conference Report, 1951, p. 61).

interests (aided by the Conservative Opposition) ever more confident that nationalization would prove a temporary and easily reversible measure,[1] but also determined that the take-over should be as difficult as possible. In the House of Commons on the 19th of September, 1950, G. R. Strauss, the Minister of Supply, related how, having invited the spokesmen of the steel interests to submit the names of 'experienced men who would be acceptable to their fellow industrialists for inclusion in the Corporation', the Executive Committee of the Iron and Steel Federation refused 'on the grounds that in their opinion the Government had no mandate to carry out the Iron and Steel Act'. 'They warned me at the same time,' the Minister went on, 'that the Corporation, deprived of such people, would be unable successfully to plan the steel industry. Further, I was informed that every effort would be made to dissuade any important man I might approach from serving on the Corporation. . . . In short, these people decided to threaten, and indeed they did carry out, a political strike.' There was in fact, in the Minister's words, a 'gentleman's agreement throughout firms in the industry not to serve on the Corporation', and this, he complained, 'is concerted action by a number of people for the specific purpose of sabotaging an Act of Parliament'.[2]

Save for the nationalization of iron and steel from which it could not retreat, the Government's main ambition was to spin out an invalid existence until some such time as its electoral prospects might, somehow, improve. But the rapid worsening of the international situation after the outbreak of the Korean conflict in June 1950 shattered its hopes of a quiet life. From then until its demise in October 1951, it was involved in a succession of crises, its responses to which rapidly accelerated its decline.

As for the Labour Left, the Korean war was a further blow to its morale. There was no disposition to challenge the Government's support for American intervention in Korea, or to criticize Britain's own contribution to what the Labour Left generally agreed to regard as an exercise in collective security, to which it now felt committed. However, there were grave fears, by no means confined to the Left, that, as a result of American policy, the Korean 'police action' might come to involve war with China, which in turn might precipitate a world war;[3] and there was also, on the Labour Left,

---

[1] 'A number of companies such as Vickers and Cammell Laird, whose steel business had been nationalized, revealed that the compensation received had been placed in separate funds which would be used for the repurchase of steel affiliates in the event of a Conservative victory.' (Rogow, op. cit. p. 169.)
[2] H. of C., vol. 478, cols. 1834-5.
[3] See Leon D. Epstein, *Britain—Uneasy Ally* (London, 1954) pp. 214 ff. The Government, it will be recalled, had recognized the Communist regime

much unease, which antedated the Korean war, but was much increased by it, at what was regarded as the British Government's failure to do more by way of restraining its American ally.

It is worth noting in how subdued a form this unease was expressed at the Labour Party Annual Conference in October 1950, where a resolution expressed 'alarm at the increasing danger of war', but was content to urge the Government to 'strive to end the differences between the five great powers, to which end a Conference should be called immediately', to renew its efforts 'to create friendly relations with the U.S.S.R.', and to pursue a number of other equally worthy aims.[1] Supporters of the resolution insisted that it contained nothing to which the Government or the National Executive could object. However, the Executive and Ernest Bevin did object, and the resolution was defeated, though 881,000 votes were cast for it (against 4,861,000).

Unease and apprehension grew to much vaster proportions with General MacArthur's drive to the Chinese border and with the entry of Chinese troops into the Korean conflict in November.[2] With President Truman's statement at a Press conference that the use of the atomic bomb was under consideration, the need for 'restraint' on the United States appeared greater than ever before, and brought Attlee to Washington at the beginning of December. From this visit grew the legend that it was the Prime Minister's intervention which prevented the use of the atomic bomb against China. What was not a legend, however, was the Government's commitment, in May and September 1951, to the possibility of military action against China.[3]

in China in January 1950. For the reasons which impelled it to recognition, see Ernest Bevin's speech in the House of Commons on the 24th of May, 1950 (H. of C. vol. 475, cols. 2082 ff.).

[1] Such as support for the outlawing of the atomic bomb and the limitation of armaments through the United Nations organization, further action to secure the representation of Communist China on the Security Council, and 'the end of dollar dependence by the year 1952' (Labour Party Annual Conference Report, 1950, p. 141).

[2] Note in this connection the 'Peace with China' campaign, support for which extended well beyond the Labour Left.

[3] See Winston Churchill's speech in the House of Commons on the 26th of February, 1952: '. . . In May of last year, before the truce negotiations began . . . the late Foreign Secretary (i.e. Herbert Morrison) replied to an inquiry (by the United States) that His Majesty's Government had decided that in the event of heavy air attacks from bases in China upon United Nations forces in Korea they would associate themselves with action not confined to Korea' (H. of C. vol. 496, col. 969); and, in the course of the same speech: 'In September last year the Americans proposed that in the event of a breakdown of the armistice talks and the resumption of large-scale fighting in Korea, certain action should be taken of a more limited character . . . Whereas in May the right of prior consultation had been required by the

It is equally worth noting, particularly in the light of later developments, how little Labour criticism there was of the Government's decision, announced in September 1950, to increase expenditure on rearmament to a total of £3,600,000,000 for the years 1951-4. Nor, despite acute misgivings on the Labour Left, was there any challenge to the upward revision of that figure in January 1951, under intense American pressure, to a total of £4,700,000,000. Indeed, Aneurin Bevan, speaking for the Government in February against a Conservative motion of no confidence, defended the new programme, and barely qualified his defence with ambiguous warnings of the dangers of too rapid a rate of rearmament. Two months later, however, the Budget was to lead to Bevan's resignation and thus provide the Labour Left with the leader it had lacked since 1945.

The Budget which Hugh Gaitskell (who had succeeded Cripps as Chancellor of the Exchequer the previous October) introduced on the 10th of April, 1951, was the logical consequence, not only of the rearmament programme, but even more of the Government's long standing policy of 'consolidation'. For the Government, having agreed to an enormous rearmament burden, also had to find ways of footing the bill. Its problem was in some ways similar to that which had confronted the Government of Ramsay MacDonald in 1931. And, like Philip Snowden before him, the Chancellor found it much easier to place the major share of the burden on the poor than on the rich. Snowden's economies on unemployment benefits had no relevance to the economic problem he faced; nor had Hugh Gaitskell's economies of £25 million on the National Health Service. Within a few months, Britain was again in the throes of a major balance of payments crisis, which the Government had entirely failed to foresee.[1] As in 1931, it was the Conservatives who found most cause to rejoice in the Budget. 'Mr Gaitskell,' the *Daily Express* wrote, 'introduces a Tory Budget. He puts a charge of 50 per cent. on teeth and spectacles. That is what the Tories would have done.

---

late Government in the specific instance, before our consent could be assumed, in the more limited proposals of September the Socialist Government did not insist upon this right' (ibid, col. 973). Though former Labour Ministers deeply objected to these revelations, nothing they said suggested that the revelations were inaccurate.

[1] In July 1951, the Chancellor told the House of Commons that the deterioration in the third quarter of the year was 'largely on account of seasonal factors' and that 'so far as I can see at present the fourth quarter's results will not be so unfavourable, though again I think it unlikely they will show a surplus' (Rogow, op. cit. p. 46). In the last three months of the year, the gold and dollar reserves fell by 934 million dollars (ibid, p. 46). This was democratic planning with a vengeance.

Now the job is done for them.' *The Times* put the same point more elegantly: 'Mr Gaitskell,' it said, 'seemed to have resisted most of the temptations which beset a Socialist Chancellor of the Exchequer.'[1]

For the meagre consolation of his own side, the Chancellor did budget for an increase of 4s. a week in the pension of some categories of old age pensioners; and a casual compliment was also paid in the Budget to the old notion of 'equality of sacrifice' in the form of a higher tax on distributed profits. The City's embarrassing welcome for the Budget did not suggest that the burden would prove very great.

Initially, Bevan's objections to the Budget had been confined to the imposition of charges on Health Service patients. Had this been all, some compromise would no doubt have been found. But the Budget served to crystallize an accumulation of discontents over the general drift of the Government's policy.[2] At the time, the Government's precarious majority prevented discontent from erupting into open rebellion. Though Bevan resigned from the Government (as did Harold Wilson and John Freeman), there was no challenge to it. As Bevan and three of his supporters on the National Executive (i.e. Barbara Castle, Tom Driberg and Ian Mikardo) wrote[3] after his resignation, 'we are determined to do nothing that may impair this unity (of the Party), weaken the position of the Government in the House of Commons, or handicap the Prime Minister's exercise of his initiative in determining the date of the General Election'; even so, they added, 'we reserve our democratic right to debate freely issues of Government policy'.[4]

[1] Both quotations from *Tribune*, 20th of April, 1951.

[2] Of that drift, a small but significant example was the Government's decision, in September 1950, to summons ten of 1,700 gas maintenance workers on strike, under the Conspiracy and Protection of Property Act of 1875 and the emergency powers provided in the Conditions of Employment and National Arbitration Order 1305. On the 5th of October, the ten strikers were duly sentenced to one month's imprisonment and on the same day their fellow strikers agreed to return to work; on appeal, the sentence was reduced to fines of £50. Despite the bitter feelings the prosecution aroused in the trade union movement, another prosecution under Order 1305, this time of seven dock members of the Transport and General Workers' Union, was initiated in February 1951. However, the jury disagreed and the prosecution was withdrawn. In August, the Order was revoked. (See Allen, op. cit. pp. 269-70.)

[3] In a letter to the Secretary of the Party complaining of a Statement the National Executive had issued after the resignations expressing support for the Government and the Budget, and calling on all members of the Party to stand firmly behind the Government. The signatories of the letter objected to the statement on the ground that, in issuing it, the National Executive had 'exceeded its proper function'. (Labour Party Annual Conference Report, 1951, p. 5.)

[4] ibid, p. 5.

However, what debate there was[1] was cut short by the Prime Minister's announcement on the 19th of September that there would be a General Election on the 25th of October.

Labour's Election Manifesto, drafted by a committee consisting of Hugh Dalton, Aneurin Bevan, Sam Watson and Morgan Phillips, and then approved by the National Executive, was an even woollier document than its immediate predecessor. This time, there was no specific pledge on nationalization. 'We shall,' said the document 'take over concerns which fail the nation and start new public enterprises wherever this will serve the national interest . . . we shall establish Development Councils, by compulsion if necessary, wherever this will help industrial efficiency. . . . We shall associate the workers more closely with the administration of public industries and services.'

Nor, for that matter, was there any specific pledge on anything else. In the main, the Manifesto was content to stress Labour's past achievements, notably the maintenance of full employment, and to contrast these achievements with the Tories' dark pre-war record.[2]

Much of the document's emphasis, however, fell, not surprisingly in the light of the world situation, on the issue of peace. Though it insisted that Britain 'must play her full part in the strengthening of collective defence', peace, it also said, 'cannot be preserved by arms alone. . . . As our armed strength grows, more attention must be given to the under-developed regions of the world'. Only a Labour Government would do this: 'the Tory still thinks in terms of Victorian imperialism and colonial exploitation'.

This last point was highly topical in the light of Britain's dispute with Persia over the nationalization of the Anglo-Iranian Oil Company. But in the light of the Government's policies in that dispute, it was a somewhat disingenuous point for the Labour leaders to make.

It was just before the General Election that the conflict over Persian oil had entered its most acute phase. For years past, the British Government had waged a tenacious battle against concessions to Persian demands for a greater share in the profits of the Anglo-Iranian Oil Company. It was only after the Majlis voted to nationalize the oil fields on the 15th of March, 1951, that the Company made an offer of a fifty-fifty share of the profits to the Iranian Government. The offer came too late to stem the tide of Persian

[1] See, e.g. the anonymous *Tribune* pamphlet, with a Foreword by Aneurin Bevan, Harold Wilson and John Freeman, entitled *One Way Only*, published in June 1951.
[2] For full text, see Labour Party Annual Conference Report, 1951, pp. 209-211.

nationalism and the assumption of the Premiership by Dr Mossadegh at the end of April directly posed the threat of the Company's eviction from Persia.

There followed a summer of abortive negotiations, of appeals to the International Court of Justice and to the Security Council, of assertions that Britain would not leave Abadan, of economic pressure, and of displays of naval strength in the Persian Gulf. Nothing of all this was of any avail. On the 3rd of October, just before the opening of the electoral campaign, Abadan was finally evacuated.[1]

The day before, Winston Churchill had fiercely attacked the Government. The decision to evacuate, he said, 'convicts Mr Attlee and the Lord Chancellor of breaking the solemn undertaking they gave to Parliament . . . in August. . . . I do not remember any case where public men have broken their word so abruptly and without any attempt at explanation'.[2]

These and similar Conservative accusations provided Labour with one of its major electoral themes—the danger of war if a Conservative Government was returned. Speaking to the Annual Conference of the Labour Party on the 3rd of October, Herbert Morrison directly challenged Churchill to say whether Britain should have gone to war with Persia or not. 'I do not accuse the average Conservative of being a warmonger, of thirsting for the shedding of blood, or of wishing to be involved needlessly in a world war. I do not say that, and I advise you not to say that, because it would not be fair, and it would not be true. But it is their temperament; it is the background of their mental outlook—the old imperialist outlook. It is the semi-hysteria of the bulk of those Tory backbenchers that really alarms one as to what a Tory Government would do if a Tory Government were put in. Therefore if the country wants peace it had better vote for the people who can most surely be relied upon to preserve peace and, if I may say so, are the most competent to frame principles and proposals for the peace and well-being of the world.'[3]

Yet, the explanation of the Government's refusal to resort to armed intervention in Persia cannot be made to rest simply on its dedication to peaceful settlements. No doubt, a Labour Government would be less inclined than a Conservative one to contemplate armed intervention and would have found it much more difficult to persuade its backbenchers to support a military venture against Persia. But

---

[1] For a detailed account of the dispute, see A. W. Ford, *The Anglo-Iranian Oil Dispute of 1951-1952* (Berkeley and Los Angeles, 1954).

[2] D. E. Butler, *The British General Election of 1951* (London, 1952) p. 113.

[3] Labour Party Annual Conference Report, 1951, p. 129.

there were other factors. One of them was intense American pressure (by no means disinterested) against such a venture. Another was the danger of Soviet intervention. But there was also the fact that the Government was advised that the necessary resources for such a venture were not available. And Lord Morrison himself has recently revealed that, had the resources been available, a resort to force would have been by no means excluded.[1]

At the time, however, Labour was able to argue that the Government's handling of the Persian dispute, as of its Egyptian difficulties,[2] was a token, not of weakness, but of its abhorrence of force, and to charge its opponents with, at the least, powerful propensities to its use. This 'warmongering' theme, though partially qualified by most Labour speakers,[3] and epitomized by the *Daily Mirror's* headline on Election Day, *Whose Finger on the Trigger?*[4] undoubtedly placed the Conservatives on the defensive, perhaps for the first time in any General Election in this century; in combination with Labour's warnings of the threats to full employment and the Welfare State which a Conservative victory were said to entail, it gave to Labour's electoral campaign a dynamic which its electoral programme alone could hardly have supplied. Without this, Labour might have fared much worse. As it is, Labour achieved its highest poll ever, with 13,948,605 votes, or 48.8 per cent. of the total votes cast, while the Conservatives obtained 13,717,538 (48 per cent.) It was not enough, however, to prevent Labour's loss of twenty-one seats to the Conservatives and the latter's return to office. In any case the Government would have found another lease of life a burden rather than a challenge. By then, it had long fulfilled its limited purposes.

[1] 'The crux of the matter,' Morrison writes, 'was that if military action was to be politically effective it should be quick . . . My own view was that there was much to be said in favour of sharp and forceful action. The Cabinet was, however, left in little doubt that mounting an effective force would take a lot of time and might therefore be a failure. In the end, we had to abandon any military project, save that we should have used force if British nationals had been attacked.' (Morrison, op. cit. p. 281.) For further confirmation of the Cabinet's attitude, see E. Shinwell, The Anatomy of Leadership—III, *Sunday Times,* 25th of September, 1960.

[2] On the 8th of October, Egypt abrogated the Anglo-Egyptian Treaty of 1936 governing the maintenance of British military installations in the Canal Zone. Again, Morrison recalls, 'it could have been that another surrender to a *minor and irresponsible Power* was imminent. I went back to Downing Street and summoned officials of the Foreign Office. I strongly advocated a stiff line with Egypt and Attlee agreed' (op. cit. p. 282). My italics.

[3] See Butler, op. cit. pp. 118-28.

[4] Churchill issued a writ for libel against the *Daily Mirror*. This was settled out of court seven months later with an apology by the newspaper.

CHAPTER X

THE SICKNESS OF LABOURISM

—◦❦◦—

1. FROM DEFEAT TO PARALYSIS

The Labour Party accepted its loss of office in 1951 with a certain complacency. This was partly due to a feeling that so much had been accomplished since 1945 that a breathing space had become natural and inevitable. But it was also the product of two basic assumptions, then quite common in the Labour Party. The first of these was that opposition would restore its energies and that it would therefore soon be ready for another period of office. The second assumption was that the Conservative Government would provide so disastrous a contrast to its predecessor that a majority of the electorate would wish to use the first available opportunity to return Labour to power with a comfortable parliamentary lead. Both assumptions were false.

The belief that Labour in opposition would soon regain its vitality not only failed to take into account Labour's steady degeneration of purpose in its last years of office, but also the fact that those who had been mainly responsible for that degeneration remained in secure control of the Labour Party after it had lost office. Even more important, it failed to take into account the fact that these men were determined, after 1951, that the course they had traced for the Labour Party in the previous years should not be reversed, or substantially modified.

This was not because they were tired, or old, or stupid. They had adopted policies of consolidation at home and bipartisanship abroad because they were convinced that these policies were necessary and right, and they continued to believe in them after they left office. Unfortunately for the Labour Party, these policies made impossible vigorous opposition to the Government and the fashioning of a new and distinctive programme.

This, from a purely electoral point of view, might have mattered less had Labour's second assumption been true—had the Conservatives, that is to say, tried to undo all or most of Labour's achievements in the preceding years. But the belief that the Conservatives would do this was a bad misreading of the impact which the experience of war, the defeat of 1945, and the years of Labour rule had had upon them. By 1951, the Conservatives had come to be well aware that the *minimal* expectations of the larger part of the electorate now included regular employment and welfare services. Nor in any case was there any reason why they should seek to deny these expectations, since the denial, and the undoing of Labour's achievements, including most of Labour's nationalization measures, were in no way essential to their purposes.

Hence the Conservatives' refusal to act according to Labour's expectations. Hence also the problem for the Labour Party of maintaining, in concrete policy terms, a clear distance between itself and its political opponents. Given the political philosophy of Labour's leaders, this was (and remained throughout the fifties) an insoluble problem : for these leaders would not venture into territory where they stood no danger of being followed by their opponents, and their opponents would not beat a dramatic retreat from the territory which the Labour leaders felt to be their own.

Unlike the Labour leaders, the Labour Left did not find the problem insoluble. The solution, it said, lay in the adoption by the Labour Party of a new radical programme, with extensive proposals for further nationalization well to the forefront; and in an attempt to reverse at least some of the foreign and defence policies pursued by the Labour Government since 1945. Even before Labour had lost office, there had been increasing dissatisfaction on the Left with these policies. The return to opposition, coupled with the departure from the scene of two powerful figures, Ernest Bevin and Stafford Cripps, now revived, in a more acute form, the conflict between Right and Left which office had helped to contain.

For a long time after 1951, it seemed that the demands of the Left were particular to the parliamentarians associated with Aneurin Bevan, and to the constituency activitists who supported them. But there is very little about Labour in the fifties which is more important than the fact that the opposition to the leadership's policies, at home and abroad, was at least as persistent in the trade unions as in the constituency parties.[1] Throughout the Bevanite controversies in the first years of the fifties. the Bevanites themselves rightly claimed that they not only spoke for the constituency activists, but for a large number of trade unionists as well.[2] Nevertheless, the conflict

[1] For a detailed analysis of the strength of trade union opposition to official policies from 1945 through the fifties, see M. Harrison, *Trade Unions and the Labour Party since 1945* (London, 1960) passim.
[2] See, e.g. Bevan: 'Do not let the union leaders think that they alone speak for their members. We speak for them as much as they do' (29th of September, 1954, in Harrison, ibid, p. 129).

between Right and Left continued to be defined as one between the 'wild men' of the constituency parties and their parliamentary leaders on the one hand, and 'sober' trade unionists on the other.

There were a number of reasons for the persistence of this definition. It was the constituency parties which, from 1952 onwards, swept Bevanite candidates on to the National Executive Committee of the Labour Party. Secondly, the fiercest opposition to Bevan and to the Left generally came from the leaders of some of the largest unions who turned themselves into a knightly order for the defence of the political leadership of the Labour Party and, with the help of the block vote, ensured the regular defeat of the Left at T.U.C. and Labour Party Conferences. Their victories served to obscure the dimensions of the pressure of the trade union left for more radical policies. In fact, the orthodox trade union leaders never spoke for the whole trade union movement, just as there was always a substantial number of constituency parties who faithfully supported the Labour leadership against its critics on the Left.

In home affairs, the conflict in the Labour movement between Right and Left was soon focused on nationalization. As early as 1952, a resolution was moved at the T.U.C. which called upon the General Council to formulate proposals for 'the extension of social ownership to other industries and services, particularly those now subject to monopoly control', and for 'the democratization of the nationalized industries and services' so as to make possible 'the ultimate realization of full industrial democracy'.[1] The resolution was carried, against the wishes of the General Council, by 4,532,000 votes to 3,210,000.[2]

At the 1952 Labour Party Conference a month later, the National Executive was faced with a similar demand that it should 'draw up a list of the key and major industries to be taken into public ownership'.[3] Though the delegates were strongly warned against rashness by such speakers as Emmanuel Shinwell, Herbert Morrison, George Brown and Hugh Gaitskell, the Executive did not, after the vote at the T.U.C., offer outright opposition to the resolution, which was carried without a vote.[4]

However, neither the General Council nor the National Executive had any intention of acting in the spirit of the respective resolutions with which they were saddled. Indeed, the manner in which both bodies dealt with the instructions they had received provided a good illustration of the fact that no such instructions, however

[1] T.U.C. Annual Conference Report, 1952, p. 438.
[2] ibid, p. 448.
[3] Labour Party Annual Conference Report, 1952, p. 91.
[4] ibid, p. 112.

imperative, could bind a leadership firmly determined to evade them. On this issue, both the General Council and the National Executive had plenty of room in which to manoeuvre, and to interpret their mandate in such a way as to nullify the expressed will of their Conferences.

The *Interim Report on Public Ownership*[1] which the General Council presented to the T.U.C. in 1953 did not express opposition to further nationalization. On the contrary, it said that there was a 'clear case' for the complete public ownership of the water supply industry. Nor was there anything in the Report, as Sir Tom Williamson put it, 'which opposes or obstructs the approach to public ownership'.[2] All that the General Council asked was that the subject should be given the most careful reflection and study. Nothing, on the face of it, could have sounded more reasonable—indeed would have been more reasonable, had the plea for further study been inspired by a genuine wish to lay plans for a future nationalization programme of the kind envisaged in the 1952 T.U.C. resolution. But the majority of members of the General Council were not eager seekers for knowledge, the better to nationalize. They were opponents of further nationalization, who found it necessary to conceal their opposition behind pleas for thinking and planning.[3] And, at the 1953 Conference, they won the day. A motion for the reference back of the Report was defeated, though no less than 2,640,000 votes were cast in favour of the motion.[4]

The tactic of the General Council was also the tactic of the National Executive Committee of the Labour Party. The programme which it presented to the 1953 Annual Conference of the Party (*Challenge to Britain*)[5] also displayed the passionate concern of its authors for further knowledge and research. It is unlikely that any document issued by any political party has ever proposed the setting up of as many committees of investigation and research as did *Challenge to Britain*; nor has any Party ever promised to set up more such committees if it was returned to office.

The document, James Griffiths, speaking for the Executive, told the delegates, reaffirmed 'that the general case for public ownership is overwhelming and remains a major objective and purpose of this

---

[1] For text, see T.U.C. Annual Conference Report, 1953, Appendix A, pp. 475-525.

[2] ibid, p. 390.

[3] *The Economist's* accurate comment was that 'the ·leaders of the T.U.C., as they express themselves in the General Council's report, could hardly go further in opposing nationalisation.' ('The Unions and Socialism', 5th of September, 1953.)

[4] T.U.C. Annual Conference Report, 1953, p. 393.

[5] For text, see Labour Party Annual Conference Report, 1953, pp. 61-80.

great movement'. But when it came to concrete proposals, the Executive was rather less bold. A future Labour Government, it said, would restore to public ownership the steel industry, then in process of denationalization by the Conservatives; as for road transport, which the Government was also returning to private enterprise, Labour would take back into public ownership 'such road haulage units as are needed to provide a co-ordinated transport system'. Water supply would be nationalized; *where necessary,* the next Labour Government would take particular sections of the engineering industry into public ownership; it would also acquire, in the public interest, a number of the key machine tool firms; in regard to the aircraft industry, it would 'take powers to acquire any firm which falls down on the job'; for chemicals, a Labour Government would 'obtain from the industry itself such information and records as will enable it to ·determine the most appropriate sections to be acquired, and the most appropriate method of acquiring it'. And, more generally, 'where private enterprise fails to act in the public interest . . . the state shall either build and operate new enterprises or acquire a controlling interest in existing enterprises or both'.[1]

It was in many ways extremely fortunate for the Labour leaders that the Conservative Government should have decided to denationalize steel and road transport. For however much they might be opposed to any serious extension of nationalization, these leaders could hardly do less than pledge themselves to the renationalization of either steel or road transport. This soon became the well-gnawed bone which the leadership regularly threw back to the hungry activists, as a token of the leadership's belief in public ownership.[2] Together with the other proposals of *Challenge to Britain,* this at least partially blurred the fundamental division between the.leadership and those in the Labour movement who believed that any talk of a socialist society must remain a feeble joke until a predominant part of the economy had come under public ownership.

As so often before in the history of the Labour Party, the Executive's programme, meagre though it was, served to neutralize the pressure from the Left. At the 1953 Conference, all attempts to strengthen the document were defeated with the help of the trade union block vote. Indeed, Arthur Deakin, who described the Plan for Engineering of the Confederation of Shipbuilding and Engineering

---

[1] Labour Party Annual Conference Report, 1953, pp. 67 ff. My italics.
[2] Note, however, the appointment (approved by the General Council of the T.U.C.) of three trade unionists to the Steel Board in 1953, one of them, Sir Lincoln Evans, as Vice-Chairman of the Board. The Steel Board was established for the specific purpose of carrying out the denationalization of the steel industry.

Unions as 'just a mumbo-jumbo of meaningless words and phrases . . . the worst abortion ever conceived in the mind of man', also warned the delegates 'not to drive us into the position of falling out and breaking with the Party on such an issue as this' (i.e. nationalization).[1] The threat was pure bluff. The fact that much of the opposition to *Challenge to Britain* had come from trade union delegates, and the vote at the T.U.C. a few weeks earlier, were sufficient proof that Arthur Deakin was not speaking for a united trade union movement. However, the endorsement of *Challenge to Britain,* which was to form the basis of Labour's next electoral programme, marked a major victory for the consolidators.

In opposing a bolder programme, these men had repeatedly invoked the prior need to improve the operation of the industries and services already nationalized—without ever indicating how they proposed to go about it. The advocates of further nationalization also wanted to improve the public sector, but insisted that so long as 'public ownership remained a marginal part of the economy, the full advantage of social ownership will be lost'.[2] And they also asked at the 1953 T.U.C. Annual Conference for 'greater participation in the management and control of nationalized industries of the workers employed in those industries'.[3] The resolution embodying this demand, which was moved by J. S. Campbell, the General Secretary of the National Union of Railwaymen, was opposed by the General Council, and was defeated.[4]

A similar demand, also put forward by J. S. Campbell, was made at the Annual Conference of the Labour Party a month later. The National Executive was also opposed to it. On its behalf, Harry Douglass, of the Iron and Steel Trades Confederation, explained that, as the resolution dealt 'specifically with workers' control—control by those employed in the industry', it was not acceptable.[5] The resolution was defeated by 4,658,000 votes to 1,488,000.[6] On the other hand, the Executive had no objection to an innocuous resolution which said that a Labour Government, in conjunction with the Trade Union and Co-operative movements, would consider 'the formulation of proposals for closer association of workers and consumers with the management of publicly-owned industry and the supervision of privately-owned industry that at present

---

[1] Labour Party Annual Conference Report, 1953, p. 125. Bevan, for his own part, described the Executive's approach to nationalization as 'defeatism and treachery to the spirit of socialisim' (*The Times,* 1st of October, 1953).
[2] T.U.C. Annual Conference Report, 1952, p. 438.
[3] T.U.C. Annual Conference Report, 1953, p. 397.
[4] ibid, p. 400.
[5] Labour Party Annual Conference Report, 1953, p. 129.
[6] ibid, p. 134.

exists'.[1] This was hardly likely to fire the imagination of those workers in the nationalized industries who had told Arthur Deakin, as he reported to the Conference, that 'if you cannot get more out of this than we are getting at this time then on the next occasion we are going to vote Tory'.[2] But the lesson Deakin drew from this was that the minds of trade unionists were not 'conditioned' to industrial democracy.[3]

Parallel to the demands in the Labour movement for the adoption by the Labour leadership of more radical policies at home, there was also pressure, much more insistent after 1951 than in the years of Labour's tenure of office, for different Labour policies in regard to foreign affairs and defence. The two main issues over which battle was joined between Right and Left were the size of the British rearmament programme, and the rearmament of Germany.

The Labour Government had left office committed to a programme of rearmament so unrealistic that the Conservatives themselves had found it necessary to begin reducing it. Former Labour Ministers were in a poor position to press for further reductions, even if they had wished to do so. But a sizeable minority of the Parliamentary Party, and a considerable part of the Labour rank and file, in the constituency parties *and* in the trade unions, felt no such inhibitions.

In March 1952, fifty-seven Labour Members (out of 295) defied the Whips and, instead of abstaining, as they were summoned to do, from voting on a Government motion asking for approval of the rearmament programme, voted against it.

At the 1952 T.U.C. Conference in September, the opponents of the leadership were badly defeated on the issue of rearmament, mainly because of poor tactics; but at the Labour Party Conference a few weeks later, a resolution from the Shop, Distributive and Allied Workers' Union called for a 're-examination and reduction of the rearmament programme', and was only defeated by 3,644,000 votes to 2,228,000.[4]

By 1953, it was German rearmament which had become the main issue of contention between Right and Left. At the Labour Party Conference of that year, the Executive itself presented a resolution, urging 'that there should be no German rearmament before further efforts have been made to secure the peaceful reunification of Germany'.[5] This was carried 'almost unanimously'. By February

[1] Labour Party Annual Conference Report, 1953, p. 130.
[2] ibid, p. 132.
[3] ibid, p. 132.
[4] Labour Party Annual Conference Report, 1952, p. 154.
[5] Labour Party Annual Conference Report, 1953, p. 151.

1954, the Labour leaders decided that further efforts had been made,[1] and justified them in now supporting German rearmament. Both the National Executive and the Parliamentary Party agreed, by slender majorities.[2] When the T.U.C. met in September 1954, the French Parliament had just rejected German rearmament as part of the European Defence Community. Undeterred. the General Council put forward an emergency resolution which reaffirmed support for German rearmament. This was carried, but only by 4,077,000 votes to 3,622,000.[3] With so narrow a majority at the T.U.C., it seemed very likely that, with the larger part of the constituency vote added to that of the trade union opposition, official policy would be defeated at the Labour Party Conference. And so it would have been, had not the delegation of the Amalgamated Society of Woodworkers switched, despite the mandate from its own Conference, from opposition to support of the platform, thus ensuring the latter's victory, by 3,270,000 votes to 3,022,000.[4]

Throughout these controversies, on home and foreign policy, the limelight was held by the Bevanite parliamentarians, and particularly by Aneurin Bevan himself. These were the years in which Bevan was constantly and bitterly denounced, by his opponents in the Labour movement as well as by his opponents outside, as an unprincipled demagogue, whose sole impulse was personal power. At the same time, the assumption was easily made that 'Bevanism' was Bevan's own creation and that the really important battle was being fought in the Parliamentary Party and in the upper reaches of the Labour hierarchy. Both notions were false. Bevan did not create Bevanism: as a refusal on the part of a substantial minority of Labour's rank and file to endorse the leadership's drift of policy and as an affirmation of the need for different policies, it had existed in the Labour Party and in the trade unions long before Bevan gave it his name and his gifts; and it endured, and grew in strength, after he ceased to give expression to it. As for parliamentary Bevanism, its challenge to the leadership was crippled by inhibitions which made it, for all the interest it attracted, a great deal less significant than the opposition of the rank and file. This is worth examining a little more closely.

When fifty-seven Labour M.P.s defied the Party Whips in March 1952, there were powerful voices, notably that of Arthur Deakin, to

---

[1] I.e., the Berlin Conference of January/February 1954.
[2] *The Times*, 24th and 25th of February, 1954.
[3] T.U.C. Annual Conference Report, 1954, p. 401.
[4] Labour Party Annual Conference Report, 1954, p. 108. For the Woodworkers' switch, see Harrison, op. cit. pp. 71-3.

press for their expulsion from the Parliamentary Labour Party. There were others to urge conciliation. It was this counsel which prevailed and the parliamentary leaders were content to place a veto on further rebellions by reimposing the Parliamentary Party's Standing Orders, suspended since 1945. This meant that only those M.P.s who could plausibly plead scruples of conscience would be allowed to abstain from voting in support of party policy, but that everyone who could not invoke a narrowly interpreted 'conscience clause' would have to fall into line with official policy. And since those who opposed official policy were only a relatively small minority of the Parliamentary Party, this meant obedience to policies with which they disagreed, failing which there would be the threat of expulsion from the Parliamentary Party, and from the Labour Party itself. To clinch matters, a resolution, clearly directed at the Bevanite group, was moved by Attlee in the Parliamentary Party after the 1952 Labour Party Conference, banning all unofficial groups within the Party and demanding an end to all 'personal attacks'. This was approved by 188 votes to 51, and it meant the end of what degree of organized opposition there had been within the Parliamentary Party. Semi-organized activity did not altogether cease, but it never was very effective. As a parliamentary force, Bevanism had, by the end of 1952, been decisively checked.

This was somewhat masked by the success in 1952 of Bevanite candidates in the election to the constituency seats of the National Executive. In 1951, Aneurin Bevan, Barbara Castle, Tom Driberg and Ian Mikardo had shared these seven seats with James Griffiths, Herbert Morrison and Hugh Dalton. In 1952, Morrison and Dalton were eliminated in favour of Harold Wilson and Richard Crossman.[1] Of the Old Guard, only James Griffiths managed to hold on,

---

[1] Immediately after the 1952 Conference, Hugh Gaitskell described the unseating of Morrison as 'not only an act of gross political ingratitude but a piece of blind stupidity which until it is put right must gravely weaken the party'. 'A most disturbing feature of the Conference,' he also said, 'was the number of resolutions and speeches which were Communist-inspired, based not even on the *Tribune* so much as the *Daily Worker* . . . I was told by some observers that about one-sixth of the constituency party delegates appear to be Communists or Communist-inspired. This figure may well be too high; but if it should be one-tenth or even one-twentieth it is a most shocking state of affairs to which the National Executive should given immediate attention.' However, the Conference, he felt, had 'come down firmly on the side of sanity and responsibility. The issues of foreign policy and defence are now settled. All the silly nonsense about withdrawing troops from Korea, breaking away from the Atlantic Alliance and going back on what the Labour Government stood for has been blown away. We are definitely opposed as a party to unilateral cuts in our defence programme, though we favour periodic re-examination with our allies . . . Loyal members of the party must now accept all these decisions, including the new members of

and the six Bevanites were again elected in 1953 and 1954.

To the Labour Left, this seemed a success of the first magnitude. This was a mistake. For the first result of the Bevanites' success was to impose upon the victors an acceptance of policies which they had no chance whatever of affecting in any significant way.

The Bevanite members of the National Executive might have found the constrictions of collective responsibility more difficult to bear had it not been for their belief that, by being members of the Executive, they *would* be able to make a difference to Labour's programme and policies. In fact, their membership of the Executive only made it more difficult for the Bevanites to give effective direction to the struggle against the Right. But their willingness, indeed their eagerness, to suffer the burdens of collective responsibility is not only to be explained in terms of an overestimation of how much could be achieved by a small minority of dissidents on a body like the National Executive. It also owed much to their high propensity to compromise. Though uneasy with the Labour Party's drift, they seldom found it possible (and where possible often did not find it politically desirable) to articulate their unease into clear alternatives. Thus, in the great controversy on the rearmament of Federal Germany, the leading Bevanites were severely limited by their reluctance to question the basic assumptions of Labour's foreign policy, of which the rearmament of Germany was a logical outcome. As for common ownership, they were ready enough to insist that there should be more of it. What they seemed unable to do was to offer an alternative analysis to the narrow Fabian view of its necessity and purpose. In other words, many of the political ambiguities of parliamentary Bevanism were but a reflection of its ideological ambiguities. Throughout, parliamentary Bevanism was a mediation between the leadership and the rank and file opposition. But the parliamentary Bevanites, while assuming the leadership of that opposition, also served to blur and to blunt both its strength and its extent. Themselves limited by their parliamentary and executive obligations, they fell back on the politics of manoeuvre, and were regularly outmanoeuvred in the process.

Bevan himself bore a double burden of responsibility without power. In addition to being a member of the National Executive, he was also elected to the Shadow Cabinet in November 1952,[1]

the National Executive.' 'It is time,' he also believed, 'to end the attempt to mob rule by a group of frustrated journalists and restore the authority and leadership of the solid, sound, sensible majority of the movement.' (*The Times*, 6th of October, 1952.)

[1] Bevan had stood for the deputy leadership of the Party against Herbert Morrison, and had been defeated by 194 votes to 82. In the election to the Parliamentary Committee, all Bevanite candidates were defeated, save Bevan.

and was re-elected to it in 1953 and 1954. After two years of ineffectual opposition in the Executive and the Parliamentary Committee, Bevan finally resigned from the latter body in April 1954. However, the circumstances of his resignation robbed it of much of its effectiveness. On the 13th of April, Attlee, speaking for the Opposition, had given a qualified welcome to the Government's announcement that the establishment of a Treaty Organization similar to NATO was being considered for South East Asia. Bevan, for his part, condemned the proposal, and thus appeared to disavow his Leader. Rebuked in the Parliamentary Committee, and threatened with rebuke in the Parliamentary Party, Bevan, without consultation of any of his associates, chose to resign his membership of the Committee. Harold Wilson, who had been the runner-up in the 1953 election to the Shadow Cabinet, thus gained automatic admission to that body. But his acceptance of the vacant seat entailed a scarcely veiled disavowal of Bevan's action and completed the disintegration of a group whose inner cohesion had always been minimal.

However, Bevan's disengagement from official responsibilities was only partial. In June, he announced that, rather than gain an easy re-election to the National Executive in October as a representative of the constituency parties, he would be a candidate for the Treasuryship of the Party, for which post Hugh Gaitskell, with the strong backing of the most powerful trade union leaders, was already in the field. But Bevan remained a member of the National Executive until the 1954 Conference was over. As a result, the Conference was treated to the unedifying spectacle of the leading Labour opponent of German rearmament remaining silent, as did the other Bevanite members of the Executive, in the debate which decided the issue. And when the Paris Treaties, incorporating German rearmament, were presented to the House of Commons in November 1954, six Labour M.P.s[1] defied the parliamentary leadership's decision that the Party should abstain from voting. and challenged a division, thus ensuring that the Treaties would not be approved by the House without any opposition being recorded against them. The six (and a seventh Labour Member, Mr McGovern, who voted with the Government) were promptly expelled from the Parliamentary Party, but readmitted some months later.

After his expected defeat for the Treasuryship,[2] Bevan announced

---

[1] Namely, G. Craddock, S. Davies, E. Fernyhough, V. F. Yates, E. Hughes, and S. Silverman.

[2] Hugh Gaitskell was elected to the post by 4,338,000 votes to 2,032,000 cast for Bevan. The size of Bevan's vote should not be overlooked.

that he would henceforth campaign among the rank and file trade unionists and seek their help in the defeat of the right wing trade union leaders. The announcement came three years too late. The time to have made it was 1951, if indeed not earlier. Nor, by October 1954, was there much in the project to cause any worry to those whom Bevan now belatedly challenged.

There was one final flicker of dissent within the Parliamentary Party before the General Election of 1955. In March of that year, the Government announced that it had decided to manufacture the hydrogen bomb. In its amendment to the Government's motion asking for the approval of the House of Commons for the Defence White Paper, the Labour Party approved the decision, while criticizing the deficiencies of the Services after a three-year expenditure of some £4,000,000,000. Despite a three-line Whip, sixty-two Labour Members, invoking the conscience clause, abstained from voting for the Party's amendment.

This opposition was too large to be disciplined. But Bevan's enemies (some of whom were by then little short of paranoid about him) thought that it might yet be possible to expel him from the Parliamentary Party, and from the Labour Party itself. In the course of the debate, Bevan had asked the Government whether it was contemplated that nuclear weapons should be used against an attack with 'conventional' weapons. But he had not only asked the question of the Government. He had also challenged Attlee to make Labour's position clear.[1] On the ground that the embarrassment Bevan had caused Attlee was only the latest of numerous breaches of discipline, the Parliamentary Party agreed (by 142 votes to 112) to Bevan's expulsion from it. It only remained for a majority to be found on the National Executive to expel him from the Labour Party itself. Such a majority might well have been found had it not been for the storm of rank and file protest which the threat evoked, and had not a General Election been in the offing.

At the General Election of May 1955,[2] the Conservatives, though they polled some 400,000 votes less than in 1951, increased their parliamentary majority from seventeen to fifty-eight. The percentage of votes cast for the Conservatives rose from 48 per cent. in 1951 to 49.7 per cent. in 1955. Labour's vote, on the other hand, showed

---

[1] It may be noted that neither Attlee, nor the Minister of Defence (then Harold Macmillan) gave a clear answer to the question. (See H. of C. vol. 537, cols. 2176 ff., 2nd of March, 1955.)

[2] Winston Churchill had resigned as Prime Minister on the 6th of April. On the 15th, Sir Anthony Eden announced that the Election would be held on the 26th of May.

a sharp decrease of some one and a half million, while its percentage of votes cast fell from 48.8 per cent. to 46.4 per cent.

Labour's election manifesto, *Forward with Labour*, had marked a retreat even from the nationalization proposals of *Challenge to Britain*. Save for the inevitable inclusion of the renationalization of steel and road haulage, the manifesto only promised that 'sections of the chemical and machine tools industries' would be brought under public ownership; and, 'where necessary', a Labour Government would 'start new public enterprises'. These proposals gave Labour the worst of both worlds. They could not be presented (and the Labour leaders had in any case no wish to present them) as forming part of a thought-out socialist programme: and this, ironically, made it easier for the Conservatives to denounce them either as a token of Labour's 'doctrinaire' clinging to outworn dogma, or as the product of an uneasy compromise between Right and Left. But neither did these proposals arouse any enthusiasm among Labour activists, or much interest in the electorate at large. The same was true for the rest of Labour's proposals. These were apposite enough for a mildly reforming party,[1] but scarcely sufficient to bring the election to life.

As for foreign policy and defence, it was the H-bomb, *Forward with Labour* said, which 'loomed over mankind'. The Labour Party, it also said, would not approach the problem in a 'party spirit'. In fact, it did not approach the problem at all, save for suggesting that Britain should propose to Russia and the United States the immediate cessation of H-bomb tests.

Labour's main problem, from a purely electoral point of view, was that four years of Tory Government had not produced the catastrophies which had been confidently prophesied in 1951. The Government had brought rationing to an end, full employment had been maintained, the target of 300,000 houses a year had been reached and surpassed, the welfare services had not been dismantled, the Government had nursed with particular care its relations with the trade union leaders,[2] and there was very little in the Government's handling

---

[1] E.g. proposals for a comprehensive schools system, for an improvement in the rates of national assistance, for the removal of taxes on sport and the living theatre, for the improvement of working conditions in shops and offices, and for the restoration of a free health service, including the abolition of all charges, amongst them those which Hugh Gaitskell had imposed as Chancellor of the Exchequer.

[2] Not that this presented any major difficulty. Immediately after the Election of 1951, the T.U.C. General Council had issued a statement referring to 'our long standing practice to seek to work amicably with whatever Government is in power and through consultation jointly with Ministers and with the other side of industry to find practical solutions to the social and economic

of foreign affairs to which the Labour Party, in the light of its own foreign policies, could have plausibly objected.[1] There was a powerful Socialist case to be made against the Conservatives, but it was not a case the Labour leaders were willing to make, or indeed would by then have known how to make.

It was to Labour's failure to put forward a bold socialist programme that the Left readily attributed electoral defeat. But there was little evidence to suggest that such a programme would have attracted greater support if it had been presented *in 1955*. The point has been made before: a socialist programme could only have enhanced the Labour Party's chances if it had been put forward, and fought for, in Parliament and outside, from 1951 onwards, and if all the resources and energies of the Party and the trade unions had been used to make it known and understood. As it is, the election of 1955 was the quietest of the century. It was also the first election since 1918, save for the special circumstances of 1931, in which the Labour vote fell below the total recorded at the previous election.

2. PARALYSIS AS IDEOLOGY

The leaders of the Labour Party were even less prepared after 1955 than they had been after 1951 to listen to pleas from the Labour Left for the adoption of more radical policies—nor indeed was that Labour Left itself able to present either a clear diagnosis of the Party's troubles or a solidly-based argument for such policies as it wanted to see adopted. In consequence, there was ready agreement with the Executive that, as James Griffiths told the 1955 Conference, the Labour Party should 'go back to the classroom'. Over the next three years, he promised the delegates, a whole series of policy reports would be prepared, ranging from Equality and the Ownership of Industry to Agriculture and The Individual and Society.[2] In addition, there would also be an investigation of the shortcomings of Labour's electoral machine.

The proposal that the Executive should engage in a prolonged

---

problems facing this country. There need be no doubt, therefore, of the attitude of the T.U.C. towards the new Government' (T.U.C. Annual Conference Report, 1952, p. 300).

[1] 'I doubt,' Hugh Gaitskell had said in October 1954, 'if foreign policy will play a big part in the next Election—not because it is not important, but because Mr Eden has, in fact, mostly carried on our policy as developed by Ernest Bevin, in some cases against the views of rank-and-file Tories' (*Tribune,* 8th of October, 1954). It will be recalled that both Sir Winston Churchill and Sir Anthony Eden had claimed, for their part, that it was Bevin who had followed Conservative policy.

[2] Labour Party Annual Conference Report, 1955, pp. 125 ff.

're-thinking' exercise, at the end of which the Labour Party would be equipped with brand new policies, had a wide appeal. But it was easily overlooked that the 're-thinking' would be directed by men who believed that it must also involve a great deal of 'de-thinking', particularly in relation to common ownership: the result of the exercise might be to provide the Labour Party with new policies, but the policies would reflect a further dilution of the Party's aims. What made this certain beyond any doubt was the election of Hugh Gaitskell to the leadership of the Party in December 1955.

By the time Attlee finally decided to resign, the only two likely contenders besides Gaitskell were hardly in the race at all. Herbert Morrison's star had long ceased to twinkle, and Bevan was wholly unacceptable both to powerful trade union leaders and to the vast majority of the Parliamentary Party. Hugh Gaitskell, on the other hand, had long enjoyed the support of the former and was also, *faute de mieux,* acceptable to the latter. So clear was his lead on the eve of the election that some of those who opposed him persuaded Bevan to withdraw in favour of Morrison if Gaitskell would do likewise. The latter refused and was duly elected, by 157 votes to 70 for Bevan and 40 for Morrison.

Though the Labour Party's shift to the right had begun long before Hugh Gaitskell assumed the leadership, his election both accentuated the shift and helped to give it a much sharper ideological and political articulation.

An older generation of Labour leaders had always set very definite limits, in their programmes and policies, to Labour's socialism. But they had also held out to their followers the promise that accommodation with capitalism was a temporary halt, however prolonged, on the journey to the Socialist Commonwealth. And, cautious though they might be about common ownership, they had not been disposed to argue that it could be divorced from any meaningful interpretation of socialism. In outward form at least, their quarrel with the Left had thus appeared as a quarrel about the pace of advance, not about the ultimate desirability of advance itself.

In contrast, a new revisionism, to which the new Leader was ideologically and politically committed, claimed not only that nationalization was an electoral liability to the Labour Party, but that in a 'post-capitalist' society, it had actually come to be largely irrelevant.[1]

In political terms, there was much in revisionism which helped to obscure the retreat it signified even from that Labourism with

---

[1] For the most articulate exposition of revisionism, see C. A. R. Crosland, 'The Transition from Capitalism', in *New Fabian Essays* (Ed. R. H. S. Crossman), pp. 33-68 (1952) and the same's *The Future of Socialism* (1956).

which the Labour Party had made do since it had come into existence. There was the amplitude of its egalitarian rhetoric; and also the willingness of the revisionists to concede, indeed to insist, that the frontiers of public ownership had not been finally drawn up: there would be cases where an industry or firm, having 'failed the nation', might be considered ripe for nationalization, or some diluted form of it.[1] But, whatever element of confusion these qualifications introduced in the debate on nationalization, they did not affect the essential difference between Right and Left, namely that the former envisaged as permanent an economic system in which the 'private sector' was to retain by far the dominant share of economic power, while the latter wanted precisely the opposite.

Just as Ramsay MacDonald had conceived it as one of his main tasks to educate the Labour movement into the conventions and niceties of the parliamentary system, so did Hugh Gaitskell consider it one of *his* main tasks to educate it into a final acceptance of the 'mixed economy'. An important, though still intermediate stage in this process of education, was reached with the publication in 1957 of *Industry and Society,* one of the 're-thinking' policy reports on the future of public ownership. Steel and long-distance road haulage, said that document, would be renationalized by the next Labour Government. 'Beyond that,' it went on, 'we reserve the right to extend public ownership in any industry or part of industry which, after thorough enquiry, is found to be seriously failing the nation.'[2] Meanwhile, *Industry and Society* also proposed that 'the community (should) acquire a stake in the expansion of industry' through the acquisition of shares by the State. But such acquisition, it was made clear, 'will be guided solely by investment considerations and will not be aimed at securing control'.[3]

No one outside the Labour movement had the least doubt that the adoption of *Industry and Society* would constitute a major retreat from public ownership, and that the document owed its main inspiration to the Leader of the Labour Party. Nor was there much doubt on the Left as to the tendencies it represented.[4] On the other hand, the erstwhile Bevanite leaders of the Labour Left did not choose to challenge the new programme.[5] Instead, some

[1] For an exposition of this functional approach to nationalization, see Hugh Gaitskell, *Socialism and Nationalisation* (1956).
[2] *Industry and Society,* p. 57.
[3] ibid, p. 57.
[4] See, e.g. the letter to *Reynolds News* of 32 Labour M.P.s expressing 'disappointment and dismay' at the document. (*Reynolds News,* 28th of July, 1957.)
[5] It was Harold Wilson, speaking on behalf of the Executive, who opened the debate at the 1957 Party Conference on *Industry and Society* with an ardent commendation of the document (See Labour Party Annual Conference Report, 1957, pp. 128-31).

of them argued that, provided it was properly interpreted, a bold nationalization programme could be extracted from it. Even if this had been true, the argument failed to take into account the fact that the interpretation of the document, when it came to the point, would not be left to those who wanted an extension of public ownership, but to those who did not.

It is notable that some of the most vigorous opposition to the spirit and to the practical proposals of *Industry and Society* came from within the trade unions. At the 1957 Labour Party Conference, it was a trade union leader, J. S. Campbell, who issued the clearest challenge to the Executive with a resolution affirming 'belief in the common ownership of all the basic industries and means of production', and deploring 'the present tendency to deviate from these accepted principles'. And the resolution also proposed the reference back of *Industry and Society* 'in order that a clear, unambiguous policy document can be prepared and issued indicating the industries to be brought under public ownership by the next Labour Government'.[1] Another resolution, from the Hornsey Constituency Labour Party, took a leaf from the document and, while asking the Conference to reaffirm its belief in nationalization, also proposed that a Labour Government should, as a first step, 'seek to transfer to public ownership all the shares of a substantial number of the companies whose assets exceed £2½ million'.[2]

In reply to the debate, Hugh Gaitskell assured the delegates that he and the Executive believed in equality, social justice, co-operation, accountability, and planning for full employment; and that, 'through public ownership and control we can achieve higher productivity'. But a future Labour Government, he reminded the delegates, was already committed to the renationalization of steel and road haulage, to a 'huge expansion of public ownership' in housing,[3] to the repeal and replacement of the Rent Act, and to a new plan for superannuation. 'Believe me,' said the Leader, 'in these measures alone, together with all the other minor pieces of legislation, we have certainly more than enough to occupy the first two or three years of any Labour Government.'

'Those who wield the weapons of economic power, wherever they may be,' the Leader further told the delegates, 'should be accountable to the community for their actions.' It was therefore intended that, 'in order to plan this economy properly', the Government should know 'all we can about investment intentions', that it

[1] Labour Party Annual Conference Report, 1957, p. 131.
[2] ibid, p. 133.
[3] I.e. the acquisition of rent-controlled houses and flats by local authorities (see *Homes for the Future. Labour's Policy for Housing*) (1956).

should have 'a fair degree of control over investment by private firms', that the latter should present their accounts as did the nationalized industries, and that they should be prevented from avoiding taxation 'in various ways'. And there was also 'a strong case', the Leader believed, 'for laying down a code of conduct which these large firms must observe'.

In the light of these rather modest proposals, it was entirely appropriate that the Leader, notwithstanding his ardent commendation of Government share buying in industry, should have categorically rejected the Hornsey resolution. 'It commits us as a first step,' he said, 'to transfer to public ownership all the shares of a substantial number of companies. Frankly, I am not prepared to accept that. I think probably it is very much more important that we should renationalize steel and road haulage as a first step and I have already said we must have inquiries before we go further in that direction.'

Finally, there was the electorate to be considered, and particularly the 'so called marginal voters', who were not convinced socialists, but 'ordinary decent people who do not probably think a great deal about politics'. and who would want to know the specific reasons for nationalizing any particular industry. The Executive, Gaitskell said, could have come to the Conference and presented a document with a long list of further industries to be nationalized without a new idea, and, 'very probably', this would have been received with acclamation. They had not done so 'because if we had done so we would have been putting something to you which in our hearts we did not believe we could carry out . . . which in our hearts we believed the electorate was bound to reject . . . we do not believe in that sort of leadership; we believe in leadership which is clear-eyed and clear-headed, which does not flinch from making the Party and the Movement face the facts of the day, both the economic and the political facts'.[1]

The Executive easily carried the day. *Industry and Society* was endorsed by 5,309,000 votes to 1,276,000. Support for the document was a great deal less enthusiastic than was suggested by these figures.[2] That it was carried by so large a majority was in fact due to a number of reasons which had little to do with the merits of the argument.

There were, in 1957, few people in the Labour movement who did not believe that the sharp decline in Conservative fortunes after the fiasco of the Suez expedition would result in the return of a Labour Government at the next General Election. And the more

---

[1] Labour Party Annual Conference Report, 1957, pp. 155 ff.
[2] See, e.g. the speech of Frank Cousins (ibid, pp. 142-3). However, his union's vote was cast in support of the leadership.

likely a Labour victory seemed, the greater grew the desire to present the Labour Party as a united party, and the greater too the authority of its Leader—not least with potential members of his administration. By 1957, most leading members of the extinct Bevanite group had edged steadily closer to Hugh Gaitskell, and none closer, to all appearances, than Bevan himself.

Bevan's reconciliation with the Leader of the Party, and with many of his former enemies in the trade unions as well, had begun soon after his defeat for the leadership in December 1955. In October 1956, he had been elected Treasurer of the Party and had thus rejoined the National Executive as an *ex-officio* member. He was also re-elected to the Parliamentary Committee in November and was then appointed 'Shadow' Foreign Secretary by the Leader. It is in that capacity that he replied for the Executive at the 1957 Labour Party Conference to a debate on a composite resolution which asked the Conference to pledge that 'the next Labour Government will take the lead by itself refusing to continue to test, manufacture or use nuclear weapons, and that it will appeal to peoples of other countries to follow their lead'.[1]

What is now remembered about that speech is Bevan's description of unilateralism as an 'emotional spasm' which would send a British Foreign Secretary 'naked into the Conference Chamber'. However, there was much else of interest in what he said.

'You may decide in this country unilaterally,' said Bevan, 'that you will have nothing to do with experiments, nor with manufacture, nor with use. With none of these sentiments do I disagree, none of them at all.' But this would mean, he told the delegates, 'that all the international commitments, all the international arrangements, all the international facilities afforded to your friends and allies must be immediately destroyed . . . The main difficulty we are in here is that in this way we shall precipitate a difficult situation with the nations that are now associated with us in a variety of treaties and alliances, most of which I do not like—I would like to substitute for them other treaties more sensible and more civilized and not chaos and a shambles. If any Socialist Foreign Secretary is to have a chance he must be permitted to substitute good policies for bad policies.'[2]

Despite its rejection of unilateralism, this was not an argument based on the proposition that the Labour Party was irrevocably committed to existing treaties and alliances, 'most of which I do

[1] Labour Party Annual Conference Report, 1957, p. 165. The resolution was defeated by 5,836,000 votes to 781,000 (ibid, p. 183).
[2] ibid, p. 181.

not like'. Indeed, said Bevan, the purpose of a Socialist Foreign Secretary would be to prevent 'that deadly negative polarization that we have been fighting for years' and to interpose 'between those two giants (i.e. the United States and the U.S.S.R.) modifying, moderating and mitigating influences'.[1]

Whether Bevan was right or wrong in insisting that the possession by Britain of nuclear weapons was essential to a Socialist Foreign Secretary's purposes is not here the point. The argument had in any case become irrelevant three years later, when a Conservative Government had to admit that Britain would not, before many years had passed, have an independent nuclear deterrent at all. More important in this context is that, in his wish to inject a degree of flexibility in the foreign policy of a Labour Government, Bevan would have soon found himself at odds with many of his colleagues. For they, and most particularly the Leader of the Party, had none of Bevan's reservations about the treaties and alliances in which British foreign policy was enmeshed.

For the time being, however, these differences were entirely overshadowed by Bevan's support for the Executive and for the Leader of the Party. With his speech at the 1957 Conference, Bevan unambiguously removed himself from the leadership of the Labour Left and appeared to accept as final his position as Hugh Gaitskell's second in command. And with the massive endorsement by the 1957 Conference of *Industry and Society,* and the equally massive rejection of unilateralism, the Right seemed more firmly entrenched than ever, with a Leader of its own persuasion in unchallenged command of the Labour Party. All that was now required was for the Labour Party to seize the initiative from the Government.

Here, however, was the rub. For the initiative was not to be seized without far greater exertions than the Labour Party's policies and political attitudes made possible. This had already been demonstrated on the issue of Suez, and it was to be demonstrated again in the following years.

Though the Labour Party had failed to acquire clear and distinctive policies in regard to the Middle East from the time it left office in 1951, it did at least express opposition to the Government's actual resort to force in Egypt. On the 1st of November, 1956, a special meeting of the National Council of Labour had declared itself 'profoundly shocked' by the British Government's attack on Egypt and had called upon the Government 'forthwith to cease all military measures' against that country. The Council also decided to organize public meetings on the theme 'Law—Not War', but set a definite

[1] Labour Party Annual Conference Report, 1957, p. 182.

limit to its opposition by calling 'upon the British people to bring effective pressure to bear' on the Government 'through normal constitutional parliamentary methods' and 'to refrain from taking industrial action as a means of influencing national policy in the present crisis'.[1] British military operations did in fact come to an end within the next few days. No one, however, has so far seriously claimed that the Labour Party's opposition had much to do with this outcome.

Nor did the Opposition behave, after Suez, as if it really believed that the Government's conduct of affairs had robbed it of its title to govern, and that it must, at the least, seek a fresh mandate. Sir Anthony Eden's successor was as deeply implicated in the Suez venture as Sir Anthony himself, and so was the rest of Mr Macmillan's Government. Yet Labour's campaign came to an end as abrupt as the Government's military operations, and Labour pressure upon the Government soon subsided altogether. It is difficult to believe that a Conservative Opposition, in similar circumstances, would have been so obliging to a Labour administration.

The same pattern was repeated in every other field of policy. It was in fact the Conservatives who went on 'the offensive in the following two and a half years. Between June 1957 and September 1959, the Conservative Party spent £468,000 in a public relations campaign which, it has been observed, 'was altogether new to British politics',[2] while a variety of business interests spent an additional £1,435,000 between June 1958 and September 1959 in anti-nationalization campaigns.[3]

The most notable fact about these campaigns is not that they were undertaken, but that they largely went unanswered. It was inevitable that they should be left unanswered, since the Labour leaders were precluded by their own ideological predispositions from countering attacks on nationalization with arguments for it. Indeed, *Industry and Society* had itself conceded much of its case to private industry. 'The Labour Party recognizes,' it said, 'that, under increasingly professional managements, large firms are as a whole serving the nation well' and that 'no organization, public or private, can operate effectively if it is subjected to persistent and detailed interventions from above. We have therefore no intention of intervening in the management of any firm which is doing a good job'.[4] It would have been unreasonable to expect the steel industry not to

[1] Labour Party Annual Conference Report, 1957, p. 9.
[2] D. E. Butler and R. Rose, *The British General Election of 1959* (London, 1960) p. 17.
[3] ibid, p. 252.
[4] *Industry and Society*, pp. 48-9.

claim that these commendations applied to it as much as to other firms, and equally unreasonable to expect the Labour Party to put forward a convincing argument, on the basis of the narrow criteria it used, for making a special case of that industry: after all, it is not very likely that the nationalization of steel would have been an item of Labour's programme in the late fifties had steel not already once been nationalized.

It was not only a fundamental disbelief in the general case for common ownership which prevented the Labour leaders from countering Conservative propaganda. There was also the fear of the electorate, over this and most other issues. By the late fifties, the Labour leaders, obsessed as they were with the thought of electoral success, had come to be more convinced even than were their predecessors that the essential condition for that success was to present the Labour Party as a moderate and respectable party, free from class bias, 'national' in outlook, and whose zeal for reform would always be tempered by its eager endorsement of the maxim that Rome was not built in a day—or even in a century. Never indeed had Labour leaders been so haunted by a composite image of the potential Labour voter as quintessentially *petit-bourgeois,* and therefore liable to be frightened off by a radical alternative to Conservatism. But the paradox of this view was that it was both self-confirming and self-defeating: self-confirming in the sense that, the more the Labour Party geared its policies to suit those whom Hugh Gaitskell had described as 'ordinary decent people who do not probably think a great deal about politics', the less interest were they likely to show in the Labour Party; and self-defeating in the sense that the less interest they showed in the Labour Party, the less likely were its leaders to be electorally successful.

The late fifties were of course years of boom, in which a more prosperous population was invited to join in the apotheosis of 'free enterprise' and forget the deep economic, social and moral ills of a society sick with the impulse to private appropriation. The final impact on the electorate of Conservative claims that 'Conservative freedom works' is a matter of conjecture. But its impact on the Labour leaders is not. Well before the General Election of 1959, they had assumed a defensive, almost a plaintive, posture, and had repeatedly felt it necessary to minimize the threat Labour might pose to Conservative freedom.[1] They had no option but to propose the renationalization of steel and long distance road haulage. But

[1] In April 1959, e.g. the Secretary of the Labour Party felt obliged officially to deny Conservative allegations that the Labour Party intended to nationalize 500-600 large firms. Save for steel and long distance road haulage, his statement said, no industries or firms would be nationalized 'unless an

only 'where an industry is shown, after thorough inquiry. to be failing the nation', said their 1959 electoral manifesto, did Labour 'reserve the right to take all or any part of it under public ownership if this is necessary'. And in the General Election itself, Mr Butler and Mr Rose have noted, the Labour Party, 'as in all recent elections . . . played down any claim to stand, as a socialist party, for a radically different form of society . . . it asked the voters to say that it could administer the mixed economy welfare state better than the Conservatives'.[1]

The adoption of *Industry and Society* by the 1957 Labour Party Conference had largely stilled the debate on nationalization within the Party. But the rejection of unilateralism by the same Conference had not ended the debate on foreign affairs and defence. In fact, the Labour leaders found themselves under increasing pressure in the following two years to depart from their rigid adherence to policies framed within the context of the Cold War. By the beginning of 1958, the Campaign for Nuclear Disarmament had been formed and the London to Aldermaston march at Easter had transformed unilateralism from an awkward word into something of a movement. It was a movement whose leaders (as distinct from many of its supporters) deliberately shunned some of the larger implications of unilateralism and sought to confine it to a purely moral protest against reliance on nuclear weapons. Nevertheless, the spread within the Labour movement of the unease the Campaign reflected was soon to pose a serious problem to the Labour leadership. In March 1958. the National Executive Committee of the Labour Party and the General Council of the T.U.C. made a first attempt to meet the problem.

In a joint document entitled *Disarmament and Nuclear War*,[2] they now proposed that the British Government should 'at once suspend thermo-nuclear tests unilaterally for a limited period, in the hope that this will hasten permanent international agreement on tests and lead on to a general disarmament convention'. The statement also expressed support for an international declaration banning the use of all nuclear weapons, coupled with an agreement for the reduction of conventional arms and forces. As for the setting up of American missile bases in Britain, the document expressed the view 'not only that these bases must be effectively under British control, but also

---

official inquiry were to show (1) that they were seriously failing the nation and (2) nationalization was in fact the best remedy for the industry's problems' (Labour Party Annual Conference Report, 1958, p. 9).
[1] Butler and Rose, op. cit. p. 70.
[2] Labour Party Annual Conference Report, 1958, pp. 5-6.

that no physical steps should be taken to set them up before a fresh attempt had been made to negotiate with the Soviet Government'. The British Government, it also said, had 'failed to show that it is necessary for British-based aircraft to carry nuclear weapons on either patrol or training flights'; these should therefore be 'limited forthwith to those necessary for the transport of weapon stocks'. Another statement, *Disengagement in Europe*,[1] also proposed the 'gradual withdrawal under effective international control of foreign forces of all kinds from East and West Germany, Poland, Czechoslovakia and Hungary', and 'pending Summit talks', it also said, 'no steps should be taken towards the ultimate equipment of West German forces with nuclear weapons'.

The retreat from previous policies which these cautious and mostly conditional proposals represented was more formal than real, save for the proposal for a unilateral ban by Britain on nuclear tests. Both statements avoided a direct answer to the question of what the Labour Party's policy would be, both in regard to the establishment of American missile bases in Britain and to the equipment of West German forces with nuclear weapons, if a Summit Conference produced no results. Nor did the statements indicate what a Labour Government would do if its allies rejected, as there could be no doubt they would reject, the proposals for disengagement in Europe. However, the answer was in fact quite clear: a Labour Government, whose proposals found no favour with its NATO allies, would not persist.[2] Nor could it have been otherwise, given the Labour Party's unqualified commitment to NATO. This gave the statements a somewhat academic air. What completed the effect was the announcement that the Labour Party and the T.U.C. had agreed to organize 'an educational campaign' on the subject of Disarmament and Nuclear War, 'consisting in the first instance of regional conferences within the Labour movement'.[3] This rather suggested that the authors of the documents were at least as much concerned to wean the Labour movement away from dangerous thoughts as to influence the British Government on such issues as nuclear tests.

For the time being, the leadership's proposals served to suggest flexibility and movement. Though 102 of the 428 resolutions on the agenda for the Labour Party Conference in September 1958 asked

[1] Labour Party Annual Conference Report, 1958, pp. 7-8.
[2] See, e.g. Hugh Gaitskell: 'If the American Government do not accept this proposal (i.e., disengagement), the proposal will not be put forward on behalf of the West. Our object is to try to persuade the American Government to accept this proposal' (H. of C., vol. 600, col. 567, 19th of February, 1959).
[3] Labour Party Annual Conference Report, 1958, p. 5.

for a unilateral renunciation of nuclear weapons by Britain, a composite resolution to the same effect was overwhelmingly defeated.[1] Another resolution, calling upon the Parliamentary Labour Party 'to oppose under any circumstances the establishment of rocket missile bases in Britain' had a similar fate, after Hugh Gaitskell had told the Conference that it went 'too far in the direction of complete unilateral action'.[2]

No more than the unilateralist defeat in 1957 did these Executive victories settle the issue. Not only was the second Aldermaston march at Easter 1959 a very much more substantial demonstration than the first; far more dangerous to the leadership was the growing opposition to official policy in the trade union movement. It was more than an accident that the National Union of General and Municipal Workers, hitherto one of the staunchest pillars of orthodoxy, should have actually passed a resolution in June 1959 (by 150 votes to 126, with 75 delegates not voting) asking that 'the next Labour Government should take unilateral action in ceasing to manufacture nuclear weapons and in prohibiting the use of all such weapons from British territories'.[3]

Nor was it fortuitous that the National Executive and the General Council should have put forward soon afterwards the proposal for the creation of a 'non-nuclear club', provided that an agreement could be reached with every country except the U.S.A. and the U.S.S.R. not to test, manufacture or possess nuclear weapons. In launching such an endeavour, the Labour Party-T.U.C. statement was careful to point out, 'we should in no way be weakening in our support for the NATO alliance or in our readiness to accept American bases in Britain subject to the veto which already exists concerning their possible use'. Furthermore, the agreement would also be subject, the statement said, 'to full and effective international control to ensure that it was carried out'.[4]

The 'non-nuclear club' sank without a trace after the General Election of October 1959, nor did it even figure prominently in Labour's campaign during the Election. Its only use was to provide a chance for the leaders of the National Union of Municipal and General Workers to recall their Conference and seek to reverse its unilateralist vote. At that recalled Conference, which met at the end of August 1959, the delegates were presented with a resolution from their Executive endorsing the Labour Party-T.U.C. statement, no amendment or alternative resolution being allowed. The Execu-

[1] Labour Party Annual Conference Report, 1958, p. 223.
[2] ibid, p. 222.
[3] *The Times*, 5th of June, 1959.
[4] ibid, 24th of June, 1959.

tive had its way: 194 votes were cast for the statement, 139 against.[1]

When the T.U.C. met in September, it had been announced that there would be an election in October, and the official policy was adopted by 5,214,000 votes to 2,690,000.[2] However, the Conference also passed, against the advice of the General Council, a resolution protesting against the decision of the British Government to provide sites for the launching of United States ballistic missiles. The vote was 4,040,000, to 3,865,000.[3]

None of these differences was allowed to appear in the Labour Party's election programme. The Party's campaign committee had concluded, Mr Butler and Mr Rose write, that 'it (the public) would be more swayed by a recital of the muddle in British defence policy than by an examination of the power-politics assumptions underlying British reliance upon NATO or the nuclear deterrent'.[4] As in the three previous General Elections, the Labour leadership, given its home as well as its foreign policy, had no choice but to trivialize the electoral debate and to help degrade the democratic process the Election was supposed to illustrate. In the end, after all the re-thinking, the pamphlets, the statements and the debates of the previous four years, the proposal which most clearly emerged as the Labour Party's main contribution to the electoral campaign was the promise that a Labour Government would immediately raise the old-age pension by 10s. a week, coupled with a pledge by Hugh Gaitskell in the middle of the campaign that there would be 'no increase in the standard or other rates of income tax so long as normal peace-time conditions continue'.

The Labour Party had also set much store by its proposal for a comprehensive national superannuation scheme, and Labour candidates devoted much time and effort in explaining to their audiences the advantages that would accrue to them under the scheme once they had reached the pensionable age. Somehow, this failed to rouse great enthusiasm.

No sooner had the results been declared than a loud chorus of revisionist voices rose to proclaim that the Labour Party had lost the Election because of its attachment to nationalization. And indeed, it may well be that Labour's half-hearted presentation of a case in which most of its leaders did not believe lost the Labour Party some votes. But the revisionist interpretation of defeat was as arbitrary as would have been the claim, had Labour won, that its victory represented a vote for nationalization, let alone socialism.

[1] *The Times*, 22nd of August, 1959.
[2] T.U.C. Annual Conference Report, 1959, p. 415.
[3] ibid, p. 415.
[4] Butler and Rose, op. cit. p. 70.

By 1959, Labour's image was much too blurred to give either defeat or victory so precise a political or ideological meaning. In 1951, 20 per cent. of people, according to the Gallup Poll, had thought that it mattered little or not at all which party was in power; by the summer of 1959, the number had grown to 38 per cent. Indeed, of Labour's supporters, only 60 per cent. recognized major differences between the parties.[1]

In fact, it was the 60 per cent. who were right. In the kind of people whose vote they mainly attracted, in the reasons for the attraction, in the traditions they embodied, most of all in the aspirations of their respective activists, profound differences continued to divide the Labour Party from the Conservative Party. Nor could these differences have failed to find *some* reflection in a Labour Government's attitude to such matters as social welfare. At the same time, it was also entirely reasonable to believe that a Labour victory in 1959 would not have produced any substantial alteration in the shape of affairs at home, or in Britain's rôle abroad.

3. THE BATTLE FOR THE LABOUR PARTY

The battles which broke out in the Labour Party after the General Election of 1959 were not only about nationalization or nuclear strategy. These were the specific expressions of a more basic question, namely whether the Labour Party is to be concerned with attempts at a more efficient and more humane administration of a capitalist society; or whether it is to adapt itself to the task of creating a socialist one.

The question is as old as the Labour Party itself. But until the fifties, it was a question which could be evaded with a Labourist programme of social reform and the public ownership of basic utilities and services. It was after the fulfilment of that programme in the years of Labour's New Deal that Labourism revealed itself altogether inadequate as a basis of policy and action, and that it became increasingly difficult to evade the question of Labour's ultimate purposes.

Because of the inadequacies of Labourism, there is at least logic both in revisionist demands for the Labour Party's retreat, in practice if not rhetoric, from Labourism to a suitably contemporary version of Liberalism; and also in the demands of the Left for socialist alternatives to Conservatism, both in home and foreign affairs.

However, revisionist Right and 'fundamentalist' Left are not the only parties in the debate: there is also the Centre, whose main purpose is to keep the Labour Party within the bounds of Labourism,

[1] Butler and Rose, op. cit. p. 19.

and whose main attribute is the invention of 'formulas' that might be all things to all men.

In a party like the Labour Party, and in an electoral system which greatly discourages political fission, appeals for unity through compromise are always likely to meet with much support, and to appear as the epitome of commonsense and political wisdom. At the same time, such appeals overlook the fact that *genuine* compromise between revisionism on the one hand, and socialist purposes on the other, is impossible; and that any verbal compromise which may be reached on the basis of ingenious formulas, not only perpetuates the paralysis of the last decade, but also ensures, in practice, the predominance of the policies favoured by a revisionist leadership.

Thus a compromise was reached in the controversy which Hugh Gaitskell initiated after the Election of 1959 with his proposal that Clause 4 of the Party Constitution should be revised.[1] In face of the violent resistance this encountered, the proposal had to be dropped, but the 1960 Party Conference was also asked to accept, as a 'valuable expression of the aims of the Labour Party in the second half of the twentieth century', a lengthy statement of aims which was said to 'reaffirm, amplify and clarify' the Labour Party's objects.[2] The statement expressed the conviction that the Party's 'social and economic objectives can be achieved only through an expansion of common ownership substantial enough to give the community power over the commanding heights of the economy'; and 'recognizing that both public and private enterprise have a place in the economy it believes that further extension of common ownership should be decided from time to time in the light of these objectives and according to circumstances, with due regard for the views of the workers and consumers concerned'.[3]

The 1960 Conference agreed to this. But it is surely naïve to think that these formulations provide the basis of genuine compromise between people who fundamentally disagree on the purpose, nature and extent of common ownership. All that such a compromise can do is to provide a temporary lull in a battle to be resumed so soon as actual programmes and policies come to be discussed.

Yet, it is not the fact that a battle between Right and Left broke out in the Labour Party after 1959 which is remarkable: that battle has gone on uninterruptedly since the Party was founded. Much more remarkable are its dimensions. Had the opposition to the leadership's policies and tendencies been confined to the traditional Left in the constituencies and in the unions, the neo-Liberals

[1] See Labour Party Annual Conference Report, 1959, p. 112.
[2] Labour Party Annual Conference Report, 1960, p. 12.
[3] ibid, p. 13.

would have had very little difficulty in imposing upon the Labour Party an explicitly revisionist image, such as has now been assumed by the German Social Democratic Party; and the Left would have been equally powerless to affect the Labour Party's approach to nuclear strategy and related questions. Indeed, there would then have been no Centre to emerge as a political factor: the Centre, such being its nature, would have readily submitted to the Right. What has made all the difference and introduced new dimensions into the conflict is the massive trade union intervention against the leadership.

There have been occasions in the past when the trade union movement has been at odds with the Party leadership over this or that particular issue—most notably in August 1931, when the unions refused to accept Ramsay MacDonald's view of what the national interest entailed. But never in the history of the Labour Party has there been serious disagreement with the unions on its fundamental aims and purpose. This is why the Party leaders, protected by the crushing power which the Constitution of the Party attributes to the unions, were always safe from the challenge of the Left. It is the withdrawal of that protection after 1959 which has created a problem of unprecedented magnitude for the Party leadership.

Unlike constituency or parliamentary rebellions, and unlike 'ginger groups' of the Left within the Party, trade union opposition cannot be crushed or threatened with expulsion. Nor can its wishes, when translated into majority decisions at T.U.C. and Labour Party Conferences, be easily ignored by the Parliamentary Labour Party. It can be induced, by manoeuvre, verbal juggling and appeals for unity, to accept artificial compromises, as was the case in the Clause 4 controversy. It may be pacified by apparent concessions on specific issues of policy. And division among the unions may even ensure the reversal of Conference decisions to which the Party leadership is opposed. But nothing of all this resolves the real problem, which is that a leadership whose purpose it is to reduce the Party's commitment to socialist policies can no longer rely on the trade unions to help it in achieving its aims.

It would be wrong to see this trade union opposition as an ideologically cohesive and politically homogeneous force. But it would be equally mistaken to underestimate the genuine and stubborn radicalism which it expresses. In this context, much of its significance derives not only from its extent but from its persistence. Had the trade unions been single-mindedly committed to a consolidating Labour leadership throughout the fifties, their opposition since 1959 might more plausibly be interpreted as a sudden eruption of bad temper following Labour's third consecutive electoral defeat. But recent history suggests, on the contrary, that this opposition is only the latest manifestation of powerful currents which have been running in the trade union movement for ten years and more and which have produced a consistent pressure for more radical Labour policies, notably for more, and more democratically controlled, nationalization, and for new Labour initiatives in international affairs. Electoral defeat only increased an impatience which had been manifesting itself over the previous years.

The apparent paradox is that this groundswell has been gathering strength precisely in the years of the 'affluent society', which was deemed to have ushered in the era of what C. Wright Mills has called the 'cheerful robot'. But the paradox *is* only apparent. For the contradiction which is so often assumed between 'affluence' and radicalism leaves much out of account. It leaves out of account the fact that the long years of slump and mass unemployment were not years of trade union militancy and radicalism, either in industrial or in political terms. It also leaves out of account the fact that the social and economic changes which have occurred in Britain since the war have not been such as to eradicate the fundamental conflict of interests which continues to divide wage earners from their employers. But most important of all, it overlooks the fact that trade unionists have behind them two decades of increased confidence in their own strength—of increased confidence generated by the experience of war, by the achievements of Labour's New Deal after the war, and by the maintenance of full employment after 1951. That confidence has not only found expression, often against the wishes of trade union leaders, in a far less defensive attitude towards employers; it has also led to the rejection of that grand reconciliation between the Labour movement and contemporary capitalism which is the essence of revisionism.

At the Labour Party Conference of November 1959, Hugh Gaitskell vigorously rejected the notion that the Labour Party should break with the trade unions. 'I have always looked upon the Trade Union Congress and the Labour Party,' he said, 'as part of the same great Labour Movement and our close integration as one of our great strengths. I see no reason to change my mind. I hope our trade union friends feel likewise.'[1] At the same time, however, the Leader also complained that, even though the Labour Party in the House of Commons was 'a far better cross-section of the community than the Tories who are still overwhelmingly drawn from a single social class', yet 'somehow we let the Tories get away with the monstrous

[1] Labour Party Annual Conference Report, 1959, p. 109.

falsehood that *we* are a Class Party and they are *not*. We must now surely attend to this'.[1]

The two statements epitomize the crucial dilemma of those who wish the Labour Party to renounce its so-called fundamentalist principles. For alliance with the trade unions is not only *one* of the Party's great strengths; it is by far its greatest strength. And attending to the 'monstrous falsehood' that the Labour Party is a class party can only be achieved in one of two ways: dissociation from the trade unions, which Mr Gaitskell excludes, or an even greater dilution of Labour policy, to which the trade unions themselves are opposed.

In fact, it is not a monstrous falsehood for the Tories to claim that the Labour Party is a class party, however false it may be for them to claim that their party is not. But the Labour Party is also a party whose leaders have always sought to escape from the implications of its class character by pursuing what they deemed to be 'national' policies: these policies have regularly turned to the detriment of the working classes and to the advantage of Conservatism. Nor can it be otherwise in a society whose essential characteristic remains class division.

One of the reasons why Labour leaders have always repudiated the class character of the Labour Party has been their fear that to admit the fact, and to act upon it, would antagonize 'floating voters'. So in many cases it no doubt has. And so indeed it should. But there is nothing to suggest that a multitude of men and women, who are not of the working classes, have in the past found the class character of the Labour Party a bar to their support for it, or that support for it would wane if its leaders were to adapt their policies to that fact.

The reverse is more likely to be true. For while Labour leaders have felt that the 'affluent society' required more urgently than ever that their Party should appear 'classless', profound unease with that society has grown apace far outside trade union ranks. If trade union radicalism in recent years is a sign of this unease, the radicalism to be found in a new generation is surely another. While lamentations have been loud at the supposed political apathy of youth, a multitude of young men and women have found in the threat of nuclear war and a host of other issues a basis of commitment far transcending the orthodoxies of Labourism. It is only in comparison with the mythical thirties that the fifties, or at least the late fifties, have been years of political disengagement. The comparison with the real thirties is not to the detriment of these past years. The real difference is that the fifties have often appeared to lack the political instrumentalities of radical change. And to this impression, a consolidating Labour Party, revisionist in practice if not in theory, has greatly con-

[1] Labour Party Annual Conference Report, 1959, p. 109. Italics in text.

tributed. If politics in the fifties have seemed a decreasingly meaningful activity, void of substance, heedless of principle, and rich in election auctioneering, the responsibility is not only that of the hidden or overt persuaders: it is also, and to a major degree, that of Labour's leaders.

Even if a socialist Labour Party had not, in the fifties, won more elections than did the Labour Party as it was, it would not have found defeat catastrophic: armed with genuine alternatives to Conservatism, it would have been able to take the longer view, and seen its electoral defeats, not as the occasion for retreat, but as a spur to greater efforts in its task of political conversion. And whether it would have won an election or not, it would certainly have provided a very different opposition to the Government in power, and made conversion more likely because of the opposition it would have provided.

If the Labour Party were to become such a party, it would be subject to attacks infinitely more fierce than it has had to endure for many a day, both from Conservative interests and a Conservative Press whose present yearning for a 'virile Opposition' would instantly vanish, and also from former members who would feel impelled to turn against it and denounce its policies and deeds. But against this, it would elicit and enlist the kind of devotion and support which a consolidating Labour Party now finds it increasingly difficult to engender. It is well to resist the urge to prophecy. But it does not seem unduly rash to suggest that the alternative to its becoming such a party is the kind of slow but sure decline which—deservedly—affects parties that have ceased to serve any distinctive political purpose.

POSTSCRIPT

I

The last chapter of *Parliamentary Socialism* was written in 1960 at the height of the struggle between Gaitskellite 'revisionists' on the one hand, and an unstable coalition of their opponents in the Labour Party and the trade unions on the other; and the concluding section of the book left open the possibility that the Labour Party might yet become an adequate agency for that radical transformation of British society to which it had for so long been formally committed.

This, clearly enough, is not what happened in the following years. The groundswell of militancy to which I then referred did grow throughout the Labour movement and well beyond it in the sixties. But this found no reflection in Labour's policies and activities, least of all during the six years in which the Labour Government was in office; or rather, this militancy produced policies and activities designed to curb and subdue it.

The natural tendency, in discussing Labour in the sixties, is to focus on the Labour Government's record between 1964 and 1970. But that record needs to be seen as the consequence of attitudes and decisions which had been adopted well before the Government came to office. The key to its performance in office is to be found in the Labour leaders' basic approach, while still in opposition, to the purposes and tasks they assigned to a Labour Government. Directions were then assumed, or rather confirmed, which fundamentally determined the course of subsequent events.

The most important of the decisions that were made in the years which immediately preceded Labour's electoral victory in 1964 was that a Labour Government, when it next came to office, would not seek to extend public ownership in any really significant way.[1] This, in effect, was the outcome of the struggle around Clause 4 in 1959–60; and though the episode is now ancient history, it was sufficiently important in its long-term implications for its more salient aspects to be reviewed here.

[1]This, incidentally, is not to be taken to imply that a vast extension of public ownership, least of all in the forms in which it was undertaken after 1945, is a sufficient condition for the transformation of a capitalist society into a socialist one or that it constitutes an instant remedy for all economic or social ills. The point is rather that it is a necessary condition for the transcendence of capitalism in socialist directions; and that the much more modest ambitions of the Labour leaders also depended, as they themselves were soon to argue, on their capture of the 'commanding heights' of the economy.

Hugh Gaitskell, it may be recalled, had not specifically asked for the excision of Clause 4 from the Party Constitution, or even for its amendment.[1] What he had proposed was a new 'declaration of aims', which would become part of the Constitution of the Labour Party alongside Clause 4. The draft 12-point declaration which he had presented to the National Executive Committee of the Labour Party in March 1960 had invited the Party to affirm that 'its aim is a classless society from which all class barriers and false social values have been eliminated'; that it stood for 'democracy in industry'; that it rejected 'the selfish acquisitive doctrine of capitalism'; and that it wanted instead 'to create a socialist community based on fellowship, cooperation and service in which all can share fully in our cultural heritage'. The reference to public ownership in the declaration went as follows: 'It [the Labour Party] is convinced that these social and economic objectives can be achieved only through an expansion of common ownership substantial enough to give the community power over the commanding heights of the economy'. This might have been taken to signify a far-reaching commitment. But the text then went on virtually to qualify it out of existence. 'Recognizing,' it said, 'that both public and private enterprise have a place in the economy it [the Labour Party] believes that further extension of common ownership should be decided from time to time in the light of these objectives, and according to circumstances with due regard for the views of the workers and consumers concerned.' Given the known attitude of the Labour leaders to the extension of public ownership, this evasive formula amounted to a commitment that nothing much would be done about it. Nor, for that matter, would a less evasive formula have made much difference in practice. What mattered was what the Labour leaders wanted, or, as in this case, what they did not want.

The proposal that the declaration be included in the Constitution of the Labour Party was accepted by the Executive. At this point, however, a difficulty arose. As one writer with strong sympathies for the 'revisionists' has noted, 'the trade union delegates to the NEC had provided him [i.e. Gaitskell] with the necessary support, but they had acted individually and without reference to their unions. The union conferences in the spring and summer of 1960 refused to ratify the decisions of their delegates, and what in March had appeared as an agreed solution had by the autumn turned into

[1] Clause 4 reads: 'To secure for the workers by hand or by brain the full fruits of their industry and the most equitable distribution thereof that may be possible, upon the basis of the common ownership of the means of production, distribution and exchange, and the best obtainable system of popular administration and control of each industry and service.'

a defeat for Gaitskell.'[1] Faced with the certain prospect that his attempt to write the declaration into the Constitution would be turned down at the 1960 Labour Party Conference, Gaitskell agreed to an Executive resolution which decided to leave the Constitution as it stood, but which also declared that the statement which it had accepted in March was a 'valuable expression of the aims of the Labour Party in the second half of the twentieth century', and which it therefore 'commended' to the Conference. The Conference duly agreed to this, and the battle of Clause 4 was thus brought to an end.

It suited the contestants to proclaim (and as far as much of the Labour Left was concerned probably to believe) that the battle had ended without a decisive victory for either side. But save in purely formal terms, it was not an accurate view of what had happened. For all practical purposes, Labour's 'revisionist' leaders had had their way. Moreover, they remained firmly in control of the day to day decision-making apparatus of the Party. Such verbal concessions as they had been compelled to make – and they had been compelled to make very few – merely served to pacify the Labour Left, and thus even to strengthen the leadership.

In 1961, the Annual Conference adopted *Signposts for the Sixties*, the document which formed the basis of Labour's electoral programme in 1964, and this too is worth a brief mention.

This document called attention to the fact that 'the economy is still dominated by a small ruling caste. For years the Tories have talked about a property-owning democracy. Yet the top one per cent of the population owns nearly half of the nation's private wealth and property. . . . But these men are not only wealthy: they are also powerful – a small and compact oligarchy . . . in private industry the directors of a few hundred great combines determine between them what Britain should produce. As their power increases, these men, together with the directors of leading insurance companies, are usurping the functions of a Government which is theoretically responsible to the whole people.'[2] In the same vein, *Signposts for the Sixties* called attention 'to the menacing growth of private monopoly and the consequent concentration of power in irresponsible hands. The giant corporations or private financial empires which dominate so much of the British economy, and which decisively influence its total performance, grow each year larger, fewer and yet more closely interlocked.'[3]

This analysis, it might have been thought, unmistakably pointed to the conclusion that major measures of public ownership must

[1] S. Haseler, *The Gaitskellites* (1969) p. 170.
[2] *Signposts for the Sixties*, pp. 9–10.
[3] ibid, p. 17.

form an essential plank of Labour's platform. But this was precisely the conclusion which the document quite deliberately failed to reach. Having located the 'commanding heights', the Labour leaders showed that they had no intention of climbing them. *Signposts for the Sixties* committed a Labour Government to the re-nationalisation of steel, which had become an unavoidable pledge; and to the creation of an 'integrated and publicly owned transport system', which, however commendable, was hardly dramatic, since so much of public transport was already publicly owned. For the rest, the document was resolutely hypothetical, and spoke of public ownership, not as a means of capturing the 'commanding heights', but, 'most important of all', as a means of 'helping to fufill our national plan for economic growth'. There was very little about this economic, 'pragmatic' emphasis, that the 'small and compact oligarchy' which was said to dominate economic life need be unduly troubled about.

By 1963, Harold Wilson was explaining to the readers of *The New York Times* ('Wilson Defines British Socialism') that 'our plans to extend the public sector – to occupy the "commanding heights" – consist mainly in the creation of new industries'. Even this was qualified: 'We shall not be dogmatic or doctrinaire about the ownership of the new industries. Some will be privately owned, some publicly owned – the important thing is to get them established'.[1]

By the time this was written, Wilson had become Leader of the Labour Party. Much, as a result, then seemed to many people to have been thrown back into the melting pot. To the Labour Left in particular, this utterly unpredictable turn of events appeared to suggest that the new chapter which was about to be written in the Labour Party's history would be very different, and much more attractive to the Left, than could have been anticipated had Gaitskell lived. From having been permanently exiled to the outer fringes of the Labour Party's apparatus of power, the Labour Left now felt itself to be represented at its very centre. After all, Wilson had challenged Gaitskell for the leadership of the Labour Party in 1960, and had therefore appeared, willy nilly, to ally himself with Gaitskell's opponents on the left. Nine years earlier he had resigned from the Attlee Government with Aneurin Bevan and John Freeman; and although he had been careful, in the following years, to keep his distance from the Bevanite group, he had also been even more distant from the Gaitskellite faction; indeed in personal terms much more so. The constituency parties had regularly returned him to the National Executive on what was generally regarded as a left slate. In short, he appeared in 1963 as the answer to the Labour Left's prayer for a sympathetic leader of the Party.

[1] The article is reprinted in H. Wilson, *Purpose in Politics* (1964).

This view of the prospects unfolded by Wilson's accession to the leadership unfortunately overlooked a great deal that was known about him, and which should have been obvious from his pronouncements and conduct over the years – notably the fact that neither over foreign affairs, nor over home policy, including public ownership, did he materially differ from Gaitskell. Their views might not be identical over this or that policy issue, but such differences as there were could in no basic sense be said to place the new leader outside the ideological spectrum in which Gaitskell moved. What separated him from Gaitskell and the latter's friends (apart from the dislike, distrust and even contempt which they felt for him) was a matter of tactics and a certain style. Wilson had an infinitely greater sense of the complex strands which make up the political culture of the Labour movement, and he realised far better than did the 'Hampstead set' that the 'unity' of the Party, which meant in effect the neutralisation of the Left, could be achieved at a very small price, indeed at next to no price, provided the leadership was willing to wrap up whatever policies it thought suitable in language which would appeal to the Left. A small but significant episode may serve to illustrate the point. Shortly after Wilson's accession to the leadership of the Party, a Tory backwoodsman sought to embarrass him in the House of Commons by referring to Clause 4. Wilson defiantly interrupted him and answered him that it was 'the position of the whole Party'.[1] It was not the kind of thing which Gaitskell would have handled well, but which Wilson could take in his stride, and gain credit for from the Labour Left, even though what he said did not actually mean anything. There was to be much of the same kind in the following years.

However, Harold Wilson said much, in the eighteen months after he became Leader of the Labour Party, which appeared to provide an answer to Labour's search for the kind of positive 'message' which it had failed to find ever since the collapse of the Attlee Government in 1951.

His most insistent and persuasive theme was the need for change, renewal, modernization and reform in every area of British life, most of all in economic life. Much of what he said sounded radical enough, as for instance when speaking for the first time in the role of Leader of the Party to its annual conference, he told the delegates that 'for the commanding heights of British industry to be controlled today by men whose only claim is their aristocratic connections or the power of inherited wealth or speculative finance is as irrelevant to the twentieth century as would be the continued purchase of

[1]House of Commons, 18 February, 1963, vol. 672, col. 106.

commissions in the armed forces by lordly amateurs'.[1] It needs to be understood, however, that what Wilson was attacking was not British capitalism as a system, but some facets of it, the 'old boy network', 'candy-floss commercialism', 'parasitic speculators', the 'grouse-moor mentality', and that what, in effect, he counterposed to this was not the vision of a socialist society, but of a renovated capitalism, freed from its aristocratic and gentlemanly accretions, dynamic, professional, entrepreneurial, numerate and efficient.

Two things may be said about this. The first is that Wilson's apparent conviction that it was possible to make a clear separation between 'patriotic' and 'unpatriotic' enterprise altogether ignored the degree to which those forms of it to which he objected and those forms of it which he approved were in fact intertwined. Secondly, that even if some such separation was possible, the kind of capitalism which appeared to meet with his approval was as socially irresponsible and greedily exploitative as any other kind. It is in this perspective that such radicalism as forms part of Harold Wilson's philosophy has to be seen. It is too simple to suggest, as has often been done in the light of subsequent experience, not least by many of his erstwhile admirers, that when he spoke before 1964 of the need for radical change, he was merely engaged in an astute public relations exercise, designed to appeal to a widespread mood of impatience with a decrepit economic and social order. No doubt, the public relations aspect of the matter was there. But there is no need to deny Mr Wilson's interest in reform. To do so is to miss the much more important point that his reforming zeal was deliberately set, for all its verbal edge, within the context of an economic system whose *basic* features were accepted by him and his colleagues as given; and that all their proposals for change had therefore to be adapted to the nature and requirements of that system. But 'adapted' is too weak – 'subordinated' would be more accurate. Whatever deficiency and dereliction Harold Wilson touched on – and he touched upon many – was directly or indirectly related to the prevailing economic system: and it followed that the changes of which he spoke, if they were to be as far-reaching as he proclaimed to be necessary, would require precisely the kind of challenge to that economic system which his whole approach precluded. Given the context which he assumed, namely one in which the 'commanding heights' of the economy would remain under private ownership and control, and in which public enterprise would continue to remain an adjunct of capitalist enterprise, the 'modernization' for which he asked could only mean the more efficient operation of the capitalist system; and this would include that ever-greater concentration of

[1] Labour Party Annual Conference Report, 1963, pp. 134.

private economic power, which he denounced, but which the Labour Government was in fact to encourage. He spoke of allying 'science to socialism': all that this could mean was the more effective harnessing of science to the purposes of capitalism. He appealed for an end to the 'system of educational apartheid' and proclaimed the need for careers to be open to talent. But what this meant, given the context, was that more talent should be channelled into the service of the going system. Nor did the Labour Government make any notable indent into the system of educational apartheid; and in the field of tertiary education, it even managed, with the adoption of the 'binary' system, to give it new institutional forms. Wilson comprehensively denounced the 'conservatism' of British life: but the only 'conservatism' he and his government tried to do much about was that of the trade union movement, which did indeed want to conserve hard-won rights of self-defence against the attacks of the Labour Government.

The fact is that, in order to acquire effective meaning, Wilson's radicalism needed to include the determination to mount an assault upon the 'commanding heights' of the economy. But he had no more wish than his erstwhile 'revisionist' opponents to do anything of the kind. This being the case, his radicalism was bound to remain mere verbiage. Without the control provided by the public ownership of strategic sections of the economy, he and his colleagues could only try and persuade those who did control the 'private sector' to cooperate with them. But they could only succeed in doing so by pursuing policies which corresponded with the purposes of capitalist interests. These purposes did not happen to include the radical aspirations by which the Labour leaders proclaimed themselves to be driven.

The attitude which the leaders held towards the question of public ownership had a significance which went far beyond that issue itself. The battle of Clause 4 had not only been about public ownership. Behind that issue, there was the determination of the Labour leadership to force upon the Labour Party the final acceptance of an economic system predominantly based upon private ownership and control, and its abandonment, for all practical purposes, of the alternative vision which Clause 4 embodied. In this crucial sense, the argument had not at all been about 'theology' as Harold Wilson had found it convenient to claim at the time. On the contrary, it had vast political implications not only in terms of the Labour Party's ultimate purpose, but also in terms of its approach to immediate problems. A leadership as thoroughly reconciled as this one was to the permanence of British capitalism could also be expected to be easily reconciled to its requirements, and to the acceptance of its particular rationality. That this was so was richly confirmed by the experience of Labour in government.

The reconciliation was all the more likely to be achieved – or at least sought for by the Labour leaders – in that they had, like their predecessors, a profound sense of their 'national' vocation. It has been said about Gaitskell that he had a 'philosophic predilection for "class harmony" as opposed to "class division" or "class war" '; and that this partly explained 'his desire to make Labour a "classless party" and his intense emotional reaction against the Conservative Party's claim that they represented all social classes whereas Labour was tied to a single class.'[1] This is no doubt quite accurate. The trouble, however, is that the search for class harmony could only be successful on two conditions: the first was that the Labour Party should not attempt to do much about the evils which its leaders were so ready to denounce on Labour platforms, since to try and do much about them involved a radical challenge to those forces which profited from their perpetuation. Secondly, it required that the Labour leaders should do their best to demobilize their own supporters and, where occasion demanded, to turn against them. Provided they were prepared to meet these conditions, and they were, there was no reason why they should not achieve a reasonable rapport with the best people.

Harold Wilson shared to the full this concern for class harmony. Indeed, his wish to cut a 'national' figure, particularly after he had assumed office, often seemed to be an almost obsessive preoccupation, only previously matched in its intensity by Ramsay MacDonald. At the 1966 Annual Conference of the Labour Party, following Labour's resounding victory at the polls, he explained the significance of that victory, as it appeared to him: 'It proved', he said, 'that the British people accepted that Labour could govern, that we had the means and the measures that the country knew were necessary. It proved that Labour could give national leadership, that we rejected the Conservative concept of cynical conflict between class and class'.[2] Of course the 'Conservative concept' was precisely the opposite, namely that there was no inherent conflict, cynical or otherwise, between class and class, and that where conflict did occur, it should be attributed to the machinations of ill-intentioned men seeking to exploit long-outmoded attitudes unfortunately still prevalent in the working class. This view, though in itself absurd, is a necessary part of Conservative thinking, since it serves important self-legitimating as well as propaganda purposes. Faced with class conflict and bent on class harmony, Wilson and his colleagues soon

[1] Haseler, op. cit. p. 164.
[2] Labour Party Annual Conference Report, 1966, p. 162.

357

adopted the same Conservative view, and acted in accordance with it.

The Labour Party's Manifesto for the General Election of 1964 was boldly entitled *The New Britain*. But the contents of the document hardly matched the promise of the title. The prospectus was breathless enough – obviously the brainwork of the public relations wizards which the Labour Party had called to its help: 'The country needs fresh and virile leadership. Labour is ready. Poised to swing its plans into instant operation. Impatient to apply the New Thinking that will end the chaos and sterility . . . restless with positive remedies for the problems the Tories have criminally neglected.' The prospectus was fraudulent. The Manifesto comprised a useful if modest list of reforms, notably in the field of welfare, which Labour promised to carry out. But what was being offered in 1964 was not a 'new Britain': rather, and at the most, a more efficient and more 'compassionate' management of the old order. The Manifesto mentioned 'socialist planning': but what this amounted to was the promise to set up a Ministry of Economic Affairs 'with the duty of formulating, with both sides of industry, a national economic plan'. But, the document asked, suppose production falls short of the plan in key sections of industry? The New Thinking had the answer ready: 'Then it is up to the Government and the industry to take whatever measures are required.'

Public ownership was dealt with perfunctorily: steel would be re-nationalised, and existing nationalised industries would be encouraged to move into new fields. A Labour Government would also establish new industries: but it would do so 'either by public enterprise or in participation with private industry.' In the election campaign itself, Butler and King have observed, 'Labour spokesmen played down the issue [of public ownership]; they tended to concentrate on the monopolistic inefficiency of the steel industry and, defensively, to deny any plans for the large extension of public ownership.'[1] By 1966, the reference to public ownership in the Labour Manifesto had come to be included in a section significantly entitled 'Helping Industry' and had even less to say on the subject than in 1964.[2] Four years later, still less. In effect, the issue had been relegated to as low a place on Labour's agenda as Hugh Gaitskell and his friends could ever have wished. Given the weakness of political formations on the left of the Labour Party, this meant in effect that it had been removed from serious political debate altogether. This

[1] D. E. Butler and A. King, *The British General Election of 1964*, p. 135 (1965).
[2] In *The British General Election of 1966* (1967), the same authors also note that 'one of the supreme ironies of the 1966 election was that the final emphasis of the Conservative leader was on the need for radical change and of the Leader of the Labour Party on the need for patriotism and stability' p. 124.

was a major contribution of the Labour leaders to the nature and substance of contemporary British politics, for which capitalist interests had good cause to be grateful. In thus disposing of public ownership, in thus turning it into a great non-issue, the Labour leaders had provided these interests with a guarantee against the one threat they had most reason to fear. Wherever else the consensus between the parties might break down, all was safe so long as it endured here; and those who controlled the Labour Party were wholly determined that it should.

What has been said so far should help to explain one feature of Labour's affairs which might otherwise seem puzzling, namely its lack of 'preparation' for office, which was in some crucial respects as marked in 1964 as it had been on previous occasions. The 1964 Election Manifesto had referred to Labour's readiness to 'swing its plans into instant operation'. But as one writer has accurately noted, 'detailed work had been undertaken on social security, land, higher education and regional planning, but on the central problem of the balance of payments and the modernization of the economy only sketch plans were available.'[1] This lack of preparation, after thirteen long years in opposition, was in no way accidental. For, as the same writer also explains, 'in order to make proper preparations, a number of different and divisive issues would have had to be raised. Any thorough examination of overseas defence expenditure, for instance, would have called into question Britain's relations with NATO and the United States. Any serious examination of the tools available to the Government in economic planning might have led to the conclusion that the amount of control which was to be exercised over privately owned firms is strictly limited. Any real attempt to work out the machinery for new public ownership might have transformed this from a useful flag to wave at Party Conferences into a positive commitment to extend the frontiers of public ownership.'[2]

This is right. But Mr Pryke goes on to say that the reason such commitments were avoided was that to try and spell them out would have shattered the 'new-found unity' of the Party. 'The Labour leaders had no wish to reopen the acrimonious debates of the early 1960's. What they were usually trying to discover in their discussions was not a policy for the future but a form of words for the

---

[1] R. Pryke, 'The Predictable Crisis' in *New Left Review*, No. 39, Sept.-Oct. 1966, p. 3. It may even be doubted whether work which had been undertaken on social security, land, higher education and regional planning was as 'detailed' as is here suggested – not to speak of the degree of 'radicalism' which the work, detailed or not, exhibited.
[2] ibid.

present. In this way Labour was able to fight the 1964 Election as a united party. If it had been disunited it would have lost.'[1] This would suggest that the lack of preparation of more radical proposals was due to the need for compromise between left and right in the top echelons of the Party. But there is no evidence that anyone among the policymakers in the Labour Party seriously pressed for a more radical programme, least of all that Harold Wilson himself wanted such a programme, and that he had to be satisfied with less for the sake of 'unity'. On the contrary, the evidence suggests that the leaders of the party, however divided they might be on personal grounds, were fundamentally at one in ideological and programmatic terms. Left and Right in relation to them are terms devoid of any really serious meaning. The real reason why more radical plans had not been prepared is very simply that the leaders had no intention of carrying out any such plans. Nor did the Labour Left, still bemused by the thought that Harold Wilson was *really* on their side, have either the will or the capacity to press for more radical policies. Those who belonged to it also accepted the argument that, particularly before an election which the Labour Party stood a good chance of winning, unity was all: what they gladly overlooked was that this unity had been achieved at their expense.

The point has an obvious bearing on the present, now that the Labour Party is once again in opposition. The call is again heard that the Party *must* address itself more seriously than in the past to the task of preparing its plans for office. But this ignores the fact that the men who will control the next Labour Government are just as determined not to be saddled with embarrassingly far-reaching plans as were the men who assumed office in 1964. There may be much to be said for working out detailed socialist policies. But there is nothing to be said for the notion that they will be taken up by Labour in office. This is not what the Labour leaders are ABOUT.

The point will be discussed further in the concluding section of this Postscript. For the moment, what needs to be stressed is that the basic pattern of the Labour Government's conduct was firmly set in the preceding years. What happened between 1964 and 1970 was not due to the unfavourable economic circumstances which the government inherited; or to the entrenched conservatism of top civil servants; or to the machinations of speculators and the hostility of capitalist interests at home or abroad. It was above all due to the particular ideological dispositions which the men who ran the government brought to their tasks. It was these dispositions which allowed all the adverse factors they faced in office to weigh upon them as heavily as they did. No doubt, these factors would in any

[1] ibid.

case have had to be tackled: but they would have been tackled very differently had these men had a genuinely more radical approach to affairs. Not only would the solutions have been different: the problems themselves would have been differently perceived. At the 1966 Labour Party Conference, Harold Wilson told the delegates that 'we cannot afford to fight the problems of the sixties with the attitudes of the Social Democratic Federation, nor, in looking for a solution to these problems, seek vainly to find the answers in Highgate cemetery'.[1] But the trouble with Mr Wilson and his colleagues was that their own answers to the problems they faced were of such a kind as to involve the betrayal of their promises and the reinforcement of the system to which they declared themselves opposed.

II

Harold Wilson has described his apologia for his years of office as 'the record of a Government all but a year of whose life was dominated by an inherited balance of payments problem which was nearing a crisis at the moment we took office; we lived and governed during a period when that problem made frenetic speculative attack on Britain both easy and profitable.'[2] Five years, however, is a rather long time for a government to be dominated by an inherited balance of payments crisis, however acute; and the fact that the Wilson government was thus dominated says much about the narrow framework of orthodoxy within which it chose to operate. It had been no secret to its leading members that a Labour Government would, in 1964, inherit a massive balance of payments deficit. What they did not seem to have anticipated was the run on the pound which occured soon after the Government was installed. When it did occur, the Prime Minister and his colleagues firmly rejected the one measure which, in the short run, would have given them some respite, namely devaluation. In August 1965, Harold Wilson explained in an interview to the *Guardian* why he had decided against it: 'Although this would have given us a year or two breathing space free from all anxiety about foreign balances, we felt that, whatever the temptation from the party point of view, the national interest was one hundred per cent the other way . . . I do not deny it would have made life more tolerable with our narrow majority; that it would have enabled us to carry through our positive generous programmes of social

[1] Labour Party Annual Conference Report, 1966, p. 163.
[2] H. Wilson, *The Labour Government 1964–1970. A Personal Record* (*1971*) p. xvii

reform, but it would not have been right.' Indeed, it would have been 'totally wrong', since 'there are many people overseas, including governments, marketing boards, central banks and others, who left their money in the form of sterling balances, on the assumption that the value of sterling would be maintained. To have let them down would have been not only a betrayal of trust, it would have shaken their faith about holding any further money in the form of sterling.'[1]

These sentiments suggest a very revealing order of priorities for a Labour Prime Minister. For in choosing not to 'let down' Britain's overseas creditors, he was also choosing to 'let down' the people whose votes had brought him to office and to sacrifice 'our positive generous programmes of social reform'.

No doubt, as Mr Wilson has subsequently argued, devaluation was 'not an easy way out'. But, as experience was to show, it could scarcely have been harder than the decision to 'defend the pound', which was in any case unsuccessful. It was above all a political decision, intended to establish Labour's credentials with the international 'business community', and reinforced by the fear, as one well-informed writer has put it, that devaluation, to which the United States was then opposed, 'would cloud prospects for future Anglo-American cooperation which Wilson hoped would form the backbone of his foreign policy.'[2]

Having rejected devaluation, the Government resorted to international borrowing to shore up sterling: in November 1964, it mounted the first of the many international 'rescue operations', to the tune of 3000 million dollars, which marked its years of office. Yet, it was only a month before coming to office that the Prime Minister himself, in words which have often been quoted, told the Trades Union Congress that 'you can get into pawn, but don't then talk of an independent foreign policy, or an independent defence policy'.[3] In actual fact, the Labour leaders had no intention of pursuing an independent foreign or defence policy, so that being in pawn made no great difference. At the 1965 Labour Party Conference, Mr Wilson indignantly repudiated the charge that his support for the United States in Vietnam had anything to do with economic dependence. 'At no time – and I say this categorically – has there been any attempt to link economic cooperation with any aspect of foreign policy . . . there have never been, whether in White House talks, in telegrams, in ambassadorial approaches, or even on the hot line, any attempts to link Vietnam with any aspect of economic or

---

[1] *The Guardian*, 6th of August, 1965.
[2] H. Brandon, *In the Red* (1966) p. 44.
[3] TUC Annual Conference Report, 1964, p. 383.

monetary cooperation . . .'[1] This is hardly conclusive: the Prime Minister did not have to be *told* that there would be retribution to be aware that it might occur, if anything he said or did proved to be a serious embarrassment to the American Administration. Still, the point need not be argued: it may well be that Mr Wilson and his colleagues were sufficiently committed to the 'Anglo-American alliance' to support American aggression in Vietnam without being forced to do so by financial necessity. More relevant are some other remarks which Mr Wilson addressed to the 1964 TUC: 'There is a warning here,' the Prime Minister had gone on to say. 'If you borrow from some of the world's bankers you will quickly find you lose another kind of independence because of the deflationary policies and the cuts on social services that will be imposed on a government that has got itself into that position.'[2] At the end of the General Election campaign, he had made the same point more specifically: 'You cannot go, cap in hand, to the central bankers of Europe as they [the Tories] have now been forced to do and maintain your freedom of action, whether on policies maintaining full employment here in Britain or even on social policies.'[3]

This was very well said and describes admirably what happened throughout the life of the Government. As Mr Maudling, the previous Chancellor of the Exchequer, put it in 1964, 'it is true the Labour Government have inherited our problems. They seem also to have inherited our solutions.'[4] It was entirely symptomatic of the climate in which the Government chose to operate that the Chancellor of the Exchequer, Mr Callaghan, who had in 1963 proposed an annual tax on all wealth over £20,000, and who had had the proposal endorsed by the Labour Party's Annual Conference of that year, should have declared in December 1964 that 'in view of the major reforms I have already announced to modernize the tax system and make it more fair, I have no plans for·proceeding with this proposal'.[5]

The Government had come to office on a pledge to end the 'Stop-Go' policies of the Conservatives. It had proclaimed itself to be 'the party of growth'. But it quickly turned into, and remained throughout, a government of deflation and economic stagnation; and before long, it had come to preside over a level of permanent unemployment unknown in Britain since the war. In his book, Mr Wilson recalls that, on being pressed in November 1964 by

[1] Labour Party Annual Conference Report, 1965, p. 197.
[2] TUC Annual Conference Report, 1964, p. 383.
[3] *Sunday Telegraph*, 11th of October, 1964.
[4] Butler and King, op. cit. p. 5.
[5] *The Times*, 16th of December, 1964.

Lord Cromer, the Governor of the Bank of England, for all-round cuts in expenditure, 'I asked him if this meant that it was impossible for any Government, whatever its party label, whatever its manifesto or the policies on which it fought an election, to continue, unless it immediately reverted to full-scale Tory policies.' On being told that it was so, 'because of the sheer compulsion of the economic dictation of those who exercised decisive economic power', the Prime Minister retorted that 'if that was the case, I was not prepared to accept it.'[1] What this means, on the record, is that Mr Wilson was not prepared to go *as far* as Lord Cromer wished. There is a Tory way of carrying out Tory policies; and there is a Labour way of carrying out Tory policies. It may readily be granted that the Government carried out Tory policies in a Labour way, with heart-searching, qualifications, exceptions and so forth. But carry them out it did, all the same, and thereby cleared the way for the more drastic application of Tory policies by their Tory successors.

In 1965, the Government presented with much flourish its National Plan for economic growth. This proclaimed a series of targets which, if reached, would have achieved a 25% increase in G.N.P. by 1970. In fact, the targets were no more than forecasts and the Government had not much more control over their fulfilment than the Meterological Office has over its weather predictions. For it was in no position to 'plan'. The planning endeavours of the Attlee Government after the war had been meagre enough. But compared to those of the Wilson Government, they were positively heroic. In any case, the government was forced into policies of further deflation soon after the National Plan was announced, which made even greater nonsense of its forecasts. The Plan was dead even before the echoes of its promise had been stilled. Edward Heath was quite right to describe it as 'the biggest publicity gimmick which the Government has so far produced'[2] – not that he was by any means the most suitable person to issue the indictment.

There was one policy which the Labour Government pursued with great consistency throughout its period of office, namely an 'incomes policy'. This had been a fixed part of the Labour leaders' purpose long before the Wilson Government was formed, as it had long been a fixed part of the purpose of Conservative governments. What that policy amounted to, stripped of verbiage, was a state-imposed curb on wage increases: a matter of people earning £1000 a month (or more) telling people earning £1000 a year (or less) that they must stop being greedy. On the other hand, an incomes policy badly

[1] Op. cit. p. 37.
[2] *The Times*, 17th of September, 1965.

required verbiage, and this certainly was not wanting. As so often in the past, when wage-earners had been asked to show 'restraint', the old and spurious cry of 'equality of sacrifice' was again raised. In 1963, Harold Wilson had warned that 'we shall have to ask for restraint in the matter of incomes', but, he had added, 'when we say incomes we mean *all* incomes. That means not only wages and salaries, but profits, especially monopoly profits, distributed dividends, yes, and rents as well . . .'[1] Once again, the rich were to be asked, without much effect, to defer cashing in their profits and dividends, while wage earners were to be pressed, with much greater determination, to forego 'unreasonable' wage increases altogether.

At the TUC in September 1964, Harold Wilson had again told the delegates that 'we have the right to ask for an incomes policy because we are prepared to contribute the three necessary conditions. First, an assurance of rising production and rising incomes, so that the sacrifice, the restraint for which we ask is matched by an assurance that it will result in increased production and increased rewards. Second, an assurance of equity and social justice, in that our policies will be directed to the benefit of the nation as a whole and not to the advantage of a sectional interest. Third, an assurance that what we ask for in wages and salaries will apply equally to profits and dividends and rent (Applause). We shall not create a free-for-all for the speculator, and land profiteer and the landlord – and then ask wage and salary earners alone to show a concern for the national interest that others are not required to show.'[2]

Whatever else Mr Wilson might claim for his government, even he could hardly claim that any of these conditions had been fulfilled three months after the election of 1964. However, it was then that the Government persuaded the TUC as well as the CBI to sign a Declaration of Intent which endorsed the establishment of a new body, which became the Prices and Incomes Board, entrusted with the responsibility to 'examine particular cases in order to advise whether or not the behaviour of prices or of wages, salaries and other money incomes is in the national interest as defined by the Government after consultation with management and unions'. When this 'treaty' was signed, George Brown, then Minister of Economic Affairs, declared that 'history was being made', and announced, somewhat prematurely, that 'the document heralded the end of the class war'.[3]

This kind of exercise was not, however, nearly sufficient to ensure effective 'wage restraint'; and as the need for further financial help

[1] *The Times*, 9th July, 1963.
[2] TUC Annual Conference Report, 1964, pp. 384–5.
[3] *The Guardian*, 17th of December 1964.

from abroad became acute, so did foreign pressure grow, notably from the United States, for an incomes policy 'with teeth'.[1] By the summer of 1965, the Government had set about persuading 'both sides of industry' to accept a 'compulsory early warning system'. The representatives of business duly agreed to do their patriotic duty, possibly encouraged by the fact that the system would above all bear upon wages. The TUC was much more reluctant, despite George Brown's dramatic announcement to the members of the General Council that 'he had just heard from Washington over the transatlantic telephone that President Johnson had authorised US participation in the vital support operation, based on the "package" proposal which included the new assurances about Britain's income policy'.[2] In the end, and after much arduous arm-twisting, the TUC did agree.

This was by no means enough either. Stronger measures were required, and the Government was fortified in its resolve to adopt them by its decisive victory at the polls in March 1966. For *Tribune*, which had earlier made the remarkable discovery that the Labour election manifesto was not only an 'interesting and stimulating document' but 'also in essence, a socialist one,' Labour's victory was taken to signify that 'socialism is right back on the agenda.'[3] What was in fact right back on the agenda was a more resolute attack on wage-earners.[4] An often-quoted remark of Harold Wilson's was that 'the Labour movement is a crusade or it is nothing'. But the crusade which the Prime Minister was about to launch was directed at the men and women who had given him his electoral victory.

A useful opportunity to display 'toughness' with recalcitrant trade unionists was soon provided by the seamen's strike, which began in May 1966. In a television broadcast, the Prime Minister made it clear that the 'toughness' was not least intended to impress Britain's foreign creditors. 'What is at issue here is our national prices and incomes policy. To accept the demand [of the seamen] would be to break the dykes of our prices and incomes policy . . . Our determination to insist on these principles when the cost is great will be taken by everyone at home *and abroad* as a proof of our determination to

[1] See H. Wilson, *op. cit*. pp. 131–2.
[2] Brandon, *op. cit*. p. 103.
[3] *Tribune* 8th of April 1966.
[4] This is how Wilson explains his decision to have a General Election in March 1966: '. . . to yield incontinently to strike threats would mean the end of any meaningful prices and incomes policy, with serious effects abroad. Nor would the legislation to which we were committed make things any easier. Sooner or later there would be a confrontation, with the likelihood of a prolonged and damaging strike. It was not a welcome prospect with a majority of, at most, three whether we were going for early legislation or not' (*op. cit*. p. 199).

make that policy effective.'[1] Finding that the NUS Executive was unwilling to back down, despite intense pressure, blandishments, minor concessions and promises of future improvements, the Prime Minister announced that the fault did not lie with the union's leaders, but with a 'tightly knit group of politically motivated men' who, for their own nefarious purposes, were 'forcing great hardship on the members of the union and their families, and endangering the security of the industry and the economic welfare of the nation.' A few days later, he 'named names', i.e. some members of the Communist Party. This invocation of the Red Menace worked: the strike was called off the following week. The national interest was safe. Not quite, though. For even before the seamen's strike, the pound had again come under pressure, and the government was again faced with a by now familiar crisis. In July, the Government announced the most drastic measures of deflation since the war, and coupled them with a legally binding wage freeze, which was to operate for six months, and be followed by a period of 'severe wage restraint'.

The Prime Minister's justification of his wages policy to the trade union movement is worth noting, since it illustrates so well the ideological miasma which dominated his administration. Speaking to the TUC in September, he expressed the hope that it would not be necessary to invoke statutory powers and that his policies would work by voluntary means. But if they did not, he warned, 'if there is breakaway action, whether in wages or prices, or by any other challenge *by any section of the community seeking to secure a privileged position for itself*, the Government will, reluctantly, have to replace voluntary action by operating the statute.'[2] Phrases of this sort have become so common a part of the vocabulary in which political debate is conducted that their double-think quality tends to be overlooked. For there were sections of 'the community' which had no need whatever to *seek* a privileged position, since they fully enjoyed it already. Mr Wilson spoke as if he was presiding over a society which was already roughly egalitarian, or at least one which was well launched on that road. Any such notion was of course absurd. But this did not prevent the Prime Minister from asserting that this was indeed the case. 'An incomes policy, the planned expansion of incomes to which we are pledged', he also told the TUC, 'could only be developed by a Government which by its social and taxation policies created the necessary climate of social justice.

---

[1] Quoted in P. Foot, *The Politics of Harold Wilson* (1968) p. 173. My italics. For the Government's handling of the strike, see also P. Foot, 'The Seamen's Struggle' in R. Blackburn and A. Cockburn, Eds., *The Incompatibles* 1967.
[2] TUC Annual Conference Report, 1966, p. 398. My italics.

This we have done. . . .[1] So well had a 'climate of social justice' been created that four years later, at the time of the 1970 General Election, it could cogently be argued that poverty under the Labour Government had actually increased;[2] and the best that Government spokesmen could do to counter the argument was that it had, at most, been marginally alleviated. Whichever the case, massive deprivation remained a permanent feature of life in Britain. As far back as 1959, before the General Election of that year, Harold Wilson had said that 'given a Labour victory, the test is this: will there be, twelve months from now, a narrowing of the gap between rich and poor, quite apart from any general upward movement there may be as a result of increased national production? The answer is, quite simply, that there will be.'[3] The Labour victory had been delayed; and six years after it, never mind twelve months, the answer, quite simply, was that Mr Wilson's government had badly failed the test. What *was* soon created by the July measures was, *inter alia*, the return of chronic unemployment. By the following summer, unemployment figures had risen well over the half million mark, and stayed there for the rest of the Government's period of office.

In November 1967, the Government was finally forced to devalue the pound. This was linked with yet another 'rescue operation', the terms of which included the pledge that the Government would continue with its deflationary policies. In January 1968, it was announced that there was to be a reduction of public spending to the tune of £300 million in the next financial year, and a further reduction of over £400 million the year after. This included economies in health services, education and housing, the deferment of the raising of the school-leaving age from 1971 to 1973, the end of free milk in secondary schools, and the re-introduction of prescription charges and an increase in dental charges. Once again, however, Tory policies were applied in a Labour way: there were exceptions for those most in need. In addition, the 'package' included defence cuts, and a decision, which the Primer Minister had resisted since he had come to office, to withdraw from Singapore, Malaysia and the Persian Gulf by the end of 1971.

In ·March 1968, the Chancellor of the Exchequer, now Roy Jenkins, presented a Budget which imposed tax increases of £923 million. This time, 'equality of sacrifices' took the form of a special levy for one year on investment income, which was expected to yield

[1] ibid, p. 398. My italics.
[2] See Child Poverty Action Group, *Poverty and the Labour Government* (1970). For a detailed survey of Labour's record in social policies, see P. Townsend and N. Bosanquet Eds., *Labour and Inequality* (1972).
[3] *New Statesman*, 3rd October, 1959, quoted by Foot, op. cit. p. 145.

£100 million. However, Mr Jenkins explained in a television broadcast that 'he had decided it was better not to raise income tax but to impose heavy increases on goods and services so that incentive would not be impaired at a time when the economy must be made to work.'[1] A Conservative Chancellor could not have put it better.

This was the 'climate' in which the Government decided to proceed with what was commonly described as 'the reform of industrial relations', which meant in effect the further curbing of wage demands and new limitations on the right to strike. It was then that began the long drawn out struggle between the Labour Government and organized wage-earners, which was to end in the Government's retreat in June 1969.

The attempt to deal more firmly with labour 'indiscipline' followed naturally from the Government's approach to the management of a capitalist economy. The tone of its approach to 'industrial relations' had been set as soon as the Government was installed in 1964. The then Minister of Labour, Ray Gunter, had inaugurated his tenure of office by proclaiming that the threat of an unofficial strike of dockers 'could only lead to anarchy'. As *The Guardian's* Labour Correspondent noted, 'this is the first time for at least thirteen years that a Government has, on its own initiative, anticipated an unofficial strike with a public warning to the men . . . Mr Gunter, on the first day at his desk, has served notice that this Government intends to pursue a forward policy in labour relations.'[2] Ever since then, the Government had indeed pursued a 'forward policy in labour relations', whose main characteristic had been to try and impose 'restraint' upon wage-earners, coupled with the shrill denunciation of their resistance to it, as when George Brown told the delegates to the 1965 Labour Party Conference that 'we have been operating the law of the jungle ourselves while condemning it for every other purpose'.[3] What presumably trade unionists should have done was to abjure the 'law of the jungle', meekly accept sacrifices while everybody else continued to act according to that law, and find consolation in its occasional condemnation by Labour ministers. The Government could have had all the support it required from trade unionists, had it been seen to be genuinely engaged in the creation of a society marked by greater social justice. Only the Prime Minister and his friends believed that the Labour Government was. So it did not get the cooperation of wage-earners; and it was therefore logically driven to move from unsuccessful restraint to statutory constraint.

Its target was not primarily the unions themselves but rank and

[1] *The Times*, 20th of March 1968.
[2] *The Guardian*, 20th of October, 1964.
[3] Labour Party Annual Conference Report, 1965, p. 227.

file trade unionists, who showed a deplorable propensity to by-pass their unions and resort to unofficial strikes, which now acquired a new and more suitably sinister name, 'unconstitutional strikes'. The Government had no objection to strong trade unions, on the contrary, provided their strength was used to contain and discipline their members. Mr Wilson and his colleagues did want good 'industrial relations': but what they meant by this was that wage-earners should forego, save on the rarest occasions, the one form of action which their employers had ever found persuasive.

In the end, the Government was forced to give up its Industrial Relations Bill, and it had to be content with a 'solemn and binding' undertaking from the TUC that it would itself intervene in the matter of 'unconstitutional strikes'. Most trade unions leaders no doubt shared the Government's wish to 'routinise' industrial conflict and to contain militancy: what they opposed, and were compelled by rank and file pressure to oppose, was the means whereby the Government sought to implement the policy. Still, the failure was qualified: it had paved the way for legislation by the Conservatives.

A few weeks after Labour's victory at the polls in 1964, Harold Wilson went to Washington. John Freeman, then Editor of *The New Statesman*, and later British Ambassador to India and the United States, reported the visit as follows: 'Wilson, Gordon-Walker [then Foreign Secretary] and Healey [the Minister of Defence] have established the right of Labour ministers to be treated as well by Washington as their more familiar Tory predecessors. It is not very important – though true – that the talks took place in an atmosphere of sound professional cordiality. Far more important is Wilson's success in allaying many of the original doubts about him in the US Administration. These doubts never concerned his good will or ability. They arose partly from the Washington experience of dealing with a Tory administration, and the inevitable inscrutability of new faces, and partly from uncertainty about the soundness of Wilson's views on both defence and economics. There is still doubt about the correctness of some of his policies in the sense that they are not all acceptable at face value to American policy-makers. But any idea that he is a flighty politician, peddling irrelevant formulae in response to domestic pressures, has been dispelled. . . . The acceptance of Wilson as a responsible international statesman is the first achievement of this week's talks'.[1]

What this meant was the 'new men' could be relied on by the American administration to continue with the foreign policy which

[1]J. Freeman. 'Wilson at the White House' in *The New Statesman*, 11th of December, 1964.

had inspired all British governments since the war; there would be no departure from unswerving support of the United States as the leader of the Western conservative coalition. So indeed it was. Mr Paul Foot has suggested that, as far as Harold Wilson was concerned, it was the advent of John Kennedy to the Presidency in 1960 which had wrought a transformation of his attitude to the United States. 'Suddenly', he writes, 'all Wilson's inherent anti-Americanism, dating back to the 1949 devaluation crisis, passed from him. In his speeches both as Shadow Chancellor and as Shadow Foreign Secretary, the former citadel of capitalism and militarism became the bright land of purposive dynamism'.[1] This would seem to make rather too much of superficial sentiments, and too little of the fact that Mr Wilson was always as basically committed to the 'Anglo-American alliance' as any other leading politician in Britain, Labour or Conservative. At any rate, the Prime Minister was in all likelihood not exaggerating much when he told the House of Commons at the end of 1965, after another visit to Washington, that 'we have reached a clearer understanding than probably at any time since the Second World War'.[2]

At the time this was said, the United States had long been involved in Vietnam, and its involvement assumed even more murderous forms in the following years. There was growing opposition in the Labour movement to the Government's support of this American enterprise. This was a source of some embarrassment to Mr Wilson and his colleagues. The Prime Minister dealt with the problem by way of a series of 'peace initiatives'. It was, or should have been, obvious that these exercises were doomed to failure by the determination of the United States to maintain a client regime in South Vietnam. The only purpose they served was to help pacify the Labour Party, or at least the parliamentary Left.

But the Government's policy on Vietnam was not an aberration: it was entirely consistent with its approach to all other issues of foreign policy. In all such issues, its bias was authentically conservative. Even the long delayed abandonment of its 'East of Suez' policy represented no change in its general approach and outlook. It did finally abandon, for reasons of economic necessity, the maintenance of a permanent military 'presence' East of Suez. But as the Prime Minister told the House of Commons in January 1968, 'we

---

[1] Foot, op. cit. p. 207.
[2] ibid. p. 214. Similarly, he stressed the 'complete agreement in Washington with the British Government's decision to continue to maintain a world-wide defence role, particularly to fulfil those commitments which, for reasons of history, geography, commonwealth association and the like, we, and virtually we alone, are best fitted to undertake' (ibid.).

have assured them both [i.e. the Governments of Malaysia and Singapore] and our other Commonwealth partners and allies concerned, that we shall retain a general capability based in Europe (including the United Kingdom) which can be deployed overseas as, in our judgement, circumstances demand, including support for United Nations operations.'[1] In other words, Britain would remain, to the limits of its reduced powers, in the business of imperialist intervention. The Government's enduring purpose was well illustrated by the fact that, at the time of the General Election of 1970, British forces were being lifted in a vast and costly exercise to the Far East, in order to demonstrate their capability to intervene in the area, notwithstanding the abandonment of permanent military bases. At no point in its six years of office was there any serious indication that the Government had any distinctive Labour policies in regard to foreign affairs.

III

What, then, is it reasonable to expect from the Labour Party in the years ahead?

There are two entirely opposed ways of answering this question. The first proceeds from the view that the Labour Party, whatever its past and present shortcomings, can eventually be turned into a socialist party, genuinely committed to the creation of a radically different social order, which would be based on, though certainly not exclusively defined by, the social ownership and democratic control of a predominant part of the means of production, distribution and exchange, including of course the 'commanding heights' of the economy. The second view is that it cannot be turned into such a party. Of the two, the second seems to me much the more realistic. The remainder of this *Postscript* is largely concerned with setting out the reasons for this.

To begin with, the point needs to be stressed that the Labour Party is no longer even a 'reformist' party. 'Reformist' socialism is the belief that a socialist society will be brought into being by way of a gradual series of structural and social reforms. This conviction lay at the core of Fabianism and it inspired, however tepidly, a long line of Labour leaders. With the adoption of a new Constitution in 1918, it became the officially sanctioned perspective of the Labour Party and it remained its official perspective until some such time as the late fourties. The question is not here whether 'reformist' socialism is or is not a realistic socialist strategy. The point is rather

[1]House of Commons, 16th January 1968, vol. 756, col. 1581.

that it is no longer the perspective which, however theoretically, informs the Labour leaders' approach to affairs.

This is not to say that reforms are no longer on their agenda. They obviously are. But such reforms as these leaders may support do not form part of any kind of coherent strategy, designed, in however long a perspective, to achieve the socialist transformation of British society. The leaders of the Labour Party have no such strategy and, except for merely rhetorical purposes, want none of it. They may occasionally prattle on about socialism, but this, on any serious view of the matter, lacks all effective meaning. The 'revisionism' which dominates their thinking does not represent an alternative but an adaptation to capitalism.

There are many people in the Labour Party who, broadly speaking, accept that this is so, but who nevertheless insist that their party *can* be turned into a suitable instrument of socialist change. They do so on a number of different grounds, which must be examined in turn.

The first such ground is that the Labour leaders can be persuaded, or if not persuaded, compelled to adopt socialist policies, and to implement them in office.

This must surely be reckoned to be a very weak argument. For it enormously underestimates the strength of the Labour leaders' ideological and political commitment to the positions they hold, and which do not include the perspectives which animate their socialist followers. These leaders are not socialists who for some reason or other have lost their way and who can be brought back to the true path by persuasion or pressure. They are bourgeois politicians with, at best, a certain bias towards social reform. They have no intention whatsoever of adopting, let alone carrying out, policies which would begin in earnest the process of socialist transformation in Britain. On the contrary, they must be expected to resist with the utmost determination all attempts to foist such policies upon them.

No doubt, they may, in opposition or even in government, occasionally be prevented, as happened with the Wilson government's proposed legislation on trade unions, from taking up or carrying out measures which closely affect the trade unions and which the latter find particularly obnoxious. But this of course is hardly the point.

It is also true that Labour leaders may have to accept this or that Conference resolution, pledging them to carry out some measures of policy to which they are opposed, or about which they have serious doubts. But neither Labour Party Annual Conferences nor Trade Union Congresses can, in practice, effectively impose such policies on their leaders, and these leaders may safely be relied upon to ignore the wishes of their activists once they are in office, with arguments such as that circumstances have changed, or that the time is not ripe, or that there is so much else to do, or that the issue requires much more thought, and so on. Alternatively, they must be expected, given their cast of mind, to defuse whatever explosive charge the policies concerned may carry – in other words, to de-radicalise their application to the point where they lose much if not most of their significance.

But even these considerations, important though they are, do not quite touch the core of the matter. The really crucial point has to do with the fact that the business of challenging British capitalism at the roots, which also implies a challenge to international capitalism, is bound to be arduous and exacting enough, even for a leadership utterly determined upon the enterprise. There cannot be much in the notion that it could really begin to get under way with leaders who do not really believe that it should begin at all, which is precisely the case with the people who now control the Labour Party.

It is at this point that many socialists in the Labour Party tend to part company with the argument, on a second ground, namely that if the Labour Party's present leaders cannot be persuaded or compelled to respond to the pressure for socialist policies and actions, they will eventually be replaced by others, who would be determined upon the enterprise, and who would offer the kind of leadership which it requires.

After all, the case goes, the Labour leaders are not the Labour Party, much less the Labour movement; and already, much has happened in the last ten years or so to change significantly the balance of forces in the Labour Party itself, as a result of changes which have occured in the Labour movement. Most obviously, the trade union leadership, which traditionally acted as a strongly anti-left wing force, and whose command of the block vote at Labour Party conferences insulated the Labour leaders from serious challenge, has undergone a substantial shift to the left; and this must eventually bring about the emergence of a new and different kind of leadership in the Labour Party. This, incidentally, has also long formed part of the perspective of the Communist Party.[1]

This expectation (it can hardly be called a strategy) strikes me, for many reasons, as altogether illusory.

Of course, the shift to the left which has occured in the trade union movement is in many ways significant, most of all because it reflects a rank and file militancy which is indeed important. But the

[1] For a Communist exposition of the case, see M. Johnstone, 'Britain: Prospects for the Seventies' in *The Socialist Register, 1971.*

evidence is entirely lacking that the new Trade Union left has the slightest inclination to bring about sweeping changes in the leadership of the Labour Party, or that it would be able to do so if it had. In 1966, when Frank Cousins resigned from the Wilson Government, Ken Coates, as he recalls, wired him his congratulations 'and wrote to him appealing for him to begin to organise the socialist opposition'. Mr Cousins replied that he had no wish to become a 'focal figure' of the left, and that his main purpose was 'to try and help find a more reasonable understanding towards the removal of our economic problems than is possible under the proposed Bill for Prices and Incomes'.[1] The reply was fairly typical of the limited role which trade union leaders, including left wing ones, see themselves as playing in the Labour Party, namely that of representatives of organized labour, involved in a bargaining relationship, notably over industrial and economic issues, with their political colleagues in the Labour Party, and not in the least as political rivals intending to capture control of the party for puposes radically different from those of the men who now control it. Some left wing trade union leaders may develop political ambitions: if so, they would most likely seek to carve a place for themselves among the leaders of the Labour Party and as members of a future Labour Government. But this can hardly be regarded as a matter of great political significance.

The kind of sweeping changes at the top which a good many socialists hope to see one day brought about in the Labour Party, and which would signify a major ideological shift to the left, would presumably, given the nature of the political system, have to be engineered from within the ranks of the Parliamentary Labour Party. But to say this is surely also to indicate how unrealistic that hope is. It is unrealistic because it ignores the perennial weakness of the parliamentary left. That weakness is not accidental but structural, which is why the indignation so often manifested by left activists at the derelictions of Labour Left M.P.'s is futile. The derelictions are real enough, but they are built into the system of which these M.P.'s are a part. Left parliamentarians operate within the rules of a game designed to limit their capacity and indeed their willingness to challenge their leaders. They are required to behave 'loyally' and to accept compromise in order to help maintain the 'unity' of the party. They must not give aid and comfort to the other side, most of all when Labour is in government, but also when it is in opposition. Accommodation is in any case made easier by virtue of the fact that the members of the parliamentary left are, and always have been, characterized by a marked uncertainly as to what, in basic ideological terms, they are really about. This too is not accidental: it is a

[1] K. Coates, *The Crisis of British Socialism* (1971) p. 131.

necessary condition of their becoming parliamentarians in the first place. Political success, in this respect, and even political survival, depends on an early ability to blunt the edge of one's dissent and to minimize the gulf which separates the would-be socialist dissenter from his leaders. There have been some exceptions: a few Labour M.P.'s have, so to speak, slipped through the net. But they have remained isolated and often pathetic figures, bitterly at odds not only with their leaders but with that large and permanent majority of the Parliamentary Labour Party which entirely shares its leaders' orthodox modes of thought. Most left parliamentarians, for their part, have learnt, more or less easily, to adjust to their ambiguous situation; and very few, when the chance has occured, have been able to resist cooptation into the Labour Establishment, at whatever cost to their proclaimed commitments: the ministerial career of former Bevanite parliamentarians provides ample testimony to the fact.

The Labour Left in Parliament can mount episodic 'revolts' on this or that issue, though with dubious effect; and it can act as a pressure group upon the Labour leaders, with equally uncertain impact. But more than this it cannot be expected to do.

What this means is that the Labour Party will not be transformed into a party seriously concerned with socialist change. Its leaders may have to respond with radical-sounding noises to the pressures and demands of their activists. Even so, they will see to it that the Labour Party remains, in practice, what it has always been – a party of modest social reform in a capitalist system within whose confines it is ever more firmly and by now irrevocably rooted. That system badly needs such a party, since it plays a major role in the management of discontent and helps to keep it within safe bounds; and the fact that the Labour Party proclaims itself at least once every five years but much more often as well to be commited not merely to the modest amelioration of capitalist society but to its wholesale transformation, to a just social order, to a classless society, to a new Britain, and whatever not, does not make it less but more useful in the preservation of the existing social order.

It is very likely that the Labour Party will be able to play this highly 'functional' role for some time to come, given its over-whelming preponderance as 'the party of the left' in the British political system. There is at present no party or grouping which is capable of posing an effective challenge to that preponderance; and this helps to explain why so many socialists in the Constituency Labour Parties, in the trade unions (and for that matter in the Communist Party) cling to the belief that the Labour Party will eventually be radically transformed. But the absence of a viable socialist alternative is no reason for resigned acceptance or for the perpetuation of hopes which have no basis in political reality. On the contrary, what it requires is to begin preparing the ground for the coming into being of such an alternative: and one of the indispensable elements of that process is the dissipation of paralysing illusions about the true purpose and role of the Labour Party.

INDEX